CITIZEN-LED INNOVATION FOR A NEW ECONOMY

CITIZEN-LED INNOVATION FOR A NEW ECONOMY

EDITED BY ALISON MATHIE AND JOHN GAVENTA

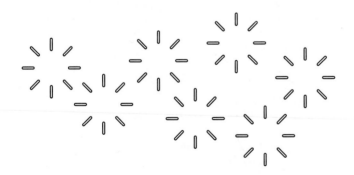

FERNWOOD
PUBLISHING

PRACTICAL ACTION
Publishing

*Everyday Good Living and the Two Row Wampum: The Vision of the Ontario Federation of
Indigenous Friendship Centres,* Linda Jones with Sylvia Maracle, copyright, 2015, Ontario
Federation of Indigenous Friendship Centres (OFIFC), reproduced with permission.

Editing: Chris Benjamin
Cover design: All Caps Design
Printed and bound in Canada

Published in North America by Fernwood Publishing
32 Oceanvista Lane, Black Point, Nova Scotia, B0J 1B0
and 748 Broadway Avenue, Winnipeg, Manitoba, R3G 0X3
www.fernwoodpublishing.ca

Published in the rest of the world by Practical Action Publishing
Schumacher Centre, Bourton on Dunsmore, Rugby, Warwickshire, CV23 9QZ, UK

Practical Action: HB- 9781853399213; PB- 9781853399220;
Fernwood Publishing: PB- 9781552667699
Lib PDF- 9781780449210; ebook- 9781780449227

Fernwood Publishing Company Limited gratefully acknowledges the financial support
of the Government of Canada through the Canada Book Fund and the Canada Council
for the Arts, the Nova Scotia Department of Communities, Culture and Heritage,
the Manitoba Department of Culture, Heritage and Tourism under the
Manitoba Publishers Marketing Assistance Program and the Province of Manitoba,
through the Book Publishing Tax Credit, for our publishing program.

Library and Archives Canada Cataloguing in Publication

Citizen-led innovation for a new economy
/ edited by Alison Mathie and John Gaventa.

Includes bibliographical references.
ISBN 978-1-55266-769-9 (paperback).

1. Sustainable development--Canada--Citizen participation--Case
studies. 2. Sustainable development--United States--Citizen participation--
Case studies. 3. Canada--Economic conditions--Case studies. 4. United
States--Economic conditions--Case studies. I. Gaventa, John, 1949-, author,
editor II. Mathie, Alison, author, editor

HC79.E5C58 2015   338.9'27   C2015-905203-3
                         C2015-905204-1

CONTENTS

LIST OF CONTRIBUTORS

Gord Cunningham is the assistant director at the Coady International Institute. He has led and participated in action research initiatives, facilitated courses and produced case studies of asset-based and citizen-led economic development in several countries. Gord has also co-developed tools for community-economic literacy, co-authored articles and co-edited a book *From Clients to Citizens: Communities changing the course of their own development* with his longtime colleague Alison Mathie.

Phil Davison is fortunate to have worked with great people in community, high school, university, college, government, and First Nations settings for over twenty-five years. He has held a variety of positions in post-secondary institutions and government and is currently the director of extension at St. Francis Xavier University in Antigonish, Nova Scotia, where he strives to secure grace, poetics, humour and compassion in his daily work.

Tom Dewar now splits his time between Baltimore and Bologna, Italy. He recently left the Aspen Institute's Roundtable on Community Change, where he co-authored "Voices from the Field III" and "Resident Led Community Building." Most recently he has become a senior associate with Nurture Development in the U.K. He also works with ABCD Europe.

Behrang Foroughi is an assistant professor at the School of Community Resources and Development, Arizona State University. His research focuses on exploring the learning dimension, learning spaces and learning outcomes of participatory social-change efforts at community level. He has the privilege of working with a variety of community development organizations in Canada and the Middle East. Behrang has graduate degrees in engineering and planning and a PhD in education (University of Toronto).

Rachel Garbary is a recent graduate of St. Francis Xavier University with an honours degree in development studies. She is interested in collaborative community engagement, activism, and building solidarity and has been an engaged citizen in the local community and university throughout her undergraduate years. Her academic work thus far has focused on Indigenous knowledge in agriculture in Ghana.

John Gaventa served as the director of the Coady International Institute, St. Francis Xavier University, from 2011–14. He is currently a fellow at the Institute of Development Studies at the University of Sussex. He has written extensively on issues of citizen engagement, power and participation in North America and internationally.

Yogesh Ghore is a senior member of the program staff at the Coady International Institute, St. Francis Xavier University. He is a course facilitator and is engaged in research initiatives and global capacity strengthening efforts in the area of sustainable livelihoods and market systems. Prior to joining the Coady Institute in 2009, Yogesh worked as a practitioner in Asia and the United States including in the Sandhills area of North Carolina, which he revisited for his case study in this collection.

Linda Jones is an independent consultant based in Canada who works in the field of sustainable and inclusive economic development. She is recognized internationally as a practicing expert in the integration of vulnerable populations — smallholder farmers, women, extreme poor, ethnic minorities — into market systems. She has published extensively on the topic with an upcoming book *Financial and Market Integration of Vulnerable People: Lessons from Development Programs.*

Elizabeth A. Lange is associate professor of adult education, St. Francis Xavier University, Nova Scotia. She has over 30 years of experience as an educator and facilitator of transformative learning in formal and non-formal settings. Her research focuses on adult education, transformative learning, sustainability education for adults, pedagogies for social change and transcultural learning and immigration. Co-written with Bruce Spencer, *The Purposes of Adult Education* is a Canadian text that serves as an introduction to the field of adult education.

Sylvia Maracle is a Mohawk from Tyendinaga Mohawk Territories, a First Nation in southern Ontario. She has held the position of OFIFC executive director for the past 35 years. She is involved in numerous agencies, boards and commissions and has made culturally competent management her focus.

Alison Mathie is the associate director of research at the Coady International Institute in Nova Scotia. She previously edited, with Gord Cunningham, *From Clients to Citizens: Communities Changing the Course of Their Own Development,* a book that explores citizen-led initiatives around the world. She has been at the Institute for over seventeen years, actively involved in asset-based approaches to social and economic change, and also teaches at St. Francis Xavier University.

Juliet Merrifield has worked as an adult educator and researcher for the last 35 years. She has written numerous articles, books, research and policy reports on topics relating to adult education, citizenship, adult literacy, assessment and accountability. She was one of the founders of the HKD Transition initiative in Sussex, England, and is deeply involved in activism on local food, energy and community resilience. She was an adjunct professor in the Department of Adult Education at St. Francis Xavier University from 2011 to 2014, during which time she mapped the green economy in Nova Scotia.

Brianne Peters is a senior member of the program staff at the Coady International Institute in Nova Scotia. She manages a multi-year partnership with organizations in Ethiopia, Kenya, South Africa, Ghana and Canada. She has produced several case studies, video documentaries and manuals on asset-based and citizen-led initiatives. Brianne also teaches in Canada and overseas.

Anne Toner Fung, former director of St Francis Xavier Enterprise Development Centre, is a management consultant who supports community economic development through her work with entrepreneurs, social enterprises and social profit organizations. As volunteer faculty and curriculum committee member for Leadership Waterloo Region, she pursues a continuing commitment to community leadership development and adult education.

ACKNOWLEDGEMENTS

This collection of case studies is the result of a collaborative effort involving the organizations and social movement leaders featured here, especially during 2013 and 2014. As editors, and on behalf of the authors of the cases, we are deeply grateful for the time those champions of change dedicated to sharing stories and insights, and we stand in admiration of their persistence in ushering in a new economy in their communities and beyond. We hope that in spreading these stories further, many more people will be inspired and influenced by their work. We also want to thank an anonymous donor and the Ford and Kettering Foundations for their financial support for this project, as well as the Indigenous Women's Community Leadership Program at the Coady International Institute for support for the two cases from Aboriginal communities in Canada.

Additional thanks to the St. Francis Xavier University's Extension Department, particularly for the role of Pauline MacIntosh, Mark MacIsaac, Phil Davison and Beverly Hemlow in helping to organize the Citizen-Led Sustainable Change conference held in June 2013, co-sponsored by the Extension Department and the Coady International Institute. These cases were first presented and discussed at this event and our understanding of the significance of these cases was enriched by lively discussions among the 150 participants.

The 2013 conference celebrated the 75th anniversary of the Antigonish Movement, an important movement for a new economy of its time. We remain inspired by this movement and appreciate how a history of co-operativism at another time of economic turbulence can be threaded into an understanding of new forms of organizing for social and economic change in the contemporary era.

The authors and editors of this collection also acknowledge the efforts of several reviewers who have offered advice and suggestions. Each author had a role as a reviewer of other cases. Our collaborators in the organizations featured in the cases also reviewed the work and contributed to discussions about the lessons learned. We are grateful to Anton Struchkov for the editing of the initial drafts of the cases and to Sue Hawkes for assistance with illustrations. Particular thanks go to Nanci Lee for background research for this project and to Juliet Merrifield, Jay Ross, Brianne Peters and Gord Cunningham for painstaking reviews in the later stages of this effort.

This book has complementary materials that can be used for teaching purposes or simply as a way to "meet" several of the people involved in the cases. There are short video interviews, webinars and other learning materials available, as well as a full report of the Citizen-Led Development for Sustainable Change gathering. These can be downloaded from coady.stfx.ca/coady/nacommdev/.

Alison Mathie
John Gaventa
May 15, 2015

PLANTING THE SEEDS OF A NEW ECONOMY
Learning from Citizen-Led Innovation

Alison Mathie and John Gaventa

The case studies in this collection provide a window onto citizen organizing for change. Together they give form and substance to the ideal of a new economy based on fairness and environmental sustainability.[1] Occurring in response to the effects of globalization on local economies, the environmental degradation brought about by industrial development as well as de-industrialization and a deep concern about climate change, these are stories of local citizens grappling with complex problems in their local communities, forging innovative solutions, prying open cracks in the system and seizing opportunities to redirect economic life. They are challenging the short-termism of our political leadership by taking action now for future generations.

Listed in the table below, the cases explore urban and rural initiatives among citizens in ethnically diverse settings — First Nations, Inuit, Latino, African American, predominantly white and mixed communities — where self-organized efforts to bring about change have generated innovation in the conduct of economic and social life. Innovation in these cases means a new way of working that "changes the rules of the game" (Fowler 2013: 13) in a realignment of power tying economic justice to the creation of multiple types of environmental, economic and social assets or forms of wealth. As indicated in the table below, examples include the development of local food systems for a viable land-based economy; the revitalization of decayed downtown areas using financing and ownership instruments that low income residents can afford; housing for people on low income created by green retrofitting of housing stock combined with a youth apprenticeship scheme; strategies to engage ethnically diverse new immigrants in building a vibrant urban neighbourhood; attempts to put the idea of a conservation economy into practice, grounded in local innovation but with the potential for proliferation, scale and nationwide influence; and Indigenous First Nations' knowledge asserting its influence by shaping mainstream thinking and offering cultural security to young people as they transition to urban centres. While starting small, several of these innovations have scaled up to regional or even national and international levels of influence. They therefore offer insights into the possibilities for local action connecting to wider networks to respond to the challenges of a broader economic and environmental crisis in which both countries are implicated. As such, this collection can also claim to be innovative: few volumes have brought together examples from both Canada and the U.S. despite their intertwined economies; nor have they included such a diversity, stretching from the deep South in the U.S. to the far North of Canada, offering examples of urban and rural, Indigenous and non-Indigenous communities and covering a range of community issues.

Table 1-1 List of Case Studies

Case	Location
Humility and audacity: The story of *Vivre Saint-Michel en Santé* New immigrants organizing to build a vibrant and stable community	Montreal, Quebec
New Dawn Enterprises: Becoming a "community instrument through which the people can do for themselves" An early adopter of social enterprise, demonstrating the possibilities of revival in depressed economies	Cape Breton, Nova Scotia
A vision of flipping the iceberg of power: The Greater Edmonton Alliance faces Big Land and Big Oil A coalition of over 50 civil society groups protecting agricultural land from urban development; promoting local food security and carbon neutrality	Edmonton, Alberta
Everyday good living and the Two Row wampum: The vision of the Ontario Federation of Indigenous Friendship Centres A province-wide Aboriginal organization supporting First Nations people as they try to retain and reclaim their cultural identity in urban settings	Ontario
A quiet movement: Inuit self-determination Claiming Inuit rights to livelihood through advocacy at the international level	Nunavut

Case	Location
Ecotrust Canada: Building the conservation economy Building local economies with local and Indigenous communities using "triple bottom line" principles	British Columbia
Resident ownership and neighbourhood transformation: The village at Market Creek Innovative models for philanthropy; urban revitalization by low-income multicultural residents	San Diego, California
Pushing for green solutions to urban neglect: The work of People United for Sustainable Housing (push) Retrofitting of old housing stock for affordable housing; raising awareness of energy issues and advocating for energy efficiency; organizing for neighbourhood greening; youth skill-building	Buffalo, New York
Permeating the mainstream: Rural Action for a sustainable future for Central Appalachia Organized action for a sustainable rural economy, including the local food system, sustainable forestry, and waste recycling	Appalachia, SE Ohio
Reclaiming land, reaffirming culture: Deep South Community Agricultural Network Rural African-American communities recognizing and building multiple forms of wealth	Mississippi and Alabama
Reaching back to move forward to a future of hope: The story of the Sandhills Family Heritage Association African Americans returning to land lost during the Jim Crow period and reclaiming cultural heritage	North Carolina

This introductory chapter is organized as follows. First, we explain the background to the collaborative research that generated these case studies and we introduce the Canadian and U.S. context in which the cases are situated. Secondly, we explain the rationale for their selection, and the collaborative process used to develop these cases for discussion and publication. Thirdly, we explore the themes emerging from the cases to understand the reasons these innovative ideas resonated with and motivated people to organize, participate and persist in their efforts. We discuss how these strategies were taken to scale, how the steps were sequenced and how the protagonists in these cases challenged the power that stood in their way or worked to expand existing spaces of influence. Finally, we ask whether these innovations are pathways to a new economy insofar as they are examples of citizen organizing for small-scale innovations that shape the system by setting precedents, and start from below to create new models of change, then expand outwards and upwards. As such, the cases reflect Speth's argument that "Systemic change must be driven both bottom-up and top-down … it requires communities, businesses and citizens deciding on their own to build the future locally as well as to develop the political muscle to adopt systems-changing policies at the national and international levels" (2012: 15). Moreover, this view sees "the growth of a powerful citizens' movement as necessary to spur to action at all levels" (ibid.).

BACKGROUND

The editors and several writers contributing to this collection are associated with the Extension Department and the Coady International Institute at St. Francis Xavier University, Nova Scotia, Canada. Both of these institutions draw their inspiration from the Antigonish Movement in Atlantic Canada in the 1920s and 30s. An example of social innovation in its day, "study clubs" motivated organizing for cooperative action among farmers, fishers and miners to secure an economic livelihood in the Depression years. Ultimately it "achieved what many people believed to be the impossible feat of establishing a network of efficient economic organizations that were created, owned, and operated by the people themselves" (Dodaro and Pluta 2012: 123). The Movement's leaders, Drs. Jimmy Tompkins and Moses Coady, had a clear vision for an economy based on cooperativism, made possible by integrating savings and credit and producer and consumer cooperatives into a comprehensive program (which they described as "The Big Picture"), that developed into a powerful movement. The vision captured the imagination of thousands in the Canadian Maritime provinces and of social innovators elsewhere, including in the developing world, who came to the Maritimes to learn. The precedent set in this relatively remote rural region spread widely, contributing to the growth of the cooperative movement in Canada and around the world.

At this historical moment in North America and Europe, the industrial revolution had generated extreme social divisions. The Russian revolution had taken place in 1917. The cooperative movement was building momentum in Europe and offered an alternative to the excesses of capitalism other than the spectre of Communism. As Moses Coady himself would write in 1958, rural North America, including the Canadian Maritimes, had been contributing millions of people to the proletariat over several decades. People had moved out of rural areas in search of work, and middlemen working for large companies increasingly governed rural livelihoods. As the Great Depression of the 1930s wore on, Coady identified a new type of feudalism: "the dictatorship of business and finance" (cited in Laidlaw 1971: 33–34). Coady and Tompkins' vision was to reverse this trend. They saw opportunity in cooperative formation, shaping legislation to permit the growth of credit unions, but most importantly having a fundamental belief in the capacities of working people to "use what they have to secure what they have not." And so, through adult education the economically poor built confidence in themselves to participate in a movement for radical change. They used their assets to build their assets, demonstrating the agency of people previously excluded from economic opportunity and security.

Just as the Antigonish movement responded to the crisis of capitalism implicit in the Great Depression some eight decades ago, the cases in this collection illustrate responses to the contemporary crisis of capitalism as felt in North America: the fragility of economic growth through globalized production and finance, a weakening of the state apparatus to provide the services that the post-war generation grew to expect, increased disparities in wealth and lost confidence in the environmental sustainability of the prevailing economic model. As Murray notes:

> The current crisis, like that of the 1930s is the hinge between the old world and new … What is needed is a radical transformation of infrastructures and institutions that will be the precondition for a new, qualitatively different period of growth[2] … In this transformation, environmental and social innovation will have a central place. (2009: 5)

In recent years, building on their roots in the Antigonish Movement, the Coady Institute and the Extension Department have been exploring how local initiatives are accelerating the social innovation required today for such socio-economic transformation. At the centre of this work has been our interest in active citizenship and how that is expressed in different contexts. This idea of citizenship is one in which "citizens are problem solvers and co-producers of public goods, not simply volunteers, voters, or consumers" (Boyte 2006: 34). With this understanding, we position active citizenship or agency[3] along two dimensions: (i) active citizenship as a horizontal phenomenon with citizens actively engaged with one another in their communities, motivated by a sense of civic duty or mutual responsibility; and (ii) active citizenship as a vertical phenomenon in which organized citizen action is oriented towards claiming rights and shaping decisions of the state. Drawing upon their own strengths and assets as well as those of their communities, active citizens demonstrate a capacity to act as agents of change along both these dimensions. In fact, both horizontal forms of solidarity and community cohesion and vertical forms of protest and advocacy are often necessary and complementary.[4] As Kretzmann (2003, cited in Green and Goetting 2010: 185) argues, and as the cases in this collection bear out, "the distinction that is often drawn between mobilizing local resources versus pressuring powerful systemic forces … may be a false one."

With this perspective on assets, agency and active citizenship, we were interested in examples of initiatives that had grown over time from organizing for local impact to having influence at a larger scale that would be reflected in a rewiring of attitudes in support of a sustainable and equitable economy. Rather than focus on institutional actors, we wanted to explore "citizenship [that] grows from action and identities in multiple spheres, not only in relationship to the state or market" (Gaventa 2010: 60), and citizen agency as central rather than marginal to social innovations. Like Cornwall and Gaventa (2001: 50), we position citizens as "makers and shapers" of their own futures, not just as "users and choosers" of services and options defined by others.

Foreshadowing an economy structured for sustainability and equity, this collection demonstrates such citizen-led change in as broad a range of contexts as possible, recognizing that connection to "place" has deep significance across the cases. As Fisher and Smith explain:

> In diverse struggles across the world, "place" and its many meanings push back against the valorization of placelessness and "virtuality" associated with globalization. Place in these varied contexts is at once a symbolic landscape of cultural tradition and human connection (the place of home) and the tangible ground that is a source of livelihood and focus of contestation (forests, watershed, farms). (2012: 1)

Reinforcing this perception of place, these cases provide multiple insights into why and how citizens in a diverse cultural landscape in the U.S. and Canada are leading change in their communities and how they interact with civil society, market and state institutions. The questions we explore are many. For example:

- What motivated African Americans in the South to reclaim their land and farming roots and how have the cultural connections to the land been converted into a broad array of economic, social and environmental benefits?
- How have local citizens in rural Appalachia sustained their efforts to challenge and reverse the social and environmental degradation caused by extractive industries and built an alternative economy based on a local food system, zero waste recycling and sustainable forestry?
- What has sparked the commitment to the idea of a conservation economy in British Columbia and how has it been put into practice?
- What insight into risk taking, new forms of philanthropic giving and innovative financing can we draw from the revitalization of the downtown Diamond neighbourhoods of San Diego, and their transformation into The Village at Market Creek with options for ownership and control by local low-income citizens?

- How have young people organized in depressed areas of downtown Buffalo to link affordable housing with green retrofitting, local apprenticeship programs and a National Fuel Accountability Campaign directed at utility companies?
- What motivated First Nations people in Canadian urban centres to form Friendship Centres to help people living in a new urban landscape and ultimately healing and reaffirming their cultural identity while pursuing their potential to survive and influence mainstream Canadian society?
- What explains the ability of an alliance of community groups in Edmonton, Alberta to prevent the encroachment of urban development on prime agricultural land and challenge the collusion of business and government in an economy booming with Canada's oil industry?
- What lessons can be drawn from the experience of building and serving low-income communities following the principles of a social economy, in an area suffering economic decline in Atlantic Canada and in a suburb of Montreal, Quebec welcoming new immigrants?
- How can a community development organization work with local citizens in such a way that it is "keeping its face to the community" rather than turning inward, so that "the membrane between them is pretty thin," as claimed by New Dawn Enterprises in Cape Breton, Nova Scotia?
- How can remote and dispersed Indigenous peoples in the Arctic form alliances to advocate for the right to a livelihood and how are they preserving their heritage while leveraging new opportunities?

These initiatives have all required agency, demonstrated by active citizens organizing for change, re-evaluating the different forms of wealth required to sustain economically and environmentally viable communities, putting innovative ideas into practice and building ever expanding networks and alliances to bring these to fruition. In other words they are demonstrating how to harness, conserve and build assets for a fairer and environmentally sustainable economic system. Their innovations are neither quick fixes nor oversimplified models for replication, but through linkages with local government, the private sector, donors and other actors, they gradually piece together the components of a significant shift away from "business as usual." They are thus achieving what Edwards (2011b: 15) calls "thick" solutions to complex crises rooted in the current economic system and turning local successes into a force for a new economy that political leaders can no longer ignore.

TIME FOR A CHANGE? THE CANADIAN AND U.S. CONTEXT

Although the U.S. position as the global superpower is faltering, it continues to have dominance as an economic engine thirsting for resources to prime its continued growth, for which Canada has been a willing and geographically convenient supplier. Together, their domestic dependence on fossil fuels and their high levels of per capita consumption place on them a corresponding level of responsibility for carbon emissions, despite the fact that much industrial production has been outsourced to other countries in a globalized economic landscape. Reluctance to cooperate on action called for by the international community has earned them harsh criticism, with neither country signing the Kyoto Protocol and Canada rebuked as a pariah state in the fight against climate change.[5] In both countries the model of economic growth has threatened land, culture and sustainability, whether African-American land loss, resource extraction on Aboriginal land or the social and environmental consequences of repeated boom and bust cycles associated with coal, oil and shale gas extraction in rural Appalachia in the U.S. and Cape Breton and Alberta, Canada. Neither country has invested significant revenue for future generations at federal, state or provincial levels.[6]

As interconnected as they are economically much is made of cultural differences between the U.S. and Canada. The role of the state differs significantly, as Canada has a relatively progressive taxation system, a national health care system that has been a source of great national pride and a narrative of a multicultural "mosaic" rather than a "melting pot." It has to be said, however, that despite Canada's celebration of diversity and the affirmation of Quebec as a "distinct society," assimilation policies with respect to Indigenous peoples and some groups of newcomer immigrants have contradicted this idea historically. On the other side of the border, U.S. exceptionalist rhetoric has masked the embarrassments of the highest poverty rates, child mortality rates, prison populations and military expenditures per capita among OECD comparator countries (Speth 2012). Moreover, the U.S. "melting pot," while diluting culture, has been unable to erase racial discrimination as witnessed once again in the events in Ferguson, Missouri and their aftermath in 2014.

Nevertheless, while the tolerance for inequality is claimed to be much lower in Canada than in the United States (Brooks 2014), wealth inequalities have grown in both countries. Both have experienced a decline in manufacturing, which companies have taken to countries south and east in search of cheaper labour, and a corresponding increase in more precarious service-sector employment (Bernard 2009; TD Economics 2014). Cuts in public expenditures in both countries have disproportionately affected the poor and paths to building wealth have tended to favour middle-income rather than low-income families. In the U.S. for example, McKernan et al. (2013) report worsening wealth disparities over the 30-year period

1983–2013, with the top 20 percent seeing a net wealth increase of 120 percent and the families in the lowest 20 percent seeing average net wealth fall below zero, meaning their assets were fewer than their debts. The racial wealth gap is even more pronounced, with whites on average having six times the average wealth of Blacks or Hispanics despite the fact that the income gap between these groups has narrowed (ibid.). In Canada, while disparities are not as great, the trend is in the same direction[7] and is compounded by regional disparities as the centre of economic gravity shifts westward from the older established industrial heartland of Ontario and Quebec.[8] More significantly, the painful experiences of Aboriginal people as they try to both reclaim cultural integrity and find a unique place in Canadian society is a persistent challenge to the Canadian ideal of egalitarianism.

Of particular relevance to these case studies are the traditions of organizing and action in the civil society sector. Both countries have a long history of social movements ranging from the labour and civil rights movements of the U.S. to the cooperative agricultural, consumer and financial movements of Canada (see MacPherson n.d.).[9] Some have argued that these traditions have been lost, or that there has been a shift in recent decades from high levels of participation in voluntary groups or associations of solidarity that cut across class and occupational divides toward a rise of public interest groups (such as environmental associations, human rights groups and so on), many of which have become professionalized groups with adherents and supporters rather than a membership base (Skocpol 2011). Similar concerns have been raised about "the growth of the service-providing not-for-profit sector diminishing the power of collective action, social movements, democratic decision-making and community-organizing" (Edwards 2011: 6). In this view, the decline of associational life is attributed to the rise of neoliberalism and its attendant cutbacks of public services in communities and the weakening of the labour movement (Fisher and Smith 2012: 5). Still others raise concerns about the public imagination of alternative futures being stifled by nationalistic hubris and isolationism or, conversely, a narrative of powerlessness in the face of the global economic and financial system, as Fisher and Smith (2012) claim for the U.S.[10]

And yet, despite growing economic and social inequalities, there are signs that the current crisis is leading to new bottom-up innovations and organizational strategies that can be shared across borders. Illustrating this, the cases show how complex challenges at the local level have been resolved by collectively learning-by-doing and combining organizational strategies with coalition and network building. Solutions have been pieced together that hark back to histories of mutual solidarity, reframed in language of "social innovation," "social enterprise," value chains for localizing the economy, "a conservation economy," and "local ownership and control," that link local imperatives to larger responsibilities in a globalized world.

In Canada, for example, a long history of non-profits, the voluntary sector and cooperatives has generated ideas for a social or solidarity economy that are being played out in different ways across the country. In the province of Quebec, the social economy has roots in francophone community solidarity that occurred prior to Quebec's Quiet Revolution and *movement populaire,* but became integrated into a government-led provincial development strategy. Even as cutbacks in public expenditure and widespread unemployment occurred late in the 1990s, the *Chantier de l'economie sociale,* a network of social economy networks, has shaped new social innovations out of the flux in state, market and civil society relations (Mendell and Neamtan 2010). Elsewhere in Canada, the idea of a social economy is entering public discourse as a way of stimulating innovation, though its roots are also deep. The example of New Dawn Enterprises in Nova Scotia, Canada, working against the trend of local economic decline, was an early adopter of the idea of social enterprise as a not-for-profit vehicle for financially sustainable projects, constructing affordable housing and establishing a college to train caregivers. Building on the principles of an innovative precedent two generations earlier, the cooperative movement, New Dawn Enterprises became Canada's first Community Development Corporation.

The U.S. is also seeing a similar resurgence of grassroots economic organizing, which is helping to shape a new economy focusing on principles of democratic ownership and sustainability. Groups like the Democracy Collective catalogue dozens of examples of citizens of what they call "community wealth building" (see democracycollaborative.org for more information). Alperovitz (2013) has argued that democratically controlled organizations like cooperatives, community land trusts and other municipal institutions provide the seeds for building a new sustainable economy from the ground up — one that will be dramatically different from capitalism or socialism, while Speth (2012) similarly argues that these efforts form the basis of a "Manifesto for a New Economy."

HOW THESE CASES WERE DEVELOPED

Despite the parallel emerging movements in both Canada and the U.S., few studies have sought to dig deeper, to document the stories and examples of change, and to link them in a common discussion across borders. This book begins to fill that gap. The inspiration for this collection followed the publication of a previous collection, *From Clients to Citizens: Communities Changing the Course of Their Own Development* (Mathie and Cunningham 2009). This earlier collection was international in scope and drew attention to communities worldwide that were organizing to bring about change on their own terms, with or without the assistance of external organizations. The innovations that arose from these citizen-led initiatives prompted us to ask a similar set of questions about what was happening closer to home.

Consulting members of our networks in the U.S. and Canada, we drew up a long list of citizen-led community development initiatives. The pivotal features were communities that had organized to address social and economic inequality and, in most cases, environmental sustainability. In so doing, their efforts not only improved the lives of significant numbers of people, but also ensured deeper and broader impact by shaping change at the systems level. Their stories tell how formal organizations of civil society, government and private sectors were involved in that reshaping. Narrowing the list, we still tried to capture as much diversity in experiences of citizen-led development as possible.

The cases were written in collaboration with the local communities and organizations featured.[11] Once the initial drafts were prepared, a three-day event for 130 people was organized at the Coady Institute in 2013, bringing participants from case study communities and organizations together with authors as well as other interested participants in innovative citizen-led work across Canada and the U.S. Through presentations and discussions, understandings of the key lessons of the case studies deepened. At the same time, participants enjoyed opportunities for developing relationships, extending networks and linking these varied local experiences. Despite travelling a considerable distance, from southeast U.S. to the Canadian Arctic (what was soon called the Deep South to the Far North), it was clear that there was commonality in the case study stories and a desire to learn and be strengthened by each other. A series of webinars on each of these cases has spread the stories further. Along with a package of learning materials, these have resulted in yet another layer of conversation and inspiration. (See <coady.stfx.ca/knowledge/publications/conferences/citizen_led_innovation>.)

Through the forums, the links and the follow-up, participants expressed a sense that something powerful is afoot, that change was happening that could offer promise of a new economy.

In the following sections we draw together some of the lessons from these citizen-led initiatives. Starting with an overview of the original motivation for citizen organizing, moving to how strategies for citizen-led innovation evolved, we then explore how these local initiatives have contributed to change at the systemic level.

CITIZENS ORGANIZING: HOW IT BEGINS

The motivations for organizing and the strategies for doing so vary across the cases. Some cases illustrate rights-based or resistance-based organizing such as the Alinsky-style organizing used by the Greater Edmonton Alliance, or the early days of struggle against the coal industry in Rural Appalachia, as well as the experience of the civil rights movement in the American South.

A second type of organizing is motivated by a desire for self-determination, the healing of past wrongs and celebration of cultural identity evident in the stories of African Americans of the Deep South and the Sandhills, North Carolina, urban Aboriginal populations served by the Ontario Federation of Indian Friendship Centres and the Inuit's livelihood adaptation in the Canadian Arctic. Achieved by reinforcing cultural norms of solidarity and mutual responsibility, these illustrate horizontal forms of citizenship in contexts where, historically, the relationship to the state through formal citizenship has been ambiguous or characterized by state oppression.

A third reason to organize is to build community among relative strangers to achieve a shared vision of change, as in the cases of new immigrants in Quebec in the Vivre San Michel en Santé (VSMS) case and revitalization in depressed urban areas such as in the Diamond neighbourhoods of San Diego and inner-city Buffalo. Once again, horizontal forms of citizenship are shown in associational life and mutual support, this time across ethnic lines.

Finally, a fourth strategy is to more deliberately carve out an economy based on principles of environmental sustainability and/or social equity, as in the case of Ecotrust Canada in British Columbia, Rural Action in Appalachia or New Dawn Enterprises in Nova Scotia. These latter three have been able to demonstrate ways in which people have organized to participate in the market while delivering services for both a social and environmental public good, thus putting hands and feet on ideas of "a conservation economy" (Ecotrust Canada) building multiple forms of wealth (Rural Action), and a "social economy" (New Dawn Enterprises).

While the starting points for organizing vary across these cases, there is similarity in their strategic intent to reframe the way we think about the economy. Over time both vertical and horizontal forms of citizenship are undertaken to challenge the state and instill a collective sense of solidarity and responsibility for achieving that end. Whether through environmental conservation, building affordable housing or reclaiming a history of working the land, the basis of all this work is asset building and the assertiveness of local citizens who want to achieve a sustainable and dignified livelihood for current and future generations. All show how even the most disadvantaged can find the space and support to contribute as agents of development. In so doing, people mobilize their own power, take advantage of small opportunities and enlarge them and challenge power that stands in their way.

Each case illustrates how different strategies are linked, how they are sequenced over time and how the initiatives are taken to scale. For example, in the case of Rural Action, its origins were in the resistance struggles against the coal industry that was leaving severe social and environmental damage in its wake. At a crucial turning point its leadership began to organize membership around an alternative economic future, and focused its organizing efforts on community building in rural communities of place and in communities of identity who shared an interest in growing a land-based, regional economy that could outlast the boom and bust cycles of extractive industries — first coal, then shale gas. Over the years, these ideas took hold in collaborations between not-for-profits, universities, local businesses and local governments, who saw opportunities for local value-added production, especially in food production, forest products and waste recycling.

The initial motivation for organizing has therefore evolved into a vision for a social and environmental economy that can function alongside and then permeate the mainstream.Obstacles — internal tensions over direction, periods of trickling funds, the slow pace of reforms in public services or the withering of state support for voluntary or non-profit organizations — are constant challenges, requiring astute negotiation and creative forms of investment. In the Rural Action case the inevitability of shale gas extraction has meant a redoubling of efforts to continue to promote a land-based economy as a viable alternative, while lobbying for a higher proportion of severance taxes to be redistributed to the counties impacted by extraction industries. In this way investment for future generations can be controlled locally.

LEADERSHIP OF CITIZEN-LED CHANGE

Regardless of the merits of an idea, program, policy or system, it is the people driving these that make them stick. An often under-appreciated aspect of all development work has been the characteristics of leadership, yet it is leaders who connect or channel organized energy to a vision or an opportunity and leadership that earns the trust of others when the unconventional or unpopular challenges to the status quo must be made (Kahane 2008).

In all these cases, a storyline of leadership that has kindled organizing for change with innovative ideas is evident, but the types and styles of leadership vary at different stages of the process. At certain times an inspirational individual has been at the forefront, the reference point for the push for change. At other times, leadership is multiplied in different nodes of a network deliberately woven to maximize innovation and collaboration, spreading a sense of collective agency as well as individual self-efficacy (Krebs and Holley 2002). And in many cases, leadership has been so understated or anonymously dispersed that it has gained less profile than it deserves.

Standing out as individual leaders in these cases are the founders of movements for change, usually "of the place" rather than outsiders, who were deeply familiar with the local community and invested extended periods of time listening to the people who would later organize. They combine the capacity for creative action with the ability to resist the pressure to conform and engender trust in innovative ideas and behaviour (Dale 2013: 2). Examples are Ammie Jenkins in Sandhills,

North Carolina, inspired by Martin Luther King, but discovering relatively late in life a yearning among African Americans to return to the land and reclaim a lost heritage; Rankin MacSween's determination in Nova Scotia, Canada to recast Cape Breton's internalized sense of economic dependency into a fierce independence and self-reliance expressed through New Dawn Enterprises; and Sheila Watt-Cloutier's fight for the "right to be cold" in her Inuit homeland, requiring a demonstration of leadership in global as well as local arenas (Watt-Cloutier 2015).

Yet, important as individual leaders were in all the cases, the ability to spread the capacity for action outwards and to keep multiple leadership nodes connected are what gives the cases their character as citizen-led initiatives. Hence the idea of "constellation leadership" in the Vivre San Michel en Santé case and the way the Greater Edmonton Alliance used Alinsky-style "relationals" to spread the power of ideas, making use of existing leadership dispersed in established church congregations, unions and other organizations, and linking these into an alliance to keep momentum going. Similarly, the Deep South Community Agricultural Network fosters leadership by helping people connect their leadership potential with their past achievements: "It gives them a strong voice … [because] the language and practices of generating wealth resonate with the longstanding civil rights activities of our past" (quoted in Davison, this volume). The Jacobs Family Foundation, whose sunset-clause committing them to withdraw once the Diamond neighbourhoods of San Diego had been revitalized, sent a strong message that legal ownership and financial investment by community members in The Village at Market Creek was an opportunity for genuine leadership by local citizens.

BUILDING COMMON CAUSE

Citizen-led initiatives are rarely a linear process; it may take years for a common cause to evolve and the cause may shift over time as well. For example, in the vsms case, the Healthy Cities Initiative funded years of community mobilizing for civic participation in a community of new immigrants on the outskirts of Montreal. From skirmishes with local authorities in order to prevent waste dumps and wrecked vehicle impoundments from spoiling their neighbourhood, people became increasingly concerned about building a desirable community where people of diverse origins would continue to live as new Canadians rather than move on elsewhere. In the case of the Ontario Federation of Indian Friendship Centres, a movement that began with supporting First Nations people when they moved from reserves to urban centres evolved into an organization that was able to affirm both the importance of Indigenous cultural identity and the ability to adapt to mainstream culture, a skill now recognized to be as important for non-native Canadians as it is for First Nations Canadians themselves. The Sandhills case started as a personal quest for Ammie Jenkins to learn about her family's history but it became a broader movement around the common issue of land loss among the African-American community. A similar evolution has started in Buffalo's diverse west side, where PUSH's community organizing activities began with door-to-door campaigns to understand issues of common concern, evolved into a community planning congress to spearhead local employment opportunities, access affordable rental housing and increase energy efficiency of housing stock, then building a broad-based political and environmental consciousness and a culture of civic activism, ready to take on government and private sector alike.

Several lessons emerge from these examples — the painstaking community building work to build common cause locally, the rally around a single issue to build solidarity and deepening of support among the allies and supporters across sectors beyond the local community. The cause cannot be shouldered by one organization alone.

IDEAS FOR A NEW ECONOMY

In this collection, the assumptions and values underlying the prevailing economic model are challenged, in keeping with Speth's claim that "With its emphasis on privatization, commercialization, and commodification, American capitalism has carried this demolition [of nature, neighborhoods, safety, and security of local food production and other raw materials] forward with a vengeance" (2012: 4). These citizen-led initiatives, explicitly or implicitly, are oriented to a new type of economy, retrieving values of sustainability and mutual solidarity.

This new type of economy may need to look back to the best of the past in order to move forward just like the Sankofa bird of the Akan people of Ghana that inspired African-Americans in the Sandhills case. In the face of growing inequalities, loss of a means to livelihood, neglect of the environment and a weakened sense of mutual responsibility, the response in these cases has often been an evocation of culturally embedded principles that pre-date capitalism. For example, the Ontario Federation of Indian Friendship Centres case just discussed, as well as the Inuit case, reminds the reader of the aspirations of balance, responsibility and right to livelihood. These same ideas have been re-crafted in the language of the "conservation economy," linking business opportunities in the fisheries and forestry with the imperative of environmental stewardship and the promotion of social equity — the "triple bottom line" or "triple E" enterprises promoted by Ecotrust Canada in British Columbia.

Similarly, both the Rural Action case in Appalachia and the Deep South Community Agriculture Network case show how independent initiatives are being streamlined into a vision of an economy that creates multiple forms of wealth — social, individual, natural, built, financial, political and cultural capital — through the construction of viable product value chains that maximize the wealth retained locally, including the income derived from primary production and secondary processing (Yellow Wood Associates and Deborah Markley 2010). The principle of balance, where one form of wealth cannot increase at the expense of others if the system is to be sustainable, resonates in these diverse contexts where the coal industry generated financial wealth for a few at the expense of environmental assets for the many in rural Appalachia, or where a history of exclusion and exploitation of African-American labour depleted cultural capital and agency, such as in North Carolina and the Deep South.

In the case of the Greater Edmonton Alliance, the encroachment of Edmonton's urban development backed by the financial wealth earned from Big Oil and Big Land was the touchstone for action against "political decision making favoring local developers, global land speculators and the global oil industry over the local public good, contributing to a shift in the public's political and environmental consciousness" (as Lange explains in this volume). The Alberta tar sands, and Canada's unapologetic stance favouring their exploitation, has prompted a response by Greater Edmonton Alliance that includes the protection of prime agricultural land from development, the promotion of a local food system that helps local producers to reclaim market share and the promotion of affordable (green) housing stock. The effort is to advance carbon neutrality in the symbolic epicentre of global carbon emissions.

In the Canadian context, until the collapse of oil prices in late 2014 and early 2015, Alberta's economy was booming because of the oil industry. By comparison, the eastern provinces have been labelled the have-not provinces, dependent on federal transfers and pushing labour out to work on the oil patch out west. What is surprising about New Dawn Enterprises in the depressed economy of Cape Breton in Nova Scotia is its resilience and growth. Rejecting the have-not moniker, New Dawn has shown how wealth can be grown locally through social enterprise — care-giving services, vocational training and affordable housing. It has also found support for its "wealth created here stays here" approach through provincial tax breaks for investment in community enterprises and local employment. A pioneer of social enterprise and a forerunner of a social economy in which such enterprises flourish, in its four-decade history, New Dawn has become "a community instrument through which the community can do for themselves," growing incrementally, "learning to remake the organization over time" (Merrifield and Toner, this volume).

This same re-imagining of local economic wealth creation through urban revitalization is evident in the example of PUSH Buffalo, where young activists, going door-to-door to find out local citizen concerns and organizing public meetings to address them, recognize the potential in vacant and dilapidated housing. Not only could such housing be refurbished and retrofitted for green energy, but by offering unemployed youth the opportunity to apprentice in such refurbishing schemes a new cadre of skilled workers for the green economy could be created, and campaigns could be launched to secure fairer rates from utility companies.

PARTNERSHIP ACROSS SECTORS

The evolution of citizen action from an informal movement to a formal civil-society organization has sometimes taken shape as a member-based organization, as in the case of Rural Action and PUSH Buffalo. From there, alliances may be built among like-minded member-based civil-society organizations, as was particularly evident in the Greater Edmonton Alliance case. Beyond this, however, as Kania and Kramer (2011: 39) argue, "complex problems can be solved only by cross-sector coalitions that engage those outside the nonprofit sector."

The historical trajectory of the examples here demonstrates how such partnerships with public and private sector institutions are crafted to sustain momentum, take initiatives to scale and broaden the receptivity to change. They offer insight into how and when local voluntary efforts partnered with local non-profits or foundations, how collaborations with government organizations were secured and how partnerships with the private sector were negotiated.

While not always successful, citizen-led initiatives had to be nimble enough to adapt to the requirements of partnership while holding fast to their own identity. In the case of The Village in Market Creek in San Diego, for example, an innovative philanthropist responded to citizen ideas to revitalize a run-down neighbourhood, taking responsibility for setting up a process for decision-making by local citizens, inviting public and private sector collaboration at strategic points in the development and then carving out the legal space for local ownership through an Initial Public Offering (IPO) that permitted the purchase of shares by low-income earners. The "next" economy tested in this case would be one that celebrated ethnic cultural diversity but ensured everyone could have "skin in the game," making IPOs accessible to all but limiting the number of shares an individual could own.

As several examples illustrate, partnership is not necessarily a smooth ride. Even with the extraordinary investment of time in collaboration, networking and communication between all players, organizational cultures can be very different and for any organizational player tensions arise between short-term expediency and fidelity to long-term goals. At times, the collaboration has surged forward as in the examples of Rural Action, Ecotrust Canada, New Dawn Enterprises and the Village at Market Creek.

At other times, some of these collaborative efforts have floundered. Maintaining funding support for the different strands of the solutions has been a challenge, as has the uphill struggle of sustaining the momentum of citizen-led action through each generation of leadership. A salient case is that of the quiet movement of self-determination in the Canadian Arctic, where Shelia Watt Cloutier's attempts to champion traditional culture and livelihoods is dovetailed with new possibilities for a younger generation connected over vast distances by social media.

NAVIGATING POWER

In tracking social innovation over a long period of time, these cases have much to say about how power is navigated in order to sustain the momentum of innovation and change. We discuss these in terms of how "power over," "power with," "power within" and "power to" play out (Veneklasen and Miller 2002; Gaventa 2006). First, the acknowledgement of "power over" in the power of the prevailing system and of vested interests in the status quo and its institutions has its corollary in passivity, inertia and quiescence. Taking on this challenge, the starting point for most of these cases was a few concerned citizens gradually garnering interest and trust of other citizens. The Alinsky-style "relationals" of the Greater Edmonton Alliance case, the door-to-door canvassing of the PUSH Buffalo case, the asset-based community building work in rural Appalachia, the tireless relationship building and organizing among new immigrants in Montreal and the culturally-based healing of the Ontario Federation of Indian Friendship Centres (OFIFC) are remarkable for the time taken to instill a sense of possibility and power among fellow citizens. Leaders and the organizations they represented also had to acknowledge their own power when trying to bridge divides of class or race — the examples of New Dawn Enterprises, Vivre St. Michel en Santé and Rural Action are cases in point.

Each case is about creating or building power, focusing on the assets that people have "within" as their individual, cultural or spiritual attributes, the power they have in collaboration "with" others, and how these combine into a sense of agency or "power to." We see this in the OFIFC case, drawing upon the strengths of Indigenous culture and the solidarity of an urban support system. We see this in the Sandhills case, again invoking cultural tradition of a connection to the land to recreate a sense of capacity and motivation for a rural land-based livelihood, as well as the strength to defend it, even in the face of the encroachment of the U.S. military's Fort Bragg. We see this in the Village at Market Creek, with a painstaking process of building participatory decision-making around a vision of a vibrant multi-cultural downtown core, owned by local residents.

Negotiating power involves tension and compromise, where protagonists have to ensure that compromise does not extend to selling out, and where the goals are held fast even if strategies to reach them bend as new opportunities for collaboration emerge. Vivre St. Michel en Santé in Quebec and Rural Action in Ohio both described the conscious steps they took to stay true to their mission even as circumstances and membership changed and unforeseen opportunities arose. Ecotrust Canada has had to balance its responsiveness to local initiative with its commitment to investment in ideas that can go to scale. Sometimes it is necessary to pull the plug on initiatives that don't have that potential. And the Inuit have to balance economic need, traditional livelihoods and rapidly changing environmental and political situations. In every case, the partnership with other organizations required such negotiations, whether these were funders or partners in other sectors. Sometimes multiple strategies are required so that, as in the Sandhills case, collaboration with powerful actors does not compromise the ability to also challenge them at the same time. Sometimes, regardless of common goals, these partnerships were threatened by the incompatibility of organizational cultures or inflexible timeframes, all of which took time and resources to resolve. Sometimes, the clearest indicator of a power imbalance is the burnout in organizations dependent on outside funding when resources to continue the work are seriously overstretched.

Experiencing success, however, is how that sense of power is replenished. Some of the cases illustrate collective power pushing back on municipal authorities, a utility company or even the U.S. military in the case of Sandhills. But it is also by confronting an internalized sense of powerlessness, as experienced in the case of Indigenous peoples in Canada featured here, and the African Americans in the Deep South and the Sandhills, North Carolina.

Systemic change, which we turn to in the next section, requires navigating power. Recognizing it, building it, using it and negotiating with others while keeping the strategy on course is the test that the players in all these cases have had to face.

PATHWAYS TO SYSTEMIC CHANGE

The cases in this collection all confront the need for an overhaul of the dominant economic system if sustainability and fairness are to be achieved. Where this is tackled, however, is at the local level with innovations — many of them social innovations — shaping an economy that builds multiple forms of wealth and ensures broad-based access to a means of livelihood. The term "social innovation," however, is not without its critics. Fowler (2013: 31), for example, argues: "The dominant story line in the social innovation field seems willfully naïve, and thin on recognizing the centrality of power and politics and realities of timeframes in processes of change." In this collection, while these stories are still unfolding, social innovation is shown in a more substantial light. We show how citizen-led innovation in these cases not only responds to deep concern about the status quo but evolves over time as people self-organize, strategize and then collaborate across institutional and cultural boundaries to achieve their ends, dealing with issues of power on a day-to-day basis.

Mulgan (2006: 149) describes how social innovation starts with "exclusion, resentments, passion and commitments ... and spreads in an S curve, with an early phase of slow growth among a small group of committed supporters, followed by a phase of rapid-take off, and then slowing down as saturation and maturity are achieved." Rarely does any pathway conform so neatly to this shape; the fluctuating energy and pace of change is a common feature in these cases, as are the periods of uncertainty of the direction taken and tensions among those trying to act as a team. Yet, distanced from the events themselves, the story is of new relationships between previously separate individuals and groups, people with ideas and expertise linked together with people and institutions with money and influence, strengthening rather than diluting or obstructing systemic change. This is how a local food system is developed, or a zero emission waste recovery system is achieved or a resident-owned downtown revitalization scheme becomes a reality. Each of these cases illustrate how particular individuals and institutions have played a critical role working along the boundaries, linking citizens without access to opportunity to financial institutions, to champions in municipal government, to other economic actors in the value chain or to supporters and allies in government, all moving the innovation to the next level.

Donella Meadows' work on systems change (1999, 2008,[12] also cited in Fowler 2013), provides a helpful framework for examining the contributions of the citizen-led innovation to deepen systems-level change in these cases. She explains the complexity of systems level change and why the quest for the legendary single lever — "a small change in one thing that can produce changes in everything" — is futile. Instead, systems change is achieved through multiple levers; the weight of existing systems can be lifted by such levers and innovation given room to grow. She lists these levers from the least to the most effective. Least effective are "parameters" such as changing the amount of land set aside for conservation, or the minimum wage or the rent charged in subsidized housing. These she says are: "Diddling with the details, arranging the deck chairs on the Titanic. Probably 90 — no 95—no 99 percent of our attention goes to parameters, but there's not a lot of leverage in them" (1999: 8).

She notes that leverage is particularly effective in parts of the system where information and control are found, when information feedback loops to decision-makers result either in corrective action (if the feedback is negative) or in reinforcement (if the feedback is positive). The visibility of growing urban and youth unemployment in Buffalo's West side in the PUSH case, popular protest against urban-industrial encroachment on viable agricultural land in Edmonton in the Greater Edmonton Alliance case or the social and political consequences of a loss of cultural identity among Aboriginal people in Ontario are examples of negative feedback that acted as levers. In the case of the Village at Market Creek, a major philanthropist realized that existing patterns of donor giving were making no difference to the loss of jobs, nor to the persistence of poverty or the blight of low-grade housing of the Diamond neighbourhood in San Diego. This negative feedback raised the possibility of an alternative strategy: local ownership by local residents of a revitalized commercial space.

Democracy is a system designed to generate the negative feedback loops that will put people out of office if self-correction does not occur. But as Meadows (1999: 10) explains: "The process depends upon the free, full, unbiased flow of information back and forth between electorate and leaders. [Instead, however], billions of dollars are spent by [political] leaders to limit and bias that flow." The cases in this collection are examples of citizens attempting to correct that bias. The Greater Edmonton Alliance case study drew attention to "organized money" trying to corrupt civic politics, especially the power of Big Oil skewing municipal, provincial and federal politics towards encouraging oil interests and land specula-tion at the expense of democratic participation. A traceability tool developed by Ecotrust Canada entitled This Fish allows consumers to purchase only fish caught by hook and line, creating a feedback loop in the market that could potentially influence the seafood industry's choice of fishing methods.

Another powerful leverage point is where feedback loops that only reward win-ners can be weakened. In the prevailing economic system, tax policies favouring the wealthy can be weakened if public opinion is mobilized to make the political case for progressive taxation on income, or taxation to cover the real costs of pollution or carbon emissions or increases in corporate tax. The Village at Market Creek case provides the example of an innovative financing mechanism allowing low-income residents to be co-owners but preventing large-scale share accumulation by a few.

Yet another lever is using underutilized regulations or government programs, as well as claiming the space to shape new laws and policies. For example, citizen-organizing in rural Appalachia was effective in convincing local authorities to use their power to compel coal companies to comply with regulations and then to protect and compensate farmers for loss of land quality. PUSH Buffalo's strategy to get municipal support for its green retrofitting strategies for affordable hous-ing under the Green Jobs — Green New York Act of 2009 is another example. By its creative use of provincial government sponsored Community Economic Development Investment Funds to build social enterprises, New Dawn Enterprises in Cape Breton illustrates this further; the social services and the training of care workers now serve as a model for provincial policy.

All these levers help to redistribute ownership, control and production of livelihoods to local levels. They also, in the process, build awareness where it is most needed in order to change the system. This awareness may then be used "to add, change, evolve or self-organize system structure" (Meadows 1999: 3), a powerful leverage point. Meadows explains, "The ability to self-organize is the strongest form of system resilience. A system that can evolve can survive almost any change, by changing itself" (ibid.: 15). Taking this further is Jane Jacobs' advice that we learn from ecology about how we should improve our economic systems, particularly their ability to self-organize, correct, and self-refuel (Jacobs 2000).

Each of these cases illustrates the transitions not only in how citizens organize themselves (informally in associations, as membership-based organizations or as formal non-profits), but also in how they collaborate with others to build networks, often in ways that create alternative systems. The effort that goes into this is often under-appreciated but when successful new interdependent local economic relationships are created through value chains that build multiple forms of wealth. Both the Deep South Community Agricultural Network and Rural Action cases demonstrate a network of allies evolving and permeating the mainstream economy. Another example is Ecotrust Canada's work in the conservation economy, forming strategic alliances with communities on the coast where the model of industrial resource development was being challenged by local groups and First Nations. Social innovations in how people communicate, collaborate and organize accompany technical innovation (such as digital mapping for community planning and visioning), social financing mechanisms used to support innovative enterprise and "proof of concept" measures used to test the synergy of these innovations.

The ability to self-organize and create or evolve new systems relies on a diversity of sources of ideas. As Meadows (1999: 16) observes, "Insistence on a single culture shuts down learning, cuts back resilience." Common themes in these cases are the importance of retrieving lost culture, celebrating diversity and learning from Indigenous ways of knowing. These feed the imagination for new ways of living.

Finally, the lever that meets with the most resistance is the one that pulls on the consciousness and behavioural changes that are necessary for systems change. When it is possible to call into question the paradigm from which the current system draws its central goals, power structure, rules and culture, there is openness to alternative possibilities and a paradigm shift can be considered. The actions outlined in many of the cases reflect a deep questioning of the economic model that sees nature as "a stock of resources to be converted to human purpose" or "economic growth as the answer to virtually all problems" (Meadows 1999: 17, 1). Whether this is influenced by Indigenous ways of knowing, the idea of multiple forms of wealth and sustainable livelihoods or simply a growing awareness of the imperative to shift to a low carbon economy, the ground is shifting. A reconnection with place and drawing livelihood from the land is part of this shift as in the Sandhills and Deep South cases. So are the ideas for "distributed systems of production" (Murray 2009) where local nodes of food production are connected through increasingly sophisticated communications networks, the potential for which is illustrated in the work of Rural Action. Deeper democratic engagement is evident in the community-building work among new immigrants in Montreal (the Vivre St. Michel en Santé case), in the Greater Edmonton Alliance case of broad-based citizen mobilization and in the securing of fair treatment by city and utility companies in the PUSH Buffalo case. The paradigm shift, then, is a new way of seeing, an articulation of a new type of economy expressed by new producers and consumers committed to environmentally sustainable and socially just practices.

CONCLUSION

This overview began with an introduction to eleven case studies from Canada and the U.S. that are featured in this book, selected because they show how innovations are taking place, led by ordinary citizens, that help answer the vexing question of how we reverse or temper the trends towards greater inequality and environmental crisis. None of these offer quick solutions, nor do they claim, by themselves, to have spread their ideas to system-wide levels. Yet, each story has elements that speak to the "thick" solutions (Edwards 2011) for the complex challenges faced in North America — thick because they are neither stroke-of-the-pen nor single project in scope, but a combination of top-down and bottom-up initiatives glued together by a growing support for "radical, practical change." The ideas and actions in these cases are not from institutions disconnected from citizens, but from citizens connecting with institutions and finding a voice. They speak of possibilities, of an emergent demand for a sustainable future in which citizens are prepared to lead. As Speth argues, examples such as these help us to envision a "new operating system" based on "new economic thinking and driven forward by a new politics" (2012: 9–10). Initiatives that may seem small and local can be starter wedges that lead to larger changes and "provide inspirational models for how things might work in a new political economy devoted to sustaining human and natural communities" (Speth 2012: xi).

This book itself is but a small step in spreading the word and inviting more discussion. By looking at the cases retrospectively, we can trace how social innovation has grown and spread through citizens acting collaboratively in the horizontal sense of citizenship and challenging the status quo though action directed at the state, in the vertical sense of citizenship. In so doing such citizens are claiming the space for social and economic inclusion but at the same time challenging politically the nature of an economy that drives growth at the expense of equity and environmental sustainability. This relationship between such economic and political forms of citizenship needs to be explored more deeply. The task ahead is to create the conditions under which such collective agency can grow and to show how allies in institutions or in social media can help accelerate the pace of citizen action and democratize the channels of information. Knowing that we are on the cusp of change, what are the most strategic actions to take in order to usher in an economy that is morally sound? If we imagine these same stories unfolding and proliferating in the coming decades, what will be their sequels?

Notes
1. As will be elaborated in more detail in the following pages, the term "citizen" is used not only as a legal term, but more broadly in the sense of a citizen as an individual who has rights and responsibilities for engaging in political, economic and civic life.
2. "Growth" here can be in technical and social innovation that can moderate or reverse unsustainable types of economic growth.
3. "Citizenship as participation can be seen as representing the expression of human agency in the political arena, broadly defined; citizenship as rights enables people to act as agents" (Lister 1998: 228).
4. See also Kabeer (2005) and other work of the Development Research Centre on Citizenship, Participation and Accountability at <drc-citizenship.org>.
5. Canada signed the Kyoto agreement under the Chretien administration (1993–2003), but pulled out under the Harper administration (2006–). At the time of writing, U.S. Secretary of State John Kerry is articulating concerns about the impending climate change "tipping point" and its consequences. Recent negotiated agreements with China to address climate change and the Obama administration's determination to veto approval of the Keystone oil pipeline from Canada indicate a shift, though this is an ongoing story.
6. In contrast to Norway, where oil revenues have largely been saved in a sovereign wealth fund since 1996 which now stands at $800 billion, Alberta has saved so little of its revenue that since 1976 it has only accumulated $15.3 billion (*The Economist*, Jan 25, 2014).
7. For income alone, rather than overall wealth, a report by Yalnizyan (2010) for example shows that the richest 1 percent of Canadians took 32 percent of growth of incomes from 1997–2007.
8. This has been slowed by the slump in oil prices in 2014–15 but it is uncertain if this is the beginning of a trend or a temporary situation caused by the combined effects of oversupply, slower demand from China and a switch to natural gas.
9. According to MacPherson, the agricultural cooperative movement dates back to the late nineteenth century. By the early twentieth century fishing cooperatives, consumer cooperatives and credit unions were making headway, followed by cooperative housing in the late 1930s. Finally, Arctic cooperatives for Inuit crafts as well as consumer products were established from the 1950s onwards.
10. In relation to the U.S., they write, "Empire as a way of life sidelines movements for progressive change and substitutes paranoid togetherness for community. By distorting

our knowledge of the rest of the world, empire prevents us from discovering how we are linked with others through common oppressions, goals, struggles, and dreams and from learning from grassroots experiments in land reform, public ownership, and democratic participation that are occurring throughout the world" (2012: 287).

11. Research for these cases was undertaken during 2013. After case study selection, authors collaborated on a common set of research questions to guide each study. The research began with a study of existing literature and website information about the case. Fieldwork was conducted in all cases in 2013 to gather information from in-depth interviews with people in the various organizations involved, as well as to glean local community perspectives. Reference to personal communication throughout these cases applies to this period of fieldwork and any subsequent follow-up communication, including during the forum Citizen-led Innovation for Sustainable Change, held in June 2013.

12. Note that Meadows' 2008 book has a chapter on leverage points (pp 145–66), which is a slightly edited version of her 1999 paper. The book itself is an edited compilation of her writing following her death in 2001. Page numbers here refer to her 1999 paper, downloaded from <donellameadows.org/archives/leverage-points-places-to-intervene-in-a-system>.

References

Alperovitz, G. 2013. *What then must we do? Straight talk about the next American Revolution.* White River Junction, VT: Chelsea Green Publishing.

Bernard, A. 2009. "Trends in Manufacturing Employment." *Perspectives,* February. Statistics Canada. Retrieved January 15, 2015 from <http://www.statcan.gc.ca/pub/75-001-x/2009102/article/10788-eng.htm>.

Boyte, H. 2006. "Breaking the Silence." *The Kettering Review* 24 (Spring). Kettering Foundation Press.

_____. 2008. "Civic-Driven Change and Developmental Democracy." In Alan Fowler and Kees Biekart (eds.), *Civic Driven Change: Citizen's Imagination in Action.* The Hague: Institute of Social Studies (ISS).

Brooks. 2014. "The Canada-United States Relationship." In J. Bickerton and A.G. Gagnon (eds.), *Canadian Politics* sixth edition. Toronto: University of Toronto Press.

Cornwall, A., and J. Gaventa. 2001. *From Users and Choosers to Makers and Shapers: Re-Positioning Participation in Social Policy.* Brighton: UK. IDS Working Paper 127.

Dale, A. 2013. "Agency: Individual 'Fit' and Sustainable Community Development." *Community Development Journal* November.

Dodaro, S., and L. Pluta. 2012. *The Big Picture: The Antigonish Movement of Eastern Nova Scotia.* Montreal and Kingston: McGill Queens University Press.

The Economist. 2014. "Canada's Year of the Ant." January 25.

Edwards, M. 2011a. "Introduction: Civil Society and the Geometry of Human Relations." In Michael Edwards (ed.), *The Oxford Handbook of Civil Society.* New York: Oxford University Press.

_____. 2011b. *Thick Problems and Thin Solutions: How NGOs Can Bridge the Gap.* The Hague: Hivos Knowledge Programme.

Fisher, S.L., and B. Smith. 2012. *Transforming Places: Lessons from Appalachia.* Urbana, Chicago, and Springfield: University of Illinois Press.

Fowler, A. 2013. *Social Innovation: New Game, New Dawn or False Promise?* The Hague: Hivos.

Gaventa, J. 2006. *Finding the Spaces for Change.* IDS Bulletin. 37: 6.

____. 2010. "Seeing Like a Citizen: Re-Claiming Citizenship in a Neoliberal World." In Alan Fowler and Chiku Malunga (eds.), *NGO Management: The Earthscan Companion.* London: Earthscan.

Green, G.P., and A. Goetting [eds.]. 2010. *Mobilizing Communities: Asset Building as a Community Development Strategy.* Philadelphia: Temple University Press.

Jacobs, J. 2000. *The Nature of Economies.* New York: Vintage Books.

Kabeer, N. 2005. *Inclusive Citizenship: Meanings and Expressions.* London: Zed Books.

Kahane, A. 2008. "The Change Lab: A Breakthrough Way for Small Teams to Unstick Large Systems." In Water Link, Thais Corral, and Mark Gerzon (eds.), *Leadership Is Global: Co-Creating a More Humane and Sustainable World.* Shinnyo-en Foundation.

Kania, J., and M. Kramer. 2011. "Collective Impact." *Stanford Social Innovation Review* Winter.

Krebs, V., and J. Holley. 2006. "Building Sustainable Communities Through Network Building." Retrieved February 15, 2014 from <supportingadvancement.com/web_sightings/community_building/community_building.pdf>.

Laidlaw, A.F. 1971. *The Man from Margaree.* Toronto: MacLellan and Stewart.

Lister, R. 1998. "Citizens in Action: Citizenship and Community Development in the Northern Ireland context." *Community Development Journal* 33, 3: 226–35.

MacPherson, I. n.d. "The History of the Canadian Cooperative Movement: A Summary, a Little Historiography, and Some Issues. <socialeconomyhub.ca/sites/...ca/files/Cdian%20Co-op%20History.doc>.

Mathie, A., and G. Cunningham. 2008. *From Clients to Citizens: Communities Changing the Course of Their Own Development.* Rugby: Practical Action.

McKernan, S., C. Ratcliffe, E. Steuerle and S. Zhang. 2013. "Less than Equal: Racial Disparities in Wealth Accumulation." April. Urban Institute <www.urban.org>.

Meadows, D. 1999. *Leverage Points: Places to Intervene in a System.* Hartland, VT: The Sustainability Institute.

____. 2008. *Thinking in Systems: A Primer.* Hartland, VT: The Sustainability Institute.

Mendell, M., and N. Neamtan. 2010. "The Social Economy in Quebec: Towards a New Political Economy." In Laurie Mook, Jack Quarter and Sherida Ryan (eds.), *Researching the Social Economy.* Toronto: University of Toronto Press.

Mulgan, G. 2006. "The Process of Social Innovation." *Innovations,* Spring.

Murray, R. 2009. "Danger and Opportunity: Crisis and the New Social Economy." Provocation 09, London: National Endowment for Science, Technology and the Arts (NESTA).

Scokpol, T. 2011. "Civil Society in the United States." In Michael Edwards (ed.), *The Oxford Handbook of Civil Society.* New York: Oxford University Press.

Speth, J.G. 2012b. *America the Possible: Manifesto for a New Economy.* Yale University Press.

TD Economics. 2014. "The Curious Case of Canada's Ailing Manufacturing Sector." <http://www.td.com/document/PDF/economics/special/CanadaAilingManufacturingSector.pdf>.

VeneKlasen, L., and V. Miller. 2007. *A New Weave of Power, People and Politics: The Action Guide for Advocacy and Citizen Participation*. Rugby, UK: Practical Action.

Watt-Cloutier, S. 2015. *The Right to Be Cold: One Woman's Story of Protecting Her Culture, the Arctic, and the Whole Planet*. Toronto: Allen Lane (Penguin).

Yalnizyan, A. 2010. *The Rise of Canada's 1%*. Ottawa: The Canadian Centre for Policy Alternatives.

Yellow Wood Associates. 2010. *Wealth Creation in Rural Communities: A New Approach*. New York: Ford Foundation. <http://community-wealth.org/sites/clone.community-wealth.org/files/downloads/paper-yellow_wood.pdf>.

HUMILITY AND AUDACITY
The Story of Vivre Saint Michel en Santé

Brianne Peters

Saint-Michel is a neighbourhood with a population of 56,000 in northeastern Montreal. From the time it became a ward of the city in 1968, it was known for all the wrong reasons: high crime rates, street gangs, poverty and unemployment; it was a neighbourhood in serious and persistent decline. But as this case study will show, this part of its history is drawing to a close. Over the past ten years, Saint-Michel residents have articulated a new vision with an ambitious and concrete action plan to turn its story around.

Today, there is a buzz of activity in Saint-Michel, with dozens of self-initiated committees, associations and roundtables[1] that bring together people of different ethnic backgrounds to address issues related to poverty, income, employment, housing, security, culture, sports and recreation, neighbourhood beautification and education. Over time, these associations have been complemented by the increased number of social services that have been established in the neighbourhood. As a result, its once highly-transient population has begun to stabilize and newcomers to Saint-Michel are increasingly choosing to settle there.

The people involved in this movement are a mix of recent and established immigrants who are members of Vivre Saint-Michel en Santé (vsms) — For a Healthy Saint-Michel — a community-led organization created in 1991 as part of the Healthy Cities Program initiated by the World Health Organization in 1986. vsms is an umbrella organization established to coordinate and support the neighbourhood's revitalization strategy. It includes dozens of members and staff from within and outside Saint-Michel, many of whom are experienced community organizers and seasoned political activists. It also includes several community-based organizations and external institutions that support its work.

This case study documents a ten-year story of ordinary citizens doing some extraordinary things. The results have been gradual and at times humbling. The real innovation of VSMS lies in initiating and leading the process of citizen engagement in a community whose residents have often not been recognized as citizens, either in the legal sense or in terms of their capacity to play an active role in determining their own future.[2] It is a story of collaboration, compromise and at times confrontation.

This case study also provides insights into the effectiveness of Quebec's progressive social policies with regard to relatively marginalized populations. The emergence of VSMS coincided with the enactment of a number of provincial policies intended to foster inclusion of new immigrants, reduce poverty, and increase employment and access to services. In a sense, VSMS is a product of these policies. The organization's experience also raises important questions about how these policies could be more meaningfully targeted to support service delivery and job creation at the grassroots level.

CONTEXT

Quebec

The province of Quebec has a long history of social and political movements. As the only province of Canada with a French-speaking majority, it has had to hold its own to preserve its identity in a predominantly English-speaking country. Quebec faced very real possibilities of secession from Canada with referendums for independence held in 1980 and 1995, which garnered 40 percent and 49.4 percent of the vote, respectively (Dickinson and Young 2008).

Quebec is known for its community-organizing traditions and strong cooperative sector dating back to the early 1900s, when Alphonse Desjardins and his wife Dorimène Roy started a network of *caisses populaires* (people's banks) aimed to provide loans and savings services for residents who were previously out of reach of these services. Today, Desjardins Group is the largest cooperative financial group in Canada and the sixth largest in the world.

In the 1960s, Quebec saw the emergence of another notable social movement as a reaction to a worldwide recession. Known as *l'animation sociale* (social animation), this movement involved the creation of citizens committees that took an active role in meeting the needs of Quebec's population and eventually started advocating for improving government-service provision. Brodhead (2008: 4) observes:

> The animation movement became characterized by two distinct approaches, one integrative and consensual, and the other integrative and conflictual. Citizens committees in Quebec practiced both approaches — one that advocated community-run social services, which would be

based on the principle of self-help, and the other on the need to make "animation" more political with the creation of pressure groups.

This tension between collaboration and self-help on the one hand, and conflictual organizing to agitate for broader structural changes on the other, is a prominent thread in the story of VSMS.

Quebec is also known for its progressive social safety net and in 2002 it became the first jurisdiction in North America to pass an act to combat poverty and social exclusion. This act included dedicated funds to support organizations working on these issues, such as VSMS. Another feature of Quebec that needs to be mentioned here is considerable decentralization of political authority, with sub-municipal units (called boroughs) being responsible for local administration and city governments focusing on larger issues. This decentralization offers opportunities for citizen participation in decision-making and responsive government support for citizen initiatives.

Given this history, it is not surprising that Quebec has a vibrant social economy, a term that came to the forefront of public discourse in the province as early as the 1990s. Today, the social economy sector in Quebec accounts for between 7 and 8 percent of GNP — 6,000 businesses and some 120,000 jobs in the cooperative, non-profit and enterprise sectors (Neamtan n.d.). This attests to the value that Quebec citizens have traditionally placed on civil-society engagement in the delivery of services and enterprise development.

It should be noted that most of the people involved in VSMS are immigrants who do not share Quebec's past. Montreal has the second largest immigrant population in Canada and over 70 percent of the households in Saint-Michel speak neither French nor English as their first language. Most people in Saint-Michel carry their expressions of solidarity from their countries of origin and have their own ways of dealing with political, social or economic challenges and opportunities that are not necessarily rooted in sovereignty movements or other forms of social organizing characteristic of Quebec. VSMS is, therefore, an eclectic movement that incorporates community building strategies from around the world.

Saint-Michel

Originally a small farming community with its own municipal status, Saint-Michel became a ward of Montreal in 1968. It experienced a rapid population increase — from six thousand to sixty thousand — in less than twenty years following World War II thanks to low-cost housing and availability of jobs created by industrial development. In Saint-Michel, industrial development included the establishment of two large quarries, which became an unattractive defining feature of the neighbourhood. Both quarries had closed by 1984 and were subsequently turned into a site for snow removal and a dump for the rest of the city's waste. The closure of the quarries had detrimental effects on employment in the neighbourhood, and their subsequent conversion into landfills is remembered as a particularly painful part of Saint-Michel's history. For many, the decision to locate two large city dumps in Saint-Michel was symbolic of how the rest of Montreal perceived the neighbourhood — as its *poubelle* (garbage can).

Saint-Michel's demographic profile also sets it apart from the rest of Montreal. It is one of the most ethnically diverse neighbourhoods in the city. The first large influx of immigrants came from Italy after the Second World War, followed by Haitians seeking asylum from the oppressive regime headed by Francois Duvalier. In the 1970s, Saint-Michel saw a significant number of immigrants from Southeast Asia — "boat people" from Vietnam, for example. During the 1980s, large numbers of people came from Central and South America. The most recent wave of immigration, originating from Northwest Africa (the Maghreb region), occurred in the late 1990s and early twenty-first century. As a result of these different influxes, Saint-Michel has become known as a juncture of cultures and religions with dozens of organizations established to facilitate the immigration and integration of newcomers.

By the time of the creation of vsms, the continuous flow of immigrants into Saint-Michel had resulted in a population density that was nearly twice as high as other parts of Montreal. Yet, over half of Saint-Michel residents stayed there for less than five years. The unemployment rate was higher than in other parts of Montreal and when people did have jobs — mostly in small mechanical and manufacturing shops, hotels, clothing stores, taxi cab companies and restaurants — they usually earned less than average Montreal wages for the same types of jobs. Crime rates were also above the city average.

Vivre Saint-Michel en Santé

In 1991, some two hundred residents of Saint-Michel gathered together to discuss how they could address issues of transiency, crime and poverty in the neighbourhood. That meeting inaugurated Saint-Michel's participation in the World Health Organization's Healthy Cities Program intended to provide spaces for citizens to discuss and act on issues of common concern. This program was locally promoted by the City of Montreal, the Ministry of Health and Centraide (United Way).

The meeting also led to the creation of vsms to coordinate and support a number of roundtables charged with designing specific actions to help the residents of Saint-Michel achieve their collective vision. The vision was this: "St. Michel, a pleasant neighbourhood within which to live, supportive of family life and multicultural exchanges, an active and unified community, which takes charge of its affairs and also contributes to the vigour of Montreal" (Vivre Saint-Michel en Santé 2004: 1).

Today, VSMS has close to fifty members from both Saint-Michel and other parts of Montreal. Some members are individual citizens acting as volunteers and some are staff of organizations engaged in Saint-Michel. Collectively, they are dedicated to supporting revitalization of the neighbourhood. Ambitious in its approach, VSMS targets multiple issues and involves networks focusing on mental health, children and families, food security, seniors, youth, housing, culture, security, sports and recreation, citizen participation, transportation and revenue generation. VSMS staff manages the human, material and financial resources of the more than fifty action plans designed by residents to meet their collective vision. They also forge relationships with partners and donors, including a number of provincial departments, private companies and family foundations.

When you ask VSMS members to describe its role, they say that it is a "coordinator of community action," an "information hub," a "networker," a "reference point for government institutions and donors," a "catalyzer," a "community-building work camp," and a "responsive investor (not just financially) in community activity." The organization's flexibility and ability to take on multiple roles simultaneously are parts of its beauty.

VSMS leaders wholeheartedly put citizen participation at the centre of everything they do. The term "citizen," in this context, refers to individuals who have legal rights and responsibilities, but also to individuals who actively engage in civic life, with or without formal citizenship credentials. According to Panet-Raymond (2013: 73), VSMS strives to achieve three types of citizen participation in Saint-Michel. The first is political: exercising direct or indirect power over decision-making in public spaces. The second is public: taking part in debates and decision-making concerning economic, political and social issues. And the third is social: engaging in informal and formal associations and movements with the aim of transforming policies, structures and social norms.

VSMS dedicates resources to support these kinds of participation and to create a special Citizen Participation Roundtable that cuts across all of the organization's activities. The members of this roundtable are the key contributors to this case study. They come from diverse parts of the world but now call Saint-Michel their home and want to make it a neighbourhood where people choose to live.

CITIZEN PARTICIPATION IN SAINT-MICHEL

Stimulating active citizen participation in civic life in Saint-Michel was not a straightforward task. First, as mentioned earlier, much of its population base was temporary, so volunteer turnover was common.

Second, it was easy to find groups sharing the same background who were willing to come together but harder to motivate people to join groups that included members with diverse backgrounds and varied interests. One community organizer observed: "We were only used to coming together to complain about others. There was a lot of prejudice. So to come together to do something productive was a new idea in Saint-Michel." As he further explained,

> I would go door to door asking people about the issues they faced and whether they would be willing to do something about them. Some people answered the door, but you can imagine in a neighbourhood with as many street gangs as Saint-Michel, I knew what people were thinking ... "Who is this young Latino guy coming to my door?" (personal communication)[3]

Third, when people from diverse backgrounds did decide to come together, facilitators had to juggle the conflicting interests and ideologies within the groups, at least initially. One of them explained:

> Not everyone involved in VSMS came from democratic societies. Sometimes the leaders that emerged defaulted to replicating those systems [autocracies, dictatorships], so we had to make sure we were not complacent on these issues either. It was a real danger and difficult to balance in the beginning. (personal communication)

Fourth, poverty was a barrier to participation. A staff member of a local organization explained: "We aren't in a rich neighbourhood where people can afford to volunteer" (personal communication). Fifth, some residents felt that apathetic attitudes and dependence on government programs had undermined citizens' motivation to act. Finally, since many residents were new immigrants, they were not always aware of the spaces that existed for engaging with the broader neighbourhood. It was partly a lack of information that prevented them from participating in political and social life.

Despite these challenges, however, many residents were willing to contribute their time and money to neighbourhood activities. One organizer observed:

> Yes, it's hard to mobilize a diverse group of immigrants, but you'll be hard pressed to find a group who is more motivated to have a better life and to integrate. Immigrants are on the move and they want life to improve as fast as possible. They are under a tremendous amount of pressure to make it happen. Yes, some may be on welfare, but transitionally, not permanently or inter-generationally. This is what sets them apart from others who were born here (personal communication).

It was in this context that the Citizen Participation Roundtable emerged to develop a greater role for citizens in realizing the neighbourhood revitalization plan.

Its members — community organizers who lived in Saint-Michel and volunteered for VSMS — agreed that they would focus on supporting civic initiatives in matters of common interest, encouraging the emergence of local leaders, promoting active participation of young people in neighbourhood decision-making processes and documenting the experiences of citizen participation (Vivre Saint-Michel en Santé 2009).

The coordinator of this roundtable, Jean Panet-Raymond, has published extensively on the issues of community organizing and social movements in Quebec. He draws much of his inspiration from decades of his personal experiences as a political activist in the province who understands very well, in a practical sense, what motivates people to take action. "The high-flying theory behind all of this is complex," he explained jokingly, as he jotted down the letters "PTA" on a napkin:

> The first thing is the push of problems and needs (*"la Poussée du malaise"*) — there must be push factors that are important enough to force people into action, individually at first and then collectively. But if people don't have the pull of hope (*"la Tirée de l'espoir"*) — a sense that they have some control and can make change, then the push factors don't matter. The third is the collective group process (*"l'Adhésion au processus"*) — finding someone like you sharing a common idea that brings you together.

He then proceeded to write down the letters "FFF," an acronym for fun, *foin* (cash) and *foi* (faith):

> The process is as important as the result in community organizing. People like to have fun. People like to feel like their contribution has made a tangible difference ... like they have a role, like they have been valued and they got to a result.... It's festive, fun and an expression of culture. But the cash has to be there to support the process. And finally, faith and hope of change has always been central to community organizing. It is a great platform for organizing the next action and for building a collective critical consciousness (personal communication).

And so, members of the Citizen Participation Roundtable put these "high-flying" theories into practice in four practical steps to foster a process to gradually and deliberately move citizens from acting as individuals ("I") to acting as a group ("US/WE") and then as a neighbourhood ("TOGETHER"). They described these four steps as follows (Chevrier and Panet-Raymond 2013):

> First, go to where the citizens are. This included canvassing door to door, meeting people in places where they had already been spending

considerable time such as schools, parks, shops and subway stations. The aim was to use these venues to listen to their needs, expectations and hopes. This was where you found "I."

Second, provide information on civic issues at common meeting places. This information was provided at events such as weekly coffees, neighbourhood parties and evening discussions. Cultural activities such as concerts, theatre or cinema were often used as a medium for relaying information and sharing opinions. This was the beginning of "US/WE."

Third, support the creation of citizens' committees to deliberate on issues of common concern and to plan action. These committees were an expression of the "WE" where groups could come together to take action and expand their influence on issues affecting the neighbourhood. This was the beginning of "TOGETHER."

Finally, provide training and support for emerging leaders. This training was practical and equipped residents with the skills to act as citizens and to "learn democracy by doing."

While these steps sound relatively neutral, there was an unspoken agenda upon which they were based. A community organizer explained:

> It's really rights-based organizing without calling it that. We are trying to become a neighbourhood that understands both our rights and our responsibilities as Canadian citizens. We don't care about the vehicle for doing it — it could be festivals, debates, culture nights, leadership training, campaigning — whatever works. (personal communication)

These processes resulted in hundreds of informal interviews with citizens, who first discussed their frustrations, concerns and fears but eventually moved to talk about their hopes and opportunities for the future. One VSMS activist observed: "It was like people were just waiting to be asked how they felt about Saint-Michel. Every door, we got an amazing response ... sometimes for hours. We asked for it, and boy, we got it" (personal communication).

These discussions led to suggestions to create six designated spaces in the neighbourhood where people could move from doorway conversations to something more structured. VSMS called these Citizen Spaces and there was usually one for every sector of three hundred to seven hundred households, where people could regularly come together to discuss issues and opportunities in a non-threatening environment. Wherever possible, organizers used existing public spaces (such as a school or day care) because these spaces provided a natural opportunity for citizens of different backgrounds to mingle and could be expected to survive if the small funds allocated for keeping newly-created Citizen Spaces expired.

Over time, maintaining these spaces helped community members to shape, contribute to and volunteer in the delivery of social services rather than simply be treated like clients or beneficiaries. This has resulted in service provision designed with and for the people who have the most stake in them. As one volunteer explained, "There are lots of organizations that do good work, but they just provide, provide, provide. The dignity is missing because we do not contribute or participate ... and that's what I wanted to change" (personal communication).

These volunteers often became neighbourhood leaders and were invited by vsms to participate in leadership trainings so they could draw other residents into local activities. Six cohorts (forty-eight people in total) have graduated from a free eighteen-hour citizen leadership laboratory run by vsms, and received 110 hours of collective coaching during which they learned about public speaking, communication, running meetings and decision-making processes. This training, coupled with ongoing individual and group coaching, has yielded a strong cadre of citizen leaders ready to take action quickly on issues as they arise.

Marie Carmel Bailey, who came to Saint-Michel from Haiti in 1974, explained how this training provided her with the skills to take action when the city authorities announced that they were going to build a new composting facility in the very place the neighbourhood had set aside to build a park:

> We came together and emerged as "little leaders." None of us came from the same place, but we had the cause. We emailed, called on the phone, we made posters, and we went to see the decision-makers. It was like a trumpet! For the first time since I moved to Saint-Michel, I felt like I was doing something not for me, but for my community. (personal communication)

Marie Carmel Bailey was not the only one who articulated the move from "I" to "WE" to "TOGETHER"; it was a common narrative that ran through each conversation with community organizers. Another local leader, Kattia Pineda, who had come to Canada 17 years earlier from El Salvador, was dismayed at the decision to construct a car impound in front of her house and across the street from the local school, and decided to prevent this from happening. She explained:

> Someone from the Citizen Space came to my door to ask me about my life, and I told her about the car impound. We started a committee with two other Italians and a Quebecoise. We went to see the mayor together. It took a long time, but that's where I learned that things can change if we engage. If I didn't have the car impound in front of my house, I may not have contributed. It has to be something personal. And then you realize

you have the power to do something bigger, to change something. So why not continue? (personal communication)

As these stories illustrate, the trigger for action was often as simple as being listened to and being connected to others who had the same concerns. These new connections eventually led to tangible changes in the neighbourhood. Community gardens were planted. Literacy, language, after-school tutoring and daycare programs were introduced. Cultural festivities involving hundreds of citizens are now an annual tradition. Several mothers created a group called *Les Anges de la Securite* (Angels of Security) to accompany the neighbourhood's children on their walks to and from school. Low-cost food programs helped hundreds of people access nutritious food at affordable prices. Some parts of the neighbourhood started their own recycling programs. And the most recent endeavour is the emergence of a housing cooperative intended to construct new and affordable units. The list goes on and on and one need look no further than the local newspaper, *Journal de Saint-Michel*, to see that the neighbourhood is bursting with activity.

While street violence still exists, anecdotal and statistical evidence indicates that it has decreased considerably. Residents report a stronger feeling of cohesion with their neighbours than they had before. The police chief of Montreal has recently presented Saint-Michel with an award for outstanding contributions of community organizations to the well-being of the neighbourhood. Community organizers describe how the police have changed the ways in which they interact with Saint-Michel residents:

> They know where there is trouble. Before, they would have entered these places on the spot. Today, they know that there are community organizations that are better placed to help them deal with the situation. We know the people. So they wait now. They are more patient. They say they could not do their job in Saint-Michel if these community-based organizations did not exist. (personal communication)

Similarly, several donors have remarked that Saint-Michel is now a less volatile neighbourhood because they "have everything in place — the social infrastructure — to avoid a crisis" (personal communication with Centraide staff). This has turned Saint-Michel into a preferred partner for government departments and donors, which noted how much easier it is to work in an area where community groups display solidarity, active participation, collaboration, coordination, vision and confidence. One official from the Ministry of Immigration and Cultural Communities observed:

> For certain, it's easier to work with Saint-Michel's citizens. Participation

is important to them. It's a neighbourhood with a very developed move-ment. Yes, there is action in other neighbourhoods, but it is not concerted action. VSMS is unique and multi-disciplinary — sports, women, cul-ture, housing — a sort of "everything" type of organization. (personal communication)

Today, there is an obvious sense of pride in the neighbourhood and residents report that although poverty is still a serious issue they no longer feel defined by it.

BROADER IMPACT

In 2004 and again in 2012, VSMS commissioned an external survey and two focus group discussions, each with 320 citizens not directly involved in VSMS's activi-ties (640 people in total). The purpose was to determine whether there had been any changes in residents' satisfaction with the quality of life in Saint-Michel. The anonymous responses collected by an evaluator revealed substantial differences in residents' perceptions of the neighbourhood between 2004 and 2012. Significantly, the residents who expressed the most satisfaction were those who had been living in Saint-Michel for ten years or more, a testament to the notable improvements over time. The table below shows the changes in the percentages of people who were satisfied with service delivery in 2004 and 2012:

Table 2-1 Levels of Satisfaction with Service Delivery in Saint-Michel, 2004 and 2012

Service	Percentage of residents satisfied	
	In 2004	In 2012
Proximity of schools and day cares	75%	83%
Provision of recreational activities for children and youth	49%	62%
Provision of recreational activities for adults	29%	52%
Number of cultural activities for children and youth	47%	61%
Availability of housing	27%	51%

Source of data: Simard 2012.

Yet another area that received an improved rating was safety. In 2004, Saint-Michel residents described lack of security in the neighbourhood as a "severe problem" and 47 percent of those surveyed felt it was unsafe to go out at night. In 2012, only 38 percent reported feeling unsafe at night, which was on a par with the Montreal average.

Overall, these developments appear to be transforming Saint-Michel from a stepping stone to a better life to a neighbourhood where people come by choice, not only by necessity. And newcomers are starting to stay. Today, 61 percent of

Saint-Michel residents have lived in the neighbourhood for five or more years and far more residents intend to stay. The availability of low-cost housing is no longer the primary reason for living in Saint-Michel and respondents now identify the ease of integration, reconnecting with their families and the availability of services as the main reasons why they opt to stay (Simard 2012).

EXTERNAL INFLUENCES AND PARTNERSHIPS

Many residents of Saint-Michel had an active political past in their home countries. As representatives of VSMS, however, they have been described by funders and government officials as being "pragmatists, not ideologists," "modest and humble negotiators," "non-militant," "respectfully conflictual," "willing to compromise" and "relatively apolitical." "It's a sort of 'yes, but with conditions' kind of neighbour-hood," explained one citizen. People seem willing to put their personal political histories behind them in their public life in Saint-Michel and work together under the coordination of VSMS if this brings improvements to their individual lives and the neighbourhood. One woman explained:

> Yes, I may be a radical or a feminist in my home life, but I live in this society. And we know the constraints, what we are left with, and what we have control over. So we do what we can with what we have, which is not extreme. Sometimes I have to leave my feminism at the door so we can make change in this neighbourhood. (personal communication)

As a result of such pragmatism, citizens and organizations involved with VSMS have cultivated positive relationships with donors and government officials and VSMS currently receives the support of nearly twenty funding agencies. Indeed, there are many external actors that have become an important part of VSMS's twenty-year history.

First, the Healthy Cities Program, funded by the City of Montreal, Centraide and the Department of Public Health quickly took root in the form of roundtables on issues of common concern across Quebec during the late 1980s and 1990s. As mentioned above, this program provided the initial impetus for the creation of VSMS. In 1994, the roundtables initiated under this program became a matter of public policy and were included in the provincial community development policy framework.

Second, given the multicultural makeup of Saint-Michel and the desire of the provincial government to stimulate active citizenship among its growing immigrant population, the Quebec Ministry of Immigration and Cultural Communities began supporting VSMS in 2005 and continues to do so until this day. As one official explained:

> We are trying to integrate people in different ways to make them feel that they belong to Quebec society, to get people to know each other and each other's cultures better, and to create an environment where people can live together despite coming from different places. (personal communication)

Third, VSMS has received some financial support from the Ministry of Employment and Social Solidarity to help implement its anti-poverty strategy. Fourth, in 2004, thanks to its achievements in Saint-Michel, VSMS was invited by the McConnell Foundation, Tamarack Institute and Centraide to participate in a ten-year partnership as part of Vibrant Communities, a pan-Canadian initiative through which thirteen community organizations experimented with innovative approaches to poverty reduction. One feature of VSMS that distinguished it from other participating organizations was its constellation governance featuring multiple leaders, paid and unpaid, that emerged to take on specific issues (Cabaj 2011: 127). Another feature that set VSMS apart was its thousand-flowers strategy that energetically set out to tackle multiple issues at once whereas other community organizations often tended to focus on a single issue that was easier to address (ibid.: 126).

The existence of external funding sources for organizations like VSMS that support community-run service delivery, civil society engagement in poverty reduction efforts and community-building in general is indicative of the importance of the social and solidarity economy in Quebec. Interestingly (and perhaps not surprisingly given that most people living in Saint-Michel have a very different history) no one articulated their work as fitting within the social economy, but VSMS nonetheless has a number of features that align well with this sector. One of these is its horizontal and democratic structure. Citizens are elected to its many decision-making bodies such as the General and Neighbourhood Assemblies, the Board of Directors, Executive Committee and Citizens College. Another feature is VSMS's emphasis on building civic skills as demonstrated through its ongoing citizen leadership laboratories (discussed above) as well as through the volunteer and employment opportunities it provides for residents willing to assist in community-run services in the neighbourhood. Related to this are the sensitive, adaptable and creative ways in which community organizations and their volunteers are responding to local priorities, particularly in the delivery of services but more recently in advocating for policy changes. Finally, it is characteristic of VSMS to blend resources from public, private and community development sectors in order to provide these services.

The social economy sector in Saint-Michel has fostered active citizenship and social inclusion and contributed towards a greater access to social services. However, these results have not come without tensions. Multi-stakeholder partnerships across different sectors can be tough but are necessary in a fiscally-constrained environment. It is difficult to manage diverse interests, particularly among populations that have not always had the luxury, power or desire to confront systems that are not benefitting them as much as they could be, which also seems to be the case here.

TENSIONS

The pragmatic approach of VSMS members has enabled them to find a common denominator that brings people of diverse backgrounds, interests and sectors together to make things happen — both within Saint-Michel and with outside partners. One member observed jokingly:

> In another time and place, I would have called my colleague a neo-fascist. He would have called me a terrorist. But we've been there, done that. There is a certain political maturity here. Now we talk. (personal communication)

In all seriousness, however, this kind of "compromising collaboration" across sectors has introduced ethical dilemmas for some of VSMS members. They have admitted to finding themselves in uncomfortable ideological grey zones as a result of their engagement in some activities and in partnerships with certain institutions and networks. One member explained:

> Yes we have festive and friendly demonstrations. These don't stir up big problems, but we can't forget that this also helps to explain the success of Saint-Michel. Residents are not dogmatic, and this has led to continued funding of our work. But it has led to some tradeoffs over the years. (personal communication)

Some members felt that the organization had become opportunistic at times and linked with partners that compromised its original collective vision. "Yes, we are in a fiscally constrained environment and some people feel these partnerships are the lesser of two evils, but it's a matter of distinguishing between 'compromise' and 'compromising'," one member explained (personal communication).

At times, following funding has also led to a dependence on formal community organizations as the conduit for local activities. These organizations are commonly staffed by people with more experience and formal education who live outside Saint-Michel and are able follow external reporting requirements. Some wonder if this has had the effect of professionalizing a grassroots movement so that it becomes too much driven by staff instead of citizens. A recent OECD report (Buckingham and Teasdale 2013) also notes that the social economy, by and large, may not be directly providing employment for relatively "vulnerable" populations in Quebec because of the high costs of training required, inconsistent funding and a reliance on subsidies.

The sustainability of these community-based organizations, as described by one community organizer, is often dependent on "the commitment of an MA graduate coming from outside Saint-Michel who accepts sixteen dollars an hour when she could be making forty dollars doing the same job in the public sector" (personal communication). Wages for jobs in the social economy are characteristically low and the provincial government reported that only one-third of social enterprises exceed minimum benefits, wages and working conditions for their employees (Shragge and Toye 2006). These sentiments are also echoed in the OECD report: "stop asking SEOs [social enterprise organizations] to do more with less" was one of its recommendations (Buckingham and Teasdale 2013: 101). This recommendation resonates with members and staff of VSMS. After ten years of working for the revitalization of their neighbourhood members continue to be inspired, but they are also very tired. It was a common concern among everyone interviewed that volunteers and staff are going to burn out. There have been suggestions to simplify VSMS's original action plan and do less, but continue to do it well.

Despite the challenges associated with taking on so many activities and forging relationships with sometimes unlikely partners, members generally feel that their pragmatic approach has brought substantial improvements to their neighbourhood. Being active citizens is something residents enjoy; they benefit from the support of their partners, and would not have access to the same level of services if they did not contribute to their delivery. However, some VSMS staff feel that the level of volunteer subsidization in service delivery is unfair and they would like to take on broader systemic issues so that more resources are directed to support citizen-led initiatives. Nonetheless, it has been the staff's conscious choice to go with the flow of Saint-Michel's citizens, even if their energy leads to compromise and collaboration rather than agitation and direct confrontation for entitlements the staff feel the neighbourhood deserves. One staff member explained:

> Political leadership has to be citizen-appropriated so I can take on a more technical leadership. I will fill in the logistical and organizational gaps in so far as I am not doing everything myself. There has to be enough political leadership at the organizational and citizen level so what I do does not jeopardize the will of those citizens. (personal communication)

ACTIONS

VSMS staff members were surprised in 2012 when citizens responded with outrage at an information night they held on the city's newest plan to build a composting plant in Saint-Michel. Of the four proposed sites for composting plants across Montreal, not only was this the only one to be constructed in a residential area but it was to be constructed at the old quarry and dump site, which Saint-Michel residents had long wanted to convert into a park, a desire for which they had finally obtained approval. One staff member observed:

> We expected people would negotiate for odour reducers and that kind of thing. But there was an explosion. We underestimated the painful history that is still very much alive in Saint-Michel about always being treated as the garbage can of Montreal. They are not against composting; they just don't want more garbage next to their homes. This is not a "not in my back yard" fight ... the point is that their backyard is already full. (personal communication)

VSMS helped organize a campaigning blitz on the composting plant and local organizations agreed to include short information sessions on the subject over a number of months. One man started a Facebook page to raise awareness. A woman who was proficient in English submitted articles to city newspapers to raise awareness in the Anglophone areas of Montreal. Residents went door to door collecting thousands of signatures on the petition against the plant construction project (see Figure 2-1), which were then presented to City Hall together with a series of questions prepared by recent graduates of the citizen leadership laboratory held by VSMS.

Figure 2-1 Citizen Petition Against Composting Plant Construction

Petition: NO to the Composting Plant in Saint-Michel!

Considering:

- That the Saint-Michel neighbourhood has an unrivaled concentration of urban nuisances related to public infrastructure: regional landfill site for more than 30 years, environmental sorting complex, dump and snow removal depot, regional car impound and the highway in the heart of the neighbourhood;
- That the Saint-Michel neighbourhood has suffered from a severe decline in social and economic conditions over the years as a result of political decisions;
- That the district has begun a process of revitalization for 10 years to make Saint-Michel a neighbourhood where life is good and conducive to family life.

We, the signatories of this petition, are asking the City of Montreal ro renounce the installation of the composting plant in Saint-Michel!

On February 14 and again on March 18, 2013, hundreds of citizens took to the streets to protest against the installation of the composting plant. Because of the positive relationships residents had established with local authorities, the police helped clear the streets and the borough mayor and local councillors marched with them and even subsequently paid for some of the costs associated with the demonstrations with government funds. Over the course of the year, the composting plant became an election issue and the decision to construct it in Saint-Michel has since been overturned.

This protest is perhaps the most concerted and confrontational action taken by VSMS over the past twenty years. It is symbolic of the pride residents now feel about their neighbourhood, the responsibility they feel to protect it and the expectations they have from the state as citizens.

LESSONS

The social economy

By and large, the literature on the social economy that has emerged since the 1990s has promoted the sector for many of the reasons demonstrated in this case study. Services in Saint-Michel are responsive to many different local concerns and opportunities, local organizations are nimble, delivery is personalized to suit the needs and circumstances of users and people who have the most at stake in these services are given the opportunity to participate in their provision. These opportunities impart skills and networking opportunities that may not otherwise be there, particularly for those with less education and employment experience. Saint-Michel is a different neighbourhood today as a result of the commitment and agency of its volunteers and staff, who are taking advantage of the enabling environment. One of the motivations behind these policies is the recognition that community-run services offer something unique and that organizations like VSMS help those operating in the public and private sectors to do their jobs better. This recognition has recently been enshrined in a province-wide act to provide support for actors operating in the social economy across all government ministries.

However, there are also a number of concerns that come out of this case study. One of the reasons that many of the services in Saint-Michel continue to run is because of voluntary labour and the low wages of staff. Many of those employed formally in these organizations live outside of Saint-Michel. Many of these organizations are run out of old buildings that need renovation. Reporting mechanisms of the many provincial departments and donors that promote the social economy are arduous and funding is inconsistent. As a result, staff and volunteer burnout rates are high and the sustainability of these organizations are at risk.

Collaboration if possible; confrontation if necessary

Living and working in one of the most ethnically diverse neighbourhoods in Montreal, residents demonstrated that in order to find common ground they had to leave their own histories of political activism in their private life and find a common denominator, sometimes collaborating on something fun like sharing cultural dances and food and sometimes confronting more serious issues such as the composting plant project. VSMS staff, many of whom come from Quebec, which had a strong history of political activism and agitation, had to make a choice to follow the energy of Saint-Michel residents, which also sometimes meant collaboration and concession with outside supporters on issues or partnerships with which they disagreed.

On the other hand, there were also several enabling collaborations without which VSMS would not be where it is today. VSMS had champions within relatively rigid institutions who were willing to fund labour-intensive, participatory processes with often immeasurable results, which are not always easy processes to sell. Funding this kind of work has required accepting that outcomes can be unpredictable, encouraging flexible monitoring and evaluation systems, allocating resources for action and learning and taking an initial risk.

A holistic and ambitious vision

VSMS articulated a vision and action plan that was rooted in the needs and hopes of Saint-Michel residents, which resulted in holistic and far-reaching change across a number of sectors. However, with ambition and audacity come some trade-offs. An evaluation report comparing Saint-Michel with other participants of the Vibrant Community Initiative across Canada (Gamble 2010) noted a number of challenges. First, the sheer size of VSMS and its range of activity made it more difficult to manage. Second, staff and volunteer burnout was more common. Third, it was difficult to prevent its volunteers from working at cross purposes. And finally, the vision required flexible funding institutions willing to pay for process and an intermediary organization to coordinate the movement, which is the central and often hard-to-describe role of an organization such as VSMS.

"I don't *do* anything," explained one staff member. "I make things happen. ... I hold the microphone while citizens do all the talking. I shut up and back up. That's my role" (personal communication). This kind of role is the grease that keeps everything in motion and is critical for achieving Saint-Michel's vision.

Simplicity of approach

Despite VSMS's multi-pronged vision and ambitious action plan, the simplicity and humility of VSMS' approach is an important success factor. Saint-Michel citizens have demonstrated that community-building, as a concept, can be quite basic. It does not take years of formal education to understand. Nor does it necessarily require a rich natural resource base, political clout, adequate physical infrastructure or wealthy citizens and institutions — although each and all of these factors would certainly help.

But it does take people with experience, patience and passion both inside and outside the neighbourhood, who are willing to invest in a deliberative process over the long term, oftentimes outside of office hours and above and beyond what donors will pay for or job descriptions can possibly capture. It's the irreplaceable x factor. It's messy, heavy, ever-shifting and requires constant face time and phone calls. There is no substitute. The good thing is that it can happen in any community.

CONCLUSION

There are ongoing attempts to facilitate the transition of newcomers to Canada, particularly in urban areas. The story of vsms stands out as exceptional because it demonstrates that with the right type of support and an appropriate timeframe, it is possible to build community, among people who would not naturally call themselves a community, with strong leaders and local organizations. vsms's story provides important lessons on how to activate the responsibilities of citizenship at the community level and how citizens of diverse backgrounds, by working on a common goal, can begin to access resources of government and even shape the broader political environment. It is a story that demonstrates the effectiveness of several unique social policies initiated in Quebec in order to foster inclusion, reduce poverty and facilitate access to services for new and established immigrants. However, it also raises some constructive questions about how people might benefit more from these policies, recognizing how immigrants are building their own kind of social economy.

At the time of writing this case study, vsms has reached an important turning point. It has just celebrated its twentieth anniversary and is in the throes of developing a new strategic plan for the next four years. The job of vsms is certainly not over but the organization and its members are on a very different track than they were years ago. Their new organizational vision, approved in recent months, provides an indication of how far they have come: "Saint-Michel, a lighthouse district, inspiring and supportive, proud of its diversity, strengthened by its ability to act collectively, where its citizens want to grow, succeed and grow old."

Notes

1. A roundtable (*table de concertation* in French) is a coordinating committee that meets regularly to discuss and act on issues of common concern. Starting in the 1980s, roundtables became a popular strategy for mobilizing citizens among government, non-profit and donor agencies in Quebec.

2. Refer to the introductory chapter discussion of citizenship.
3. All references to personal communication are for interviews conducted in January 2013.

References

Brodhead, D. 2008. "Neighbourhood Change and the Role of Centraide/United Way of Greater Montreal in Saint-Michel." Waterloo, ON: Tamarack Institute. <http://tamarackcommunity.ca/downloads/index/centraide_final_071408EN.pdf>.

Buckingham, H., and S. Teasdale. 2013. *Job Creation through the Social Economy and Social Entrepreneurship.* Paris: OECD Publishing. <http://www.eco.public.lu/attributions/economie_solidaire/ocde2013.pdf>.

Cabaj, M. (ed.). 2011. *Cities Reducing Poverty: How Vibrant Communities Are Creating Comprehensive Solutions to the Most Complex Problem of Our Times.* Waterloo, ON: Tamarack Institute.

Chevrier, E.-I., and J. Panet-Raymond. 2013. « La participation citoyenne pour développer un quartier. » *Nouvelles pratiques sociales* 26, 1: 67–83.

Dickinson, J.A., and B. Young. 2008. *A Short History of Quebec* fourth edition. Montreal: McGill-Queen's University Press.

Gamble, J. 2010. "Evaluating Vibrant Communities, 2002–2010." Waterloo, ON: Tamarack Institute. <http://tamarackcommunity.ca/downloads/vc/VC_Evaluation.pdf>.

Neamtan, N. n.d. "The Social Economy." <http://tamarackcommunity.ca/g3s10_M4C2.html>.

Shragge, E., and M. Toye (eds.). 2006. *Community Economic Development: Building for Social Change.* Sydney, NS: Cape Breton University Press.

Simard, F. 2012. « Repère communication et recherches. Étude qualitative auprès des citoyens du quartier Saint-Michel. » Unpublished manuscript.

Vivre Saint-Michel en Santé. 2009. « Gouvernance, tables et clubs. » <http://www.vsmsante.qc.ca/index.php?page=gouvernance-tables-et-clubs>.

____. 2010. "St. Michel's Community Plan." <http://tamarackcommunity.ca/downloads/trail_builders/stmichel_plane.pdf>.

Wright, E.O. 2010. "The Social Economy — A Niche in Capitalism or a Pathway Beyond?" <http://www.ssc.wisc.edu/~wright/Social%20Economy%20PDFs/EOW--Social%20economy.pdf>.

NEW DAWN ENTERPRISES

Becoming a "Community Instrument through which the People Can Do for Themselves"

Juliet Merrifield and Anne Toner

This case study maps the learning journey of the oldest Community Development Corporation (CDC) in Canada. New Dawn Enterprises started thirty-seven years ago in Cape Breton, Nova Scotia with a big idea: to be a "community instrument through which the people can do for themselves" (MacIntyre 1995: 79). Working in the poorest area of one of the poorest provinces in Canada, the journey has been a long and slow process of finding the way, building the skills and developing the confidence needed to act in the interests of the community. Along the way, New Dawn has created a network of 20 companies under the governance of a not-for-profit company employing over 175 people in the areas of affordable housing, commercial real estate, healthcare services, social care-giving and vocational training. But the successful projects are only part of the story of New Dawn Enterprises. It has not just created jobs and services but has become over the years a trusted partner in a wide range of community projects, an increasingly strong voice speaking out for community assets and a forum for community conversations about what the future should be.

This case study will look at some of the key moments that shaped New Dawn's journey and enabled it to move forward. It will look at how the journey has changed, how New Dawn sees itself, how it is seen in the wider community and the opportunities that have become possible because of its history and accomplishments. There have been many challenges to overcome and there are more challenges yet to be faced. New Dawn's history in the Cape Breton context of economic and social deprivation provides important insights for wider debates about community economic development.

THE CAPE BRETON CONTEXT

New Dawn's home base is the area once known as "Industrial Cape Breton," including the city of Sydney and surrounding former coal mining communities of North Sydney, Sydney Mines, New Waterford and Glace Bay. Such an environment provides both opportunities and challenges. Like many island communities, Cape Breton has a strong sense of identity. New Dawn's president MacSween (1997b: 16) says that "Cape Bretoners believe themselves to be a distinctive people." He credits this "special identity" for the foundation of community purpose that underpins New Dawn.

Cape Breton Island is a place where the mainstream economy over the last sixty years has mostly failed to create employment or maintain living standards. Based on coal mining from the 1830s until after the Second World War, along with a large steel industry, it has been an area of industrial decline since the 1950s. Rankin MacSween describes Cape Breton as a "depleted community." In its economic sense, that depletion is obvious. Nova Scotia as a whole had a lower Real GDP than any other Canadian province between 1990 and 2009 and the second lowest per capita income generation (OneNS 2013). Average wages are lower and unemployment is higher than in Canada as a whole (Nova Scotia Finance and Treasury Board 2013a). Nova Scotia's population is declining and ageing (OneNS 2013) and that decline is most pronounced in Cape Breton. Between 1987 and 2012, its population decreased by 17.6 percent, the labour force dropped by 8.2 percent and employment by 3.1 percent. More significantly, employment has shifted from production in goods and industries (down by 46.8 percent in this period) to health, education and public administration (an increase of 58.9 percent in this period) (OneNS 2013). Cape Breton has moved from its industrial past of producing goods to sectors dependent on the public purse. These do not replace the earlier economy: Cape Breton unemployment is high — 16.2 percent in July 2013 compared with 9 percent for the province as a whole and 7.2 percent for Canada (Nova Scotia Finance and Treasury Board 2013b). Cape Bretoners leave in order to find work and some say 25 percent of the island's income comes from off-island work.

There is social depletion in the sense that the social infrastructure is not well developed, but also "psychological depletion" meaning that the community has "lost a sense of possibility" (R. MacSween interview). The core of the problem is that, "For the past 100 years, almost all important decisions about the Island have been made elsewhere" (MacSween and MacPhee 1996: 11). Industrial Cape Breton's history is one of exploitation and control by a succession of powerful outside interests. The coal mine and steel mill owners may have left when those industries were deemed no longer profitable, but the federal government took up the reins of decision-making for the area. Strain and Grant (1999: 174) summarized research on government failings in Atlantic Canada: "federal policy taken in its totality rarely promoted regional development." However, in areas where the mainstream economy is not working to generate jobs and well-being, there is often room for innovation and experimentation. Cape Breton's twentieth century social history is distinctive because in the 1930s and 40s the area was an important part of the Antigonish Movement of adult education for self-generated community economic development. The Extension Department of St. Francis Xavier University convened social action study groups that mobilized people to form credit unions and cooperatives (Coady International Institute n.d.). New Dawn sees itself as building on that earlier movement, with an emphasis on the value of cooperation and the "potential of each community to determine its economic destiny" (MacIntyre 1995: 80). There has also been a thread of alternative leadership to the powerful outside interests in the community clustered around what is now Cape Breton University (CBU). Much of the early leadership in New Dawn came from individuals associated with this educational institution and indeed the struggle to establish a university in Cape Breton inspired those early leaders to take on more.

The history of industrial Cape Breton has resulted in complex and contradictory community characteristics. Its sense of independence and special identity sit alongside a lack of experience with internal community leadership because of the long history of external control: "We don't have a history of leading our own affairs" (New Dawn staff interview). Indeed there is an expectation that "somebody will come in and save us" (New Dawn board interview). Its history of social solidarity grounded in the Antigonish Movement sits alongside what New Dawn members describe as a divided and partisan community, one in which there is a lot of fear: "There's a dependency we've had a long time, a long, long time" (R. MacSween interview).

In the challenging context of industrial Cape Breton, New Dawn has demonstrated that community enterprises can work, and has told the story that the community can "do for itself." In a partisan community New Dawn has worked to build relationships and partnerships. In a dependent community it has spoken out in the community interest and built the opportunity for community conversations about its future.

NEW DAWN ENTERPRISES: THE LEARNING JOURNEY

New Dawn Enterprises was first incorporated in 1976, an offshoot of two earlier initiatives launched by a group of local residents mainly associated with the University College of Cape Breton (later Cape Breton University). The first was the Metropolitan Alliance for Development (MAD), started in the early 1970s to develop alternative economic drivers for Cape Breton. In 1973 Greg MacLeod and other MAD leaders each contributed $200 to form the Cape Breton Association for Cooperative Development. This was later incorporated as New Dawn Enterprises, a not-for-profit vehicle for financially sustainable community projects and Canada's first Community Development Corporation (CDC).

Being the first CDC meant that New Dawn had to find a viable legal structure as well as the language and concepts to convey its vision. The Antigonish Movement had promoted cooperatives but this organizational form was seen by the New Dawn founders as too narrowly focused. They saw the corporation as the most powerful institution of the day and wanted to create a corporation that wasn't just about making money but had a community development intent, and which could be enabling rather than limited — "something with tentacles," as MacSween puts it.

While the work was to be practical and useful, the founders emphasized the values underpinning New Dawn from the beginning and these continue to be alive and guide the organization today. Rankin MacSween (1997b: 17) wrote that New Dawn had been grounded in the values critical to community building: hope, faith and love:

> The founders acted on the basis of hope for New Dawn and its possibility. They acted on the basis of faith: faith that, if the energy of the community was focused and structured within a New Dawn-style organization, good will and perseverance could lead to a significant process of community problem-solving. They acted on the basis of a love for their community.

A former board member said, "This organization clearly understands the struggles of those in our community that are in need, and by understanding that it has really been able to speak to that with all its power as much as it can" (board interview). Through its history New Dawn has been gathering the power to speak to community needs, building its skills and gaining confidence in the process, changing how it sees itself and how it is seen in the wider community. This section outlines some key moments of that development.

Finding the path: real estate, healthcare and a college

In its early years New Dawn tried an array of projects, some of which worked and some didn't. Community needs abounded but New Dawn founders saw they could only be met through financially-viable mechanisms. Two early projects contain the seeds of what became New Dawn's approach: identify a community problem, find a response that can be sustainable, evaluate and move on. The first project acquired a building in Sydney to provide a home for a local craft school. Constructing four apartments generated rental income that enabled New Dawn to provide a ground-floor facility to the craft school rent-free for five years (Perry 1987).

Next, New Dawn Enterprises decided to tackle the lack of dental services available to the community by attracting dentists to work and live in Cape Breton. The business plan was to build fully-equipped dental clinics and recruit new dentists directly from the Dalhousie School of Dentistry to lease or buy the clinics. The new dentists were attracted by the state-of-the-art facilities, advantageous lease terms and clear evidence of unmet demand in the community. As a result, they established thriving practices in Cape Breton, local residents gained better access to dental care and New Dawn began to grow (R. MacSween interview).

Building and managing community assets required New Dawn to build its skill set: "We had to learn how to do financial management, how to run a small business. We tried things, all to get a footing. Some stuck and some didn't. They gave us the background and understanding so we ended up growing" (R. MacSween interview).

The need for affordable housing in the area was identified early on. Many of the houses in Industrial Cape Breton were "company houses" built at the turn of the twentieth century by coal and steel companies for their workforces (MacSween 1997a: 4). The housing stock was improving by the 1970s but there were few apartment blocks or buildings for people with special needs. The community need, New Dawn's desire to be financially sustainable, the availability of a government subsidy for construction of affordable housing and the status of real estate as a sound investment all combined to create an opportunity. Over a twenty-year period following its launch, New Dawn collaborated with the Canadian Mortgage and Housing Corporation and the Nova Scotia Department of Housing to generate an average of $1 million per year for construction, resulting in development of over 200 units of affordable housing (ibid.: 5). Real estate became a key means for New Dawn to attain a sound financial footing and to create community assets (ibid.: 6).

New Dawn's real estate projects began to create one of the seven forms of community wealth (or capital) identified in the Wealth Creation in Rural Communities initiative, "built capital," defined as "the stock of fully functioning constructed infrastructure" including buildings (Hoffer and Levy 2010: 6). The community wealth creation framework provides a different way of thinking about community development:

A key principle of the wealth creation approach is broadening the traditional focus on economic and financial wealth to include many kinds of wealth that benefit individuals and communities. These include physical and mental health, individual skills that create income, shared knowledge, political clout, and more. A rural development process aimed at building many forms of wealth tied to place is more likely to create rural livelihoods that are sustainable over the long term, and more likely to benefit the many rather than the few.[1]

Carrying out smaller projects over fifteen years prepared New Dawn to embark on a much more ambitious project to develop built capital, the Pine Tree Park Estates. The federal Department of National Defence (DND) was divesting surplus property including a former military radar station. The relationship with the Cape Breton office of the Nova Scotia Department of Housing, developed while building earlier housing units, led to its support for some of the costs involved in assessing the property (MacSween 1997a). New Dawn acquired it in 1991 for a dollar (community interview) and embarked on a $3.5 million redevelopment and re-purposing of the military housing and other buildings for residential, healthcare and commercial use. Once completed, New Dawn's Pine Tree Park Estates included sixty residential units (later reduced in number), a guest home, mini-home park, New Dawn Home Living , a curling club, a bridge club and New Dawn College's welding school (EarthFuture n.d.). These projects addressed severe housing shortages, especially for marginalized or under-served people including seniors and people with physical or mental disabilities. They provided the community with quality, affordable housing and New Dawn with financially viable real estate ventures (R. MacSween interview).

New Dawn's leadership recognized that lack of access to affordable housing is a complicated, demographically varied issue which often has more to do with available support networks than with physical space requirements and the cost of housing itself. Mental health needs can be as big a barrier to affordable housing as lack of employment. New Dawn's staff understood that real estate and financial capital alone were not enough to meet complex community needs; they also had to develop people. In doing so they began to create another form of community wealth, "individual capital," defined by Hoffer and Levy (2010: 5) as "the stock of skills and physical and mental healthiness of people" in the community. Individual capital has been an important area for New Dawn in terms of both support for physical and mental health and vocational skill development. New Dawn has worked in partnership to develop innovative support for people with mental health needs.

One example is its Supported Housing for Individuals with Mental Illness (SHIMI) project, carried out in partnership with Cape Breton District Health Authority. For a number of reasons, persons with mental illness, especially those living on fixed incomes, have difficulty finding and holding on to decent, affordable housing. As the New Dawn website indicates, "persons with mental illness continue to experience discrimination in their community. They are often shunned because of the visible signs of poverty, the presentation of symptoms, and the general misconceptions that many have about mental illness" (New Dawn Partnerships n.d.). An illness requiring even short-term hospitalization could cause people to lose their homes when the rent went unpaid (New Dawn staff interview). As of June 2013, the SHIMI project had a total of thirty-seven units in Sydney, Glace Bay and Sydney Mines — the first ten developed by Cape Breton District Health Authority (Mental Health Services) and an additional twenty-seven by New Dawn.

A New Dawn board member gives SHIMI as an example of identifying a gap, a community need, where individuals do not need 100 percent full-time care, but neither are they ready to be entirely independent and on their own (board interview). A staff member observed: "The idea was if somebody was hospitalized New Dawn would get along without the rent until the person came back to their home.... Folks love them and feel empowered and actually nobody has been re-hospitalized" (staff interview). She suggested that the project had an impact on the health and self-esteem of the residents (some research on the impacts is currently underway). There remains a significant local need: New Dawn estimates that 200 people in the greater Sydney area live with severe and persistent mental health problems and a quarter of them still need safe, affordable housing.

Another part of the New Dawn network of companies, Home Living Ltd., offers living options within the Pine Tree Park Estates that uniquely address the needs of seniors and people needing emotional, physical or mental support. Residents are housed in duplexes alongside caregivers and their families. The caregivers rent their side of the duplex and are contracted by Home Living Ltd. to care for two or three individuals in the other half of the duplex, rented by Community Services for their clients. These are people with physical, mental or emotional challenges who would be unable to live independently without twenty-four-hour access to support and care (New Dawn staff interview). The side-by-side model allows residents to live independently within a home environment, with constant access to assistance and personal care from trained caregivers. This arrangement is unique in Nova Scotia and the substantial waiting list of caregiver families eager to participate is a testament to its effectiveness. In conversation, a New Dawn staff member described the program with obvious enthusiasm and then added, "I can't understand why people haven't copied it!" (staff interview).

Housing led to other developments for New Dawn, including healthcare. New Dawn Health Care, established in 1988, offers professional healthcare services including foot care, blood collection, homecare and residential care for elderly people. These services were not previously provided locally. New Dawn Health Care is the only registered private healthcare service in the area. In turn, these services need trained staff. In 1983 New Dawn registered as a private career college with the Nova Scotia Department of Labour and Advanced Education. The college created a Personal Care Worker Program to train people to work for New Dawn Health Care. In 2000 the Personal Care Worker Program became the Community

Care Assistant (CCA) program accredited by the Province of Nova Scotia and additional training programs were offered including welding. Early in 2012 New Dawn College moved to a downtown campus and is expanding into other skills training areas, which allow students to obtain diplomas in fields of study that have been identified as having available employment opportunities in Cape Breton. The programs related to beauty services also offer student-provided services to the public at discounted rates. This provides students with real work experience while making their services more affordable to local residents.

Meanwhile, the circumstances that had enabled New Dawn to develop affordable housing were changing. In the late 1990s the Canadian Mortgage and Housing Corporation was restructured and its budget for new construction was removed; the Nova Scotia Department of Housing did not have the budget to subsidize new housing construction (MacSween 1997a). Downturns in the housing market meant that New Dawn's real estate portfolio was no longer a growing asset: it was no longer the case that whatever building New Dawn constructed or bought one year was worth more the next, so that New Dawn could raise capital by selling or leveraging its property (MacSween 1997b). MacSween foresaw the need for New Dawn to find new means of creating capital. Real estate projects continued, though with less focus on housing, but working capital was sought through generating financial capital directly.

Creating financial capital to support community enterprises

Hoffer and Levy (2010: 6) define "financial capital" as "the stock of unencumbered monetary assets invested in other forms of capital or financial instruments." Within any community, the availability of financial capital is important in supporting projects that increase other forms of capital. New Dawn had ventured into community investments in a small way in the mid-1980s. But it is Nova Scotia government's Community Economic Development Investment Funds (CEDIFs) that now serve as New Dawn's main vehicle for increasing financial capital. Since 2004 CEDIFs have become an important source of capital to develop New Dawn's own projects and more recently have been structured to support other community enterprises.

CEDIFs were set up to address the problem of capital outflow from Nova Scotia (to other parts of North America). According to Statistics Canada, approximately $678 million was contributed to Registered Retirement Savings Plans (RRSPs) by Nova Scotia taxpayers in 2011 (The Daily 2013: 3). Less than 2 percent of that is estimated to have been re-invested in the province (Nova Scotia Department of Economic and Rural Development and Tourism 2008). To encourage more local investment, the Province created a framework for CEDIFs and offered attractive tax credits to support them. The intention was to support economic development projects that have a measurable financial return:

> A CEDIF is a pool of capital, formed through the sale of shares (or units), to persons within a defined community, created to operate or invest in local business. It cannot be charitable, non-taxable, or not-for-profit, and must have at least six directors elected from their defined community. (ibid.)

New Dawn's leadership was quick to recognize a vehicle that would keep investment dollars close to home and provide a pool of capital to fund the type of projects and investments the organization had become known for. Initially New Dawn created a CEDIF called New Dawn Holdings to raise capital for investment in the New Dawn group of companies. In 2011, New Dawn Holdings raised almost $2.5 million, at that time the highest one-year CEDIF offering in Nova Scotia history. More recently, in 2012, New Dawn established New Dawn Community Investment Limited, a CEDIF that allows people to invest in locally-owned private sector businesses, keeping their investment capital in the community and contributing directly to the creation of local jobs and wealth (New Dawn Invest Local n.d.). To date New Dawn's various CEDIF funds have paid dividends of $630,000 to investors.

As a former board member explains, the importance of the community investment CEDIF is keeping money circulating locally. His vision is to grow the fund to $100 million in order to support "companies, organizations, community endeavours, start-ups, and what have you" (board interview). New Dawn staff were concerned about CEDIF's reputation for failure: "People considered these things to be charitable donations that they weren't expecting to get their principal back … people invested in high-risk things that fell apart" (ibid.). To avoid this, New Dawn staff wanted to invest conservatively in "Grade A" investments. That meant the fund started small, with a loan to just one company in the first year, but that company used the funds to take on a new building, develop a new manufacturing line and grow from forty-five employees to seventy-five. In the second year (2013), $1.4 million was raised for investment in three companies. The ultimate goal is a fund that generates a return on investment that can be continuously re-invested in the community.

A New Dawn staff member places the CEDIFs in the wider context of New Dawn's vision: "What's interesting about the CEDIF, it's not so much the money that has changed things, it's the story Rankin [MacSween] has used to promote the CEDIF. That's the story that changed things" (staff interview). The story of how money leaves the community and doesn't come back, the story of dependence on handouts from the federal government, is challenged by the demonstration that industrial Cape Breton can generate capital for itself, from within, and use it to develop the community.

Creating social capital to build the community

"Social capital" is "the stock of trust, relationships, and networks that support civil society (Hoffer and Levy 2010: 5). New Dawn's purpose from its beginning was "community building" (MacSween 1997b: 16) and building community requires development of social capital. Through much of New Dawn's history, social capital has been created through the networks of relationships created by its work. Recently it has started a more deliberate effort to engage the wider community. Three main categories of people form New Dawn's networks.

First, New Dawn's long history has created an "orbit" of people who have con-nections with it: friends and partners, present and past board members, people linked with Cape Breton University, local businesses and government agencies. In interviews, board and staff members told of evolving relationships in which someone involved in one community project might be recruited for a board role and subsequently join the staff. Or vice versa. As a former board member suggested, relationships established for one purpose can develop into something different over time: "So the relationship might develop for one purpose but the opportunity or the need ... might appear as a result of that relationship but be unconnected to the original intent of that relationship" (board interview). The orbit of friends and partners around New Dawn continues to evolve. A current board member noted the growing number of younger people getting involved in the New Dawn board over the last few years:

> People with young families. People who are trying to stay in the com-munity and they care about New Dawn and the area around because this is the community they want to live in, and they feel that if they want to be here, they're going to have to take action and improve the place. (board interview)

The second important relationships are those with local residents developed through New Dawn's services. According to New Dawn's website, its companies and projects service some 600 people each day (New Dawn Enterprises n.d.). The Meals on Wheels service alone delivered ten thousand meals in 2012 (and is expected to deliver twelve thousand in 2013). Through service provision, key social relationships are developed "between the organization and the people receiving the service and accepting the fact that it was being delivered in a little different way, and appreciating that" (New Dawn staff interview).

Finally, New Dawn has been building partnerships and collaborations with other organizations in the community through its work in the areas of afford-able housing and healthcare. Partnerships created for one purpose often lead to further collaborations. For example, recently New Dawn has begun a partnership with Mental Health Services, the regional hospital and the local Credit Union to establish a new organization to link together the wide range of services available for people with mental health needs, and smooth people's path through them. In the last few years partnerships have accelerated as New Dawn has needed community support and as it has moved more into the public eye. The process through which that happened will be outlined in the next section.

Creating political capital to stand up, hold our ground

Hoffer and Levy (2010: 6) define "political capital" as "the ability of an individual or a group to influence the distribution of resources within a social unit, including helping set the agenda of what resources are available." Like most community organizations, New Dawn has needed to create its own stock of political capital in order to secure various assets over the years. But the wider community political capital was not the explicit focus of its work for most of its history. Like many community development organizations, New Dawn did not see its work within the political arena and kept a low profile in terms of political activism. As one staff member observed, the organization "kind of kept its head down and did really good work, did a lot of things in a more quiet, private way" (staff interview). Staff say they were concerned about the Cape Breton pattern of "vainglorious announcements of what was coming" that never delivered the promised solutions; in reaction New Dawn's president said "there's going to be no glorious declarations, just put your head down, OK, do the work" (R. MacSween interview).

But the guiding belief was always that the community should be involved in determining where it wants to go. To help that happen New Dawn had to step out into the public eye. There was a long process of learning and doing to reach that point of organizational capacity: "It certainly took us a long time to get to a level of maturity in terms of how the organization functions and to move beyond or to get it to a certain capacity" (MacSween interview). Several moments along that learning journey stand out as key to the process of organizational learning and capacity building.

Acquiring Pine Tree Park Estates was New Dawn's first step into a bigger and more public role:

> It was a new audience for us; they didn't know us well. It was our first partnership with a 'big animal.' Going out to the community and raising money was a big step — we had to be trustworthy and to know what we were doing. We had to get the community with us — we had never done it before. (R. MacSween interview)

Even more public was a lawsuit over a palliative care unit at the Pine Tree Estates. Some nurses had approached New Dawn about the need for non-hospital-based palliative care. There was space at the Pine Tree Estates and the duplex model for care giving that had been established there looked a promising model for end-of-life care. However, at the time there was a freeze on licences for new nursing homes. A nursing home was defined as having four or more beds, so New Dawn built a set of four apartments with three beds in each. The fire doors between the apartments had to be kept closed to avoid being defined as a nursing home. The provincial health minister came to visit, loved the place and committed to help get a nursing home licence for the newly-built facility. But his suggestion of how much nicer it would be with the fire doors open to allow residents to visit each other had unintended negative consequences. The fire marshal did an inspection, found the fire doors open and said the building had to be closed down. As a result, the metropolitan planning department's building inspector issued an eviction order. The legal fight to keep the palliative care unit open eventually went to the provincial supreme court. It was one of the first times that New Dawn had been in the public eye, fighting for the community.

New Dawn's developing community relationships and social capital were called upon again when it was immersed in a battle with the DND over the contamination of the Pine Tree Park Estates, another key moment on its learning journey. In 2004 it was discovered that the military homes had been built on top of old oil tanks, which were now leaking (New Dawn staff interview). When approached about remediation, the DND was very slow to respond or take responsibility although at the time of sale it had accepted legal responsibility for existing environmental conditions. Absorbing the cost of remediation would have ruined New Dawn financially, compounded by the impact of lost rental revenue on the forty homes that had been vacated upon discovery of the contamination (and later had to be demolished). Over the years, New Dawn had obtained mortgages on Pine Park Estates to restore existing housing stock and build new units. Without the rental revenue, the cost of carrying those mortgages became problematic. In addition, once it was known that the site was contaminated, banks refused to extend any further credit to cover accumulating costs associated with the legal process and New Dawn could not renew mortgages or take out additional loans. Many of the volunteer board members were afraid that it might mean financial ruin for New Dawn Enterprises and were understandably concerned about personal liability.

The largest of New Dawn's real estate ventures had become one that provided the greatest threat to the organization — indeed, one that could have closed it down. Pine Tree Park Estates "almost became the equivalent of a black hole that consumed the entire organization forever and a day" (community interview). An extended legal and political battle aimed to get the DND to take responsibility for remediation and compensation. But when New Dawn had to stand up against the federal government, they found they were not alone. People who had been supported by New Dawn in the past rallied to their defence. Supported by a skilled consultant, a community coalition was formed to work on New Dawn's behalf. The coalition included key local groups such as the Chamber of Commerce, the Council of Churches, the Bras d'Or Stewardship Society and others.

Eventually New Dawn won: in 2010 the DND agreed to invest $11.2 million in cleaning up the site and compensated New Dawn with $7.3 million for lost operating revenues and the capital loss of the forty homes that had to be demolished. It took years and a lot of resources of New Dawn staff and board time and money but it also inspired and encouraged the organization to feel it had the capacity and the power to engage more politically in the future.

The next step taking New Dawn into a much more visible role in the politics of the Sydney metropolitan area involved the development of the Sydney Port. In this slowly evolving process New Dawn's advocacy for community ownership of its assets remained consistent while the situation developed in a way that they could not have foreseen. In the late 1990s the federal agency, Enterprise Cape Breton Corporation (ECBC), decided to sell the assets of the former naval base located on the North West Arm of Sydney Harbour, which included wharfs, buildings, a 240-acre (97 hectares) industrial park known as SydPort and adjoining land. New Dawn developed a bid in partnership with the Cape Breton Regional Municipality (CBRM) but this was not successful and the site was sold for $3.2 million to a group of Cape Breton businessmen who had formed a company called Laurentian Energy Corporation (LEC). ECBC's expectation was that the businessmen would invest more in the development of the site. LEC expected to capitalize on offshore oil development but the expected bonanza did not happen, the oil remained offshore and by 2004 LEC was seeking development funds from the Province of Nova Scotia. It was told that in order to get government funds it needed to open up for community investors. New Dawn and other community investors responded and invested $200,000 each. The new investors had seats on the LEC board, which gave them a "community voice at the table" (staff interview).

Some people in the community were puzzled about New Dawn's motives as a not-for-profit taking shares in a for-profit company. Although New Dawn's intent was to see this asset used in the best interests of the community, some of its friends were concerned that it was just providing a "community front." One of those individuals now says, "New Dawn was absolutely right in what they did: the property, because of New Dawn's efforts, ended up coming back to the municipality" (community interview).

The involvement of community investors, along with others, led to LEC assessing the potential for a port development on a greenfield part of the site that would create an important community asset and enable economic growth for the region. LEC funded a feasibility study for the development of a container terminal, which would create large numbers of jobs. The terminal would require dredging the port. Subsequently a group of port operators formed another group, the Sydney Marine Group, and secured $38 million for the dredging project, which has recently been completed.

New Dawn's involvement became more public and visible when LEC ran out of money again in 2010 and owed debts to, among others, ECBC. The federal agency proposed to take back the SydPort land but New Dawn strongly and publicly articulated the importance of making it a community asset. This brought them into conflict with ECBC. New Dawn then petitioned the Cape Breton Regional Municipality to intervene and buy the 200-acre site designated for the container port as a community asset, rather than allowing it to be bought by a for-profit company. New Dawn staff recall, "We did a lot of publicity, we did a lot of education, we did a lot of awareness," (staff interview). New Dawn's position on the Sydport land was based on the following principles:

- that the community should lead in determining its future;
- that the community should own its key assets;
- that the community has the capacity to make the best use of its assets; and it has the responsibility to do so. (New Dawn Enterprises 2011)

New Dawn's proposal was for "a new model of economic development; a model where wealth created here stays here" (ibid.). Initially the cash-strapped local government was not in favour of committing funds to buy the Sydport assets, but after three days of deliberations, a presentation by MacSween on the purchase and being "inundated" by communications from the public, councillors voted to buy the greenfield site for $6 million. Subsequently LEC sold its remaining assets and operations to a group of local business people and New Dawn is no longer associated with LEC. While New Dawn was not alone and doesn't claim full credit for the successful outcome, its staff and board believe that it played an important role in making sure there was community discussion about the options, that the debate was had (board interview). New Dawn's President reflects on its changing political relationships over the years:

> There was a day when we were having a very difficult time, a long time ago, even getting a seat at the table, we would be like a little child trying to make elbow room to get in to have a say. Then we went through a period of time when we probably had a seat at the table but nobody expected us to do too much or say too much or contribute too much or cause too many problems. I think today we're at the table and our voice is heard. (MacSween interview)

The successes of the Sydport battle led to a decision by MacSween to run for office in the CBRM mayoral election of 2012 when Mayor John Morgan announced he would not run again. A New Dawn board member, Mike Targett, also ran for town council during this election. Both ran on a platform of community ownership and control of key community assets. Neither won their election but MacSween captured 40 percent of the vote, which a community leader said was a surprisingly high percentage for a newcomer to politics running against two well-known political candidates (community interview). New Dawn staff report a high level of interest in the campaigns, with election meetings well attended and a small rise in the popular vote at a time when it is declining in many places (staff interview). They feel that the election demonstrated a strong core of interest in the community in the debate about community assets.

The LEC and Sydney Port debates have enabled New Dawn to reach beyond its circles of friends and service users and gain credibility with the business community and other organizations. Its history of increasingly confident ventures into the community eye has brought both New Dawn and the community to a place of readiness to engage in community conversations about the future.

Ways forward: Conversations and collaborations

New Dawn's learning journey has changed how it sees itself and how it is seen in the wider community. From the early years of "keeping our heads down" and getting on with projects, New Dawn has moved into a more public place. Its history has laid the groundwork for community conversations and collaborations that would not have been possible before.

The newest development that symbolizes the way forward for New Dawn is the Holy Angels project. In May 2013, New Dawn announced its purchase from the Congregation of the Sisters of Notre Dame their property in the North End of Sydney, including a school, convent, house and 2.77 acres (1.12 hectares) of land. Holy Angels is New Dawn's most ambitious real estate project to date. New Dawn's early vision for the site is focused on the concept of mixed-use spaces — "converting the property into a vibrant and inclusive place where the community can live, work, learn, play and converse" (New Dawn Enterprises 2013). Possibilities include a centre for the arts and creativity (performance and studio space); a centre for social innovation; co-working spaces; public, private and non-profit offices; an early childhood development centre; a café/restaurant; a local fresh grocer; private and/or post-secondary education classroom space; affordable and market housing and a community kitchen.

Exciting as the potential of this property is, the Holy Angels site stands for more than a real estate project for New Dawn. Its staff are imagining what can be possible for community engagement, building on established and new relationships. The development offers opportunities to work with theatre groups in the area, which are not only interested in using the performance space but also considering forming a coalition in order to work together to make the best use of the space. As New Dawn's Director of Operations Norma Boyd comments, "For them to think of that is more important than anything in this building: they identify the values, sense the dream and want to get on board" (staff interview). People are coming to New Dawn and seeing the organization as an "enabler."

Partnerships and collaborations are part of engaging the wider community. New Dawn has also begun a series of community conversations. The "IDEAS: Powered by Passion" project, modelled on TED Talks, is a speaker series in which creative people in the community are given eighteen minutes to talk about their passion, their ideas, their projects. Each session begins with a "news bite" (a short presentation by a community member about a project they're working on and what motivates them). There is then live music from a local singer/songwriter before the keynote speaker and Q&A. Many participants then adjourn to the pub for a "meeting of the minds" (New Dawn Community n.d.). As a staff member suggested, the project has attracted a different group of people, "people that probably wouldn't have had much to do with New Dawn otherwise" (staff interview). For New Dawn staff, the IDEAS initiative has been particularly valuable in linking them with young people who have swum against the tide of out-migration and stayed in, or returned to, Cape Breton.

MacSween comments that the Holy Angels site will tie into the New Dawn Foundation's ambitions for community engagement. It provides opportunities to get beyond the silos that separate people and organizations in the community, "so we can learn to work together, not to be afraid, cooperate, negotiate our differences and find the common ground" (R. MacSween interview). In a sense one can see all of New Dawn's long history as leading up to this moment when the work of community dialogue and debate about its future can begin.

NEW DAWN'S ACCOMPLISHMENTS AND IMPACTS

There was no "grand plan" at the beginning. MacSween says that New Dawn started so early in the evolution of CDCs that "there wasn't a whole lot of language, so you were incoherent all the time about what it was you were trying to do" (R. MacSween interview). He credits three key factors as enabling New Dawn's evolution: its "fierce" independence and freedom from outside control, a privilege that many in the community didn't have; "keeping its face to the community" rather than turning inward, so that "the membrane between the organization and the community is pretty thin;" and finally, its ongoing process of learning: learning about the community, how to talk to the community in a more deliberate way, learning from mistakes, learning to survive and learning to remake the organization over time (R. MacSween interview).

New Dawn has worked to create different forms of community wealth, some as a deliberate strategy, others as part of responding to needs and opportunities as they arose. It started with real estate as a means of meeting community needs for affordable housing, branched into financial capital as a tool to gain working capital for itself and then for other community enterprises, recognized that buildings and money were not enough without developing people so moved into individual capital, developed social capital as an adjunct of community services and found itself engaged in political capital when it became clear that social investment in community assets required political activism.

At the heart of any form of community wealth is the community's sense of itself, "the stories we tell ourselves," and New Dawn's stories have been as important as its activities. The stories told about themselves by people in Cape Breton have often been about dependency and looking for outside leadership (the coal barons, the steel mill owners or the federal government). A former board member of New Dawn said: "The stories that we tell ourselves, in the context of Cape Breton, either [say] that there's no hope, abandon ship, move to Alberta ... or we grasp onto whatever hope we can find and wait for the next political announcement for a ribbon to get cut" (board interview). New Dawn's story from its beginning was a different one, a story about self-reliance and community values. A board member feels New Dawn's story is saying, "We have to take charge, we want to be more self-sufficient than that" (board interview). New Dawn's President talks about challenging the long-standing culture of fear in the Cape Breton community: New Dawn members "have learned to believe that we can do anything" (R. MacSween interview).

Transforming the culture of an area is not something that happens quickly or can be accomplished by any one organization on its own. But New Dawn's board members and staff see signs of change and think that the organization has made a contribution to these. One board member says:

> There's a whole bunch of interesting activity that goes on that never gets noticed. I think one of the things that New Dawn has been really good at is noticing these things, acknowledging them, calling them together, and saying, "There are a lot of assets here and we could do better things as we build on strengths." (board interview)

The "IDEAS: Powered by Passion" series of talks is a good example of New Dawn accentuating the positive. A new staff member talked about having lived away from Cape Breton and on her return going to her first IDEAS talk: "I thought, oh, this is the kind of vibrancy, people thinking out-of-the-box ideas, this is where they get together" (staff interview). By its actions and by the stories it tells, New Dawn is changing the prevailing story of a weak, dependent and helpless community to one that can "do for itself."

New Dawn's long history has required an ability to move with the times. It has responded to multiple needs in the community, from mental health to political work. It has made changes to its programs — sometimes because it had to (like the move away from affordable housing development) and sometimes because it could (like the battle to secure the Sydney Port as a community asset). Its work has been shaped by the challenges of working in a "depleted community," but also by the opportunities that context offers for innovation and experimentation.

In developing over time, New Dawn has faced and continues to face some challenges that are not unique but are widely shared among community development organizations. The next section explores some of these challenges and how New Dawn has responded.

CHALLENGES FOR THE FUTURE

New Dawn Enterprises has faced many challenges over the years. Three current challenges raised by the members interviewed shed a light on community economic development more broadly. One is the challenge of New Dawn's central purpose of building community: how to engage the community, how best to encourage it and what New Dawn's role should be in community leadership. The second is how to manage the tension between financial sustainability and a social vision, which includes organizational development and leadership within New Dawn itself. The third challenge is how to build multiple partnerships in the community, with government agencies and for-profit companies as well as other not-for-profits, while maintaining autonomy.

Nurturing strong and confident community leadership

While building the community was part of the original intent for New Dawn, it has become an explicit focus only during the last few years, as New Dawn has begun to look more deliberately at how it can engage with the community and support community leadership. As one staff member observed, New Dawn is not only about business development but also "how do you mobilize this community, how do we as citizens begin to shape the direction of this community, because of the whole history of this community as always led from the outside" (staff interview). While its earlier work was about identifying community needs or problems and finding solutions, New Dawn is now beginning to engage actively with community members about future directions.

Engaging and encouraging community participation and dialogue was the objective of the New Dawn Community Development Educational Foundation, established and registered as a charity in 2002. Absorption in the battle with the DND over cleaning up Pine Tree Park Estates prevented much work on the Foundation, but it has recently been revived. As one former board member describes it, the Foundation's work now is to "ask around, engage in the community, really speak to what the needs of the community are, find out where New Dawn can help, where they can play a role." The Foundation is considering two areas of work: community research and community engagement.

Community research is needed, staff feel, because there is no mechanism to do that right now. They see individual institutions, such as Cape Breton District Health Authority, ECBC or Cape Breton University as evaluating themselves or their projects but not the overall health of the community. "Individually they may be doing fine, but no one looks at how the whole community is doing; these institutions are not typically talking to each other on a significant level" (staff interview). Community research activities are needed to provide a more holistic view of the community and as a basis for planning ahead: "How do we need to be thinking now in order to take us into the next fifty years, which are going to be radically different from the last fifty years" (staff interview).

The proposed community engagement activities relate to one of New Dawn's earliest visions for itself: "To create leaders in the community, we want the community to take responsibility for themselves" (board interview). How to do that is not always clear or agreed. Some staff and board members emphasize fostering community leadership outside of the organization. For example, a former board member says, "New Dawn is best when it doesn't try to lead itself but creates the space for the community to find its own leadership" (board interview). But others, including some former board members and community allies, suggest that New Dawn or its president, MacSween, should step in as a community leader. One former board member said that the Sydport issue "was an opportunity for someone else to step in and take a leadership role and speak for the community and engage with the community. I felt that New Dawn really had and does have a role to play in that area" (board interview). The Sydport issue has seen New Dawn speak out about policy issues and it did take a leadership role, acting in the community interest.

There are important differences in approach to how New Dawn should work: how much it should speak for the community and assume leadership itself, how much it should be creating space for the community to develop its own voices. These differences illustrate the deep challenges of any community work that is based on values that do not necessarily come from the community. New Dawn's staff and board are agreed on its core values of standing up for the community, building community assets and helping the community take responsibility for itself. The means are more difficult to grasp than are the ends.

Building partnerships and maintaining autonomy

Most community development work cannot be done by one organization in isolation but requires partnerships. Over its long lifetime and with the expansion of its
activities New Dawn has had to create multiple partnerships with governmental
institutions and other organizations. The challenge is always to partner effectively
while maintaining autonomy and staying true to its values.

According to MacSween, the New Dawn founders originally saw the organization functioning in partnership with government but they soon discovered that
"cooperative action with government was not possible" (MacSween 1997: 5). He
says the difficulties arise from the nature of their perspectives: government works
within separate departments while New Dawn takes a more comprehensive view;
government programs try to meet the needs of individuals while New Dawn's aspiration is to "rebuild the community" (ibid.). In interviews, New Dawn's staff and
board talked of the importance of their independence from government: "One of
the things that we always tried to do is remain free" (staff interview). Some of the
need for independence comes from the history of the area and the powerful presence of the federal government in particular. As a staff member says, "The reason
why New Dawn was established in the first place was to hold up the community in
the face of the powerful government influence in this community" (staff interview).
There are some good reasons for New Dawn's skepticism about the effectiveness
of government interventions.

At the same time, New Dawn from its beginning has been linked to government though its need for capital. The $1 million per year of construction funds
through its first twenty years came from government (federal and provincial). New
Dawn's CEDIF offerings are only possible because of the provincial government's
tax incentives. Pine Tree Park Estates was built on federal land acquired for a song.
New Dawn has government contracts for service delivery (community services,
home health care, nursing home). When New Dawn spent years trying to secure
the Sydport land as a community asset the goal was getting local government
to buy it. Historically New Dawn has been ambivalent about government but
elected government is still the only way to secure community assets. MacSween
ran for election on a ticket calling for more community assets to be secured by
the municipality. So there is a challenging path to tread in which government can
be a partner, a funder, a way to secure community assets but not dominant. "We
participate in government programs but we do not allow ourselves to be directed
by government or controlled by government" (staff interview).

New Dawn's partnerships have extended as it has grown and especially as it
ventured beyond service delivery into the mainstream economy. In LEC, New Dawn
partnered with private sector players that would normally be seen as a very different
kind of animal. Someone familiar with the project said that creating relationships

on a complex issue required sitting at the table with the port operators "to really understand things," to "take the time to develop relationships by demonstrating more adaptability and a greater level of sincerity than perhaps rabid partisans would be used to" (community interview).

Becoming a trusted partner who is respected for working in the community interest rather than for private profit is central to New Dawn's ability to fulfil its mission. "With New Dawn in the room the principles are not how to make a buck off it; it's how do we do something for the community" (board interview). The Holy Angels site offers the possibility of new partnerships and collaborations with a wider range of groups. New Dawn's leadership feels that its past work has positioned it well and given it the capacity to engage in new partnerships.

Balancing financial sustainability and social vision

In order to sustain themselves, community development organizations have to get the leadership right in terms both of effective operations and vision and values. New Dawn's president describes the two dangers that have accompanied its history as "one, we go bankrupt; or two, we lose our soul … those are the two horses you've got to ride" (R. MacSween interview). Many community development corporations and similar groups face these dangers and they illustrate an important point about organizational development and leadership: groups need both competent operational management and a vision and sense of strategy. How organizations solve this dilemma varies. In the case of New Dawn, for most of its history there has been a single strong leader (first Greg MacLeod and then for the last twenty-five years Rankin MacSween) who has been able to ride both horses.

There is no doubt among New Dawn's staff and board members, current and past, about MacSween's crucial role as a visionary leader. They describe him as "an incredible visionary, a great communicator" (board interview); "a genius [who] has this ability to make very complex things simple for people to understand" (staff interview). He combines vision and a sense of direction with an ability to communicate effectively, engage people in conversation and tell stories that help people understand what New Dawn is trying to accomplish. This talent has allowed MacSween to build strong community ties, to attract board and staff members and inspire in them a strong loyalty to New Dawn. According to one new staff member, "That is what drew me to the organization, the opportunity to work with strong leaders. It's great that the community has an organization like this that provides leadership in big important issues" (staff interview). A danger for an organization with a visionary and charismatic leader is how to sustain the organization beyond him or her. A former board chair suggests that "if Rankin wasn't around there would be a real loss in terms of vision and leadership" (board interview).

New Dawn's continued growth suggests successful operational management, the mastery of the skill sets of financial management, personnel management and project management. That wasn't always the case: New Dawn's earlier organizational structure and operational systems were generally hard for outsiders to understand. One former board chair said that "as a board member it was really tough to grab on to anything within the organization or to get comfortable with any piece. It took a number of years to get that sense of comfort to really understand what was going on" (board interview) The organizational chart looks like a mind map as a result of what another former board member called "not practising organizational family planning: every time a new idea comes up a new organization comes out" (board interview).

MacSween's recent election bid for the office of mayor has put succession planning back in focus. One outcome has been the development of so-called hedgehog committees of board and staff to "jointly plan specific strategies for specific areas of their organizations" (board interview).[2] As a former board member said, "I think the organization is moving from very organic, very personality-driven to being more of a systematic organization, strategically driven" (board interview).

Over the years, the need to impose a better management structure on the sprawling organization became apparent. A former board member recalled identifying the need for better management systems as far back as 2001 and trying "to bring some order to the management levels in the organization, reporting structures, financial reporting, system of metrics and accountability" (board interview), but this effort was sidetracked by the DND battle. Board members realized that organizational knowledge needed to be captured and systems made more formal and understandable. After intensive internal planning sessions, New Dawn Enterprises was organized into four business units (Rental Properties, Healthcare, Education and Investments), each with its own management, under one governance board.

The role of the board has shifted over time, from earlier years when it was more involved in day-to-day work and hands-on management to a clearer focus on governance. Boards need to look both outwards into the community and the wider vision and inwards to ensure that finances and operations are effective. A former New Dawn board member describes the challenges for a small, volunteer board in balancing the outward-facing mission with internal governance:

> You've got a mandate, a mission, a vision that are external to the organization, so you've got this responsibility to do work for the community. But how do you measure that? How do you know when you've had the influence? How do know if you've achieved the mission? At the same time you have to work on the organization, you have to continue to build the strength and capacity of the organization. So you're always looking in two different directions. Rather than being able to do both of those well,

I think we swing back and forth. The DND issue came up and we all went external. The port issue came up and we all went external. I get the sense now that the organization shifted back to looking at its internal functioning and structures and strengthening itself on the inside. (board interview)

New Dawn has had strong leadership and effective operations. It has ridden the two horses of financial sustainability and vision. Its challenge is to keep them both alive into the future. The prospect that MacSween may step down at some point is fearful but also exciting: New Dawn staff and board members feel that they have the capacity to manage the transition and that it could bring change and renewal.

CONCLUSIONS

Over its thirty-seven-year history the oldest CDC in Canada has more than survived; it has evolved, responded to changing needs and contexts, done what it had to and what it could. New Dawn has been criticized from different perspectives: for being undemocratic and non-transparent in its operations, for not practising "organizational family planning," for being too quiet and for putting its head "above the parapet." Criticism goes with the territory, whether justified or not. This case study suggests some of the important lessons New Dawn provides to other community development efforts.

Its survival over a long period of time demonstrates the importance of being able to evolve and change as needs and opportunities develop. The New Dawn of today may not be exactly what its founders expected of it but it has held true to the core values of working in the community interest and being financially sustainable. Its ventures into different forms of wealth creation were part of responding to community needs. Providing affordable housing to vulnerable sections of the community required care-giving services, which in turn required vocational training. Securing working capital to develop new activities required new financial instruments. Protecting community assets required political activism. MacSween's emphasis on learning seems crucial: part of what it takes to "make it up as you go along" is an ability to learn from mistakes, listen to others and be aware that despite thirty-seven years of history you don't know everything.

New Dawn's growth and development into a significant local employer and an advocate for the community has put the organization into the public arena and created new demands. It has formed partnerships with groups that have different agendas and values. It has mobilized public support, taken on community leadership. It faces a future in which it will continue to move out of safe spaces into the public eye.

Much of New Dawn's history, like that of many CDCs and social enterprises, has been in what a community partner called the "white spaces" — filling the gaps in the social fabric that the market and state do not cover. Usually those white spaces are at the margins, in the areas that provide too little profit for private entrepreneurs and are too difficult for governments. New Dawn's agenda was not, in the early stages at least, radical in the sense of creating a new economy. Only in the last few years has New Dawn moved into the mainstream economy through LEC and the ownership of the Sydport, and now with the Holy Angels site. But from the beginning it has been consistent in making the case for community ownership of its assets. It is in fact calling for a "new model of economic development; a model where wealth created here stays here" as the Sydport battle illustrates.

In the context of Industrial Cape Breton, where wealth has been seen in an extractive resource model, New Dawn's more holistic approach to building community wealth has been quietly radical. It has seen community wealth as more than resources and money that can be taken away but as an array of assets that the community can and should control. New Dawn's work has helped create several forms of community wealth: the built capital of its real estate projects, the individual capital of its training and care-giving work, the financial capital of its CEDIFs, the social capital of its networks and the political capital of its advocacy for community control of its assets. New Dawn has been pursuing a kind of economic development different from that traditionally followed in Atlantic Canada, moving from an extractive model (in which resources and finances are taken out to benefit people elsewhere) to a model of creating many forms of wealth that stay.

New Dawn has prospered as an organization, developed successful projects and created innovative responses to community needs. But industrial Cape Breton has not prospered through these last thirty-seven years. A community partner questions whether projects can be sufficient on their own and argues that impacting government policies are fundamentally important to community development (community interview). He feels there are no coherent or effective economic development policies for declining regions at either the federal or provincial level in Canada. He argues the importance of moving beyond a traditional municipal government to take on a broader scope of economic responsibilities. He believes that MacSween decided to run for office because "he fundamentally understands that you've got to make these policy changes or else the place is not going anywhere" (community interview). One might expect that the success or failure of a CDC would mirror the success or decline of the community in which it works. The fact that New Dawn has grown and prospered but Industrial Cape Breton has not suggests that there is much more to be done working within the mainstream on policy and political change, advocating for a new model of economic development where "the wealth created here stays here."

New Dawn's approach offers the beginning of a solution, the precursor of something that can grow in scale and influence. Its leaders understand that transformation of a community at its core requires it to see itself differently. People need to change the stories they tell themselves about who they are and what they are capable of. New Dawn's stories are about community agency, about independence, keeping true to community values. It has demonstrated itself as "community instrument through which the people can do for themselves."

Notes

1. This quote was taken from the WealthWorks website <creatingruralwealth.org> but the section containing it was taken out in the subsequent revision of the website.

2. The hedgehog concept was used by Jim Collins and his team of research students to mean "piercing clarity about how to produce the best long-term results, and then exercising the relentless discipline to say, 'No thank you' to opportunities that fail the hedgehog test" (Collins 2005: 115). The creation of a company's hedgehog concept comes from a small group process that identifies the overlap between the three circles of what are your core values, what can you be best at and what is your economic engine.

References

Coady International Institute. n.d. "The Antigonish Movement." <http://coadyextension. stfx.ca/antigonish-movement/>.

Collins, J. 2005. *Good to Great and the Social Sectors: Why Business Thinking Is Not the Answer.* Boulder, CO: Author.

EarthFuture. n.d. "Sustainable Community Initiatives: New Dawn Enterprises, Cape Breton." <http://www.earthfuture.com/economy/sei/sei09.asp>.

Hoffer, D., and M. Levy. 2010. Measuring Community Wealth: Report for the Wealth Creation in Rural Communities Project of the Ford Foundation. <http://community-wealth.org/_pdfs/news/recent-articles/04-11/report-hoffer-levy.pdf>.

MacIntyre, G.A. 1995. *Active Partners: Education and Local Development.* Sydney, NS: Cape Breton University Press.

MacSween, R. 1997a. "New Dawn's Quest for Affordable Housing (II): The Critical Role of Partners." *Making Waves* 8, 1: 4–6. <http://communityrenewal.ca/sites/all/files/resource/MW080104.pdf>.

____. 1997b. "New Dawn Enterprises (III): Cape Breton's Famous CDC Heeds the Call to Evolution." *Making Waves* 8, 3: 16–17. <http://communityrenewal.ca/sites/all/files/resource/MW080316.pdf>.

MacSween, R., and J. MacPhee. 1996. "New Dawn Enterprises and the Quest for Affordable Housing (I)." *Making Waves* 7, 3: 9–11. <http://communityrenewal.ca/sites/all/files/resource/MW070309.pdf>.

New Dawn Community. n.d. "IDEAS: Powered by passion." <http://newdawn.ca/community/ideas-powered-by-passion/>.

New Dawn Enterprises. 2011. "A New Model of Community Economic Development: New Dawn's Principles." <http://archive-ca.com/page/1023257/2012-12-20/http://newdawn.ca/2011/02/port-development/sydney-harbour-assets-laurentian-ecbc-new-dawn/>.

____. 2013. "New Dawn Enterprises Announces Holy Angels Purchase." <http://newdawn.ca/new-dawn-enterprises-announces-holy-angels-purchase/>.

____. n.d. "About New Dawn." <http://newdawn.ca/about/>.

New Dawn Invest Local. n.d. "2012 CEDIF: New Dawn Community Investments Fund." <http://newdawn.ca/invest-local/2012-cedif-new-dawn-community-investment-fund/>.

New Dawn Partnerships. n.d. "SHIMI: Supported Housing for Individuals with Mental Illness." <http://newdawn.ca/partnerships/shimi-supported-housing-individuals-mental-illness/>.

Nova Scotia Department of Economic and Rural Development and Tourism. 2008. "What Is a CEDIF?" <http://www.novascotia.ca/econ/cedif/background/>.

Nova Scotia Finance and Treasury Board. 2013a. "Key Economic Indicators." <http://www.novascotia.ca/finance/statistics/analysis/default.asp?id=1&sid=6>.

____. 2013b. "Labour Force Survey (August 2013)." <http://www.novascotia.ca/finance/statistics/analysis/default.asp?id=23>.

OneNS. 2013. "NS Economics 101 — A Discussion Primer." <http://onens.ca/ns-economics-101-a-discussion-primer/>.

Perry, S.E. 1987. *Communities on the Way: Rebuilding Local Economies in the United States and Canada.* Albany, NY: State University of New York Press.

Strain, F., and H. Grant. 1999. "What Can a Region Do? The Debate on Economic Development Options in Atlantic Canada. *Acadiensis* 28, 2: 167–88. <http://journals.hil.unb.ca/index.php/Acadiensis/article/download/10822/11626>.

The Daily. 2013. "Registered Retirement Savings Plan Contributions, 2011." February 11. Ottawa, ON: Statistics Canada. <http://www5.statcan.gc.ca/access_acces/alternative_alternatif.action?teng=The%20Daily,%20Monday,%20February%2011,%202013&tfra=Le%20Quotidien,%20le%20lundi%2011%20f%C3%A9vrier%202013&l=eng&loc=dq130211-eng.pdf>.

A VISION OF FLIPPING THE ICEBERG OF POWER

The Greater Edmonton Alliance
Faces Big Land and Big Oil

Elizabeth A. Lange

Alberta is the heartland of Big Oil, conspicuous since the opening up of the oil sands between 1967–1978. The 2010 greenhouse gas emissions now register at 9 percent of Canada's total output (Englander, Bharadwaj and Brandt 2013), constituting over 0.1 percent of global output. The wealth-producing brashness of industry in Alberta generates big booms, when money flows freely, workers flood over provincial borders and suburbs of super-sized homes erupt from the landscape; but it is also accompanied by cyclical big busts, when homes are foreclosed, tent cities grow quietly on urban borderlands and panhandlers circulate supermarket parking lots. Despite the beliefs in tough self-reliance, this boom and bust cycle is common to dependent raw-resource economies, fuelling "redneck" cynicism, anger, fear and bigotry. The impact of the 1970s oil boom on Alberta was summed up in the popular bumper sticker, "Dear God, give us another oil boom and this time we promise we won't piss it away." They got another chance in 2004-8 and again in 2012.

The historic waving wheat-engorged prairies have been home to bold innovation, not only industrial and technological but also cultural, from politics to the arts. Alberta has been a political economy defined as a petro-state run by an oil oligarchy resulting in a democratic deficit, particularly reflected in a weak political party system. Yet, Alberta has solid counter traditions of social movements, progressive think tanks, union organizing and community development, continuously claiming spaces for citizen voice. From the Famous Five who achieved legal personhood for Canadian women in the 1920s to the germination of new political parties — United Farmers of Alberta, Social Credit Party, Reform Party and the Wildrose Party — innovation has emerged across the political spectrum, challenging the traditional party structure.

More recently, Alberta citizens mobilized against the Free Trade Agreement in 1988, the North American Free Trade Act in 1993, the provincial health care and education cuts in the mid-1990s, the 2002 G8 meeting in Kananaskis Village with its locked-down, army-guarded perimeter and then against Bush's 2003 Iraq War. Vibrant inner city community organizing has politicized and activated working-class folks and immigrant neighbourhoods, shaping the more left-leaning political character of Edmonton as a capital city. Yet the province has been ruled by rightwing parties for over eighty years and the Progressive Conservative Party since 1971, with ideology and policy changing only with new party leaders. This party has staked the province's future on oil, with strong federal backing since 2006, despite market volatility and international protest. This single premise is now the primary constraint on political discourse and civic engagement. Called the "resource curse" theory (Auty 1993), it explains how the oil industry has distorted Alberta's political economy: in boom times, by decreasing competitiveness through corporate concentration and undermining economic diversification and dissent; and in downturns by increasing interventionist economic policies and short-term labour strategies, all reducing the capacity for long-term economic sustainability.

This case study describes an Edmonton broad-based community organization, which initially organized resistance to the neoliberal government reforms of the 1990s.[1] Called the Greater Edmonton Alliance (GEA), it built dialogue across associations of transit workers, public school teachers, immigrant serving agencies, government workers, small businesses, building trades, inner city organizations, Muslim mosques and service agencies and many Christian churches, service agencies and religious orders. This is arguably the first organization in Alberta that is multi-sector, multi-issue and mobilizes disciplined social action. Identifying common concerns, GEA works as a collective power for social justice and the greater good. While it has made significant policy gains and is elevating the political consciousness and civic engagement of Edmontonians, it has inevitably come up against Big Land and behind that, Big Oil, the sometimes more covert but encompassing power that pulses through the capillaries of the province.

While GEA is considered young in the North American history of broad-based community organizations, it exhibits potential for deepening Albertan democracy over the long term and contributing to the foundational work needed for a sustainable society. The vision of GEA, says paid organizer Madhu Sood, is to flip the iceberg of elite power upside down, exposing the power of the people and the brilliance of their passion for the greater good, not only to themselves but to the hegemonic powers of Big Oil and Big Land (personal communication).[2] So far, GEA has exposed the ideology of incessant economic growth and corporate privilege that reinforce the paradigm of fossil fuel reliance. It is also achieving incremental change at the systems level, by holding the private sector and the state accountable for policies and practices not considered to serve the long-term public interest. Yet, as Jose Ortega y Gasset (cited in Barber 1992: 62) has previously noted, "Everyone sees the need of a new principle of life. But as always happens in similar crises — some people attempt to save the situation by an artificial intensification of the very principle which has led to decay." GEA is hybridizing broad-based organizing in this unique Canadian context and generating new principles of citizen engagement. Nevertheless, the challenge it faces is absentee power holders, some of the most significant global players today who maintain a grip on old principles and systems of power that further the decay of the late modern industrial era.

ALBERTA AS THE CANADIAN NEOLIBERAL FLAGSHIP

Alberta was the first provincial experiment of New Right ideology in Canada, dovetailing with the earlier reforms of Mulroney's federal Conservative government, which mimicked Thatcher's Britain, Reagan's United States, Pinochet's Chile and Rogernomics in New Zealand. Neoliberalism arose to address Western inflationary stagnation, the international debt crisis, corporate profit crisis and the electronic revolution by returning to laissez-faire concepts of free trade and free markets. Contradictory in theory and practice, particularly when coupled with neoconservative morality and state authoritarianism, neoliberal economics seeks to free capital for global mobility and away from labour and environmental regulation established to protect the public good. It breaks the social pact between labour and business negotiated during the Keynesian social welfare era and seeks to reduce the power of the "interventionist" state, which considers social services dysfunctional — too bureaucratic, generating dependency and bankrupting the state (Harrison 2005) even though in Canada it was calculated that social programs contributed only 2 percent to Canada's debt (Statistics Canada as cited in Ecumenical Coalition for Economic Justice 1993).

In 1993, newly-elected Conservative premier Ralph Klein initiated the dramatic restructuring of the public sector that would become known as the Klein Revolution, using the rationale of a debt crisis and the inevitability of a global economy (Harrison 2005; Flanagan 2005; Harrison and Laxer 1995). Under the banner of the Alberta Advantage, populist Klein reduced the role of government in providing social services and market regulation and attempted to fire individual entrepreneurial initiative and competitiveness by reducing social programs and curbing the excesses of "too much union power and too much democracy"

(Harrison and Laxer 1995). Klein implemented austere cutting of all government services by at least 20 percent and crafted market solutions to public services (Flanagan 2005), such as selling crown corporations, deregulating public services including utilities and daycares, reducing government regulatory functions, cutting public sector wages and undermining union power. Klein wanted to restrict public education and healthcare to core services and encourage P3s (public-private partnerships) or more importantly, the full privatization of "non-essential" services, to re-establish market dynamics.

The outcome was intended to be two-tier access to social services based on wealth and a significant increase in private sector involvement as part of re-establishing the power of economic elites and corporate freedom (Harvey 2005). The steps of the legislature were filled regularly with thousands of protesters, to no avail. As Harvey (2005) explains of neoliberal proponents, generating public fear and insecurity and using assertions of a crisis in the welfare state were strategies to manipulate consent in the majority. Dissent was marginalized by Klein, pejoratively called "special interest groups," connoting a threat to social stability, an effective divide and rule strategy. Ignoring public outrage reveals authoritarianism rather than an interest in democratic engagement and negotiation.

Klein did eliminate Alberta's $23 billion debt in a compressed time frame, incurring substantial surpluses only six years later in 2000. Feeble reinvestments in social services were the response to mass protests, fuelling the skepticism that it was an ideological agenda for gutting the social welfare state, mobilizing the power of capital, protecting the interests of private property, re-establishing hierarchical power and rebuilding the power of elites (Harvey 2005). In the mid-1990s, Alberta recorded its highest unemployment ever at 9.7 percent and the ranks of the poor doubled, reaching almost 20 percent of the population, resulting in a heavy increase in food-bank usage, child poverty and homelessness (Kolkman, Ahorro and Varlen 2000). As the confluence of neoliberal economics and neoconservative social policy has done elsewhere, it reversed decades of social progress and created persistent increases in social and economic inequality (Harrison 2005; Harvey 2005). This reality was the entry point for GEA.

ALINSKY COMES TO CANADA

In 1991, Sue and OJ Scott came to Edmonton from Lincoln, Nebraska for positions as a professor in adult education and United Church minister. In the 1970s, Lincoln community developers, including Sue, heard Saul Alinsky speak in Chicago and were inspired to create a citywide broad-based organization, the Lincoln Alliance, which successfully tackled many issues as part of the War on Poverty. In 1997, as the worst impacts of the Klein Revolution were felt, Sue put out feelers around

Edmonton to explore interest in an Alinsky-style broad-based organization. Sue met Ed Laboucane, a Métis inner city organizer, and Don Mitchell and John Riley, who were associated with the inner city Community Action Project. Don, a transit driver turned labour organizer with the Coalition of Edmonton Civic Unions, was instrumental in prompting labour unions to join the newly forming alliance and John gathered together neighbourhood community groups. OJ became the force behind churches joining such an alliance, hosting training sessions and dialogues. Bob McKeon and Linda Winski from the Roman Catholic Social Justice Commission were able to bring in the organizational and financial support of the Edmonton Archdiocese.

Initially this group explored the characteristics and strategies of broad-based organizations (see Scott 1992, 2000, 2001) while remaining wary of importing an American model into Canadian social conditions — a context characterized by a less confrontational political culture founded on negotiation rather than revolution, a different history of voluntarism, provision of state funding for civic organizations and a constitutional parliamentary system rather than a constitutional republic (B. McKeon personal communication). While there was a strong history of funded local neighbourhood organizing in inner city Edmonton as well as church-labour collaborations on specific provincial issues, this initial group agreed on the wisdom of creating a citywide organizing model, the importance of collective direct action and the desire for a sustainable multi-issue organization.

For Saul Alinsky (1946; 1971) and his colleague and successor Ed Chambers (2004), politics is not a game but the ancient concept of sovereign citizens gathering to deliberate and act for the common good. Alinsky believed that social justice could still be attained within the American democratic system despite centripetal forces toward power concentration. As a criminologist in the 1930s Chicago Back of the Yards neighbourhood, one of the largest slums amid the stockyards and factory complexes, Alinsky crafted a hard-nosed, confrontational political style based on the "formula of agitate, antagonise, educate and organise" (Ledwith 2005: 93). He developed an "organization of organizations" — embracing churches, labour unions, small business and youth committees — to foster mass participation in the democratic process. Organizing this first neighbourhood across differences to achieve political gains and then developing mass or broad-based organizations across an urban region they generated power across multiple sectors, multiple issues and over time. The independence of broad-based organizations is sustained by membership dues supporting paid professional organizers. Based on these pioneering concepts and structures, Alinsky formed the Industrial Areas Foundation (IAF) in 1940, subsequently influencing the union movement, farm workers movement and the struggle for civil rights.

Chambers (2004: 18; 71) asserts we are political beings by nature and thus public life should be a natural vocation as part of citizenship. Thus, extensive leadership training is a key element of Alinsky organizing, meant to kindle a sense of political vocation and educate leaders in civic skills and the exercise of power in public life. Intensive and long-term mentoring is designed to support the self-development of those who have never played a political role, a form of adult education (Sirianni and Friedland 2001). In 1969, Alinksy, Chambers and Dick Harmon established an IAF training institute to teach concepts related to participatory democracy as well as political and organizing skills. They began building a national network, achieving fruition in sixty-two IAF organizations in twenty-five American states today, including expansion into the United Kingdom, South Africa, Germany, Australia and Canada.

Four critiques of Alinsky organizing have been the confrontational tactics, the prevailing focus on narrow self-interests rather than broader values (particularly spiritual values and an inclusive political vision), a tendency toward dependence on paid, charismatic organizers and the reduction of organizing to technique (Sirianni and Friedland 2001). After Alinsky's death, Harmon, Ernie Cortés and Chambers reversed a key element of Alinsky organizing, putting relationships before issues (Chambers 2004: 46). For them, building common cause across social differences emerges through disciplined listening. The first step in building a broad-based organization is fondly called "relationals" — one-on-one thirty-minute meetings carried out three to four times with each person. Individuals share personal stories with public significance. True listening makes no assumptions about how institutions function, how power flows within them, what people's passions and commitments are or where self-interests of individuals or organizations may lie. Thousands of these individual relational meetings take place, identifying potential leaders. House meetings, pioneered by Fred Ross, bring these people together to more systematically form a network of power with deep and diverse roots in the community (Sirianni and Friedland 2001).

Alinsky organizers understand power not only as negative ("power over" compelling another to act) but also as positive ("power to" as the capacity to act that is always created in relation to "power with"). The purpose is to transform unilateral power into relational power: "It's not the power you possess, but using the power of the opposition against itself that changes things. It's called political jujitsu" (Alinsky as cited in Chambers 2004: 12). Thus, the second step is leadership training, including the IAF ten-day leadership workshop which trains the body, spirit and mind in the use of power, including overriding normal deference to authority and expertise, which is a form of internalized powerlessness (Gaventa 2006) and moderating physical reactions to high stress situations. It teaches the virtues of self-control, discipline and trusting intuitive understandings for use in difficult public situations. To effectively build the power and confidence of people, a key Alinsky rule has been "never do for others what they can do for themselves" (Industrial Areas Foundation 1990: 17).

Related to this is the third step of learning political capacity, namely the abilities to withstand heat and tension, through which one must travel toward real change. Another IAF rule is "change means movement; movement means friction; friction means heat; heat means controversy;" in other words, "there is no nice, polite way to get change" (Chambers 2004: 31). Alinsky and Chambers consider controversy and conflict as the tools that can till the ground for change. Organizers work across the divides of class, race, ethnicity, religion, age and ideology, learning to identify common community issues, harnessing individual and organizational interests and examining where the controversy exists.

Once an issue has been determined through listening to members, the fourth step is the cycle of organizing — research, action and evaluation. A power analysis includes mapping the leaders involved in the issue, who they influence, how they relate to each other and who determines decisions, including monetary spending. A power analysis also involves identifying the opposition, potential allies and their relative strengths. Actions are targeted to where a concrete winnable action is likely. Relationals with allies, public officials and corporate leaders help in identifying the target of the action or who will be put on the "hot seat" in the public drama that plays out, to capture media attention and generate public support. Finally, after a public action, an evaluation is immediately carried out. "Happenings become experiences when they are digested ... reflected on, related to general patterns and synthesized" (Alinsky 1971: 69).

BUILDING THE GREATER EDMONTON ALLIANCE

In 1997, Sue, OJ, Ed and Don began with an orthodox IAF process for building a broad-based organization, fanning out to do "relationals" with a wide range of people who in turn did their own relationals. Their conversations expanded into church social action networks, labour unions and inner city organizations. Consistent with traditional Alinsky organizing, the goal was to identify people who were moderates, had large informal social networks, would be effective public leaders and could bring in the support of their organization.

This growing group of leaders formed a pre-sponsoring committee and generated enough interim funds to galvanize and train others. The top IAF trainers were brought in: Sister Christine Stephens did the first training in 1997, Ernie Cortés did the second in 1998, Ed Chambers did the third in 1999 and Dick Harmon did the fourth in 2000, each with thirty-five to one hundred people attending. Many also attended the ten-day IAF leadership training in the U.S.; reporting it "lit a fire," changing their lives. In 2000, a formal sponsoring committee was established which continued to offer two or three local training weekends per year and created an organizational growth strategy.

Part of the challenge of the IAF model is that broad-based organizations are not built on philanthropic, government or individual donor funding but on a membership base of formal organizations that pay 1–2 percent of their annual budgets to support the alliance. According to the IAF founders, power is built through "organized people and organized money" (Chambers 2004). Financial independence provides the ability to control their destiny. The biggest task, then, was to convince various institutions that the IAF could help build their internal organizations, largely through leadership training of their members as well as build their external alliances with other organizations as part of a developing solidarity. Yet even having meetings located in a church, it was felt, would alienate labour union members; so historical divides, deep prejudices and enmity had to be overcome.

The purpose of the alliance was framed for each organization using its institutional discourse. For instance, within the Roman Catholic Church, a session was held on "Jesus and Saul Alinsky," drawing similarities between Jesus organizing his disciples and IAF organizing. Leaders conveyed that they could enact the Catholic social teachings of social justice and human dignity through IAF membership (B. McKeon personal communication). They also felt that the action opportunities and leadership training could perhaps reverse decades of member loss in churches by providing a compelling outlet for faith in action. Warren (2001: 12) describes how the IAF itself, and derivative groups such as the PICO National Network and Gamaliel Foundation, evolved into congregational-based community organizing, drawing on powerful connections between personal faith, biblical values, ethical imperatives and political action. These groups also effectively built upon the social capital and volunteer traditions in faith communities (Sirianni and Friedland 2001).

In the case of unions, Don Mitchell realized their isolation and defencelessness during the extensive 1997 job cuts to municipal unions, with no recourse and no allies. To avoid a repetition, he became "a fisher for a better way of doing things." He appealed to unions "in terms of their own interests and traditions," maintaining that they could do far more in a citywide alliance "because we can actually bring allies to the table" (D. Mitchell personal communication). He was troubled by reliance on the social democratic political party to represent union interests; he said, "we shouldn't be contracting out our politics … we should be taking care of … developing … public leaders — leaders in their institutions, leaders in their community, or their city, and not depending on somebody else to do that for us" (D. Mitchell personal communication).

He felt union folks could be better negotiators and stronger leaders by knowing their constituencies and being connected both inside and outside their union.

Personal relationships forged between organization leaders, such as the Alberta Union of Provincial Employees president and Roman Catholic Archbishop, proved most effective for overcoming divisions. They both understood the mutual gains in sharing power, perspectives, skills, constituencies and leadership. Don came to believe that "state or political power is not central.... I became much more interested in citizen power than in the wheels of political power." For him, leadership training was vital for strengthening unions and he considered GEA training as "schools for public life" (D. Mitchell personal communication).

Leadership training also has potential for harnessing passion capital to address the burn out of a small band of overworked leaders. For instance, OJ Scott witnessed his United Church congregation doubling in size over the next ten years as word of the training and new sense of purpose spread (S. Scott personal communication). Another church minister, Chris New, found the opportunity for impact on social justice issues compelling. He recalls the power of relational meetings, when Monique Nutter invited him into conversation:

> I'll never forget it, because it was a really meaningful conversation.... She asked me why I became a minister.... She said, "I don't know that many ministers, how do you spend your days, what do you do?"... A little later she said,... "Is that the way you want to spend your days? ... Like there's quite a difference in the ideal of the passion that you had for doing this kind of work and the way you spend a typical day, does that gap ever bother you?" (C. New personal communication)

Chris was floored but realized these conversations were getting at the heart of his vocation. Monique wasn't asking for money or volunteer time for her inner city organization as he had expected; rather, the conversation had "to do with utilizing passions and a sense of the world as it could be." This example exhibits the compelling power of relationals to attract members, build a network of power across sectors and convince folks that GEA could "use the strength of our people and our organizations to make a difference" (C. New personal communication).

Church leaders also saw the opportunity to dialogue around a vision of what the role of churches could be in relation to a changing social welfare state. While churches had been service providers historically, then sidelined in the era of public social agencies, religious leaders such as Chris New wanted dialogue on "what's our place now?", particularly as churches were being asked to pick up the slack of government social service cuts. Chris felt it was a time to tear down church walls to "discourse outside of our bubbles that we usually live and breathe in" (C. New personal communication). Thus, various leaders became convinced that their growing web of one-to-one relationships not only held participants personally accountable but was as transformative as the systems change they could achieve together as they rethought the roles of the public, private and civil sectors.

Nevertheless, this remained a time of touch and go as core leaders were never sure if they would meet their targets and advance to the next stage of organizing. It always felt like they were one meeting away from disbanding. They were unsure how to organize — by topical caucuses, geography, action teams or mixes of institutions. It proved difficult bringing in service organizations, particularly inner city or immigrant-serving agencies, who were often on the edge of finances and energy themselves. Some people could not envision what the relational meetings were building toward or were uncomfortable asking for financial commitments. People were lost along the way. As Debbie Hubbard, a longtime member of OJ's church and GEA's board, summarized, "Unless it's being pushed from the pulpit or the [union] executive committees ... it's been a real struggle for us to [bring in and] keep these organizations." At times, when the dreams were bigger than their capacity, people grew tired. Monique said core leaders continuously reassured each other, "It is a slow building process ... it's generational work ... we are not going to create massive change overnight and we're not going to build an organization like this overnight" (D. Hubbard personal communication).

Then, in the early 2000s, the Ursulines of Jesus had to close their convent and retreat centre, giving the developing alliance $30,000 to attract dues-paying organizations as part of their investment in long-term systemic change. To do this, John Reilly was hired in 2004 as the lead paid organizer and later Michael Walters joined him as the associate organizer. The challenge given by IAF mentors was to raise three years' worth of budget monies, after which a founding assembly could be held. While they did not quite reach the full amount, the organizing momentum led to an early but exciting founding convention in May 2005, with over 1,000 individuals and fifty institutions attending, including the mayor and some city councillors. The newly-minted organization, the Greater Edmonton Alliance, was publicly launched with a traditional IAF board structure, including caucuses and action teams. It would double its dues-paying members over the next five years to over thirty-five member organizations.[3] In sum, it had taken seven years to achieve significant organized money and organized people through relationals, leadership training, network building and a strong vision of revitalizing democracy through citizen action.

GEA CUTS ITS TEETH ON AFFORDABLE HOUSING

Yet, with only talking and training, the momentum soon appeared to be waning. People gravitate to action or, as Ed Chambers said directly to GEA, "Action is to the organization as oxygen is to the body." Thus the next step in IAF-style organizing is to listen to your membership, choose an issue, do background research and a power analysis, then undertake and evaluate a calculated, aimed social action (Gecan 2008). Most important, this enables institutions to act in unison as a functioning unit focused on the same goal.

Typically, core leaders bring together small groups of people from the relational meetings to identify pressing issues. Called "house meetings" or "listening campaigns," they allow a key issue to emerge across member organizations. A listening campaign asks questions such as, "What voices need to be heard? What is not being taken care of? Where should we place our energies for social justice and sustainability?" The first issue pursued by GEA was affordable housing. However, it unfolded in an unorthodox IAF manner rather than through cross-sector "listening" and action.

In 2006, tenants in a north end lower-income neighbourhood heard that their 1950s rental housing complex, Ascot Gardens, was to be upscaled into luxury condos. A local church, St Edmunds Catholic Church, approached GEA for help, explaining the tenants' fear, uncertainty and sense of powerlessness. While the majority of tenants said they would just leave, a vocal group of long-time neighbourhood residents wanted to stay but their limited income ruled out home ownership. The newly-created action team of GEA volunteers did a survey through a door-knocking campaign to gauge the interest of tenants in contesting gentrification. The team gathered their stories and perspectives and then organized a small group of tenants brave enough to become leaders. Chris New explained GEA's motivation: "How could these very limited-income people utilize this circumstance to make an improvement in their life ... [For GEA, it was] a process of accompaniment, searching for a way that folks could stay in the neighbourhood and even own a home" (C. New personal communication).

The tenants called their group RAGE (the acronym for Remodel Ascot Gardens for Everyone), a name which polarized the players, as did a rally and media coverage. With controversy stirred up and an active media gaze, the tenants' paid organizer and volunteer action team approached the developer, who now construed them as the enemy stalling his project. As they entered into negotiations, he came to meetings flanked by a band of staff and lawyers. Yet tenants shared their views and goals and GEA leaders emphasized their intention for a win-win solution. In its background research, GEA found that a year earlier the city had approved "Cornerstones: Edmonton's Plan for Affordable Housing," mandating any development or redevelopment to provide 5 percent affordable housing of the total units. While meeting with the developer, GEA simultaneously organized tenants to speak at the rezoning application hearings. As the mayor said later, it was the first time in Edmonton history that tenants impacted by a redevelopment spoke at City Hall. It would also become the first implementation of the City's new policy.

Worried about the controversy approach and the impasse created, GEA decided to try a more relational approach. They adopted creative storytelling, hoping it would overcome the tenants' sense of intimidation by the fancy boardroom and lawyers. One resident told a personal story of what it meant to live all those years in the neighbourhood and what a home meant to her. Next, they invited the developer to share a personal story, particularly where he grew up and what home meant to him. They were surprised to hear that he was the son of a single mother who had to work multiple jobs to support her family. He watched her save waitressing tips for years to purchase a home. He felt passionate that families should have a home as a result of their hard work, where they feel secure. The oppositional nature of the discussion shifted, the lawyers vanished from future meetings and the developer voluntarily agreed to include at least 5 percent affordable housing units. GEA arranged for these units to be purchased and managed by the Capital Region Housing Corporation as purchase or rental units. With the 2008 global market crash and lack of economic confidence, the developer stalled the plan but is expected to move ahead in the near future (M. Nutter and C. New personal communication). To "keep the deal," GEA members say they will remind the developer of his commitment.

Following the IAF precept, GEA showed its power, got to the negotiating table and made a deal. However, GEA also learned that issues may emerge from outside the organization and that there is a delicate balance between controversy and staying in relation to get results. While confrontation is a tactic that stirs up media attention and public pressure to get the developer to the decision-making table, staying in relation creates the mutual win. As GEA found, this was particularly effective with power holders that are locally based. In this case, the win included: community-building among tenants; tenants learning civic engagement and empowerment as they impacted both the City Council and developer; using storytelling with public significance to reframe the discussion and re-establish a relation; "chauffeuring the conversation" to broker a three-way negotiation between the tenants, developer and a government-funded nonprofit corporation to devise a workable solution that manifests social justice; holding the city accountable to its new affordable housing plan and through this process creating "a real ally" willing to build affordable housing. Most importantly, for GEA, this represented an innovative and inclusive model of housing redevelopment in Edmonton. Such partnerships could, in the future, involve the city's housing division and community service workers in housing redevelopments (M. Nutter personal communication).

GEA used this model in its next housing action on the city's south side when another 1950s stock row housing and apartment complex was to be redeveloped into a mixed housing urban village. The tenants offered support to the developer if the 504 units were guaranteed as low-cost housing. The developer would only agree to give 88 units, until GEA brought in Habitat for Humanity[4] to plan how 450 units, or 25 percent of the complex, could be made affordable housing, re-emphasizing GEA's ability to foster innovative partnerships between sectors. Eventually, this plan was approved at City Hall in February 2008 with the council chambers full of GEA supporters; recent news indicates this redevelopment will be built in the next several years (C. New and M. Nutter personal communication).

By these two actions, citizens held the City to account for implementing their new municipal policy on affordable housing, also affirming the need for social protections by the state. Through coordinated actions in different city locales, GEA broadened claims for low-income housing, brought multiple stakeholders to the table and included diverse perspectives and interests never represented before in deliberations and resolution. These examples illustrate how confrontational tactics and relational strategies have both been used in community organizing, along with an emphasis on building community and social capital.

GEA GENERATES A SUSTAINABLE SOCIAL ENTERPRISE

When GEA was officially launched, it became part of the IAF Northwest region which included Washington, Oregon and Australia. Later, in 2009, the only other Canadian member, the Metro Vancouver Alliance, would join. Centered in Seattle, the IAF Northwest was creating a subsidiary nonprofit called SustainableWorks to address high unemployment through home energy audits and energy efficiency renovations in residential and commercial buildings. In 2008, GEA adopted SustainableWorks, not as a result of a listening campaign but for the ability to engage a large number of building trades, some of which were core members of GEA. As Debbie Hubbard explains: "Always when we do an action, we're trying to build power, we're trying to bring in new dues and new leaders" (D. Hubbard personal communication). Further, environmental sustainability was a key value shared by member organizations. According to board member Kirsten Goa, one of GEA's goals was to generate green jobs and economic diversification as well as decrease housing costs and greenhouse gas emissions (K. Goa personal communication).

Kirsten explains that, while the original idea was to incubate SustainableWorks to become a separate entity, GEA members felt this venture could add to their financial self-sufficiency and be an important entry point into neighbourhood organizing. With assistance and training from the Northwest IAF, the new SustainableWorks team[5] began engaging partners in the trades, government, financial sector and the utilities. Seed funding was garnered through several large foundations, a director hired and a legal structure enacted. In 2009, five renovation projects were piloted just prior to the official launch of SustainableWorks in November to a packed house of 500 people, including 100 who signed up for home audits. This project was well supported by unions of electrical and sheet metal workers, plumbers and pipefitters whose representatives sat on the SustainableWorks team, and by a local power utility, local bank, contractors and other funding agencies. Soon, complexities began to emerge with the pilots, as did the risks of running a business. Further, the economic context that generated SustainableWorks in the USA did not exist in Alberta. Alberta did not have an employment crisis and thus the importation of this model proved problematic. Three elements began to converge to take SustainableWorks in a new direction.

First, the Social Enterprise Fund had been established in 2008 to provide financial support in the form of loans and training to organizations growing a social enterprise.[6] It was a unique collaboration between the City of Edmonton, its arms-length Edmonton Community Foundation and other contributors such as the United Way, Alberta Real Estate Foundation and private funders. In May 2010, GEA asked the Social Enterprise Fund to complete a feasibility study and comprehensive business plan for developing SustainableWorks as a stand-alone operation.

Second, in 2007–8, the City of Edmonton crafted its forty-year strategic plan, "The Way Ahead," to build a vision of a sustainable and resilient city. A subsidiary draft plan, "The Way We Green," was the city's environmental strategic plan, eventually approved in July 2011. One of its key goals is to make Edmonton a carbon-neutral city where there is no net increase in greenhouse gas emissions. The city followed this with a "Green Building Policy and Plan" in 2012, supporting the design, construction and retrofitting of high performance green buildings.

The third element came from an innovative couple, Godo Stoyke and Shanthu Mano, who had a vision of greening the existing Edmonton housing stock through their small eco-business, Carbon Busters. They had developed an extensive energy efficiency retrofit program (see Stoyke 2007) with sophisticated audit software and supply sourcing and had also designed a zero carbon village.

In 2010, it was clear from an internal organizing capacity survey that GEA did not have the capacity to run SustainableWorks. The Social Enterprise Fund assisted by casting around for innovators who could make it a viable business. A coalition was developed between Anna Bubel, a sustainability business consultant and community planner, and the eco-business couple Shanthu and Godo, with start-up funding from the City of Edmonton and the Social Enterprise Fund. By combining and leveraging these support systems and expertise, the spin-off non-profit social enterprise called C-Returns was created.

C-Returns was launched in April 2012 with the intent of helping homeowners "see returns" in terms of community revitalization, carbon savings, cash savings, comfort and increased resale value. It provides a one-stop service centre that includes: thorough audits of homes and community-owned buildings;

introductions to the maze of innovative green products; research on the best retrofit devices; soliciting and evaluating retrofit bids; determining pay-back information; arranging financing; supervising construction; scheduling inspections and applying for rebates. The goal of C-Returns is to complete almost 3,500 audits and 1,700 green retrofits in three years. As a collaborator, the city is paying for the first 100 audits. The Edmonton Federation of Community Leagues has now started a Solar and Energy Savings Program for homeowners, further scaling up the reach of the innovation. If successful, C-Returns will inject $21.4 million into the Alberta economy over these three years while contributing to the city's carbon neutral future and the health of the planet.

The C-Returns story illustrates GEA's capacity for involving layers of public, private and civil society sectors over time resulting in a partnership of over a dozen players representing the quasi-government and government sector, the civic-minded nonprofit sector, unions and the private sector including construction, banking, utilities, business consulting, eco-business and funders interested in generating a social enterprise. Further, human need and environmental integrity are held in balance with participation in the market, anticipating the possibility of a new economy. Finally, C-Returns tested GEA's ability to allow a new, independent organizational form to emerge under its auspices, scaling out the innovation.

Yet, as Edwards (2009) suggests, social enterprises cannot address fundamental economic change and thus GEA maintained its focus on public and private sector responsiveness and accountability, as demonstrated by its next action.

GEA FACES BIG LAND AND BIG OIL

GEA's next initiative, which became its signature action, started small and innocently enough. In the end, it would put GEA on the map as a significant political player which could rouse civic engagement and shift public consciousness, the political agenda and ultimately public policy. However, it would also bring GEA face to face with the most powerful global players at work in Alberta, sharpening its political education.

Soon after the Klein government deregulated and privatized the utility companies in the early 2000s, one of the founding GEA members, Ebenezer United Church, participated in a GEA listening campaign in 2007. The paid organizer asked the ten congregational participants, "What are our hopes and what are the pressures today?" Their first concern was the impact of rising energy costs on seniors and those with fixed incomes. The second was the environmental legacy left for their children and grandchildren. These participants were concerned about the impact of deregulated, hence increasing, utility prices on food prices, which were also rising in late 2007 (Smythe 2012). With GEA guidance, the participants discussed possible actions, but through a preliminary power analysis realized they did not have the power to force the government to re-regulate energy costs or address the larger problem of climate change.

To identify a specific actionable issue, they examined utility use in grocery stores, particularly open freezers and fridges, finding them relatively energy efficient according to the local United Food Commercial Workers union. The GEA organizer then began using Alinsky-style agitational techniques with congregational participants that search out controversy, stir up anger and frustration, disrupt taken for granted explanations and reveal contradictions (Alinsky 1971). He asked, "Where does all the food in our grocery stores come from and what impact does that have?" The conversation turned toward the origins of food, particularly the importation of 80–90 percent of all foodstuffs consumed in Edmonton, incurring significant transportation costs and greenhouse gas emissions. The participants discussed sourcing food locally and pricing the cost of a local meal. Shopping at the farmer's market, the congregation held a local foods dinner on the hundred-mile diet principle, asking a local gourmet chef to prepare the congregational meal for about sixty people.[7] They were pleasantly surprised at the freshness and taste of the meal.

In 2008, Edmontonians had relatively little local food or sustainability consciousness, yet many congregational people remembered growing up on the perimeter of the city, now paved-over farm land. In a survey of their eighty households, congregational leaders asked, "What do you spend weekly on groceries in your household? If you could buy more local food, would you?" Collectively, the congregation found they spent around $400,000 annually and that members were indeed interested in local food. Realizing their economic leverage, the leaders thought this food buying power could be translated into pressure on grocery stores for change. Once they did another power analysis with GEA help, they realized that the buying desks for major grocery stores were far removed from their community.

In response, GEA then established a volunteer local foods team and met with the Ebenezer leaders. Imagining what change they could realistically make, the congregation decided to have a second local foods meal with a broader invitation list, including all GEA member institutions as well as people involved in food across the city — from farmers, farmers' market associations and restaurateurs to small businesses like meat and cheese stores and government ministry employees from Alberta Agriculture and Rural Development. Congregational leaders did an audit to see how much local food they could procure from local chain stores and shared the findings with 115 participants in April 2008. The keynote speaker described non-industrial farming, including holistic management of his farm and direct sales of his produce. From small group discussions, this broader group generated action ideas. One farmer, Jim Visser, explained how the soils in Edmonton's northeast are some of the best in the world, especially for garden vegetables. The story of his efforts since 1981 to protect his farmland from development into residential housing stirred frustration and revealed contradictions in what could be considered the public good. This story would catalyze the main part of GEA's action strategy.

In evaluating the event, the GEA team decided that the issues generated in the discussion, such as higher prices for organic food, could be addressed through a leadership training event, which was held in June of 2008 with thirty-five people. The event included discussions about the global food system, particularly the concentrated corporate power in agribusiness, as well as the world as they would like it in terms of local food. Finally, members of this group analyzed their capacity to act. Using an hourglass diagram, they visualized a mass of farmers at one end narrowing to a handful of food processing companies and distributors then widening out to a mass of consumers at the other end, noting that most consumers had no direct relationship to producers. This leadership group hypothesized that if they could facilitate direct relationships between producers and eaters they could make a difference.

Under GEA, the core action team of eight organized a public event called Shake the Hand that Feeds You during the September 2008 harvest time. The event had several goals, including support for local producers and raising public awareness about food security and local food. It brought together local farmers and urban eaters, using stories to illustrate and spread the word, resulting in the sale of 300 baskets of food and broad media coverage.

GEA's vision was to generate a vibrant local food economy with significant economic, social and environmental benefits through action impacting municipal land use policy. At the time, the City was developing a comprehensive ten-year land-use plan, which would be incorporated into the municipal development plans. Therefore, GEA launched a larger campaign called This Land is our Land, springboarding from an iconic folk song. The campaign goals included: protecting prime agricultural land to re-establish local control over Edmonton region food supplies; ensuring access to quality food for citizens over multiple generations; promoting environmental stewardship by reducing the transport of food between field and fork; promoting the strength and sustainability of local farmers and producers as part of the local economy and strengthening citizen leadership in civil society sector organizations and communities.

At the Shake the Hand that Feeds You event, GEA identified working teams to do background research and identify potential allies. These working teams were trained to open dialogue with each city councillor about the plan, asking, "Where do you think our food is going to come from in 50 years?" Most of the councillors were puzzled by the question, except one who was already thinking about local food, a potential ally. GEA was building on existing relationships with specific councillors and creating new ones, augmenting its social capital. But, when GEA members tried to arrange meetings with the mayor (a former land developer) and the city planning department, they were unsuccessful.

GEA also tried to get a meeting with the Walton Group, which they determined owns about 80 percent of the land around the perimeter of Edmonton intended for development but not yet part of an area structure plan, which would be folded into the Municipal Development Plan. As key organizer Debbie Hubbard described it, "They just blew us off because they have no need to meet with this citizen group, because they have all the power" (D. Hubbard personal communication).

Such land bank speculators buy hundreds of acres of farmland adjacent to North American cities on behalf of absentee, largely offshore investors. Those who purchase land on speculation often rent it back to farmers dictating commodity production for export until the land is rezoned and purchased by developers for urban expansion, creating windfall profits for speculators. Declining farm incomes make this option attractive to farmers and nearby acreage owners want enhanced services, both factors which promote the likelihood of development. However, in the IAF philosophy, organized money can be countered with organized citizens, who have the capacity to carry out disciplined actions. It was clear that GEA needed to demonstrate its power in order to have impact at the negotiating table.

Analyzing their conversations with city councillors, GEA members determined what their ask would be and what the negotiable and nonnegotiable points were. Then, the first public hearing related to the area structure plan for the northeast region was announced. The city was trying to integrate its industry, transportation and housing development plans, entitled "The Way We Grow," "The Way We Move" and "The Way We Green" into the area structure plans that would constitute the overall Municipal Development Plan, a process carried out every ten years. Initially, there was no consideration of regional food security or a food and urban agriculture strategy. GEA produced a brief for the November 2008 hearing and organized nine presentations, rehearsing them numerous times before formal delivery. It also tapped its networks to deliver 500 people to Edmonton City Hall, the largest number of citizens to ever attend a public hearing. They garnered media attention as City Hall staff moved people into overflow rooms to accommodate them all. GEA's ask was for city councillors to get solid research and information about urban farmland and food security before moving ahead with the existing plan.

The power of organized people well briefed on the issues made an impact. The mayor's office and the planning department called GEA for a meeting, as did the Walton Group. However, GEA discovered that the planning department, in a reactive stance, decided to eliminate any reference to food and agriculture from its plans. So GEA responded through citizen research, by writing its own detailed policy analysis of food security, local food systems and urban agriculture, calling it "The Way We Eat." In it, GEA identified the issues implicit in the global food economy and sketched out a holistic vision for creating a vibrant and sustainable local food economy, referencing successful municipal policies elsewhere. "The Way We Eat" enumerated the environmental, economic, social and health opportunities and described the needed leadership for such a shift.

GEA was able to turn out more than 500 citizens for each successive hearing. In addition to presenting its policy paper, it crafted a new ask, requesting that city council demonstrate leadership by integrating local food and urban agriculture into the Municipal Development Plan, suggesting amendments. To add weight, GEA created a citizen pledge as part of their local food survey, where 712 Edmonton households representing over 2,000 individuals committed to shifting 40 percent of their food dollars to local food (representing $2.3 million of annual food spending) when access barriers were resolved.

In September 2009, GEA organized the Great Potato Giveaway, where at least two thousand Edmontonian cars lined up on freeways and roads into the northeast for the chance to pick fifty lbs (twenty-three kgs) of free potatoes, freshly dug at Gordon Visser's Norbest farm. When the potatoes were gone three hours before the event's end and lines persisted, organizers from the Edmonton Potato Growers Association made another 8,800 lbs (4,000 kgs) of storage potatoes available, in addition to the original 100,000 lbs (45,000 kgs). Organizers were shocked by the interest, knowing they turned away as many as those satisfied with their fifty lbs of potatoes. With media assistance, this tactic helped city residents appreciate the proximity of local food, become educated about the origin of food and the value of these farmlands and generated support for GEA's proposed amendments.

These events converged into GEA's first and most important victory on food and city development (Smythe 2012). After it turned out over 500 people for another hearing in November 2009, the city administration passed, on first reading, a progressive policy that included a full chapter on food and urban agriculture in the Municipal Development Plan. It included the vision of "a resilient food and agriculture system that contributes to the local economy and the overall cultural, financial, social and environmental sustainability of the city" (City of Edmonton 2010: 57). A key clause tied the completion of development plans and rezoning of agricultural land to adherence with a city-wide food and agricultural strategy and a growth coordination strategy, still to be developed. It was the first time in Edmonton's history that local food and food security were included within planning parameters. This was a significant but initial system-level win. GEA was helping set the public agenda and had successfully changed the policy-making process.

The celebrating was barely over when, months later, one councillor advanced an amendment to delete the development of a food and agricultural strategy. Astonishingly, city staff revealed that the writing of development plans is typically led not by the city itself but by key interests involved — in this case, the land speculator. This new amendment was barely defeated in a seven-six nail biter, illustrating that council support of a food and agriculture strategy could not be taken for granted. In fact, the councillor who made the proposal quipped that GEA had "no skin in the game" (land ownership) and therefore no right to a voice (Smythe 2012). While GEA was not a property holder, the perspective that perhaps food-producing land within city boundaries was vital to the public interest and not just to propertied interests was not acknowledged. To increase its "skin in the game," GEA invited farmers to organize into the Northeast Agricultural Producers (NEAP) as GEA dues-paying members.

A year later in September 2011, GEA was invited into the advisory group for the "Horse Hill Area Structure Plan" in the northeast area. However, membership of this group was weighted heavily in favour of developers and oppositional property owners (calling themselves NEEA — the acronym for Northeast Edmonton Alliance — as a parody). GEA sent two representatives but their contributions to the group were ignored. The area structure plan came to resemble what had originally been proposed by the major landowners rather than what farmers indicated they needed for sustainable farming and a prosperous agricultural community. In other words, by inviting GEA, NEEA was able to neutralize dissent and gain legitimacy without permitting authentic participation.

The following month, the Food and Urban Agriculture Project Advisory Committee was struck by the city, populated with members handpicked by the mayor's office, including a European Union trade official, an international financier, the largest Edmonton-area land speculator, one developer, consulting technicians, representatives of the opposing community league, the city's community league federation, Agriculture and Agri-Food Canada as well as several industrial-scale producers. Less than half of the members were small-scale food producers or advocacy groups for local food and food security. GEA was asked to provide one representative, an agonizing decision after its previous experience of marginalization. The mandate of the newly-formed committee was to create first a food charter, second the terms of reference for a new food policy council and third an implementation strategy. Timelines were rushed and transparency lacking, essentially creating a stalemate among members. When the process imploded, GEA held two public meetings before the release of the strategy to explain to city councillors and members of the public that rejection of the strategy was advisable until stronger research information was available. No councillors attended either public meeting. Eventually, GEA was blamed for the stalemate and pejoratively labelled "radicals" and "nuisances" by opponents.

At that point, GEA members realized they were playing in a complicated game involving powerful, multi-layered interests that had been hitherto invisible in municipal planning. As Elkin (1987: 100) has described, "The battlefield of city politics is not flat but is tilted toward an alliance of public officials and land interests." While they had an early policy win, some GEA members described that their somewhat naïve expectations were giving way to a hard political education, demanding far more political sophistication. They were exposing the concentrated and hidden processes of power, the upper reaches of the iceberg, but were also emboldening citizens to flip the iceberg to expose their own power and claim a space for their voice.

As Monique Nutter explained, "This is what Saul Alinsky would say ... at least know why we're losing." She elaborated that "developers contribute, on average, 46 percent of the campaign funds that councillors use to get elected, ranging anywhere from 26-62 percent" (M. Nutter personal communication). While some councillors reported they had sleepless nights about environmental degradation, they would not act as GEA allies given their obligations to campaign donors. As Monique concluded, "corrupt processes" that place land speculators and developers in a room helping develop a food and urban agriculture policy reveal "a fifty-year tradition in the city, of a culture of developers running City Hall" that "we did not have the power to stand up against."

A related development was the approval of a new industrial park in the northeast, including new oil upgraders for the tertiary processing of the Fort McMurray oil sands crude. It was a lynchpin priority growth area for the city, with global vested interests not only from Big Land but also Big Oil. While the City may have had a vision for a carbon neutral future, they wanted to ensure short term oil revenues.

Early in 2012, GEA decided to make a different formal ask. Edmonton had already lost three quarters of its agricultural land since 2006. The land in question was less than 10 percent of the remaining agricultural land around the city and only about 30 percent of the northeast area, so GEA asked for six hundred hectares of contiguous land to be preserved in perpetuity. Yet, the onus was placed on GEA by the city to make a "business case" for this, clearly a difficult task for a volunteer-driven organization (Smythe 2012). Nevertheless, GEA carried out house meetings with over 550 northeast area citizens and developed its analysis through an ecological as well as an economic lens. It carried out another local-foods training event and sponsored guided bus tours of the northeast farmlands, both for public education and media attention. In September, GEA sponsored a workshop for all city stakeholders to explore policy tools to preserve agricultural land, including conservation easements, land swaps and the transfer of development credits. Few decision-makers attended.

In October 2012, the final draft of the food strategy was released. Half of the committee members were concerned about its non-committal language and many refused to sign the document. "FRESH: The Food and Urban Agriculture Strategy," as it was titled, did not stipulate any recommendations for preserving agricultural land. One date was set for a public hearing but so many presenters showed up that a second date had to be set. In the end, the city voted to accept the strategy "as is" to the great disappointment of GEA members and supporters. Even with the thousands of people GEA mobilized to preserve urban farmland, who according to Monique, "had never set foot in City Hall in their life, who have now been into City Hall," the land will not be preserved at the moment (M. Nutter personal communication). City-led citizen panels, stakeholder focus groups and surveys all conveyed the overwhelmingly clear message that citizens recommended preserving prime farmland. Monique concludes that:

> speculators and developers still have free rein.... It's about organized money; they're stronger than us still. I thought maybe civic politics could still be ours, and it probably can be, but not on land-use issues yet.... We didn't have the institutional wisdom to know we were taking on the richest, most powerful people in Edmonton. (M. Nutter personal communication)

Indirectly, GEA was also taking on one of the most significant global powers today — Big Oil, at a time (editor's note: pre 2015) when municipal, provincial and federal politics are skewed in favour of oil interests.

THE SECOND GENERATION: RENEWING LEADERSHIP

In the end, GEA's broader vision of a local food system was lost to the more immediate land question. Yet, this analysis points to the conundrum of priorities for GEA: what matters most — the action goal sought or the leadership training, public consciousness-raising and citizen empowerment that occur through participatory research and education? The first generation of GEA leaders express the primary GEA mandate as choosing actions that build power, thus they took this loss hard despite the early victory. Yet the second generation leaders identify the primary mandate as leadership building, which is facilitated by civic action and education. While this difference in priorities may reflect different organizational needs over time, it represents a substantially different focus and a growing internal critique of the Alinsky model. This critique echoes a debate between Saul Alinsky and Myles Horton of the Highlander Centre on whether "organizing educates" or "education makes possible organization." As Horton stated:

> If you were working with an organization and there's a choice between the goal of that organization, or the particular program they're working on, and educating people, developing people, helping them grow, helping them become able to analyze — if there's a choice, we'd sacrifice the goal of

the organization for helping the people grow, because we think in the long run it's a bigger contribution.… Organizing implies that there's a specific, limited goal that needs to be achieved, and the purpose is to achieve that goal.… [In education] you may not actually get that problem solved, but you've educated a lot of people. (Horton and Freire 1990: 116, 119)

Organizing and educating are dialectically related in the service of social and political change, but often the educational processes are unrecognized or subsumed. This story illustrates the role that education has played in GEA's development, reflecting a Freirean cycle of popular education — discussing reality, problematizing it through questioning that unsettles, building a social and power analysis through dialogue that transforms understanding, taking collective action to change political and economic structures and reflecting for another cycle of action, all toward the development of a critical consciousness and active citizenry. Educational activities are critical to later organizing success but are also required on an ongoing basis for organizational health and coalition building.

Since 2010, GEA has been in a renewal phase as many original leaders have moved on or withdrawn temporarily. In this succession phase, there is now significant pushback against the IAF driving the local agenda through a highly scripted, controlled training process. While the IAF has historically engaged low-income neighbourhoods and non-white populations, to date GEA's membership has largely been white and middle-class with high levels of education, leadership skills and voluntarism. As in asset-based community development, GEA leaders assert that IAF leadership trainers should not assume they lack education and experience but scaffold from their existing level of knowledge and skills. This is also considered best practice in the adult education field (Merriam, Caffarella, and Baumgartner: 2007).

Citizen empowerment should create spaces for local leaders to develop their own solutions to issues rather than adhere to organizer-directed or IAF solutions. In its evolving model, GEA is now utilizing more collaborative, less directive processes. It only invites thought leaders and technical experts in at specific times when this does not interfere with the development of citizen voice. Further, GEA is critical of the shaming, judgmental and impositional training strategies of the IAF that are intended to build discipline for public confrontations. Many current GEA leaders consider the confrontational approach and related training as part of a patriarchal model. Importantly, the two most recent paid organizers have been women, as are numerous team leaders. The current paid organizer and board chair are visible-minority women. Together, they are striking a very different leadership stance — leading from behind, building the collective identity of the organization and inspiring a higher level of political morality.

The current leaders see themselves enacting the four pillars of leadership development differently, including the relational listening, power analysis, political skills and the organizing cycle components. Now, as a hybrid model, they are adhering to the foundational IAF principles but also inserting more flexible and organic processes. This includes creating space for leaders to grow and a higher tolerance for unlearning and actions that fail, all as part of learning. They also foster additional spaces for critical reflection as well as space for projects to be spun off into innovative forms. This potentially diffuses citizen empowerment and their social capital more broadly, outside the GEA network.

Some of the larger dues-paying unions have felt disengaged from the action issues to date, largely because they may not be directly related to their organizational interests. So, it is clear that GEA leaders will likely need to re-engage in relationals, remake the case for membership, carry out regular listening campaigns to identify actions of interest to the wide diversity of membership and communicate GEA's impact more effectively. This requires community building that continuously builds collective identity as well as trust, respect and reciprocity among the member organizations as the necessary foundations for community organizing. GEA is again offering leadership training to reduce membership drift but resource issues are growing. Thus, its current leaders are considering fundraising through fee-based training for the public and may perhaps move beyond the traditional focus on formal organizations. They are thinking of allowing individual as well as organizational memberships and granting observer status for some organizations that allow for charitable tax write-offs.

GEA leaders are also taking up new lines of action — on senior care and human dignity in work — and trying to broaden membership inclusivity across race and class lines. They are engaging immigrant newcomer groups as well as visible minorities and agitating around justice issues related to temporary foreign workers and other employment ghettos. Like the IAF, GEA has been dominated by Christian organizations, but it is deliberately working across faith lines, particularly in Muslim communities. Similarly, while GEA had largely been comprised of the baby boomer generation representing traditional institutions, it is now reaching out to people under thirty and to community groups particularly within visible-minority communities. It is building on the strong social capital found in these communities, their intergenerational connections and social media as their place of association. This appears to be facilitating a plurality of voices although finding common ground will continue to be a profound challenge.

As Madhu repeats, "you are GEA and GEA is you," emphasizing the woven layers of identity, leadership and relational power that comprise a collective sense of self and deepen a coalitional consciousness (Hart 2010). In reality, GEA's approach is a hybrid of the traditional Alinsky confrontational, charismatic, accountability and issues-driven approach with a more relational and balanced approach that focuses on Freirean pedagogy, multiple sector collaborations, community building as well as power building and a complex brokering role. The hybrid approach, however, generates ongoing internal tensions and contradictions such as a backlash to new leadership styles, questions about committee involvement with powerful stakeholders and constantly generating the energy needed for community building, leadership development as well as public action.

LESSONS IN DEMOCRATIC REVITALIZATION AND THE PROMISE OF A NEW ECONOMY: THE SIGNIFICANCE OF GEA

GEA represents a significantly different way of organizing to achieve social change in Alberta. It emerged in response to the recalibration of public, private and civil society sector responsibilities as part of neoliberal economic globalization.

While the private sector has expanded its range of power, the public and civil society sectors have been left to rethink their shrinking role (Smith and Beazley 2000). GEA has provided a broad-based space where this rethinking dialogue and social solidarity can be kept alive. Guided by the values of social justice and environmental sustainability that evoke solidarity among its membership, GEA's leaders still use confrontational tactics demanding private and public accountability but also animate solutions for mitigating the harms of the existing capitalist system, whether through affordable housing, green retrofits or urban agriculture. They also concentrate on capacity building of citizens and citizen organizations, bridging partnerships across sectors to create complementary roles in the provision of public goods and services. GEA works between corporate elephant legs fostering a new model of enterprise that equally values social, financial and environment sustainability, generating new tools and relations of business along the way.

Tarrow (2005) defines scale shift as "change in the number and level of coordinated contentious actions to a different focal point, involving a new range of actors, different objects and broadened claims" (as cited in Gaventa and Tandon 2010: 121). GEA coordinates an agenda of action among diverse organizations, thus multiplying the impact of smaller, single-issue organizations. Its leaders take the long view rather than aiming for the short win, understanding social change as intergenerational work that constantly involves new actors. Further, GEA is creating a power bloc of citizen voice that compels attention and this enables it to work at the policy level so that changes are not single events but mutually reinforcing over time. GEA has scaled out its activities through the creative engagement of Edmontonians — through experiential farmland tours, potato giveaways and food baskets connecting growers and eaters as well as through multiple learning and deliberative opportunities in public spaces. Through its capacity to quickly mobilize a trained constituency, GEA is shifting public consciousness as well as rejuvenating a sense of political agency in a petro-state marked by a sense of political futility.[8]

While GEA was successful at engaging local power-holders and confronting global power-holders, challenging the interests of international land speculators or transnational oil companies will be a more complex task. GEA will require broader alliance building with new local, regional, national and global players. As Edwards (2009: 104) emphasizes, "Overlapping memberships, cross-interest coalitions, hybrid organizations and the appropriate mix of bonding and bridging [capital], grassroots groups and intermediaries, advocates and service providers are more likely to make associational life a handmaiden to broader social progress."

Most GEA participants report they now have a new view of politics and what political life can be. Current board members explain that GEA is changing the conversation about power: how power grows, flows, and hides. They have all felt the power of an organized and unified voice. The quiet, behind-the-scenes relationship building has created a web of citizen power that becomes boldly visible at times as ordinary people claim unused entry points and create new entry points for citizen participation. GEA leaders realize they are one of the only organizations that has filled City Hall numerous times, trained people to prepare research and speak, tapped into citizen concerns and, on this basis, claimed a space to speak. They are adept at presenting the heterogeneous views of their members while voicing common concerns but they have also been excluded and their views devalued.

There is now a new imagination for participatory politics, alongside a cold anger. As Debbie Hubbard noted over the last city vote, "everybody [the general public] was enraged about it; it wasn't even GEA people that we are connected with" who were enraged (D. Hubbard personal communication). Cold anger is a productive anger, in response to a revealed injustice, where people are passionate but remain reasonable, intentional and strategic (Rogers 1990). As Don Mitchell explains, GEA demonstrated that "Edmontonians actually care … about agricultural land. They care about food and our ability to sustain ourselves. Anybody that ignores that at the political level, is doing so at their peril" (D. Mitchell personal communication).

Importantly, while GEA leaders use conflict tactics, they strive to build relationships, always considering opponents as potential allies. GEA has animated public support for protecting local land and food, recognizing human interdependence with these conditions of life. Primarily, it is helping to change the current logic, from profits to principles, from patriarchy and hierarchy to radical democracy, from separation to relationality. GEA has only begun.

Notes

1. This case study was written before the Alberta provincial election of 2015, when the New Democaratic Party was elected to power.

2. All references to personal communication are for interviews conducted between Feburary 8, 2013, and February 28, 2013.

3. Thanks to Debbie Hubbard and Bob McKeon for their documents tracing early GEA history.

4. Habitat for Humanity Canada is a national nonprofit organization that mobilizes volunteers and community partners for building affordable housing and promoting homeownership as a means to breaking the cycle of poverty.

5. Thanks to Kirsten Goa for her historical account and Omar Yacub as an oral informant.

6. The Canadian Task Force on Social Finance has defined social enterprise as "any organization or business that uses market oriented production and sale of goods and/or services to pursue a public benefit mission" (Social Enterprise Fund n.d.).

7. Thanks to Nancy Siever, Linda Robinson, Monique Nutter and Debbie Hubbard for piecing together the early part of this action through various personal communications.

8. Arguably, this kind of organizing capacity contributed to the significant shift in political culture where a centre-left party was elected to govern for the first time, in 2015, ending over forty years of Conservative Party rule.

References

Alinsky, S. 1946. *Reveille for Radicals*. New York: Vintage Books.

____. 1971. *Rules for Radicals*. New York: Vintage Books.

Auty, R.M. 1993. *Sustaining Development in Mineral Economies: The Resource Curse Thesis*. London: Routledge.

Barber, B.R. 1992. "Jihad vs. McWorld." *The Atlantic Monthly* 269, 3: 53–65. <http://www.theatlantic.com/magazine/archive/1992/03/jihad-vs-mcworld/303882/>.

Chambers, E. 2004. *Roots for Radicals*. New York: Continuum International Publishing.

City of Edmonton. 2010. *The Way We Grow: Municipal Development Plan*. Edmonton, AB: Author.

Ecumenical Coalition for Economic Justice. 1993. *Reweaving Canada's Social Programs: From Shredded Safety Net to Social Solidarity*. Toronto, ON: Our Times.

Edwards, M. 2009. *Civil Society*. Cambridge, UK: Polity Press.

Elkin, S.L. 1987. *City and Regime in the American Republic*. Chicago: University of Chicago Press.

Englander, J., S. Bharadwaj and A. Brandt. 2013. "Historical Trends in Greenhouse Gas Emissions of the Alberta Oil Sands (1970–2010)." *Environmental Research Letters* 8. Doi:10.1088/1748-9326/8/4/044036

Flanagan, G. 2005. "Not Just About Money: Provincial Budgets and Political Ideology." In T. Harrison (ed.), *The Return of the Trojan Horse: Alberta and the New World (Dis)Order*. Montreal, QC: Black Rose Books.

Gaventa, J. 2006. "Finding the Spaces for Change: A Power Analysis." IDS Bulletin 37, 6: 23–33.

Gaventa, J., and R. Tandon (eds.). 2010. *Globalizing Citizens: New Dynamics of Inclusion and Exclusion*. London, UK: Zed Books.

Gecan, M. 2008. "Effective Organizing for Congregational Renewal." Skokie, IL: ACTA Publications.

Harrison, T. (ed.). 2005. *The Return of the Trojan Horse: Alberta and the New World (Dis) Order.* Montreal, QC: Black Rose Books.

Harrison, T., and G. Laxer (eds.). 1995. *The Trojan Horse: Alberta and the Future of Canada.* Montreal, QC: Black Rose Books.

Hart, M. 2010. "Radically Democratic Learning in the Grounded In-Between." *New Directions for Adult and Continuing Education* 128: 37–45.

Harvey, D. 2005. A Brief History of Neoliberalism. Oxford, UK: Oxford University Press.

Horton, M., and P. Freire. 1990. We Make the Road by Walking: Conversations on Education and Social Change. Philadelphia, PA: Temple University Press.

Industrial Areas Foundation. 1990. *IAF: 50 Years Organizing for Change.* Franklin Square, NY: Industrial Areas Foundation.

Kolkman, J., J. Ahorro and K/ Varlen. 2000. "Time for Action: Working Together to End Poverty in Alberta." Edmonton, AB: Public Interest Alberta and the Edmonton Social Planning Council. <http://pialberta.org/sites/default/files/Documents/Alberta-Poverty-Report_2010.pdf>.

Ledwith, M. 2005. *Community Development: A Critical Approach.* Bristol, UK: Policy Press.

Merriam, S.B., R.S. Caffarella and L.M. Baumgartner. 2007. *Learning in Adulthood: A Comprehensive Cycle,* third edition. San Francisco, CA: Jossey-Bass.

Rogers, M.B. 1990. Cold Anger: A Story of Faith and Power Politics. Denton, TX: University of North Texas Press.

Scott, S. 1992. "Personal Change Through Participation in Social Action." *The Canadian Journal for the Study of Adult Education* 6, 2: 47–64.

____. 2000. "Recovering Civil Spaces for Citizen Action." Presentation at the Learning for Life Conference. Saskatoon, SK.

____. 2001. "Transformation through Imagination in Community Action." Presentation at the International Conference on Transformative Learning. Toronto, ON.

Sirianni, C., and L. Friedland. 2001. *Civic Innovation in America: Community Empowerment, Public Policy, and the Movement for Civic Renewal.* Berkeley and Los Angeles, CA: University of California Press.

Smith, M., and M. Beazley. 2000. "Progressive Regimes, Partnerships and the Involvement of Local Communities: A Framework for Evaluation." *Public Administration* 78, 4: 855–78.

Smythe, E. 2012. "Resilient Local Food Systems: How to Build a Movement by Asking a Simple Question." Panel presentation on food movements, civic engagement and the struggle over Edmonton's Food and Agriculture Strategy. Edmonton, AB.

Social Enterprise Fund. n.d. "Homepage." <http://socialenterprisefund.ca>.

Stoyke, G. 2007. *The Carbon Buster's Home Energy Handbook.* Gabriola Island, BC: New Society Publishers.

Warren, M.R. 2001. *Dry Bones Rattling: Community Building to Revitalize American Democracy.* Princeton, NJ: Princeton University Press.

EVERYDAY GOOD LIVING AND THE TWO ROW WAMPUM

The Vision of the Ontario Federation of Indigenous Friendship Centres

Linda Jones with Sylvia Maracle

> The vision of the Friendship Centre movement is to improve the quality of life for Aboriginal people living in an urban environment by supporting self-determined activities which encourage equal access to and participation in Canadian society and which respect Aboriginal cultural distinctiveness. (Ontario Federation of Indigenous Friendship Centres n.d.)

The Ontario Federation of Indigenous Friendship Centres (OFIFC)[1] is the culmination of a grassroots movement in Ontario that began in the homes of urban Aboriginal people in the first half of the twentieth century. Today, with twenty-nine centres offering a wide array of programs and an annual budget of over $47 million, this not-for-profit plays a pivotal role in the provincial service-delivery system. The OFIFC has not only taken on a service delivery role within the mainstream[2] system; it has shifted the system by providing services from a uniquely Aboriginal perspective incorporating a healing process that "returns Aboriginal people to themselves" (Lawrence and Anderson 2003: 12).

In this case study, Linda Jones relates the story of the OFIFC in consultation with Sylvia Maracle, the current and long-time executive director of the OFIFC. They describe the reason why Friendship Centres were formed, how they were formalized, the role they play in the healing of Aboriginal people in urban areas and the role they also play in influencing non-Aboriginal cultures.

EVERYDAY GOOD LIVING

For the OFIFC, returning Aboriginal people to themselves means creating the space for "everyday good living" — the OFIFC's definition of culture. Everyday good living places the emphasis on what a person does rather than on what a person says and on one's interrelation with others in a spirit of trust, friendship and respect (M. Chacaby personal communication)[2]. Everyday good living reflects wholeness and peace and living in balance with the natural and spiritual worlds. It is this everyday good living that was all but destroyed through colonization and assimilation. These assaults on traditional life have contributed to maladaptive behaviours and urban migration and resulted in the need for Friendship Centres and the transformation of the social services system to include Aboriginal programming.

Another aspect of Aboriginal everyday good living is maintaining the balance of responsibilities and power between female and male members of society. Historically, the two genders had different spheres of responsibility that complemented one another and were regarded as equally important. This case study describes the significant role that women have played and continue to play in the OFIFC and the Friendship Centre movement, highlighting the leadership and contribution of one woman in particular, Sylvia Maracle. Ms. Maracle is credited with playing a decisive role in the healing movement by unifying disparate Friendship Centres into a force for change felt at the individual and community levels and contributing to the advancement of an empowering environment for urban Aboriginal people (M. Campbell personal communication).

According to the vision of the OFIFC, everyday good living also means that urban Aboriginals and non-Aboriginals should live with respect for one another and allow each other to follow their own path in harmony. OFIFC leaders explain that this message was conveyed in the Two Row wampum (The *Kaswentha* in Mohawk) representing the 1613 treaty between the Dutch and the Iroquois.[3] Two rows of purple beads illustrate how Aboriginal and non-Aboriginal people would proceed together down the river of life but on distinct paths, while rows of white beads represent how trust, friendship and respect would connect the two. Each party would honour the other's laws, languages, customs and cultures. Despite the history between Aboriginal and non-Aboriginal peoples over past decades as discussed below, the OFIFC upholds the vision of the Two Row wampum today, promoting respect for Aboriginal history and culture and the implementation of service programs according to the distinct needs of urban Aboriginals. In the final message of this paper, we reflect on the Two Row wampum and the harmony that it symbolizes.

THE FRIENDSHIP CENTRE MOVEMENT

> Their services started with tea and talk, and ultimately grew into sophis-
> ticated counselling and referral agencies. (Sylvia Maracle 2013: 316)

The Friendship Centre movement that led to the formation of the OFIFC began as a grassroots response to the migration of Aboriginal people to urban settings; as Aboriginal women became established in cities, they would welcome newcomers to their homes, creating meeting places and providing shelter to those who needed it. Other venues such as garages, church basements and community centres provided further spaces to gather (Maracle 2013), share news of home, play a game of cards or drink a cup of tea in the company of other Aboriginal people (Lowe 2006–7). Originally, these gatherings were sustained by the volunteer efforts of women, including fundraising activities such as the sale of raffle tickets, handicrafts and baked goods.

The first official Friendship Centre — the North American Indian Club — was registered as a society in Toronto in 1951. Its formation was made possible after amendments to the Indian Act removed or altered the most repressive sections, including those that forbade Aboriginal people from meeting in groups or conducting traditional ceremonies (First Nations Studies Program 2009b). The next year, the second Friendship Centre opened in Vancouver and in 1959 the third opened in Winnipeg (Native Friendship Centre n.d.). The number continued to grow from then until today when there are 119 Friendship Centres across Canada (National Association of Friendship Centres n.d.). The growth of the Friendship Centre movement had a lot to do with its informal organizing principle: "The [early] success of the movement hinged on the fact that even though the focal point changed from a private home to a social agency, this agency still operated on an informal basis providing a home-like atmosphere" (Ontario Federation of Indian Friendship Centres 1978: 8).

As Friendship Centres were established, many women, often working as volunteers, contributed to their growth and success. One example among many is LuVerna Delores (Delo) Clause, a pioneer of the movement:

> A Seneca, born in 1939 to Peter Thomas and Blanche Adell (Gibson) Thomas on the Six Nations Reserve in Ohsweken, Ontario, Ms. Clause was trained as a registered nursing assistant and became involved with the Hamilton Indian Centre as it was known then. Ms. Clause and her husband opened their doors for children to be taught Native Arts and Crafts. She and a few parents who attended the Indian Centre then established a temporary Cultural Centre as a gathering place in Hamilton

to offer services to the Aboriginal community. Ms. Clause helped the founding members with the Letters Patent enabling them to become what we now know as the Hamilton Regional Indian Centre. She served as a Board member for many years and eventually as President. (National Association of Friendship Centres Memorial n.d.)

In the late 1960s, the grassroots Friendship Centres began to organize into Provincial/Territorial Associations and the OFIFC was incorporated as a not-for-profit organization in July 1971 to represent the collective interests of its member Friendship Centres within Ontario. During the subsequent four decades, it has grown from six founding-member Friendship Centres to twenty-nine Centres across the province (Ontario Federation of Indigenous Friendship Centres n.d.). Over this same time period, the OFIFC has increased from a staff of five to seventy-six, and from an operating budget of about $1 million per year to over $45 million in 2013 (Ontario Federation of Indian Friendship Centres 2013: 47). Despite its growth, the OFIFC continues to remain an organization that belongs to and serves the community.

The Friendship Centre movement made a significant impact at the enabling policy level in the 1970s when the federal government officially recognized the need that these grassroots organizations filled. In 1972, the government, through the Department of the Secretary of State, established the Migrating Native Peoples Program which provided core funding for Friendship Centres (Ontario Federation of Indian Friendship Centres 1978). This supported the growth of the Friendship Centre movement discussed in more detail below, but first we turn to the underlying causes of urban migration and the need for Friendship Centres and the culturally-grounded services that they offer.

THE NEED FOR FRIENDSHIP CENTRES

It is generally accepted that the often conflicting goals of "civilization," assimilation, and protection of Indian peoples that have been pursued throughout the history of federal Indian legislation have their origin in (primarily British) colonialism. (Wendy Moss and Elaine Gardner-O-Toole 1991: 2)

In order to understand the Friendship Centre movement, the founding of the OFIFC and the emphasis that the OFIFC places on appropriate services and healing it is necessary to first understand the history of colonization and the migration of Aboriginal people to urban centres. This history is long, complex and fraught and we can only briefly examine it here.

Prior to contact and colonization, most Aboriginal peoples migrated according to the seasons to their customary hunting, fishing and trapping grounds. They followed established routes along riverways and across land. Some of these traditional Aboriginal routes provided the network for the fur trade (Aboriginal Affairs and Northern Development Canada 2013) and passed through the sites where major cities now stand (Lowe 2006–7). In recent decades, Aboriginal people have followed these same routes as urban migrants, seeking a home off-reserve or away from small and isolated communities.

According to the Canadian Royal Commission on Aboriginal People, the Aboriginal population in Canada at the time of initial sustained contact with Europeans in the early seventeenth century is estimated to have been between 210,000 and 2,000,000, with 500,000 as the most widely accepted estimate (O'Donnell 2008). By the first national censuses of the late nineteenth and early twentieth centuries, it was reduced to around 100,000 people (Romaniuc 2003). A number of post-contact factors combined to set off the spiral of depopulation over a period of three hundred years: changes in access to land, inter-tribal warfare spurred on by Europeans and social upheaval that grew during this time. These intensified the most significant factor in the depopulation of Aboriginal communities — the introduction of new contagious diseases by European colonists (ibid.).

Pre-contact Aboriginal peoples in Canada had a strong oral tradition and a rich culture that was closely tied to the land they inhabited. Stories of creation taught people about where they came from and their role in the world — that we are all spiritual beings who have entered the physical realm and that we need to learn how to be human. These narratives taught people how to live appropriately, with gratitude, and to "fulfill the sacred responsibility back to creation" (M. Chacaby personal communication April 19, 2013). As their population declined and communities were damaged, Aboriginal people were uprooted from their traditional land and moved by their colonizers, which further destroyed their communities along with traditional values and livelihoods. As historian Olive Dickason observes, following the Royal Proclamation Act of 1763, "the administration of First Nations in Canada took on a different character, involving the systematic removal of natives from the land they occupied" (as cited in Oliver 2010: 4–5). Removal from the land took people away from their social space, destroying the foundations of Aboriginal cultures (M. Chacaby personal communication).

In the decades that followed, "enfranchisement" became a dominant feature of the Canadian federal government's assimilation policies for Aboriginal people. "Voluntary enfranchisement" was introduced in the Gradual Civilization Act of 1857 on the assumption that Aboriginal people would want to give up their identity (legal as well as cultural) to become Canadian citizens and integrate with mainstream Canadian society. However, very few Aboriginal people took up this offer by choice and enfranchisement became compulsory with the deepening of European colonialist control and the Indian Act of 1876 (First Nations Studies Program 2009b). The Indian Act allowed the government to control most aspects of Aboriginal people's lives. In addition to controlling Indian status, land ownership, use of resources, access to education, band administration and so on, it incorporated compulsory assimilation policies (Montpetit 2011).

Aboriginal people were no longer able to practice their cultural traditions, participate in ceremonies or meet in groups. Many were excluded from treaty processes and became displaced persons while yet others lost their Indian status as defined under the Indian Act (Lowe 2006–7). The loss of Indian status could occur for a number of reasons: earning a university degree (Montpetit 2011), leaving the reserve during the depression, serving in the military and, in the case of a woman, "marrying out" to a non-Aboriginal man (Lowe 2006–7). Other Aboriginal people were victims of the residential school system, which alienated them from their home community and was designed to erase their language and culture. Many children suffered abuse of all kinds at residential schools (Montpetit 2011) and did not return home or left the reserve after they no longer felt like they fit in.

Since 1876, the Indian Act has undergone numerous changes. The amendments made between 1876 and 1950 strengthened the assimilation policies of the original Act. However, after 1950, although the philosophy of assimilation remained, certain changes have been made to provide Aboriginal people with greater control over their own lives. One of the best-known changes came in the form of Bill C-31 in 1985, which responded to the Canadian Charter of Rights and Freedoms that prohibited discrimination based on race, ethnicity, religion, sex, age or mental or physical disability. This meant that First Nations women who "married out" no longer lost their status.

Through these upheavals and shifts, Aboriginal people have continued to leave the reserves and migrate to urban settlements (often starting from smaller towns and then moving to larger towns and cities). By 1972, 30 percent of Aboriginal people in Ontario lived off-reserve (S. Maracle personal communication), while today, over 80 percent of the approximately 300,000 Aboriginal people living in Ontario are urban dwellers. Although many have thrived in an urban setting, the adjustment to a different way of life was a struggle for many others (Ontario Federation of Indian Friendship Centres 1978). Based on the 2007 Statistics Canada "poverty line," over a quarter (29 percent) of urban Aboriginal families live below the line as do over half (53 percent) of single urban Aboriginal people (Dinsdale 2010). These problems, compounding the trauma associated with the residential school system, have in turn given rise to domestic violence and abuse. Scores of victims and their families have turned to Friendship Centres for support and healing.

The OFIFC reports put a human face on these statistics:

A front-line worker told the story of a woman — B — who is a survivor of sexual, physical, and emotional abuse suffered from childhood to adulthood, including in the residential school system. In the beginning of her healing journey, she sought out different services for help, but finally her journey brought her to the Friendship Centre's Aboriginal Mental Health Program. The program was able to provide B with services that supported her healing. The worker reports that B has started to mend the dysfunction in her life and her relationships with her family. She has "learned to open up her heart to listen; bringing love, trust, and wisdom back into her life," and now "continues on her journey of healing and has started to learn her native language through the songs and Full Moon ceremonies." (personal communication)

In migrating, Aboriginal people are seeking positive change in terms of employment and education, greater availability of services, better housing and association with an established urban Aboriginal population (Lowe 2006–7). Over 22 percent are earning a middle-class income now (S. Maracle personal communication) and urban Aboriginals fare better in most social and economic categories than their rural counterparts do (Helin 2006). There are many highly successful role models and there is much optimism that urban Aboriginal people will continue to prosper. Services offered by Friendship Centres provide the necessary support for those who are struggling with this transition to urban life.

REALIZING THE VISION:
THE OFIFC AND FRIENDSHIP CENTRES' ROLES

The OFIFC and the Friendship Centre network grew out of a grassroots movement evolving from tea and talk in people's homes to a large Aboriginal institution. Over time, the OFIFC has developed a pivotal role in the service delivery system and is now recognized by the government as a critical service provider to urban Aboriginals.

Today, the roles of the centres and the Federation are distinct from one another. Friendship Centres are autonomous not-for-profit corporations, which are mandated to serve the needs of all Aboriginal people regardless of legal definition. Their activities depend on the community and the capacity of the individual centre but may include, for example, education programming, economic development and children and youth development initiatives. In addition, programs supported by the OFIFC include those related to health, justice, family support and employment and training. The range and complexity of services offered have grown significantly since the early years, requiring strategic plans, staff with a range of capacities and skill sets as well as sophisticated lobbying/advocacy and operational processes.

This growth is illustrated by the current executive director of the United Native Friendship Centre of Fort Frances, Sheila McMahon. She relates how when she was first employed with the local Friendship Centre, they administered five programs. In the 1970s and 1980s it was mainly a drop-in centre but today when families come into the Friendship Centre they are more often in situations of crisis in all aspects of their lives with housing, employment and educational supports at the forefront. The working poor make use of the food bank and rent bank through the Centre's homelessness program and the centre is taking a more proactive role in advocacy so that children are not taken out of the home by the social service agencies. Now the centre offers nineteen programs out of three buildings.

As members of the federation, the centres "first and foremost must show respect and honour all Native beliefs and customs ... must be committed to information sharing, referrals, recreation and social activities, cultural reinforcement, community development and all other such activities which ensure Native people a better quality of life through Native self-determination" (Ontario Federation of Indian Friendship Centres 1997). The Timmins Native Friendship Centre, for example, operates more than twenty programs delivered by thirty-four staff. The director, Veronica Nicholson, emphasizes how many of the people they serve are timid, cannot speak up for themselves and are strangers in their own land. The system they have to navigate is different from the one they are used to on the reserve and they need support to tap into programs such as Ontario Works or the housing list.[4] The centre therefore plays an important advocacy role and every person coming to the centre is given information on services available and help accessing them. In fact, the Timmins Friendship Centre has a checklist of supports that they go through to ensure clients can function in the new urban environment.

The following example reported by a front-line worker at a Friendship Centre illustrates the multiple levels of support offered, in this case to a family in crisis:

> She [the frontline worker] met K and her family in the Intensive Care Unit at the hospital. K's grandmother was ready to take her journey to the spirit world. While the family was all there, they had prayers and teachings on how to let her go. When she took her last breath, it was K who was seen as taking it the hardest. Her grandmother had raised her because of her mother's addiction.
>
> Shortly after her grandmother's passing, K started to do drugs and eventually her two boys were taken by the Children's Aid Society (CAS). She and her partner were referred to a Friendship Centre by CAS and their long process of becoming healthy began. Front-line workers helped them plan some lifestyle changes and once they made these changes they could see their life improving. K started to come to the sweats every two

weeks and she felt so good she continued regularly. She started attending other programs within the Friendship Centre and also volunteered to help wherever she could. This past winter, K and her partner got involved with their two sons to make Grass Dance Regalia and now both Mom and Dad want to make Regalia so they can dance in the pow wows too. K commented [to the worker] that she prays every day and says thank you for what they have, asking spirit helpers to help them to have a good day and stay on the good path. (personal communication)

The expanding role of Friendship Centres at the community level is complemented by the OFIFC. As a federation of member centres, the OFIFC takes the lead in representing the needs of urban Aboriginal people in Ontario to the government through the establishment of long-term relationships, advice on policy and facilitation of respectful communication between government officials and urban Aboriginal people (J. Riggs personal communication). The OFIFC also has a responsibility to support the development of the Centres and to represent their specific interests to a broader public. In the words of one executive director, "OFIFC does not tell us what to do. OFIFC tells us what they can do to support us" (V. Nicholson personal communication). This support includes assistance with developing more cohesive partnerships within their communities and advice in the areas of health, education, justice and housing based on the OFIFC's interaction with provincial and federal authorities (S. McMahon personal communication). One of the main ways in which this is accomplished is by raising awareness of partners (such as government, civic and religious organizations) about Aboriginal cultures, the trauma that Aboriginal people have suffered and the healing that is occurring through Friendship Centres. In this way an empowering environment is created for the Friendship Centres (M. Chacaby personal communication).

An example of how this works is the Strategic Framework to End Violence Against Aboriginal Women. Friendship Centres and the OFIFC were repeatedly being invited to discuss the issue in the community or with the government. However, such discussions were frustrating and time consuming and had limited results. As an alternative, the OFIFC created a framework document in partnership with the Ontario Native Women's Association correcting the absence of an adequate reflection of urban Aboriginal history in more mainstream documents.

The OFIFC set the context for the policy discussion so that it incorporated Aboriginal experience and perspective; worked with the government to shape relevant policy; engaged with the government to influence resource decisions and set priorities for funding investments and facilitated the participation of individual Friendship Centres in these processes, helping them develop their own capacity at the local level (J. Riggs personal communication). Over time, other Aboriginal organizations in Ontario have joined the End Violence against Aboriginal Women Initiative, which now influences much of the policy and planning discussion in the province related to this issue.

In order to address the many and varied needs of urban Aboriginal people and Friendship Centres that support them in a cohesive way, the OFIFC has adopted its second twenty-year strategic plan. This is adapted every five years and progress is reviewed on an annual basis. In its 2005 strategy, the OFIFC identified five focal areas: governance and political involvement; self-sufficiency; leadership and leadership development; programs and service delivery and culture and education. In the case of the latter, the focus is on developing the means for non-Aboriginal people to recognize Aboriginal cultures and traditions so they understand these ways and appreciate their importance to Aboriginal people (Ontario Federation of Indian Friendship Centres 2010).

The OFIFC now places significant emphasis on its policy role and must be vigilant about shifts in government policy that will have an impact on the OFIFC and Friendship Centre programs and, therefore, on the Aboriginal people that they serve. In the executive director's report to the OFIFC's forty-third annual general meeting in the fall of 2012, the policy environment as well as specific policy issues are discussed (Maracle 2012). Based on this strategic policy analysis, the OFIFC offers a wide range of programs for its membership (e.g., prevention of violence against women, youth programming, addiction services), while the centres not only implement some of the Federation's initiatives but also carry out specific programming tailored to the needs in their regions.[5]

As described above, there have been significant systems-level changes over the decades promoted and implemented by the OFIFC or adopted by the government: the endorsement of Friendship Centres; the transfer of service delivery to the centres; the growth in the number and sophistication of centres providing services; the OFIFC's increased role in engaging with donors, ministries and a range of partners (impacting the way they deliver services) and, above all, the emergence of an empowering environment for Aboriginal people.

A MAINSTREAM ABORIGINAL INSTITUTION GROUNDED IN CULTURE

The OFIFC has become a brain trust for strength-based programming and creative policy development, and an established leader in innovative, cutting-edge community-driven research. This is how the institution is being perceived by its partners, including governments, academic institutions, and private sector. (M. Smolewski personal communication)

The OFIFC continues to represent the collective interests of its twenty-nine members resulting in change at many levels in the lives of people and in the enabling environment. As described above, the OFIFC is about much more than service delivery: it is about healing, cultural revitalization and everyday good living. Why is this cultural grounding so important and what does it mean on a day-to-day basis? This question brings us back to the traumas of European contact, depopulation, colonization, displacement, "enfranchisement" and migration — resulting in the loss of community, identity and traditions. The accumulated pain, loss and injury over 400 years led to

> communities ... struggling with rampant addictions, low education levels, poor housing, few employment opportunities and numerous family stresses ... people whose lives had been profoundly scarred by the violence of residential school, training schools, adoption and other child and family service interventions, people who were apologetic for who they were. (Maracle 2013: 315–16)

By developing programs that are culturally sensitive, culturally appropriate and, as one Executive Director told us, "culturally safe" (V. Nicholson personal communication), Friendship Centres and the OFIFC serve an essential role in a cultural revitalization movement, since, as Kim Anderson (2000: 34) notes, "reclaiming our Indigenous ways is the only way we will recover ourselves as individuals, families and nations."

The OFIFC uses Aboriginal sacred items and practices to teach and reinforce Aboriginal cultures and beliefs, to integrate them into everyday life and work and to provide people with a rudder for caring and respectful behaviour. In the OFIFC office, Eagle feathers, tobacco pouches, sweetgrass, sage, cedar, drums and other sacred items are present and part of day-to-day use in ceremonies; practices such as smudging and offering prayers of thanks are carried out on a regular basis and values such as sharing are put into action, modeling behaviour for those who enter the OFIFC doors. These practices and responsibilities for caring for the sacred are not limited to physical items but include knowledge and teachings that nurture an understanding of how Aboriginal people should go about everyday good living.

The medicine wheel is an example of an Aboriginal cultural tool.[6] It provides a guide for living as well as a tool that can be used in designing programs and carrying out work. For the individual, the medicine wheel teaches, "Who we are, where we come from, where we are going and what our responsibility is" (S. Maracle personal communication) and thereby offers a path for Aboriginal people to live with a sense of wholeness, harmony and peace. The medicine wheel symbolizes the belief that throughout our life, we are continuously learning who we are in relation to the spiritual, physical, mental and emotional realms. For the OFIFC, it is a tool for culture-based programming. For example, spiritually-oriented programming is translated into cultural teaching, reminding Aboriginal people that everyday living as well as ceremonial life are imbued with spirit. Physical programs are concerned with corporeal well-being including housing, recreation and safety. Mental aspects of programming involve knowledge transfer, understanding contemporary issues and developing skills. And emotional matters include a sense of belonging, connecting to others and feeling wanted and loved.

Cultural revitalization also requires non-Aboriginal appreciation of Aboriginal cultures and support for sustaining them — which, in the view of the OFIFC leaders, has been seriously lacking. Now, with advice from the OFIFC, Friendship Centres offer assistance to non-Aboriginal service delivery partners so they can become more culturally aware and deliver appropriate services to Aboriginal clients. Friendship Centres offer trainings to organizations such as the Canadian Mental Health Association, various school boards, child and family services and justice programs (V. Nicholson personal communication).

Repairing some of the mistrust that resulted from previous experience of the tokenistic reciprocity by non-Aboriginal people when joint endeavours were undertaken, the emphasis is on respectful mutual obligations, agreed upon "with a good mind" (M. Smolewski personal communication). The OFIFC research director, Magdalena Smolewski, explains:

> Any of our allies is expected to proceed with kindness, which denotes respect that we have for each other. Coming together in honesty sustains our relationships over time. Sharing what we know and understand supports our positive emotions and inner strengths. Being strong, we can care for each other and conduct any collaborative project in good faith, with respect and trust. (personal communication)

With a focus on helping individuals create a healthy cultural identity and build a strong urban Aboriginal community, the OFIFC's urban Aboriginal programs and services have been designed with cultural revitalization as their organizing principle.

WOMEN'S LEADERSHIP

The Friendship Centre movement is unique in that women have been its leaders from the start and continue to lead it today. From LuVerna Clause, described at the beginning of this case study, to executive directors of Friendship Centres quoted in the previous section to Sylvia Maracle who now heads up the OFIFC, urban Aboriginal women have taken a significant role in the establishment of the movement and the delivery of services to urban communities. In the following section,

Linda Jones, one of the co-authors, writes of the important contribution of Sylvia Maracle, who is the other co-author, as one of these women leaders.

Sylvia Maracle's life and leadership

> I have witnessed tremendous community development over the last thirty-five years, and much of it has been led by women. (Sylvia Maracle 2013: 315)

Ms. Maracle was born on the Tyendinaga Mohawk Territory in 1955 where she is a member of the Wolf Clan. She is the oldest of six children and was only five years old when her mother died in childbirth as a result of complications from diabetes. Ms. Maracle and her brothers and sisters were subsequently separated and placed in the care of the Children's Aid Society. After some time, Ms. Maracle moved to live with aunts and uncles in the village adjacent to the reserve or in the nearby city of Belleville. As a result, she had regular contact with her grandparents, who profoundly affected her understanding of life, family and responsibility. "I was greatly influenced by my paternal grandmother and maternal grandfather who taught me to believe I was magnificent, that we all were, and that we could do anything we want," she remembers (as cited in Indspire Institute n.d.). Ms. Maracle also observed the modelling of gender-specific skills by male and female members of the family, her grandmother's leading role in defining how children should be instructed and her grandfather's gentleness and patience in trying to instill understanding of those instructions (Castellano and Hill 1995).

By the time Ms. Maracle enrolled in journalism at Ryerson Polytechnic Institute, she was consciously trying to bridge the two worlds in which she lived. Her grandparents helped her by introducing her to an Elder woman who lived on the Six Nations Reserve near Brantford and who became the first of many Elders who would carry on the education Ms. Maracle's grandparents had begun. When she was nineteen years old and attending Ryerson Polytechnical Institute Ms. Maracle began working with the OFIFC. She noticed a lack of initiatives for young women at the local Indian Centre and so she volunteered and put together some programming teaching young girls recreation. Soon after, she was invited to join the board of directors (ibid.; Indspire Institute n.d.).

Ms. Maracle has been involved in Aboriginal Friendship Centres for over thirty-five years and has served as the executive director of the OFIFC for much of that time. Under her leadership, the federation and the centres have expanded programs, increased impact and developed a well-administered institution that is true to its Aboriginal traditions. She has negotiated transfer of several programs and service agreements from the federal and provincial governments' authority to the OFIFC's responsibility. For example, she has contributed to the development of the

Aboriginal Health Policy for Ontario and was a member of the national facilitation team for the Roundtable on Aboriginal Peoples for the federal government and national Aboriginal organizations. She is a founding member of the Native Studies PhD Council at Trent University and a lecturer on urban development, women's issues and the cultural revitalization of her people (Biidwewidam Indigenous Masculinities n.d.). Ms. Maracle won the National Aboriginal Achievement Award for Public Service in 2008 and was awarded an honourary doctorate from the University of Guelph in 2012. As a leader, she acts as a mentor for those who work with her, deeply committed to the cause of the Friendship Centres and the people they serve. She can be tough when she needs to be and calls it the ways she sees it. In particular, "She will be remembered for setting the bar high, and asking for more because we deserve it" (V. Nicholson personal communication).

According to Maria Campbell, a widely respected Elder who conducts cultural training for the OFIFC, Ms. Maracle has led the OFIFC and Ontario Friendship Centres to a level of success that has not been achieved in any other province. Maria Campbell attributes this success to Ms. Maracle's ability to network, keep the Friendship Centres connected, engage with the community and with officials and always put culture at the core — "not a few feathers tacked on" (personal communication). Ms. Maracle demands a lot from others, ensures that Elders from across the country are involved in the OFIFC. Not only does she listen to them, she also listens to the community, responding to real needs of people (M. Campbell personal communication).

Sylvia Maracle on women's and men's leadership

> The wolf, she is the leader; it's a pack. We work together, we cannot be alone, but the wolf is the one who creates new relationships, who makes the trails, who finds fresh water, and renews us that we might be magnificent. (Sylvia Maracle as cited in Hiles and Anderson 2013)

Historians have emphasized the various capacities in which women were able to hold positions of power and leadership in Aboriginal communities — from the household level through to political structures. Motherhood was respected for the biological role it entailed and the leadership and responsibility that came with it. Also, women across many Aboriginal communities were responsible for the allocation of land and other resources among the band or tribe members. In some societies, such as the matriarchal Haudenosaunee, women had the power to both select and remove a male chief. And in the same nation the Clan Mother had a powerful political role within the Six Nations confederacy (First Nations Studies Program 2009a).

Ms. Maracle explains that the relegation of women's leadership to the back benches in Aboriginal communities occurred as part of the colonization process — European colonizers were mostly men and they did not want to deal with women who were leaders of families, clans or communities (Maracle 2013). Typically, men were awarded official positions of power such as chief and band councillor and this was internalized by people, seeing those who were given power as the leaders (ibid.). For example, the Indian Act of 1876 gave only males aged twenty-one and older the right to vote for a chief and even status women were unable to vote in band elections until the Indian Act of 1951 (Harry 2009: 22).

From Ms. Maracle's perspective, real community development means that people have to work hard and for long hours without real compensation. Women working in community development and emerging as leaders themselves did so because they were becoming aware of their responsibilities and were beginning to believe in their own power to recreate everyday good living for their people. Early community development allowed women to express who they were and to fulfill their role in society. They had been driven out of their home communities but they were able to create a sense of community elsewhere, especially in urban areas, which provided anonymity and safety that allowed women to freely express their creativity and vision of a better life (Maracle 2013).

Women's leadership in this context has to be situated in a larger discussion of gender roles and in particular men's role and sense of identity. The OFIFC is a key contributor in the launching of the Kizhaay Anishinabe Niin (I am a Kind Man) program and the Biidwewidam Indigenous Masculinities project. The latter is building research capacity in Indigenous masculinities and identities that contributes to the health and wellness of Indigenous communities and peoples, and the Kizhaay program is directed at helping Aboriginal men end violence against Aboriginal women and children. Recently the OFIFC has also launched a Healthy Indigenous Male Program. The program coordinator observes:

> We began with nine participants, and four young men completed the program. Of these four men, three are in a relationship where there was some degree of domestic violence before.... [As a result of this program] they explained that their self-esteem was much higher and that they had acquired a clear understanding of what a healthy, equal relationship is.... The Elder who co-facilitated had a wealth of traditional knowledge as well as his own life experiences which he shared with the group. The men stated that they really identified with these stories.... We had four sweat lodges during our sixteen weeks together and these were a first time experience for three of our participants. They really enjoyed the ceremonies and stated that the program had given them a spiritual foundation that was missing in their lives. (personal communication)

Thus, while most of the work related to decolonization and recovery has been led by women, it is also necessary to understand and find support for men's healing as well. As the program coordinator observes, our job as adults will be to create safe spaces for both men and women to develop.

CHALLENGES THAT LIE AHEAD

The following outlines a few of the main issues that are currently being faced and addressed to ensure greater success in the years ahead.

Poverty of urban Aboriginal people and serving the homeless at some Friendship Centres are ongoing challenges. Stopgap measures such as soup kitchens and food banks are implemented, but funding for long-term solutions such as affordable housing or homeless centres is not always forthcoming (V. Nicholson personal communication April 4, 2013). At the 2012 annual meeting, the OFIFC Executive Director noted that "Addressing this issue is capital intensive which holds little sway in the current economic climate" (Maracle 2012: 17).

More generally, the continuation of funding is a concern for both the local Friendship Centres and the OFIFC:

> Generally this last year has seen a severe increase in fiscal restraint on the part of government.... This is driven largely by global economic realities but also by the release of the Drummond Report and the general trend towards fiscal conservatism regardless of political stripe.... The public service at the federal level is being gutted ... and the provincial government is also enacting a variety of austerity measures. (ibid.: 5)

The lack of funding and ability to expand programs relates, at least in part, to the lack of recognition that over 80 percent of Indigenous people in Ontario now live off-reserve. The neglect of this reality results in planning in favour of on-reserve First Nations communities (M. Smolewski personal communication).

Another major challenge for the OFIFC and Friendship Centres is the high percentage of youth in the Aboriginal population and their frustrations seeking employment and a meaningful identity. The projected growth rate in the Aboriginal youth population is 37 percent compared with 6 percent for the general Canadian population (Aboriginal Affairs and Northern Development Canada 2010). The unemployment rate was three times the rate for non-Aboriginals in 2006; one quarter of young people (age twelve to seventeen) in correctional services are Aboriginal, even though they average only 6 percent of the youth population in the same regions. Suicide and self-injury are the leading causes of death for Aboriginal youth (Health Canada 2011) and there are more Aboriginal children in the child welfare system and away from their families than there were children in residential schools at their height (Evenson and Barr 2009).

Friendship Centres have been helping Aboriginal youth at risk become integrated back into the community through holistic initiatives such as the Cultural Connections for Aboriginal Youth programs — initiatives that deal with the whole person and focus on creating harmony and balance but recognize that more must be done to provide opportunities to young people.

Successes and challenges have been uneven across the centres, reflecting the ongoing challenge of equipping the centres with adequate staff capacity as well as resources. One Friendship Centre has been in a constant state of transition over the last ten years with at least five executive directors and three acting executive directors. While the centre's role is to provide a cultural presence and to offer specific programs to the community, this role has been inconsistently realized because of capacity issues (J. Riggs personal communication).

CONCLUSION

> We recognize that Indigenous knowledge comes from all relations, it manifests itself in the voices and actions of people, it is generated when people get together, it arises simultaneously from the past, present and future, it lives in words, stories, movement, dance, feelings, concepts and ideas (Sylvia Maracle and Magdalena Smolewski 2012: 3).

Despite the trauma experienced by Aboriginal people in Canada, the development of community-based groups has led to a strong and cohesive Aboriginal institution that promotes active healing. Whereas trauma associated with colonization has occurred for hundreds of years, conscious healing appears to have been occurring at a rapid pace for just forty years. The Friendship Centre movement has played an important role in this healing. Its programs and the policy changes it helps forge are building healthier individuals and communities on all levels: spiritual, physical, mental and emotional — in keeping with the values embedded in the medicine wheel. In a sense, they have co-opted this system to create the OFIFC and its network of service delivery on Aboriginal terms.

However, it is important to note there have always been Aboriginal people who were healthy — exceptional individuals who by dint of their own personality, the guidance of an Elder or some other good fortune were able to rise above their people's pain to help others and to heal a nation. These include the women who opened their homes in urban centres, people who started informal programs for children, men and women who had a kind word and held out an encouraging hand. Because of their spirits, the healing movement could begin and it could grow.

This healing movement towards the achievement of everyday good living is embodied today in the OFIFC and Friendship Centres as well as in other institutions. And the impact of the OFIFC is immense: non-Aboriginal partners have been mobilized to learn about and offer culturally appropriate services; government ministers and civil servants have transferred the administration and operation of existing social programs and supported the development of new ones; Friendship Centres themselves have proliferated from six to twenty-nine in a few decades; culturally-relevant programming and symbols such as the medicine wheel are widespread and the understanding of them is deepening and broadening; leaders are nurturing new leaders; and the number of Aboriginal people directly helped by Friendship Centres each year exceeds 50,000. Many more people participate in workshops, community events, presentations and cultural activities.

For the OFIFC and Friendship Centres, knowledge of the self and society at large will continue to be power, enabling Aboriginal people to overcome the challenges and realize even greater success. For example, the Utility, Self-Voicing, Access, Inter-Relationality (USAI) Research Framework has been developed recently to guide research projects by the OFIFC and Friendship Centres in a way that offers mutual learning by Aboriginal and non-Aboriginal partners. The USAI Framework welcomes principled partnerships, ethical cooperation and meaningful collaboration, providing guidelines to protect integrity of Indigenous knowledge from the community perspective (M. Smolewski personal communication). This enhances the ability of Aboriginal and non-Aboriginal people to live together in respect for each others' values.

In embracing their cultural heritage and revitalizing it, Aboriginal people have gained the strength and wisdom to build their future, to become whole once again and to contribute valuable knowledge and understanding to the world that we all share. By raising the awareness of non-Aboriginal partners and government agencies about Aboriginal people and their culture and history, they have shifted the larger system to meet the needs of urban Aboriginal people and to create an empowering environment.

Success may bring additional challenges. As Ms. Maracle (2013: 320) herself states, "As the numbers of Aboriginal people on the healing path increases, there will be questions and challenges about what to do after the healing is completed." Some Aboriginal thinkers such as Calvin Helin or Thomas King offer potential next steps. For Helin (2006) it is economic development; for King (2012) it is, at least in part, educating non-Aboriginals so that they understand Aboriginal history and the reason for events such as Oka,[7] Caledonia,[8] Akwesasne[9] and the Idle no More movement.[10]

It is indeed a brave new world for all, and alongside cultural revitalization Aboriginal people must deal with the challenges of international economic upheaval, the threats to the world's environment, widespread urbanization and life in an age of technology and information. And yet these are challenges that cannot be navigated in isolation from one another; we must all pull together to achieve everyday good living for future generations.

Returning to the meaning of the Two Row wampum, we revisit its message of living in harmony through respect for each others' different paths and traditions. Today, we are recognizing that we must move beyond the separate paths to learn from one another and to live together with many shared values and beliefs. Perhaps we can hope that we are on the path to achieving even greater harmony and interconnectedness. Ultimately, the Aboriginal experience in Canada is about us all — for in the infinity of creation, the dividing line between Aboriginal and non-Aboriginal is an illusion and the violence committed by one against the other is a violence that destroys us all. This case teaches us that we must all learn to live in harmony, with each other and with our natural/spiritual world.

Notes

1. Originally called the Ontario Federation of Indian Friendship Centres, it was renamed in 2014.
2. All references to personal communication are for interviews conducted between March 15th 2013 and April 30th 2013.
3. There is debate over whether the treaty exists — in large part because those who dispute it point to the lack of written evidence. However, the physical Two Row wampum belt and the oral history are not in dispute. Therefore, scholars have recently concluded that the treaty is valid if we respect oral tradition (see Parmenter 2013).
4. The OFIFC and the Friendship Centres offer a wide range of programs to Aboriginal people, spanning early childhood development, housing, addiction, cultural awareness, job counseling and more.
5. For more information on each of these programs, see Ontario Federation of Indigenous Friendship Centres (n.d.).
6. The origins of the medicine wheel are pre-contact and although not traditionally used by all Aboriginal peoples it has a powerful meaning for contemporary Aboriginal communities and therefore has achieved broad cultural legitimacy.
7. The Oka Crisis was a violent land dispute between a group of Mohawk people and the town of Oka, Quebec that took place in 1990.
8. A land dispute between members of the Six Nations of the Grand River and the Canadian government in Caledonia, Ontario that took place between 2006 and 2011.
9. Akwesasne is a Mohawk Nation territory divided by the U.S.–Canada border. From 1969 on, it has been the scene of several disputes on the rights of the Aboriginal residents to cross the border unimpeded. From time to time, the political feuds have led to outright violence.
10. Idle No More is an ongoing protest movement of the Aboriginal people across Canada, which began in December 2012 as a reaction to alleged abuses of Indigenous Treaty rights by Canada's Conservative government.

References

Aboriginal Affairs and Northern Development Canada. 2010. *Fact Sheet: 2006 Census Aboriginal Demographics.* <http://www.aadnc-aandc.gc.ca/eng/1100100016377/1100100016378>.

____. 2013. *First Nations in Canada.* <http://www.aadnc-aandc.gc.ca/eng/1307460755710/1307460872523>.

Anderson, K. 2000. *A Recognition of Being: Reconstructing Native Womanhood.* Toronto, ON: Sumach Press.

Biidwewidam Indigenous Masculinities. n.d. "Biographies." <http://www.indigenousmasculinities.com/who-we-are/biographies.html>.

Castellano, M.B., and J. Hill. 1995. "First Nations Women: Reclaiming Our Responsibilities." In J. Parr (ed.), *A Diversity of Women: Ontario, 1945–1980.* Toronto, ON: University of Toronto Press.

Dinsdale, P. 2010. "National Association of Friendship Centres." Presentation at the Best Start Conference (March 9). <http://beststart.org/events/detail/poverty/Peter%20Dinsdale.pdf>.

Evenson, J., and C. Barr. 2009. "Youth Homelessness in Canada: The Road to Solutions." Toronto, ON: Raising the Roof. <http://www.raisingtheroof.org/RaisingTheRoof/media/RaisingTheRoofMedia/Documents/RoadtoSolutions_fullrept_english.pdf>.

First Nations Studies Program at University of British Columbia. 2009a. "Marginalization of Aboriginal Women." <http://indigenousfoundations.arts.ubc.ca/home/community-politics/marginalization-of-Aboriginal-women.html>.

____. 2009b. "The Indian Act." <http://indigenousfoundations.arts.ubc.ca/home/government-policy/the-indian-act.html>.

Harry, K. 2009. "The Indian Act and Aboriginal Women's Empowerment: What Front Line Workers Need to Know." Vancouver, BC: Battered Women's Support Services. <http://www.bwss.org/wp-content/uploads/2010/06/theindianactaboriginalwomensempowerment.pdf>.

Health Canada. 2011. "A Statistical Profile on the Health of First Nations in Canada: Vital Statistics for Atlantic and Western Canada, 2001/2002." Ottawa, ON: Author. <http://www.hc-sc.gc.ca/fniah-spnia/pubs/aborig-autoch/stats-profil-atlant/index-eng.php>.

Helin, C. 2006. *Dances with Dependency: Out of Poverty through Self-Reliance.* Woodland Hills, CA: Ravencrest Publishing.

Hiles, D., and J. Anderson. 2013. "Wynne Takes Ontario Helm with a New, Larger Cabinet." *Toronto Observer,* February 11. <http://torontoobserver.ca/2013/02/11/wynne-takes-ontario-helm-with-a-new-larger-cabinet/>.

Indspire Institute. n.d. "Ms. Sylvia Maracle." <https://indspire.ca/laureates/sylvia-maracle/>.

King, T. 2012. *The Inconvenient Indian: A Curious Account of Native People in North America.* Toronto, ON: Doubleday Canada.

Lawrence, B., and K. Anderson (eds.). 2003. *Strong Women Stories: Native Vision and Community Survival.* Toronto, ON: Sumach Press.

Lowe, E. 2006–2007. "Urban Villages for Urban Settlers." *Transition* 36, 4: 11–14. <http://www.vanierinstitute.ca/include/get.php?nodeid=743&format=download>.

Maracle, S. 2012. *Executive Director's Report to the* OIFC *43rd Annual General Meeting.* Ontario Federation of Indigenous Friendship Centres, Toronto, ON.

____. 2013. "The Eagle Has Landed: Native Women, Leadership and Community Development." In M. Hobbs and C. Rice (eds.), *Gender and Women's Studies in Canada: Critical Terrain.* Toronto, ON: Women's Press.

Maracle, S., and M. Smolewski. 2012. "Background." In *Utility, Self-Voicing, Access, Inter-Relationality (USAI) Research Framework.* Ontario Federation of Indian Friendship Centres, Toronto, ON.

Montpetit, I. 2011. "Background: The Indian Act." *CBC News,* May 30. <http://www.cbc.ca/news/canada/background-the-indian-act-1.1056988>.

Moss, W., and E. Gardner-O'Toole. 1991. *Aboriginal People: History of Discriminatory Laws.* Ottawa: Library of Parliament, Research Branch. <http://publications.gc.ca/collections/collection_2008/lop-bdp/bp/bp175-e.pdf>.

National Association of Friendship Centres. n.d. "Our History." <http://nafc.ca/about/our-history/>.

National Association of Friendship Centres Memorial. n.d. "Luverna Delores (Delo) Clause." <http://mail.nafc.ca/luverna.html>.

Native Friendship Centre. n.d. In *Wikipedia.* <http://en.wikipedia.org/wiki/Native_Friendship_Centre>.

O'Donnell, C.V. 2008. "Native Populations of Canada." In G.A. Bailey and W. C. Sturtevant (eds.), *Handbook of North American Indians. Vol. 2: Indians in Contemporary Society.* Washington, DC: Smithsonian Institution.

Oliver, T. 2010. "A Brief History of Effects of Colonialism on First Nations in Canada." <http://manitobawildlands.org/pdfs/TonyOliver-BriefHistory_2010.pdf>.

Ontario Federation of Indian Friendship Centres. 1978. "Strangers in Our Own Land. A Discussion Paper Prepared for the Honourable Robert Welch, Q.C., Minister of Culture and Recreation." Toronoto, ON: Author. <http://www.ofifc.org/sites/default/files/docs/1978%20STRANGERS%20IN%20OUR%20OWN%20LAND_0.pdf>.

____. 1997. *Ontario Federation of Indian Friendship Centres Policy and Procedure Manual.* Toronto, ON: Author.

____. 2010. *Ontario Federation of Indian Friendship Centres Long-Range Plan Report.* Toronto, ON: Author.

____. 2013. "Annual Report 2012/13." <http://www.ofifc.org/sites/default/files/annualreports/OFIFC%20Annual%20Report%202012.pdf>.

____. n.d. "OFIFC Overview." <http://ofifc.org/about-us/general-information/ofifc-overview>.

Parmenter, J. 2013. "The Meaning of *Kaswentha* and the Two Row Wampum Belt in Haudenosaunee (Iroquois) History: Can Indigenous Oral Tradition Be Reconciled with the Documentary Record?" *Journal of Early American History* 3, 1: 82–109. <http://honorthetworow.org/wp-content/uploads/2012/01/The-Meaning-of-Kaswentha-and-the-Two-Row.pdf>.

Romaniuc, A. 2003. "Aboriginal Population of Canada: Growth Dynamics Under Conditions of Encounter of Civilisations." *Canadian Studies in Population* 30, 1: 75–115.

A QUIET MOVEMENT
Inuit Self-Determination

Linda Jones

For over 11,000 years, the Inuit of the Canadian Arctic survived in one of the most challenging environments in the world — a harsh region of permafrost and a prolonged winter season of ice and snow. The adaptive capacity (Ford, Pearce, Duerden, Furgal and Smit 2010) and technological ingenuity of the Inuit that respond to the livelihood demands of the Arctic have long been documented by outsiders — for example, early explorers and whalers,[1] and anthropologists (Boas 1888). Today, their ingenuity continues to be recognized in modern media — movies such as *Atanarjuat: The Fast Runner* (Kunuk 2001)[2] and art exhibits such as "Arctic Collections — Inuit, Ingenuity, Resilience and Riches" (at the *Nationalmuseet* in Copenhagen) as well as by academic researchers.

However, in recent decades, traditional livelihood opportunities for the Inuit have been rapidly diminished by climate-warming trends along with political forces and new forms of economic development. In just one generation, the Inuit people in Canada have been moved from semi-nomadic hunting households living in scattered camps to settled communities that are increasingly reliant on "the south"[3] for their day-to-day survival. The speed and scale of change has come with a cost to the individual, to the community and its shared culture and to the land that has been inseparable from traditional Inuit livelihoods, all contributing to increased vulnerabilities (Ford, Pearce, Duerden, Furgal and Smit 2010; S. Watt-Cloutier personal communication May 7, 2013). And, although these changes bring new economic opportunities in resource extraction, it is unclear how these opportunities might contribute to reduced vulnerability and improved well-being for Inuit households.

Despite this situation, the general attitude is that the Inuit will continue to adapt and succeed as they have always done. But when asked about the proverbial Inuit adaptability during discussions in Nunavut one Inuk woman posed the rhetorical question: "Why do the Inuit need to be so good at adapting?" That is, the Inuit did not choose to live in settlements, go to residential schools, lose hunting grounds or be affected by the melting of permafrost and ice sheets. Rather, how can the Inuit have greater control over the forces that are impacting their lives?

This case study deals with these questions and examines the Inuit response to livelihood threats. As part of exploring these questions, the case highlights the efforts of one Inuk woman in particular, Sheila Watt-Cloutier, who has been fighting for many years to curb environmental threats affecting traditional land-based livelihoods of the Inuit. The case also briefly describes the work of the Inuit Circumpolar Council that was formed in Alaska in 1977 to bring Arctic peoples together in their struggles around land rights, resource extraction and, more recently, climate change. The Council is the institution to which Ms. Watt-Cloutier was elected to represent Canadian Inuit concerns and where she undertook much of her climate change work from 1995 to 2006. Finally, the case describes other ways in which the Inuit are organizing to deal with livelihood challenges, comments on new economic opportunities and shows how this quiet assertiveness is shifting ideas about vulnerability and adaptive capacity.

Geographically, the case is relevant to and references pan-Arctic peoples and activities but zeroes in on the Nunavut territory of Canada where Ms. Watt-Cloutier has lived and worked throughout most of her time as an advocate for Inuit livelihoods, and where primary research for this case took place.

CONTEXT

> Our language contains the memory of four thousand years of human survival through conservation and good managing of our Arctic wealth.
> (Eben Hopson 1977)

The Arctic setting

The Arctic spans the circumpolar regions of eight nations — Canada, United States, Russia, Finland, Sweden, Norway, Iceland and Denmark. Although the Arctic is almost three times the size of Europe (Arctic-info n.d.) there are only four million inhabitants living in scattered communities across this region. While Indigenous people are estimated to make up about 10 percent of the total Arctic population worldwide (Arctic Centre n.d.), in Canada their share rises to two-thirds (Bogoyavlenskiy and Siggner 2004). The Canadian Arctic accounts for over 40 percent of Canada's landmass (Arctic Council 2011), but is sparsely populated with just three people per hundred sq km on average (Bogoyavlenskiy and Siggner 2004).

This area is comprised of frozen sea and isolated islands, and includes the world's second largest archipelago — the Canadian Arctic Archipelago. Approximately 50,000 Canadians are Inuit, many of whom live in hamlets of between 100 and 499 people (ibid.). For example, Grise Fiord, Nunavut, is Canada's most northern community with a population of 150 Inuktitut speakers, dependent on one another and on marine mammals for their survival (Grise Fiord n.d.). Nunavut, the Canadian territory on which this case mainly concentrates, makes up about half of Canada's Arctic area, is located beyond the tree line and is snow-covered most of the year, exposing rocky tundra during the brief summer months. Nunavut's total population was 35,591 as of July 2013 (Nunavut Economic Forum 2013), with over 7,000 living in the capital Iqaluit and most of the others in twenty-five tiny hamlets across the territory (Government of Nunavut 2012).

As we will read in the following sections, the Arctic context poses some unique challenges to livelihoods.

Nunavut: A changing socio-economic context
Before European contact, the Inuit lived in semi-nomadic groups dependent on hunting and fishing for their livelihood. Europeans impacted traditional livelihoods through the introduction of intensive whaling and the fur trade, establishment of missions and the spread of diseases for which Inuit had little or no immunity.[4] Nevertheless, throughout these often devastating waves of contact, the Inuit were able to adjust and maintain a relatively independent existence, continuing to live off the land in dispersed camps across the Arctic region. A more profound change took in the 1950s and 60s, when "former semi-nomadic hunting groups were re-settled into centralized communities and incorporated into a colonial relationship with the Canadian state" (Ford, Pearce, Duerden, Furgal and Smit 2010: 179).

Modern homes were built for Inuit families in communities where they would have access to healthcare, education and social services. Although this sounds beneficial, within thirty years of settlement the Inuit became almost completely dependent on government assistance and were no longer supporting themselves. Children were sent to residential schools and the sick were sent away for medical treatment. Unfortunately, the Inuit report that these decisions were made by government officials without consultation and with little direct knowledge of Inuit people.

Many people — academics, government officials, the Inuit themselves — believe that the far north settlement of Inuit people was a bid for Canadian sovereignty in the Arctic. A report commissioned by Indian and Northern Affairs Canada states that "Canada has maintained an assertion of Arctic sovereignty through its investment in the North, including its continued expansion of communities, as well as federal government services and infrastructure" (Bonesteel 2006: 30). Extreme cases such as the High Arctic Relocation attest to the government's desire to settle people further north — enticing a number of families from Inukjuak in Northern Quebec with promises of abundant wildlife and improved livelihoods to move 2,000 km north to Ellesmere Island, which was to become the home of Canada's most northern communities — Grise Fiord and Resolute Bay (McGrath 2006). As it turned out, the reality the resettled Inuit encountered there was a far cry from the government's promises:

> The Inuit soon learned that marine mammals were scarce, as were caribou, fox and fresh water. Their clothing wasn't warm enough, and their sleds and harnesses were all wrong for the rocky terrain. The rough waters made hunting by kayak impossible, and the dry wind made their dogs' lungs bleed. Sufficient snow for snow houses arrived late, leaving the settlers in flimsy canvas tents until late winter. There wasn't enough fuel for fires. (Royte 2007: 2)

Despite ample evidence of the hardship the relocated Inuit families had met on Ellesmere, it was not until 2010 that the federal government issued an apology for this relocation program (CBC 2010). Remarkably, the Inuit proved capable of adapting to its polar desert environment:

> As the years wore on, the Inuit gradually learned how to survive on Ellesmere. They constructed huts from scrap wood, revamped their sleds and dog harnesses. They learned the beluga's migration route and would eventually hunt over a range of 6,864 square miles each year. (Royte 2007: 2)

For the Inuit, one of the most controversial actions of the Canadian government was the slaughter of their sled dogs that took place during resettlement in the 1950s and 60s (J. Mike personal communication May 8, 2013; S. Watt-Cloutier personal communication May 9, 2013). At best, officials claim that dogs were killed for health and safety issues, without awareness of the devastating impact this would have on the livelihoods of people who were dependent on dogs for survival. At worst, there is believed to have been a systematic process to slaughter dog teams and to force the Inuit off the land into settled communities (Qikiqtani Truth Commission n.d.). Although the Inuit of Nunavik in Quebec have received compensation and an apology for this, the people of Nunavut are still seeking justice (Brennan 2012). Local sources observe:

> The wounds are still felt today ... People remembered seeing the dogs, their friends, being killed, and noting that after that they could not fish or

hunt because they lacked transportation. They describe how, trapped in their communities, people turned to alcohol — and thus began a spiral of cultural degradation. (Indian Country Today Media Network 2011)

It must also be noted that the socio-economic challenges associated with settlement of the Inuit continue to the present day. Many homes in Iqaluit, for example, are overcrowded with two families living in a two-bedroom house (J. Mike personal communication May 8, 2013; S. Watt-Cloutier personal communication May 9, 2013); people struggle to put food on the table, particularly if they do not have access to "country food"[5] (A. Johnston personal communication May 8, 2013; Mackay 2013); the sick or expectant mothers are still sent far away for medical care and Inuit youth and children are particularly afflicted by the challenges of living in today's Arctic. For example, according to a recent Statistics Canada report, children and teens are at a much higher risk of premature death:

> They are 11 times more likely to succumb to an infectious or parasitic disease and twice as likely to be killed by a non-communicable one [than children and teens in the rest of Canada]. Their risk of dying from an injury is nearly 11 times higher than [among] children and teenagers in the rest of the country. But the biggest driver behind the staggeringly higher death rate among Inuit children and teens is suicide. The report ... found that the suicide rate among children and teens in the Inuit homelands was 30 times that of youth in the rest of Canada during the five-year period from 2004 to 2008. (Branswell 2012)

These statistics underline the growing vulnerability of Inuit people that has come about as a consequence of rapid socio-economic change in recent years. Extractive industries are promoted as holding significant promise for Inuit employment but this has yet to be realized. Currently, Nunavut has only one mine in production, the Meadowbank Gold Mine, and one other that is in the initial stages of construction, Mary River Iron Project (Nunavut Economic Forum 2013). Although other mines are expected to generate thousands of jobs it is unclear how many will be taken by Inuit workers. The Meadowbank Gold Mine, which contributes over $200 million to GDP annually, has a staff of 675, about 30 percent of whom are Inuit. Mining is not the only employment opportunity for the Inuit, with government being the largest employer and growth in both fishing and construction sectors.

Despite these opportunities, and although the middle class is growing with more wealthy Inuit than ever before, the recent report of the Nunavut Economic Forum (2013) indicates that the poverty situation is worsening across Nunavut, supporting the observations of the Inuit people who were interviewed during primary research for this case study. Both the report and our interviews have highlighted decreased ability to earn a living off the land, deficits in education and mobility and households stuck in a welfare trap as the principal constraints preventing Inuit from taking greater advantage of the growing Nunavut economy. Under these circumstances, migration into Nunavut has increased in recent years (Nunavut Economic Forum 2013). This trend is recent, however, and although no studies of the factors making Inuit leave Nunavut have yet been conducted[6] they did so increasingly until the past two years. For example, while the total population of Nunavut grew about 20 percent from 2006 to 2011, the percentage of Inuit who live in the south rose from just over 20 percent to over 26 percent (ibid.). Today, it appears that more are returning home and with the fertility rate remaining high, the overall population of Nunavut has increased by 33 percent since 1999 (ibid.).

As a result of relocation and continued loss of traditional livelihoods (caused by settlement into larger communities and climate change), the challenges to food security are particularly grave. A recent report by the Council of Canadian Academies supports what Nunavut residents told us about their food concerns, indicating that "people in Nunavut have the highest food insecurity rate for any indigenous population in a developed country" (*The Huffington Post* 2014), with 35 per cent of Inuit households not having enough to eat. This is not surprising in view of the report's finding that "the average cost of groceries for a family of four in Nunavut is $19,760 per year while almost half of Inuit adults earn less than $20,000 annually" (ibid.). The prices for food in Nunavut are often more than ten times the same items cost in the south: green peppers at over $10 a kilogram, a small cauliflower $8.15 and a two-kilogram box of macaroni elbows nearly $14 (ibid.). This confirms the statements we heard about dependency on country food — if people cannot hunt and fish to feed their families they cannot afford to eat properly.

We will return to a discussion of livelihoods and vulnerability later in this case study, following a more in-depth examination of climate change, its impacts on the traditional economy and the Inuit response to these challenges.

Nunavut political context

In 1999, the Nunavut Settlement Area of the Northwest Territories became the first majority Inuit territory, providing a political pathway to self-determination (Hicks and White 2000: 20). Nunavut has a public government and land claim agreement, reportedly linked on several key issues. For example, the Nunavut Land Claims Agreement (NLCA) specifies that the number of Inuit employed in the public service be directly proportional to the number of Inuit in Nunavut society (Vlessides n.d.). Also unique to the government of Nunavut as a result of the land claim agreement is its ability to make decisions in certain areas that are reserved for the federal government in Canada's other territories: that is, along with federal government representatives, Inuit also sit on such bodies as the Nunavut Wildlife

Management Board, Nunavut Planning Commission, Nunavut Impact Review Board, the Nunavut Water Board and the Nunavut Surface Rights Tribunal (ibid.).

Jurisdiction over some territorial matters was transferred to the new government, including wildlife management, land-use planning and development, property taxation and natural resource management. Inuit exchanged title to their traditional land in this region for the rights described in the nlca. This agreement supports rights to the use of lands and other resources as well as to participate in decision-making concerning the use, management and conservation of these resources. It also gives the Inuit wildlife harvesting rights (and rights to participate in decision-making concerning wildlife harvesting), offers Inuit financial compensation for participating in economic opportunities, and encourages self-reliance and the cultural and social well-being of Inuit (Nunavut Land Claims Agreement Act 1993).

The establishment of Nunavut and the NLCA have provided Inuit people with certain mechanisms for control over their collective lives and self-determination as a people. Interestingly, leverage comes less from mainstream political processes and structures which are based on consensus politics (Henderson 2007) and more from organizations such as Nunavut Tunngavik Incorporated. As will be discussed later in this case study, the latter organization and other bodies are being utilized more than ever as extractive industries are moving in and further threatening the traditional land-based way of life.

The federal government provides the government of Nunavut with approximately 90 percent of its annual budget through Territorial Formula Financing (intended to ensure a certain degree of equality in the provision of public services across Canada) and through health and social transfer payments. While the total amount of these three transfers per capita has increased considerably over the last decade — from $28,050 in 2005–6 to $40,622 in 2013–14 (ibid.), the situation for many individual households has worsened as described above.

MOBILIZING AROUND CLIMATE CHANGE AND LIVELIHOODS

> It's interesting that it is our shared troubled atmosphere that is connecting us as a shared humanity. (Shiela Watt-Cloutier as cited in Rockel 2010)

This section begins by briefly examining the effects of climate change on the Arctic and Inuit livelihoods and then introduces the Inuit Circumpolar Council (ICC) and its founder Eben Hopson. This provides a backdrop to the work of Sheila Watt-Cloutier, who has been a key spokesperson for the environmental concerns of the Inuit and whose role in the climate change movement is examined in greater detail.

Climate change and the Arctic

The greenhouse effect was described in the early 1800s by the French physicist Joseph Fourier. At the end of the same century, the Swedish chemist Svante Arrhenius concluded that industrial-age fossil fuel consumption increased the natural greenhouse effect and might eventually result in enhanced global warming (Black 2013). Over subsequent decades, scientists puzzled over cause and effect, often citing human contributions to CO_2 concentrations and their warming effect. Despite this early awareness and even though other environmental concerns had already been broached and dealt with on some level, it was not until 1988 that the Intergovernmental Panel on Climate Change (IPCC) was formed to collate and assess the evidence regarding climate change. Almost twenty years later, in 2007, IPCC concluded it was "more than 90% likely that humanity's emissions of greenhouse gases are responsible for modern-day climate change" (Black 2013). The IPCC report published in 2014 strengthens this position[7] and focuses on assessing and managing the risks of climate change.

Scientists are continually revising their predictions for loss of ice cover in the Arctic, with projections on warming that now forecast an ice-free Arctic during summer months by the middle of this century (Overland and Wang 2013). But for the Inuit, the loss of ice due to climate change is not a prediction; it is real and it is now. In fact, Inuit hunters have observed and reported on climate change effects for decades. The *Petition to the Inter American Commission on Human Rights Seeking Relief from Violations Resulting From Global Warming Caused by Acts and Omissions of The United States* (2005: 2) initiated by Sheila Watt-Cloutier states that "For the last 15 to 20 years, Inuit, particularly hunters and Elders who have intimate knowledge of their environment, have reported climate-related changes within a context of generations of accumulated traditional knowledge." The petition includes numerous first-hand Inuit accounts such as the following one by Ronald Brower of Barrow, Alaska:

> One of my sons … was going to visit the next crew.… And he fell right through the ice half-way out to that camp. I've seen my fellow whalers trying to go whaling break through the ice, because it's melting from the bottom, and our snow machines have fallen through the ice. (ibid.: 40)

Some of the petition signers, for example Pitseolak Alainga of Iqaluit, have also pointed to the impact of climate change on food resources:

> The food for the caribou is less abundant. Exact same things with rabbits … Different grasses, different plants. These sort of things are changing. New plants are growing up here in the north that the rabbits have never seen … These are the changes that the Elders are seeing. (ibid.: 55)

Interestingly, Inuit hunters are also reporting that the sun is higher in the sky and rises in a different place than it used to in earlier years (S. Nattaq and M. Wilman personal communication May 8, 2013). This has caused a lot of debate involving lay people and scientists alike but the consensus appears to be that this is an optical illusion created by temperature inversions that did not exist in the past (Dixon 2010).

The response of the Inuit to climate change is discussed in the next section, with an emphasis on the leadership of Sheila Watt-Cloutier.

History of the Inuit Circumpolar Council

The Inuit Circumpolar Council (ICC), originally called Inuit Circumpolar Conference, was founded in 1977 by Eben Hopson, an Inuit leader from Alaska. Hopson had been an advocate for Inuit rights in Alaska and across the Arctic for many years. His political career began in 1946 when at the age of twenty-four he was elected to city council in his native town of Barrow, Alaska, followed ten years later by election to the territorial legislature and then to the first state senate (A short biography of the Honorable Eben Hopson n.d.). Hopson was a leader in community development, land claims, local governance, civic improvements and climate change activism. Concern over the degrading environment related to oil and gas development led Hopson to use "his Congressional campaign to draw national attention to the need for both a national and international Arctic policy to facilitate environmentally safe Arctic energy development" (ibid.). Because of his active role in raising public awareness of the impacts of extractive industries on the Inuit communities in Alaska, Hopson was invited to address the Government of Canada on a controversial pipeline development. Hopson concluded his address with an invitation to the presiding judge to attend the first meeting of ICC: "We will ask you to comment upon your experiences in your assignment of establishing the criteria for justice to Canada's Arctic people in the face of the world's energy crisis" (Hopson 1976).

ICC has grown into an international non-government organization representing approximately 150,000 Inuit across Alaska, Canada, Greenland and Russia. Its principal goals are to strengthen unity among the Inuit of the circumpolar region; promote Inuit rights and interests on an international level; develop and encourage long-term policies that safeguard the Arctic environment and seek full and active partnership in the political, economic and social development of circumpolar region (Inuit Circumpolar Council n.d.).

Important to this case study and the organizing of Inuit people throughout their vast territory, ICC is a representative organization. It holds elections every four years with delegates from across the circumpolar region who attend the general assembly that elects a new chair and executive council. This body also develops policies and adopts resolutions that guide the organization for the next four-year term (ibid.). The general assembly also provides an opportunity for "sharing information, discussing common concerns, debating issues and strengthening the bonds between all Inuit" (ibid.). Representatives from the Inuit Circumpolar Youth Council and the Inuit International Elders Council attend, thereby improving communication and creating synergies with these important affiliated organizations. ICC headquarters are located in a national-level office that each member country maintains, depending on the country from which the ICC chair is elected (ibid.). ICC's principal activities involve facilitating dialogue and sharing experiences across the Arctic, including those experiences relating to new forms of self-government (as exemplified by Nunavut). In Canada, the ICC national office is set up as a non-profit organization led by a board of directors who are elected leaders from the four regions: Inuvialuit (Northwest Territories), Nunatsiavut (Northern Labrador), Nunavik (Northern Quebec) and Nunavut.

Sheila Watt-Cloutier

Sheila Watt-Cloutier served as president of ICC (Canada) for two terms between 1995 and 2001, and as chair of the International ICC from 2002 until 2006. During her tenure at ICC she was known as a tireless advocate for Inuit rights and the leader who, among her many other achievements, brought the issue of climate change and Inuit livelihoods to international attention. In this section, we will learn more about Ms. Watt-Cloutier's background and then examine a historic petition she spearheaded that changed the way the world views climate change, human rights and livelihoods.

Ms. Watt-Cloutier was born into a hunting and fishing family in Kuujjuaq, a coastal Inuit community in Northern Quebec's Nunavik region. For the first ten years of her life, she travelled only by dogsled and spoke no English until she started school. "It shaped me completely — that's the foundation upon which I do my global work," she says of her early childhood (cited in Rockel 2010).

In a 2007 interview with CBC Radio, Ms. Watt-Cloutier observed that her life-defining and greatest personal test started in February 1999, when her beloved and only sister died suddenly of a massive heart attack at the age of forty-eight. "My entire world stopped. For a very long time I could not let her go" (as cited in Ng 2008). Over the next five years, she lost four more close family members and thought that she would never stop grieving. "I wept literally for years — in foreign countries, in strange hotels, in airports — whenever the waves of sadness would overcome me" (ibid.).

Ms. Watt-Cloutier observed that in those places of deep grief she deepened her personal journey. "Each loss held me in a place I needed to be until I gained insight and clarity" (ibid.). She was able to translate her new perspectives into opportunities for personal change and growth, and she came to see in a vivid way that all things are interconnected and that all things happen for a greater cause. "I came to know trust in the life process. I came to know courage, tenacity and commitment. I needed these character skills in order to survive my grief." And as she eventually discovered she also needed these traits to "strengthen and raise the volume of my own voice on the global stage" (ibid.).

While her healing journey began at the end of the 1990s, Ms. Watt-Cloutier's political leadership had begun in 1995 when she was elected corporate secretary of Makivik Corporation in her native Nunavik region. Makivik (which means "to rise up" in Inuktitut) was established to protect the rights and interests provided by land claim agreements to the Inuit of Nunavik (Makivik Corporation n.d.). Building on her past work with youth and social issues, Ms. Watt-Cloutier worked with Makivik on land claims including the 1975 *James Bay and Northern Quebec Agreement*, the first comprehensive Inuit land claim in Canada, that covered economic and property issues as well as establishing a number of cultural, social and governmental institutions for the Aboriginal communities involved (*James Bay and Northern Québec Agreement* and complementary agreements 1998). Her performance in this position led to her election as president of ICC (Canada) and then international chair of ICC where she carried out her work as an environmental advocate.

In her early work with ICC, Ms. Watt-Cloutier was instrumental in international negotiations that resulted in the 2001 *Stockholm Convention* to ban or severely restrict the use of persistent organic pollutants (e.g., DDT) that had been found in high concentrations in the Arctic food chain. Then, as will be described in more detail below, she led Inuit people to fight for their rights with regard to the environment and to raise awareness of the connectedness of the earth and all humanity.

Human rights petition for Inuit livelihoods

On December 7, 2005, Sheila Watt-Cloutier, along with sixty-two Inuit hunters and Elders from across the Canadian and American Arctic, filed a ground-breaking petition with the Inter-American Commission on Human Rights, which stated that the rights of Inuit had been violated by global warming caused by the United States (Petition 2005). The petition outlined the impacts of climate change including violation of Inuit rights "to the benefits of culture, to property, to the preservation of health, life, physical integrity, security, and a means of subsistence, and to residence, movement, and inviolability of the home" (ibid.: 5).

The Center for International Environmental Law and Earth Justice were the main architects of the petition itself. Providing evidence of support from across the Arctic region required significant innovation and effort. Ms. Watt-Cloutier recruited two young American scholars to support the development of the petition on a pro bono basis and had them trained on relevant Inuit issues at her house by an

Inuk lawyer, Sandra Inutiq. These researchers then travelled to Inuit communities in four regions of Canada (Nunavik, Labrador, Inuvialuit and Nunavut) as well as to Alaskan Inuit communities. Illustrating the intent to Inuit hunters and Elders with a mock petition that showed where their testimonies would be incorporated, the researchers captured their testimonies on video and subsequently transcribed them into the petition.[8] At the end of the interviews, each hunter and Elder was asked if they would like to add their names to the petition as well as have their testimonies included. All the people interviewed, except one, opted to sign the petition (S. Watt-Cloutier personal communication March 23, 2014).

The petition was also based on the findings of the Arctic Climate Impact Assessment, which highlighted the same conditions that had already been recognized by the Inuit hunters themselves. The assessment indicated that Inuit hunting culture might not survive the changes caused by global warming — in particular, the melting of sea ice so critical to safe and successful hunting. The petition stated that "Because Inuit culture is inseparable from the condition of their physical surroundings, the widespread environmental upheaval resulting from climate change violates the Inuit's right to practice and enjoy the benefits of their culture" (ibid.: 5). The petition explained that the transformation of the Inuit's physical environment due to the individual and cumulative effects of climate change has undercut their ability to maintain their traditional livelihoods. It emphasized that these effects are projected to accelerate, "seriously threatening the Inuit's continued survival as a distinct and unique society" (ibid.: 67). The petition also underscored that it is not just change, but an unpredictable and rapid change that can be very dangerous to Inuit hunters. The testimony provided by David Haogak of Sachs Harbour indicates the speed of change they are currently facing and the difficult conditions under which they are challenged to predict timings for safe crossings across ubiquitous water bodies:

> When we go out hunting, we usually expect we've got a couple of days to get our load of snow geese, and still be able to cross without having the water levels go high. Every year it's high, it's just that now we can't judge or we can't estimate ... we can't predict when to leave because of that rain. It'll be a constant. You figure that it's going to stop, we still could travel, but the water level comes up as it rains, the rivers break. We can't cut across, even with our snow machines alone, we can't make it home in the spring-time. That's just in the last 2 or 3 years. No one goes very far now, whereas long ago, even a few years ago, we used to go 40 or 50 miles. Now we don't even go 20. It's just not worth the risk. (ibid.: 44)

The petition to the Inter-American Commission on Human Rights established that climate change issues are human rights issues and this has subsequently become a common stance since its introduction by Ms. Watt-Cloutier and the sixty-two hunters and Elders from the Canadian Arctic. The *Globe and Mail* recognized Ms. Watt-Cloutier as one of twenty-five transformational Canadians for linking "the devastating effects of climate change on the Arctic to the human rights of her fellow Inuit. At the time, such a view wasn't exactly accepted wisdom. In fact, it sounded downright odd" (Rockel 2010). Soon after, however, others started identifying climate change as a human rights issue around the globe. In 2009, Archbishop Desmond Tutu and Mary Robinson, former U.N. commissioner for human rights, "delivered a global verdict on the human cost of climate change" (Oxfam 2009). With the support of testimony from 1.5 million people, this judgment was delivered to the executive secretary of the United Nations Framework Convention on Climate Change and ultimately reached the 192 countries currently working on negotiated solutions to climate change (ibid.).

At the signing of the *Stockholm Convention on Persistent Organic Pollutants* in 2010 Ms. Watt-Cloutier said of her fellow Inuit and their contribution to a sustainable environment for all of humanity: "We remain guardians of the natural environment. As we continue to navigate rapid social change it seems highly appropriate that Inuit provide advice to the world on issues that affect the health of our planet" (S. Watt-Cloutier 2012: 14). For her role in this endeavour Ms. Watt-Cloutier was nominated for the Nobel Peace Prize in 2007 and has received numerous awards, including the Orders of Canada and Norway, over a dozen honourary doctorates and United Nations' Champions of the Earth and Human Development Awards, to name a few. She was also named one of Canada's "nation builders" by the *Globe and Mail* in 2006 and included in the 2008 "Heroes of the Environment" list published by Time magazine.

Despite these accolades, Ms. Watt-Cloutier has left elected politics because she does not want to be in a state of conflict and feel under pressure to compromise her beliefs by political forces. She wants to be free to express her views and to focus on the right direction and the protection of a way of life that she lived and observed (S. Watt-Cloutier personal communication May 9, 2013). She continues to move forward with the Inuit people along their path to self-determination, with her main areas of focus in recent years including public speaking engagements and the writing of a memoir, *The Right to be Cold* (2015).

Other citizen responses to livelihood threats
While Sheila Watt-Cloutier has been a strong individual champion for the Arctic region, there also are institutions that represent the Inuit in livelihood-related issues in Nunavut today: the Inuit Tapiriit Kanatami (or, in English, Inuit United with Canada) and Nunavut Tunngavik Incorporated.

The Inuit Tapiriit Kanatami (ITK) was formed in 1971 (as the Inuit Tapirisat of Canada) as the national Inuit organization in Canada representing four Inuit regions — Nunatsiavut (Labrador), Nunavik (northern Quebec), Nunavut and the Inuvialuit Settlement Region in the Northwest Territories. ITK campaigns for the interests and control of Inuit communities on environmental, social, cultural and political issues through promoting, lobbying and negotiating changes in government policy and program delivery. At its very first meeting, Inuit talked of the need to organize to regain control of their lives: "we have to find an organized voice amongst ourselves so we may direct our lives the way we want them to be" (Jacob Oweetaluktuk in transcript of first ITK meeting 1971). In keeping with this goal, ITK played a major role in achieving recognition of Aboriginal rights in the *Constitution of Canada*, based on the fact that Inuit are a founding people of Canada known to have settled within the present-day boundaries of the Canadian Confederation thousands of years before it was formed (Inuit Tapiriit Kanatami n.d.). More recently, ITK has represented Inuit people in opposing the U.S. and E.U. bans on seal product imports, raised awareness about the high rates of Inuit teen suicide and actively participated in a multi-stakeholder dialogue concerning appropriate education for Inuit.[9]

Nunavut Tunngavik Incorporated (NTI) was established to oversee the promises made under the *Nunavut Land Claims Agreement* (NLCA), the mission that involves coordinating and managing Inuit commitments as well as ensuring that the federal and territorial governments fulfil their obligations (NTI n.d.). Inuit exchanged Aboriginal title to all their traditional land in the Nunavut Settlement Area for the rights and benefits set out in the NLCA (ibid.). This agreement was signed in 1993 and led to the establishment of the Canadian territory of Nunavut in 1999. NTI is a representative body with three directors elected by Inuit and other members serving as the heads of Inuit associations in Nunavut. As such, NTI acts on behalf of the people. And although many think that the NLCA gave up too much control and land (Iqaluit residents personal communications May 2013), this agreement and the work of NTI provide a framework for negotiation that has been used to the benefit of the Inuit people (Okalik Eegeesiak personal communication May 10, 2013). As observed by Henderson (2007: 124), "the resources that it accords and the role it has adopted have turned NTI into a second political authority in Nunavut."

In order to carry out its mission, NTI has developed processes and protocols and takes advantage of new technologies. For example, its Department of Land and Resources maintains an online database on Inuit-owned lands containing various information related to Inuit land rights under NLCA. The multi-layered maps pinpoint all Inuit hunting camps, whether disused, newly established or in ongoing use across Nunavut, identifying the exact areas where Inuit hunters are based (NTI Department of Land and Resources n.d.). At the same time, NTI also tracks current and proposed resource exploration activities and, based on the information obtained from Inuit hunters, raises concerns with authorities about the appropriateness of resource exploration in specified locations. For example, when an exploration request comes in, NTI can contact hunters known to be in that area and get a status update on local wildlife essential to Inuit livelihoods, such as caribou herds. By paying close attention to resource exploration, NTI is translating the Inuit's detailed, up-to-date knowledge of their surroundings into control over and protection of their traditional livelihoods.

Nunavut is also characterized by consensus politics (Henderson 2007) — that is, all nineteen members of the legislature run as independents, not connected to a political party. Once elected, the members select the premier, cabinet and speaker of the house. Without party politics, it is not surprising that many candidates for seats in the Nunavut Legislative Assembly, when they were interviewed by the CBC during the last election, focused on issues at the local level while only a small percentage spoke of territorial issues (ibid.). Nevertheless, the local issues raised by candidates were consistent across the Nunavut territory — with housing, education and infrastructure being the most commonly mentioned concerns. Despite this consistency, the views of the candidates appeared to be somewhat at odds with those of the citizens: specifically, the latter tended to place a much greater emphasis on the territorial, rather than local, economy (ibid.). Indeed, Henderson (2007: 128) quotes a local newspaper editorial reporting on "a frustrated public fed up with their inability to influence government policy at election time." This makes the role of NTI even more important for citizens who are asserting their rights as set down in NLCA.

VULNERABILITY, ADAPTIVE CAPACITY AND WELL-BEING

The people interviewed in Nunavut during field research for this case study were very concerned about the growing vulnerability of individuals and households — they spoke of poverty, cost of living, families going hungry, despair and teen suicide. Ms. Watt-Cloutier relates this vulnerability to a loss of traditional livelihoods and the inability of Inuit families to take care of themselves through hunting and fishing for country food. In academic literature, Ford, Pearce, Duerden, Furgal and Smit (2010: 181) define this vulnerability as "a function of exposure-sensitivity to climate risks and adaptive capacity to deal with those risks" and examine the interplay between climate change and a community's ability to adapt to this change through the use of non-climatic factors such as technology, information and institutions.

In their important study into the increased vulnerability of Inuit people, based on an extensive field research (443 semi-structured interviews with people in fifteen communities, twenty focus group discussions and sixty-five meetings with policymakers), Ford, Pearce, Duerden, Furgal and Smit (2010) identified specific vulnerabilities and characterized the factors that affect vulnerability. Their research confirmed the observations of Ms. Watt-Cloutier and the people interviewed in Nunavut for this case study: namely, the factors shaping climate change vulnerability include the loss of land-based skills and knowledge, reduced availability of food resources due to quota systems, location of new Inuit settlements, inadequate access to finance and health issues including substance abuse.

In our interviews with Inuit people in Nunavut, they explained how Inuit households and communities are adapting to meet the livelihood challenges they face. For example, they are adopting new internet technologies to connect with one another, share information and support livelihoods. As well as NTI's online Inuit Owned Lands system described above, there is extensive use of the internet and social media connecting people from Alaska to Greenland (J.A. Kunuk personal communication May 9, 2013). Now even smaller remote communities have internet access, although it can be slow and expensive. Facebook has become a common way of sharing knowledge among the Inuit — there are regularly updated Facebook pages providing information related to hunting (for example, "Inuit hunting stories of the day" <facebook.com/groups/inuithuntingstoriesoftheday>) and those dedicated to selling or swapping country food (for example, "Inuit Country Food Sell/Swap" <facebook.com/groups/420571741315856/>). Other Facebook pages provide socio-cultural information about sealing <facebook.com/InuitSealing.org> and youth initiatives (for example, "Nanisiniq: Arviat History Project" <facebook. com/pages/Nanisiniq-Arviat-History-Project/129308460430338>).

A former mayor of Iqualuit explained that social media is an important tool for Inuit adaptation to current realities — an "instant information site" (J. Kunuk personal communication, May 9, 2013). Youth are also making use of other media such as YouTube to communicate with one another across the vast Arctic region and to express their Inukness in unique ways (for example, "Building a qajaq to the future" <youtube.com/watch?v=qp3t_ovUwfs>). And television and radio remain important means of sharing information (although not as immediate as the new social media technologies). These observations corroborate those of Ford, Pearce, Duerden, Furgal and Smit (2010: 187), who stated that "communities are autonomously adapting to climate change, mostly using behavioural and technological adaptive strategies." This is in line with the fact that "Adaptation involving changing resource use patterns and technology in response to environmental circumstances has defined the very nature of Inuit survival in the Arctic for millennia" (ibid.: 184).

However, similar to Ms. Watt-Cloutier, these authors offer a cautionary note that autonomous adaptations have their limits and that intervention is necessary to allow the Inuit to assert greater control over their livelihoods to reduce vulnerability and manage risk. In their view, these interventions should concentrate on supporting Inuit communities in adapting traditional livelihoods practices to a changing climate through such means as access to information, new technologies, network development and financial support for these activities. Wage income opportunities and out-migration for jobs are considered to be of minor importance as sources of adaptive capacity (Ford, Pearce, Duerden, Furgal and Smit 2010). Ms. Watt-Cloutier would like climate change to be curbed and the "right to be cold" preserved.

Younger people interviewed for this case study spoke about what could be done to embrace change rather than to look back — and how to use the Nunavut government and other institutions to secure the Inuit's future, including meaningful employment. They often expressed that too little was being achieved by their current representatives and that the situation was getting worse for many households — an observation supported by the recent report of the Nunavut Economic Forum (2013: 18). At the same time, they talked about the importance of protecting the distinctive Inuit culture and adapting the current educational system, including the urgent need for more Inuktitut instruction in Nunavut schools and for teaching about the land and traditional ways. They also expressed their respect for the contributions of Sheila Watt-Cloutier and the necessity of country food in sustaining Inuit families (personal communications May 7–10, 2013). Overall, while reinforcing the importance of preserving Inuit cultural traditions, young people also appeared to highlight the necessity of developing new solutions to overcome livelihood vulnerability.

Echoing the comments of young people about the need for jobs, the 2013 report of the Nunvaut Economic Forum focuses attention on wage labour. Interestingly, this report moves traditional livelihoods out of the economic realm and into the development realm, stating that "The new approach [of the Forum] ... elevates the importance of the traditional economy by placing it within the context of Nunavut's *development* rather than as a part of Nunavut's *growth*" (Nunavut Economic Forum 2013: 18).[10] The traditional economy (hunting and fishing) is described in terms of its role in preserving Inuit culture as well as promoting social and community cohesion and providing an alternative to the wage economy through income substitution and greater food security. It is also interesting to note the value the report still places on the traditional economy; even as wage labour is being promoted for economic gain there is still a strong sensibility that Inuit well-being does not depend on income alone.

Ms. Watt-Cloutier adds to the debate by explaining that wage labour has to fit with the culture and that if people do not have control over resources and cannot contribute traditional knowledge to economic development then it is not likely to succeed to the benefit of the community (personal communication May 9, 2013). She is particularly concerned about extractive industries, which she finds very intrusive. Although the proponents of these industries make promises to be inclusive of local knowledge and people, she wonders how "the hunters, who have held land sacred for millennia and are nourished by hunting, will be able to contribute to digging up the land" (ibid.). Fortunately, if and when more Inuit turn to wage employment, sectors such as fishing, tourism and construction are also growing and may offer alternatives to extractive industries (Nunavut Economic Forum 2013).

Both viewpoints agree that preservation of traditional livelihoods and culture is vital for the well-being of Inuit, providing them with much more than an income. Both recognize the severity of impact on culture and livelihoods of climate and economic change. The quiet movement of cultural assertiveness, now reinforced by communications technology connecting people across the Arctic, is challenging the assumption that the Inuit will adapt passively to external forces and insisting instead that hard won self-determination for a political future should be matched by meaningful employment and livelihoods compatible with a robust culture.

FINAL MESSAGE

> Economic growth does not, by itself, provide the magic bullet that guarantees society will reach its goals. It must be made to do so. Policy, planning, coordination and cooperation are all very important. (Nunavut Economic Forum 2013: 2)

There are no easy answers for the Inuit of Nunavut and the Arctic more generally. Climate change is happening and their livelihoods have been and will continue to be affected — not only due to climate change, but also due to socio-economic and political forces.

Inuit leaders such as Eben Hopson and Sheila Watt-Cloutier have fought hard to maintain the right of the Inuit to a traditional livelihood — to ensure their economic well-being and to preserve their unique way of life. The Inuit of Nunavut and across Canada have responded by establishing various institutions such as ITK and NTI and processes such as NLCA and are utilizing these to advocate for their rights to traditional and new livelihood options.

On the other hand, other institutions, such as the Nunavut Economic Forum, are moving forward with an economic growth agenda that focuses on extractive industries as well as other non-traditional sectors such as tourism. The forum is attempting to balance out the potential of these economic options with traditional livelihoods and states in its 2013 report that traditional livelihoods are important not only for economic well-being but also for maintaining community cohesion and for cultural preservation.

Young people in Nunavut — presumably the future, as we like to say — is taking a more balanced middle road. They are talking of a measured way forward that welcomes thoughtful change while upholding traditional livelihoods on par with economic advancement. Their discussions of the importance of integrating the Inuktitut language and Inuit culture into school curriculum, of the desirability of hunting and fishing to maintain a steady supply of country food and of the need for young people to understand their roots illustrate the value that they place on the many aspects of being Inuit. Yes, livelihoods are key, but being a prosperous Inuit is not just about earning money, it is about being an Inuit who can earn a livelihood in the current environment while placing a value on both traditional livelihoods and other elements of the Inuit cultural heritage.

New technologies can contribute to this vision of a future that sees traditional livelihoods accompanying the way forward. Use of the internet across the vast Arctic region, for example, enables people to stay in touch about hunting and fishing and country food — adapting a modern technology to preserve a land-based approach to livelihoods and to strengthen community networks.

Indeed, the Inuit's ability to preserve their way of life may be a gift to us all. But let us give Sheila Watt-Cloutier the last word on this: "That's always been my message, to signal that everything is connected, and it's interesting that it is our shared troubled atmosphere that is connecting us as a shared humanity" (as cited in Rockel 2012).

Notes

1. For example, the whaler George Comer survived winters in the Arctic with the support of Inuit and was a keen collector of their artifacts and ethnography (Ross 1984).
2. As noted by Michael Evans (2010: 1), "When Zacharias Kunuk and others at Isuma created *The Fast Runner*, one of their goals was to show audiences the resiliency of Inuit and the ingenuity with which they have long faced the physical and social challenges of living in the Arctic."
3. Inuit in Nunavut and elsewhere commonly refer to the Canada below the Arctic which is mainly non-Inuit as "the south."
4. For more details see Inuit Tapiriit Kanatami n.d.
5. "Country food" is a term used by people in Nunavut to denote food from the land — from berries and fish to different types of meat.
6. Some sources point to education and job opportunities as the factors attracting Inuit south (Budak 2010).
7. Its recently approved *Summary for Policymakers* states: "A key finding of [the report] is, 'It is *extremely likely* that human influence has been the dominant cause of the observed warming since the mid-20th century'" (IPCC 2014: 3, fn. 1).
8. The videotaped testimonies are available from the IsumaTV portal (IsumaTV 2009). The petition itself contains excerpts from some of the testimonies (Petition ... 2005).
9. The "News Releases" section of ITK's website <itk.ca/media/news-release> demonstrates the various aspects of its recent work.

10. Membership of the Nunavut Economic Forum is made up mainly of economic and government bodies (Chambers of Commerce, Sector Representatives, Government of Nunavut, Government of Canada, business development organizations), and there is no indication that consultation beyond these bodies has taken place as part of preparing its 2013 report. This is not to dismiss the excellent statistical information and narrative presented in this report, but to raise a question regarding its perspective.

References

"A Short Biography of the Honorable Eben Hopson." (n.d.). In *Eben Hopson Memorial Archives.* <http://www.ebenhopson.com/bio/ChurchBio.html>.

Arctic Centre. n.d. "Arctic Indigenous Peoples." <http://www.arcticcentre.org/InEnglish/SCIENCE-COMMUNICATIONS/Arctic-region/Arctic-Indigenous-Peoples>.

Arctic Council. 2011. "Canada and the Arctic Region." <http://www.arctic-council.org/index.php/en/about-us/member-states/canada>.

Arctic-info. n.d. "The History of the Arctic." <http://www.arctic-info.com/Encyclopedia/Rubric/The%20History%20of%20the%20Arctic>.

Black, R. 2013. "A Brief History of Climate Change." *BBC News.* September 20. <http://www.bbc.com/news/science-environment-15874560>.

Boas, F. 1888. *The Central Eskimo: Sixth Annual Report of the Bureau of Ethnology to the Secretary of the Smithsonian Institution, 1884–1885.* Washigton, DC: U.S. Government Printing Office. <http://www.gutenberg.org/files/42084/42084-h/42084-h.htm>.

Bogoyavlenskiy, D., and A. Siggner. 2004. "Arctic Demography." In *Arctic Human Development Report.* Akureyri: Stefansson Arctic Institute. <http://www.svs.is/AHDR/AHDR%20chapters/English%20version/Chapters%20PDF.htm>.

Bonesteel, S. 2006. *Canada's Relationship with Inuit: A History of Policy and Program Development.* Ottawa, ON: Indian and Northern Affairs Canada. <https://www.aadnc-aandc.gc.ca/DAM/DAM-INTER-HQ/STAGING/texte-text/inuit-book_1100100016901_eng.pdf>.

Branswell, H. 2012. "Death, Suicide Rates Among Inuit Kids Soar Over Rest of Canada." *Globe and Mail,* July 18. <http://www.theglobeandmail.com/news/national/death-suicide-rates-among-inuit-kids-soar-over-rest-of-canada/article4426600/>.

Brennan, R.J. 2012. "Inuit Communities Finally Get Compensation for Dog Slaughter." *Toronto Star,* June 29. <http://www.thestar.com/news/canada/2012/06/29/inuit_communities_finally_get_compensation_for_dog_slaughter.html>.

Budak, J. 2010. A Modern Migration: Inuit Go South. September 15. <http://jasminebudak.com/2010/09/15/inuk-tropolis/>.

CBC News. 2010. "Inuit Get Federal Apology for Forced Relocation." August 18. <http://www.cbc.ca/news/canada/north/inuit-get-federal-apology-for-forced-relocation-1.897468>.

Dixon, G. 2010. "New Documentary Recounts Bizarre Climate Changes Seen by Inuit Elders." *Globe and Mail,* October 19. <http://www.theglobeandmail.com/arts/film/new-documentary-recounts-bizarre-climate-changes-seen-by-inuit-elders/article1215305/>.

Evans, M. R. (2010). *The Fast Runner: Filming the legend of Atanarjuat.* Lincoln, NE:

University of Nebraska Press.

Ford, J.D., T. Pearce, F. Duerden, C. Furgal and B. Smit. 2010. "Climate Change Policy Responses for Canada's Inuit Population: The Importance of and Opportunities for Adaptation." *Global Environmental Change* 20, 1: 177–91. <http://www.uoguelph.ca/gecg/images/userimages/Ford%20et%20al.%20(2010)_GEC.pdf>.

Government of Nunavut. 2012. "Nunavut, Our Land." <http://www.gov.nu.ca/sites/default/files/files/FINAL%20GN%20Info%20Package-%20%20Nunavut%2C%20Our%20Land.pdf>.

Grise Fiord. n.d. "Community." <http://www.grisefiord.ca/eng/community.html>.

Henderson, A. 2007. *Nunavut: Rethinking Political Culture*. Vancouver, BC: UBC Press.

Hicks, J., and G. White. 2000. "Nunavut: Inuit Self-Determination Through a Land Claim and Public Government?" In J. Dahl, J. Hicks and P. Jull (eds.), *Nunavut: Inuit Regain Control of Their Lands and Their Lives*. Copenhagen: International Work Group for Indigenous Affairs. <http://www.iwgia.org/iwgia_files_publications_files/0131_102_Nuvanut.pdf>.

Hopson, E. 1976. "Mayor Eben Hopson's Testimony before the Berger Inquiry on the Experience of the Arctic Slope Inupiat with Oil and Gas Development in the Arctic." In *Eben Hopson Memorial Archives*. <http://www.ebenhopson.com/papers/1976/BergerSpeech.html>.

____. 1977. "Welcoming Address, First Inuit Circumpolar Conference." In *Eben Hopson Memorial Archives*. <http://www.ebenhopson.com/icc/ICCKeynote.html>.

Huffington Post. 2014. May 27. "Inuit Go Hungry More Than Any Other Indigenous Group: Report." <http://www.huffingtonpost.ca/2014/03/27/inuit-food-insecurity-report_n_5041508.html>.

Indian Country Today Media Network. 2011. "Qikiqtani Inuit Association Wants Ottawa to Apologize for Dog Slaughter." August 11. <http://indiancountrytodaymedianetwork.com/2011/08/11/qikiqtani-inuit-association-wants-ottawa-apologize-dog-slaughter-46739>.

Inuit Circumpolar Council. n.d. "Inuit Circumpolar Council." <http://inuitcircumpolar.com/index.php?ID=16&Lang=En>.

Inuit Tapiriit Kanatami. n.d. "Vision of Self-Government." <https://www.itk.ca/about-inuit/vision-self-government>.

IPCC. 2014. *Climate Change 2014: Impacts, Adaptation, and Vulnerability. Summary for Policymakers*. Geneva: Author. <http://ipcc-wg2.gov/AR5/images/uploads/IPCC_WG2AR5_SPM_Approved.pdf>.

IsumaTV. 2009. "International legal action on climate change." <http://www.isuma.tv/en/international-legal-action-climate-change>.

"James Bay and Northern Québec Agreement and Complementary Agreements." 1998. <http://www.gcc.ca/pdf/LEG000000006.pdf>.

Kunuk, Z. (eirector). 2001. *Atanarjuat: The Fast Runner* [motion picture]. Canada: Isuma Igloolik Productions.

Mackay, T. 2013. "Focus on Food Security." *Canada's Arctic Journal* (May–June): 10–12.

Makivik Corporation. n.d. "Makivik Mandate." <http://www.makivik.org>.

McGrath, M. 2006. *The Long Exile: A Tale of Inuit Betrayal and Survival in the High Arctic*. New York: Alfred A. Knopf.

Ng, D. 2008. "This I Believe. Words from Sheila Watt-Cloutier." *The Terry Project.* February 14. <http://www.terry.ubc.ca/2008/02/14/this-i-believe-words-from-sheila-watt-cloutier/>.

NTI Department of Land and Resources. n.d. "Inuit Owned Lands." <http://gis.ntilands.com/iolis/>.

Nunavut Economic Forum. 2013. "2013 Nunavut Economic Outlook. Nunavut's Next Challenge: Turning Growth into Prosperity." Iqaluit, NU: Author. <http://www.neds2.ca/documents/2013_Nunavut_Economic_(FINAL)_Jan_28_2014.pdf>.

Nunavut Land Claims Agreement Act. 1993. <http://laws-lois.justice.gc.ca/eng/acts/n-28.7/FullText.html>.

Nunavut Tunngavik Inc. n.d. "About NTI." <http://www.tunngavik.com/about/>.

Overland, J.E., and M. Wang. 2013. "When Will the Summer Arctic Be Nearly Sea Ice Free?" *Geophysical Research Letters* 40, 10: 2097–2101.

Oxfam. 2009. "Climate Change Undermining Human Rights on an Unprecedented Scale." December 15. <http://www.oxfam.org/en/pressroom/pressrelease/2009-12-15/climate-change-undermining-human-rights-unprecedented-scale>.

Petition to the Inter American Commission on Human Rights Seeking Relief from Violations Resulting From Global Warming Caused by Acts and Omissions of The United States. 2005. <http://www.inuitcircumpolar.com/files/uploads/icc-files/FINALPetitionICC.pdf>.

Qikiqtani Truth Commission. n.d. "Inuit Sled Dogs in the Baffin region, 1950 to 1975." <http://www.qtcommission.com/actions/GetPage.php?pageId=39>.

Qilavvaq, B. (eirector). 2012. *Feel the Inukness* [motion picture]. <https://www.youtube.com/watch?v=iawDXQGQsr0>.

Rockel, N. 2010. "Sheila Watt-Cloutier Made Climate Change a Human Rights Issue." *Globe and Mail,* October 4. <http://www.theglobeandmail.com/report-on-business/sheila-watt-cloutier-made-climate-change-a-human-rights-issue/article1216160/>.

Ross, W. Gillies (ed.). 1984. *An Arctic Whaling Diary: The Journal of Captain George Comer in Hudson Bay, 1903–1905.* Toronto, ON: University of Toronto.

Royte, E. 2007. "Trail of Tears. [Review of the book *The Long Exile: A Tale of Inuit Betrayal and Survival in the High Arctic,* by M. McGrath]." *New York Times,* April 8. <http://www.nytimes.com/2007/04/08/books/review/Royte.t.html?_r=0>.

Transcript of first ITC meeting. 1971. February 18. <https://www.itk.ca/about-itk/origins/transcript-first-itc-meeting>.

Vlessides, M. n.d. "A Public Government." <http://www.nunavut.com/nunavut99/english/public_gov.html>.

Watt-Cloutier, S. 2012. "Wake-Up Call." *Our Planet* 12, 4: 12–14.

____. 2014. *The Right to Be Cold: One Woman's Story of Protecting Her Culture, the Arctic, and the Whole Planet.* Toronto, ON: Allen Lane.

ECOTRUST CANADA
Building the Conservation Economy

Gord Cunningham and Juliet Merrifield

Throughout the different phases of its history, Ecotrust Canada (EC) has looked for practical ways to build an economy that integrates the principles of social equity (including recognition of Aboriginal rights and title) with environmental protection and restoration without forfeiting sustainable livelihoods for households and communities. EC calls this alternative economic model a "conservation economy."

Over the years EC has developed its own way of defining and articulating the idea that it is possible to reorient a resource-based, industrial extraction model of economic development with its single bottom line of profit for shareholders to a new kind of economy that is "triple bottom line" or "3E" (environment, equity and economy). The set of beliefs that underpin its work are articulated by the current EC President:

> First, there are limits to growth. The world cannot continue in the way it's growing. We have to do things differently if we want to be here long term. Second, in spite of the best attempts at it, the trickle-down theory of economics is fundamentally flawed. Third, the economy is a tool, not a beast that we have to feed. It can be redesigned to get what we want. And, fourth, there are increasingly cracks in the system that we can exploit. (Reid-Kuecks 2013)

Central to EC's approach is building relationships of trust with active groups of citizens and communities (the term EC personnel use is "people and place") so that the movement for a different kind of economy is shared and collaborative. Issues and solutions in many cases originate with the organizations, communities and producer groups with which EC works. EC demonstrates what it takes to be an organization that is truly responsive to communities.

Innovations require risk-taking and not all of EC's innovations have worked. Innovative organizations must be able to accommodate and learn from failure. Successful projects pose other challenges, like how to grow these initiatives within the organization or whether to let others take them to scale. The ways in which EC has evolved reflect an organization that learns and adapts.

Over the past two decades EC has been involved in many different initiatives and projects. EC's footprint over this period is greater than the sum of the initiatives and projects with which it has been engaged. While no single initiative holds the potential for transformation to a conservation economy, taken together this body of work helps communities see their assets and agency in a new light and envision how their resources and economies could be managed differently. A senior EC staff member describes the challenge:

> Building a conservation economy is a huge undertaking. We can't do it in its entirety, especially not overnight. We have to focus our energy on where we can have the most value and can make the most change, and over time, that shifts according to the people and places we are working with because of the responsiveness of our approach. (personal communication[1])

EC has been creating new narratives and supporting ways for First Nations, associations of fish harvesters, alliances of woodlot owners and small businesses to tell their own stories about a different kind of economy and of community action for "radical, practical change" (S. Beebe personal communication).

Background

EC's home base is the Pacific coast of British Columbia. The coastline is indented with bays, inlets, lengthy fjords, rivers and islands and contains most of the intact temperate rainforest watersheds in North America. The population of some 450,000 is spread thin, especially in the north coast region. The economy of coastal British Columbia is similar to the national economy in its dependence on resource extraction mainly for export, in the case of B.C. on forest products and seafood. Both industries have reduced their labour force steadily since the 1990s. Much of the wealth is owned by, and benefits, people residing elsewhere,[2] so much of coastal B.C. is relatively poor.

While Aboriginal people make up 4.8 percent of B.C.'s total population, in some regions the percentage is much higher. In 2006 in the North Coast Development Region, for example, Aboriginal people made up 35.3 percent of the population (B.C. Multiculturalism and Immigration Branch 2008). Roughly one-third of Canada's close to six hundred First Nations reside in B.C., many of these in the coastal region, living on their traditional territory that has never been ceded to, or recognized by, the Canadian government despite years of treaty negotiations. Most coastal communities have experienced significant population declines in the past two decades as people (particularly youth and skilled workers) migrate to urban areas for jobs. In contrast, most First Nations have seen population growth during this period. Between 1996 and 2006, Canada's First Nations population grew 3.5 times faster than did the country's non-Aboriginal population (Statistics Canada 2006).

EC was born into a well-publicized conflict centred in Clayoquot Sound, on Vancouver Island. This conflict, known colloquially as the "war in the woods," pitted environmentalists against forestry companies for more than a decade. It culminated in 1993 with ten thousand protesters blockading logging, followed by the arrest of over eight hundred people and what was at that time the largest trial in Canadian history (Stefanick 2001). Two years later the B.C. government accepted the recommendations of a scientific panel that, for the first time in Canada's history, was made up of both scientists and hereditary Aboriginal leaders. The panel made recommendations that restructured the scale and scope of forestry activity in the region, reducing the total allowable harvest by one third, with the loss of close to four hundred forest sector jobs (Goad 2007). The current President of EC recalls the sense of both opportunity and crisis that resulted from that decision:

> An industrial forest landscape that had historically created good union-ized jobs and regional wealth, at a serious cost to the environment and with very limited benefit to First Nations in the region was suddenly over. A new economy was needed — and fast! The void created by massive reductions in logging was serious and threatened the very viability of these communities. (personal communication)

The polarization of interests ran deep, feelings were intense and constructive ways forward had yet to be created. EC came into this chasm with a vision of an alternative way of doing business, which combined community building and economic development with a strong environmental ethic. It was established as a Canadian registered charity, inspired by an American non-profit, Ecotrust, which was created in 1991 by conservationist Spencer Beebe to test ideas about conservation-based development across the ecoregion of Pacific temperate rainforests.[3] The current EC president explains:

> EC came up the middle ... and said, "Let's look at this, it doesn't have to be either/or. We already know that protection won't work; we already know that mass industrial-scale resource extraction won't work. Is there any way to marry the interests of Aboriginal people, local

communities and industry to design an economy for this place that works
for the environment, for the citizens and for financial success?" (personal
communication)

A brief history

There are three distinct stages in EC's history. These phases represent the shifts the
organization has made as it navigated in a polarized and ever-changing geopolitical
landscape. Through all three phases the organization's mission objective of triple
bottom line development did not waver, but the path that EC took was not linear.
There is clearly a belief within EC that the process of citizen-led innovation must be
iterative, learning from what works and what doesn't, and this process has required
that the organization have an adaptable institutional frame.

Phase one: (1996–2002)

Until the mid-to-late 1990s, resource extraction was occurring in coastal B.C. at an
unprecedented rate, largely at the hands of international corporations operating
with the single bottom line objective of making profit. Local communities were
captive to boom and bust cycles of commodity prices and Aboriginal communities, on whose unceded territories much of the industrial activity was occurring,
were largely ignored. In this context, EC focused on forming strategic alliances with
a number of communities on the coast where the model of industrial resource
development was being challenged by local groups and First Nations. The leading
edges of this resistance were: in the north on the islands of Haida Gwaii led by the
Haida Nation; on Vancouver Island in Clayoquot Sound supported by a coalition
of environmental groups and Nuu-chah-nulth Nations; on the Central Coast in the
Kitlope, a sacred place for the Haisla Nation and in the Koeye, where the Heiltsuk
Nation claims its home.

The Heiltsuk First Nation saw land-use planning as a way of being proactive in
dealing with pressures from resource industries to get access to their lands. They
asked EC to help them develop a plan of their own. The Heiltsuk's intention was
to develop their own Nation's land use vision which they hoped would influence
the larger lands and resource management process taking place in B.C. at the time.
Over five years, EC worked closely with both the leadership and the community
members of the Heiltsuk Nation and in 2005 their land-use vision entitled *For our
Children's Tomorrow* was publicly released. It called for the protection of 827,000
hectares of land as areas of natural and cultural significance and established zones
of use for forestry and economic development. This work has continued to guide
the Nation's decision-making to this day.

EC's objectives in its work with communities were to: (1) provide excellent
information for decision-making; (2) create and hold a space for the articulation

of an alternative land and resource use vision and (3) bring private and foundation capital into play to support the realization of each community's vision. During this period, EC published *More Than the Sum of our Parks* (1997), *Seeing the Ocean Through the Trees* (1997) and *North of Caution* (2001). These publications helped establish EC's profile. EC was asked by the Council of Haida Nations and the Nuu-chah-nulth to help their organizations create mapping departments and to assist in the raising of capital for the repatriation of the Koeye. EC relied on a combination of geographic information systems (GIS), mapping and storytelling tools that enabled these communities to define and present their interests. This approach also provided communities with facilitation and negotiation tools aimed at strengthening alliances and communications tools that allowed local and regional stories to gain attention like never before. This first phase of EC's history defined the organization as a friend and ally of communities and First Nations in coastal B.C. that were trying to chart a different course from the industrial resource extraction model.

Phase two: (2003–2009)

Early in the new millennium some space was gradually being carved out for community and Aboriginal interests in large resource development projects. This was catalyzed by several successful B.C. Supreme Court challenges that, in the absence of treaty settlements, recognized the inherent right of self-government of Aboriginal people in their territories.

While this gave the potential for a bigger slice of the resource pie for local communities and First Nations, it did not lead to a significant shift from an industrial resource-extraction model to a 3E model. To catalyze this shift EC saw a need to change their focus from "visioning" to "demonstrating" a conservation economy.

This second phase of EC's history was defined by actively working with communities to support the development of new kinds of enterprises. Business planning, developing markets, facilitating producer/consumer interfaces and brokering capital were the central activities of this phase. One of the organization's most significant undertakings was the creation of a $4 million loan fund that focused on mission-based lending to entrepreneurs engaged in 3E businesses (more details on the Coastal Loan Fund below).

Another major undertaking was the Working Sound initiative in Clayoquot Sound, begun at the request of eleven shellfish growers. Clayoquot Sound was a good place to demonstrate the possibility of a conservation economy: radical reductions in logging had left a significant hole in the local economy; the region had been declared a UNESCO biosphere reserve; oyster farming was present albeit in a marginal way; 50 percent of the resident population was Aboriginal and the region boasted at least a million tourists annually. As a result of EC's work over a five-year period in organizing and helping finance small oyster producers in the area, oyster production nearly doubled, new farms owned by First Nations came online and zero-discharge regulations were enacted to protect the marine environment.

In 2005, EC brokered over $1 million CDN to purchase the last remaining fish plant on the Tofino waterfront, bringing together local investors to own the plant, local fishermen to supply it and local restaurants as the primary market outlet, thus creating a "circle of local wealth." In Clayoquot Sound, EC has supported Iisaak Forest Resources (100 percent owned by five Nuu-chah-nulth Nations) in a number of ways over the years: providing a low interest loan to enable the company to obtain the Forest Stewardship Council (FSC) certification;[4] raising philanthropic capital to support their communications and marketing efforts internationally and ultimately stepping into direct management of the company for nearly two years at a critical stage. This experience is also one of EC's best examples of how conservation economy principles could be successfully embedded in business and yield triple bottom line results. EC's more active and direct involvement in enterprise development during this phase also included support for businesses that added value to forest products, a fishing-licence bank that allowed small-boat hook-and-line fish harvesters to share and get access to quota they could not afford to acquire on their own and the creation of an enterprise to help businesses measure, reduce and offset their carbon emissions (Climate Smart).

Phase three: (2009–present)
The 2008 financial crisis created challenges and opportunities for EC. Philanthropic funding was tight, communities were focused on jobs as a top priority, often at the expense of the environment and many traditional institutions and businesses upon which people had come to rely began to show signs of instability. It was a challenging time for EC as well as for the communities with which it worked: its 2009 Annual Report described some hard decisions that had been made, including selling 50 percent of the Climate Smart enterprise, winding down the coastal loan fund, selling the Trilogy fish plant and restructuring the staff time (Ecotrust Canada 2009). With the founding President moving to establish Ecotrust Australia, a new president was appointed to lead these changes. As she now points out, there were also opportunities that accompanied these challenges. One of these opportunities was that the financial crisis generated a public mood that was becoming more receptive to new economic models:

> The global financial crisis gave us an opening that we did not have before. When the economy was buzzing along quite fine, it was difficult to get traction for our ideas about alternative approaches to business and economic development. Nobody needs a new idea when the current one is working just fine! Prior to the recession, we had "openings" only where

there was a crisis; usually a crisis caused when industry threatened community well-being and we could intervene and demonstrate a different approach. The recession meant that suddenly everybody was alert to the need for a new way of doing business — and we have been able to advance our work much more quickly now as a result. (B. Reid-Kuecks personal communication)

Being at the forefront of demonstrating an alternative approach to economic development suddenly gained cachet in unexpected places (such as the provincial government) and opened up room for EC to emerge as a leader in the field of social innovation. EC was well positioned, based on more than a decade of experience, to be a leader in the field of how to craft an economy that creates human and ecological health alongside wealth.

Since 2009, Ecotrust Canada has focused on working with communities and industry stakeholders to harness innovation and design proof-of-concept initiatives that act as a blueprint for others. From new electronic systems for fisheries management to forest carbon sequestration to product tracking and traceability, the body of work that underpins EC today holds clues to an alternative kind of future and has given EC increasing levels of scale and influence in B.C. and across Canada.

Four themes are consistent across the history of EC: innovation; developing trust relationships with communities; learning from what works and what doesn't and creating new narratives about the possibility of a new kind of economy. The next sections review these themes.

SOCIAL INNOVATION FOR CITIZEN-LED CHANGE

EC's vision of a conservation economy can only be realized through innovation. But innovations don't just happen: EC looks for opportunities to innovate in the everyday experiences, knowledge and challenges faced by people in the communities in which it works; it incubates, nurtures and manages these innovations through long-term relationships of trust with communities who share in the creation of the conservation economy. In this section we review three kinds of innovation that have been important in EC's history: mapping for a new kind of community planning and visioning; social finance to support a new kind of enterprise and "proof of concept" for a new kind of economy.

Mapping for a new kind of community planning and visioning

The early mapping work of the organization was rooted in the desire of communities (Native and non-Native) to take a lead in describing and documenting their home territories and in discerning how they want these territories managed, as well as in EC's vision for new ways of managing natural resources for the conservation economy. Mapping was a way for communities to first articulate their vision for how their land and resources should be utilized and then negotiate with governments and industries for a more sustainable use of land and resources adjacent to their territories. It was necessary for helping First Nations respond to proposed development on their territories by the resource extraction industry. Mapping was also a way for communities to tell their stories and imagine their futures. A professional forester who worked with First Nations said: "The maps became ways that the First Nation could lay out not only what existed but what their vision of the future was" (personal communication).

In the Clayoquot Sound area, for example, EC worked with one of the Nuu-chah-nulth First Nations, Ahousaht Nation, to use GIS technology to create maps of their forests. Where conventional maps describe jurisdictional boundaries (who owns what) and natural features, the EC maps "describe ecologies in relationship to economies — where is the timber that looks the same; where is the water that could provide potential for micro hydro; where are the Aboriginal territories that need to be developed differently; where do the fish go; where are the eco-tourism possibilities?" (EC staff personal communication). These kinds of maps can only be created from community knowledge and require in-depth work, as the publication *Chief Kerry's Moose* indicates (Tobias 2000).

EC's mapping work has fused participatory mapping with the latest in GIS technology. The EC approach had two guiding principles. First, it recognized that it was important for community members to see maps not only as documents created by others (experts) but also as something that "ordinary" people could make themselves. Second, EC focused its efforts on providing training and technology as a way to build the capacity of communities to manage the mapping themselves (see McIntosh 2005). EC's early mapping work led to creation of the Aboriginal Mapping Network in 1998 as a joint initiative with the Gitxsan and Ahousaht First Nations. The Aboriginal Mapping Network is still maintained as a support system for Aboriginal and Indigenous peoples to map their traditional knowledge in support of land claims, treaty negotiations and their own land-use development plans.[5]

The mapping work has enabled EC to build long-term trust relationships with communities, incorporate traditional knowledge, ideas and visions into formal community plans and support a sense of collective agency. A good illustration of this are two mapping tools EC has built from its years of experience in GIS mapping with communities: the Living Atlas and Terratruth. The Living Atlas is an online tool that combines spatial information with narrative and other material such as charts, photos and video and audio clips (Ecotrust Canada n.d.[b]). In the B.C. interior, the Okanagan Nation Alliance has created one example of a living atlas they call Voices on the Land, which includes video clips of Elders talking about each location. This tool has provided a way for these communities to capture the

Indigenous knowledge of their lands possessed by elders in ways that can help inform future decisions on land use and development.

Terratruth is a land-use planning tool that allows communities to superimpose the shape of any proposed development onto their map to visualize its potential impact on, for example, natural features or cultural heritage sites (Ecotrust Canada n.d.[a]). EC recently provided the Terratruth application to the Carrier Sikani Tribal Council and they are using it to look at the potential impacts of the Northern Gateway Pipeline (for example, to determine where it crosses salmon streams).

But EC has always known that information democracy alone is not enough. Maps don't stand alone but are part of the process of shifting the ground towards a conservation economy, enabling communities to understand their assets, think about how they want them used and participate effectively in planning, negotiations and decision-making. The strands of mapping and economic development are intertwined.

Supporting a new kind of enterprise with social finance

Alongside the ability to envision a new future, communities need capital to use their resources in a different way, to create enterprises and employment within a conservation economy. The founding President of EC explains:

> The ability to see a future of your own design is potentially very frustrating if you don't have any way of implementing that future. The key is having the ability to connect the stories to some way to activate that vision. So, the community needs to see itself as having assets and then it needs a way of deploying these assets and for this it often needs capital. EC's understanding that we needed to bring new assets and new ways of thinking about assets to the table in these communities was an innovation. (I. Gill personal communication)

EC realized very early that for communities and regions to transform their economies would require significant financial resources deployed in numerous ways. Financial resources would be needed for "everything from early proof-of-concept pilots that require incubation instruments, to large-scale, established businesses positioned to attract commercial impact investment or mainstream conventional financing" (Ecotrust Canada 2013: 11). EC realized it could not meet all of these social finance needs through one instrument alone. Sometimes it played an important intermediary role by engaging senior commercial finance players or raising capital for incubating new ideas (ibid.: 12). Other times it supported burgeoning conservation economy enterprises by providing strategic and business planning as well as technical assistance to fishery, aquaculture, forestry and timber products ventures, convening groups to form cooperatives and alliances and carrying out assessments and feasibility studies for community initiatives. EC's most significant foray into the social finance field, however, was the creation of the Coastal Loan Fund (CLF).

The CLF was established by EC in 1998 in partnership with Ecotrust (based in Oregon) and their partner ShoreBank (based in Chicago). The fund was aimed at providing loan capital and business development support services to triple bottom line businesses. Over a ten-year period between 1998 and 2008, the CLF made eighty-seven "mission related" loans totalling $10.7 million and in the process helped its clients leverage $40 million in additional loan capital while creating close to nine hundred jobs (ibid.: 2).

The CLF explicitly targeted "rural entrepreneurs involved with conservation-based businesses and First Nations interested in shifting their local economy toward a conservation economy" (ibid.: 11). Its clients ranged from large First Nations-owned run-of-river hydroelectric systems to micro- and small-scale enterprises, from cultural and heritage tourism businesses to high-value-added wood products firms (e.g., producers of flooring or tonewoods for musical instruments) and community-owned fishery operations.

The innovation of the CLF consisted of lending solely to businesses that incorporated environmental and social practices that would advance a conservation economy. A former EC staff member observes:

> We began in a very practical way to take this concept of a conservation economy, which is very nebulous (whenever we got in a room and discussed it, nobody ever knew what it meant), but we had to translate it in our day-to-day business in our lending with potential borrowers and people we wanted to work with in the communities. We had to say, "Well, what is it about your business that is innovative and has environmental or social value, as well as being a viable business?" (personal communication)

Until the financial crisis of 2008, the CLF achieved high repayment rates and loan losses "at the low end of the range for comparable institutions in Canada" (Ecotrust Canada 2011: 1),[6] but still required grant funding to cover a significant portion of operating costs. Projections by EC determined that to break even at their current size and cover all costs they would have to charge interest rates of 20-25 percent, too high for borrowers to accept or for businesses to absorb. To break even at the 9 percent interest rate EC was charging without operating subsidies or contributed capital would require a loan portfolio of at least $20 million.

There appear to be several reasons why the CLF got into difficulty when the financial crisis hit in 2008. The resultant economic downturn hit the forestry sector particularly hard and this put a number of the CLF's clients under financial stress.

The struggling economy also meant that several foundations that EC depended on had less money they could loan or grant. In addition, an important loan loss reserve that had been provided by the federal government's Western Economic Diversification Fund ended unexpectedly and abruptly. This confluence of factors resulted in a significant rise in the CLF's risk profile and ultimately, in 2009, to a decision by the EC Board to begin winding down the CLF.

Some former EC staff also believed that the severing of ties with Craft3 (a U.S. organization created by EC and ShoreBank in 1994, which operated the CLF for the first few years and later provided technical assistance and training to the CLF staff) had weakened the CLF. EC staff felt they had little choice but to "repatriate" the CLF at that time, because of the regulatory environment in Canada that restricted a charity's ability to participate in lending as well as the "donor and community optics of a U.S. loan fund being lender of record for EC" (EC board member personal communication). A former EC staff member suggested that, while the CLF continued to make good loans after this point, it was never able to create the same rigour and discipline in terms of risk and portfolio management that Craft3 had in place:

> As an organization EC was stretched to be able to take on what was needed in the back room; I can now see that what we were getting from [Craft3], an established financial institution, was far closer to what was needed than what EC could provide. (personal communication)

The recent EC report on the CLF observes:

> In retrospect, it seems clear that even given more time, there was limited likelihood that the CLF could have simultaneously retained its attention to mission, and met its goal for break-even or profitable operations in the absence of financial support from government. Lending in areas with low population density, combined with the limited diversity of economic sectors in its operating geography, and the high costs associated with serving remote communities was a tough proposition at best. Achieving self-sufficiency would likely have required some combination of an expanded geography, a more diversified client base, an increase in lower-risk anchor loans, and a curtailing of higher-risk mission lending activities, such as micro-lending. (Ecotrust Canada 2013: 33)

Although the loan fund was wound down in 2009, EC continues to play an innovative social finance role in terms of brokering capital, incubating new ventures and providing strategic and technical support to 3E enterprise development.

Toward a new kind of economy

The main focus of EC's work since 2009 has been "proof of concept" work to demonstrate the viability of a new kind of economy. Its projects have spanned fisheries, forestry and other sectors. The traceability initiative, ThisFish, is one of the larger projects with a good potential to scale up nationally.

EC sees small-boat, local fishing fleets as a lynchpin for healthy coastal economies and communities, marine stewardship and job creation. EC was closely involved with Vancouver Island fish harvesters over many years and had developed a number of projects collaboratively with them. By 2008, it began to look likely that seafood traceability was eventually going to be required by the E.U. and other governments (Magera and Beaton 2009). Fish harvesters were interested in understanding whether an affordable system could be designed that would meet the anticipated regulatory requirements for traceability and at the same time add value to their businesses.

EC's work with groups of fish harvesters over many years provides a glimpse into the key factors its work relies on: maintaining relationships over time; the identification of problems and opportunities faced by those groups and the desire to jointly find solutions that could work. A EC staff member observed:

> We very quickly realized that something like [traceability] could really hit all the marks for 3E. If done right it could contribute to economic benefit for coastal communities, it could contribute to great gains for the environment through enhancing transparency, it could lead to a fairer distribution of benefits and a lot of things in social equity. So we were quite interested in pursuing [ThisFish]. (personal communication)

EC staff worked with Vancouver Island fish harvesters in designing and testing a fish tagging and tracking system, ThisFish. Its aims are to:

- "ensure an authentic, meaningful experience to consumers hungry for trusted information on the authenticity, quality and sustainability of their seafood;
- provide real-time market intelligence and branding advantages for every business in the seafood supply chain from fishermen to fishmongers and
- create an easy-to-use and low-cost traceability system that is accessible to small operators and rural fishermen." (Thisfish n.d.)

ThisFish works to meet regulatory requirements and educate consumers and create a premium market for small boat catches. The tagging code that identifies seafood at time of capture on the boat travels with the seafood right into the customer's hands. This forges a direct connection between producers and consumers.

ThisFish was officially launched in 2011 and currently over four hundred fishing vessels in B.C. and in the Atlantic Canada lobster and haddock fisheries are taking part. A large grocery chain, Sobeys, has taken on the system in its stores across Canada along with smaller fish retailers and restaurants. ThisFish is being used by the community-supported fishery project "Off the Hook," an award-winning initiative to connect consumers to locally and sustainably harvested seafood, carried out by the Ecology Action Centre in Nova Scotia.

Another example of the way in which EC is demonstrating "proof of concept" is testing the viability of a community forest to generate income by storing carbon and selling carbon credits in the marketplace. EC has long argued that forest practice must be about more than the extraction of timber. The current business model in Canada, where large tracts of forestland are tied by a multi-year fibre contract to a sawmill or pulp mill, results in an economic system that is fundamentally flawed. The vital ecosystem services associated with these large tenures, including water, medicinal plants, wildlife, recreation and carbon sequestration, go uncounted, undocumented, unutilized and unprotected. In 2010 EC set out to prove that ecosystem services could be quantified in economic terms in the hope of building support for a more comprehensive approach to forestland management. In partnership with the Cheakamus Community Forest, a joint venture between the Municipality of Whistler and the Lil'wat and Squamish First Nations, EC is currently developing a forest-carbon sequestration project that will document carbon stored in the forest, link this stored carbon to the company's forest management plan and take it in the form of carbon credits to market for companies and organizations that wish to purchase the stored carbon as an offset to their carbon emissions. If successful, this initiative promises to open a whole new discussion in Canada about how to maximize and diversify revenues associated with forestland management.

EC's innovations depend on relationships within the organization, with communities and with external partners. Without those relationships many of the innovations described here could not have happened because the need or idea would not have been identified, or the innovations would not succeed because they didn't build "ownership" of the solutions by the communities themselves. In the next section we examine how EC has established relationships of trust with communities.

DEVELOPING TRUST RELATIONSHIPS, LEADING, AND TAKING A LEAD FROM OTHERS

EC's mission of creating a conservation economy depends on developing and maintaining relationships of trust and respect with local communities. Innovations emerge from conversations in which community challenges, ideas and opportunities are articulated and community knowledge and resources uncovered. A

Vancouver Island fish harvester says that EC staff "don't tell people what to do, they ask them what they need and want" (personal communication). A First Nations member, whose community has worked with EC, talks about the importance of trust: EC "puts value on relationships. That is the main basis for anything, to build up good relationships. If you build good relationships there is some trust there. When people trust you they will look to you for advice or to help develop something in the community" (personal communication).

EC's presence in communities is often longstanding. Most staff have worked in the area for other organizations and brought with them their relationships from earlier roles and projects. Projects come and go, staff and offices change but partnerships with some communities have persisted. EC is now working with a hereditary chief of a First Nation whose father and grandfather worked with EC. Building trust happens through collaborative work, a lot of discussion and respect for community knowledge and values.

EC's longtime work and relationships in the Clayoquot Sound area have already been illustrated. Looking back, its president feels the experience with the Nuu-chah-nulth First Nations around Clayoquot Sound illustrates what it takes for EC and the communities it works with to develop innovations on the ground:

> The mapping helped people to articulate their vision and opportunity. Then the economic development planning helped to take this vision into action. And the loan fund [CLF] provided some of the necessary capital to realize these opportunities. The innovations that we are currently working on are the fourth level of development, or the fourth tier of growth and adaptation in the organization. We now know that we can not only help to create businesses that are conservation based, but we can actually turn economies around with strategic interventions. (B. Reid-Kuecks personal communication)

Another example of EC's approach to building relationships of trust with people and place is found in the Prince Rupert area of the north coast of B.C. Although EC has not always had an office in Prince Rupert, it has found ways to engage with communities on the north coast since its formation. In 1999, Skeena Wild, a "quality seafood co-op," was established by fish harvesters on the north coast with some technical assistance from EC staff. In the same period, EC's Prince Rupert office explored the feasibility of MSC certification[7] for sustainable fisheries in the area and supported local community forestry initiatives. The intensity of EC's relationships with communities in the Prince Rupert area grew when EC hired a local fisheries activist who had built a strong reputation and nurtured a wide range of relationships with Aboriginal and non-Aboriginal groups.

In 2008, EC's Skeena office was engaged by the Sustainable Marine Fisheries and Communities Alliance, a group formed by municipal leaders, First Nations, fish harvesters' associations and others to revive the commercial fisheries of the area. EC supported the alliance in the creation of a unified vision and strategic plan for sustainable fisheries on the north coast. One of the alliance members described how EC brought community leaders and hereditary leaders together to identify their concerns and what could be done: "[our people] are more reactive than proactive. And it really made us proactive, EC bringing us together to talk about our concerns and what we could do to improve things" (personal communication).

A new area of work that developed from that process was EC's fishery monitoring. As a result of solicitation from the federal Department of Fisheries and Oceans (DFO), industry and members of the Sustainable Marine Fisheries and Communities Alliance, EC used its staff's previous experience in this field to leverage contracts as a monitoring service provider. EC has built local capacity by developing and delivering training programs to local First Nations and employing those individuals in the delivery of the contracts for DFO and industry.

Additional work in this field then evolved to include electronic monitoring of fisheries. On-board electronic monitoring had become mandatory for the Area A[8] crab fishery on the north coast. Placing video cameras on board was initiated by fish harvesters as a way to stop gear theft but electronic monitoring expanded to continuously record vessel data during fishing. The DFO saw it as a way to regulate the industry at a lower cost than the previous human observers. When the DFO contract for electronic monitoring came up for renewal, the crab fish harvesters asked EC to bid. EC saw this as an opportunity to be responsive to local fish harvesters and work with them to create a better system at a lower cost. The fish harvesters voted on the contract and EC was successful (by one vote).

EC staff then worked with the fish harvesters and DFO in redesigning electronic monitoring systems to respond to the needs of fish harvesters while ensuring the sustainability of the fleet, healthy crab stocks and communities. Now the relationships EC has built with crab fish harvesters are being put to the test. DFO has begun changing the reporting requirements for the fishery and some of these changes are more costly. EC was chosen by fish harvesters to run the electronic monitoring program, partly because as a non-profit it could keep down its costs to fish harvesters. Now, if EC has to go back to the fish harvesters requesting a fee increase to meet the new requirements, this could erode the trust that it has carefully worked to build. EC hopes to mitigate this by working hard to ensure new costs are offset by overall program savings. EC does have credibility in this regard: in 2012 it provided fish harvesters a rebate on their fees because of cost savings in the program.

Creating and nurturing long-term relationships with local communities is challenging in itself. Managing these relationships as part of a deliberate process of innovation for social change is even more challenging. The first relationship-building challenge that the fledgling EC faced was how to communicate its idea of a conservation economy in communities that were polarized by conflict between environmentalists and businesses. One local fish harvester recalls his first impressions:

> I came in here thinking these guys were all "Greenpeacers." I wasn't quite sure where they were coming from. It was a learning curve for me. I thought it was going to be a diehard "looking after the environment and screw the jobs," and then all of a sudden it was "no, we want to have jobs and look after the environment." So I said, "OK — prove it to me." (personal communication)

EC's response to this challenge was to work in depth in a small number of places, building relationships and supporting those communities' visions. Through this work, it hoped to "prove it" to other communities, inspiring proliferation of innovations that further a conservation economy.

A second challenge lies in maintaining trust relationships over time, over projects and over places. While relationships developed during one phase of work can live on and form the basis for later work, new relationships have to be created too. A senior EC staff member explains:

> We need to constantly maintain and rebuild trust. It is not earned and then there forever. You need to prove yourself, your intentions, and integrity over and over again with every new face and every new project … or you lose your relationships fast. (personal communication)

EC has now been going long enough to span generations. One First Nation leader said that he is always wary of engaging with outside organizations but the fact that EC had built and maintained relationships with his father and grandfather provided a base of trust for him. Nevertheless, trust relationships need to be built again with each generation and he suggested that process would be easier if EC hired more Aboriginal staff. Finding intermediaries within the communities is another way in. One fish harvester talked about his role as an intermediary: "I was the guy saying, 'Hey these folks are a non-profit, they are trying to make it more financially viable for the fishermen'; and I thought this is a hell of a good idea" (personal communication).

It is also important to have the right kind of staff on the ground: not every professional is successful at community relationships. EC staff includes skilled, committed and experienced community developers and facilitators. One of them described how important it is to listen as a way of finding out what is important to people in the community: "When you are in the community, going to weddings and funerals and celebrations is so important. If you are a community development practitioner, get ready to throw yourself right in." In this case the EC staffer used his love of cooking as a way to immerse himself in community life:

> So, one of the things I have taken to doing is having a lot of dinners. And I don't really talk that much during those dinners. I cook, they love my food, and when I am cooking people will share their food (they will bring a salmon over and I will cook it). We can talk about personal stuff, or a lot of the time those community members just need someone to hold them to talk about a death in the family or to drive someone somewhere that they really need to go. (personal communication)

Nurturing relationships takes time, work and long-term investment. How to fund that is yet another challenge. In its earlier days EC was well-funded and, as a former staff member says, had the luxury of being able to work on very interesting projects and didn't have to worry about where the money was coming from. Ample funding meant staff could be fully responsive: "We learned not to be rigid in what we do but to be able to adapt to what communities wanted, and to try new things" (personal communication). Since 2008, finances have become tighter and investment in long-term relationships rather than projects more difficult.

The fourth relationship tension is between responsiveness to communities and focus on work that demonstrates a conservation economy. The financial crisis of 2008 forced some thinking within EC about what was most important in their work and approach. The focus has become more on proving a conservation economy and EC needs to be more selective about ideas and places that can demonstrate that elements of a conservation economy can work. EC's president explains:

> This [new focus] doesn't take us away from our strategic relationships and having integrity on the ground but rather we see that we can't have that integrity and follow through unless we have that focus. Otherwise we just become deliverers of a wide range of pieces without really being able to commit to and follow through on our promise as an organization of trying to make change that sticks and will provide a benefit to communities. We can't just be everything to everyone all the time, we have to focus and if we really want to prove the conservation economy can work in places we have to pick those pieces we can build up and scale. (personal communication)

Sometimes EC has to make a decision to wind down or close one of its initiatives. This is never easy for any organization but is especially difficult for an organization that depends so heavily on relationships of trust with communities. As EC's president explains, "We had to learn when to pull the plug because we all love the projects we have created. It is painful to do it. We learned to do it in a respectful way" (personal communication).

The EC management team has learned that in order to enable the kind of risk taking required to generate something really new, it is essential not only to have good instincts and market intelligence guiding go/no go decisions but also to move to a predictable process to which every initiative and every initiative manager is accountable. By being clear from the outset that every idea is just an idea until it becomes something more and by sticking to a principled approach that examines every idea in a timely and consistent way, EC has created an environment where innovation is welcome and where it thrives. EC continues to be a place-based organization, committed to learning about the challenges and opportunities that community members face. But it is less about broad community development in those places than it was and more about testing ideas in order to create "proof of concept" that can be scaled and replicated. That inevitably shifts community relationships and requires some careful analysis and decisions about priorities.

EC has experienced successes and failures in its innovations. Success and failure each present different kinds of challenges to the staff, management and board of EC. In the next section we review some of the challenges of success and failure and how EC has been learning from both.

LEARNING FROM WHAT WORKS AND WHAT DOESN'T

Failure is a necessary part of risk-taking: not all innovations work. Some fail because of a lack of funding, some because they are ahead of their time, others because the context shifts. One example in the history of EC with elements of all these factors was a project to build an energy-efficient fishing boat that could be produced in B.C. Like most EC projects, the idea came from working with community members, in this case coastal commercial fish harvesters, who identified a problem for the small-boat fishing fleet: the boats were all old and needed to be replaced over the next twenty years. EC staff began thinking about creating a new economic sector that would build fishing boats using locally-resourced materials and an energy-efficient design (fuel is a major cost element in fishing):

> So we raised the capital to work with a famous vessel designer in Maine who gave us blueprints for a fishing boat that could be launched on the west coast, flat bottom, super energy efficient, made with local materials, really inexpensive to make. We lined up a boat builder who was very excited to build one, but we never got the capital. (B. Reid-Kuecks personal communication)

But the story doesn't end there. Recently, EC's president was on the east coast meeting with Aboriginal fish harvesters who were putting together proposals to the federal government for funding to build a fishing fleet. "One of the chiefs said what we really need is a boat that is flat bottomed and really energy efficient. So I have put the plans in the mail to them" (B. Reid-Kuecks personal communication).

Communities are not always ready to take advantage of tools even when they would help them in the longer term. One knowledgeable outsider who works with First Nations said that some people from the Heiltsuk First Nation had told him they are now doing the kind of GIS mapping that EC introduced years ago, but not with the original people EC had trained. The community had gone through a period of inactivity with GIS mapping and those individuals who had been trained left. The First Nation is now recruiting and training new people in GIS after deciding they wanted to continue the work. This suggests that the timeframe for measuring impact in communities has to be long.

As part of the process of institutional learning within EC, the organization produced a reflection report that identified lessons learned from the experience with the CLF (Ecotrust Canada 2011) and commissioned an external review of the CLF published in March 2013 (Ecotrust Canada 2013). The latter identifies several important lessons for others interested in establishing similar ventures, and a number of elements that need to be in place for successful social finance instruments, including changes to the national regulatory framework. A current board member explains:

> Ecotrust Canada experimented for ten years in direct lending through its loan fund; it has engaged with program-related investments for years; it has invested directly in social enterprises [companies with mission alignment to EC]; it has even taken a management contract with a First Nation-owned forest products company that had earlier been a CLF borrower. Therefore, the organization has amassed experience in both the thinking and doing of social finance, not so common in Canadian charities. EC needs an improved social finance landscape to activate its own work and those of its partners. EC's own operations are deeply challenged by the limitations of both the amount of grant money available and the nature of its extension, which tends to be program focused and short term. (personal communication)

An innovative project that succeeds for ten years is not a failure, even if it was unable to continue long term, but the loan fund history suggests the lines between success and failure are not set for all time. A project may not succeed in its original place but may be taken up elsewhere or the innovation may not take root locally for a long time.

Success brings challenges as much as failure does but of a different kind. Three challenges in particular recur in EC's successes. The first challenge is in how to keep the innovative edge once an idea has become the "new normal." Mapping is a good example: EC was ahead of its time in bringing GIS mapping to First Nations and making this new technical tool accessible and useful for community planning and visioning. A staff member notes that, although EC had been a pioneer in GIS mapping, "the rest of the world is catching up with us" (personal communication). What makes EC different is not so much the technology itself as the way it works with partners, adapting the technology to respond to what communities want to do.

A second challenge of success is how to replicate ideas beyond their original people and place. This is illustrated by the work with Vancouver Island fish harvesters to establish a licence bank.[9] In 2006, EC partnered with a group of Vancouver Island fish harvesters to found the Pacific Coast Fisheries Conservation Company as a way to own fish quotas and lease to its members, pooling risk and sharing benefits. With financing from EC and its subsidiary, Ecotrust Canada Capital, and a start-up foundation grant, the group invested in rockfish and halibut licences and quotas and signed a "conservation covenant" for responsible fishing practices to minimize habitat damage. A shareholder agreement outlines each fish harvester's obligations to the bank, to each other and to the resource. The fisheries licence bank is an example of a successful project in which EC goes beyond demonstrating the viability of the concept to pushing for a wider impact. As EC President says, "we could have stopped there" with the original project:

> It is a small, proven demonstration that is really benefiting ten guys. That, in and of itself, could have been enough, a good community development proof of concept that changed the lives of ten people. We said that's not the objective here. The objective here is to say, "Look everybody else, here's something you could do, regardless of where you are in the world." So we published a how-to guide for creating a licence bank and it has been taken up. (personal communication)

Now EC is being invited to offer workshops on licence-bank development in other parts of Canada. However, requests from other places to learn from EC's experience place additional demands on staff time and could take away from work on new innovations in its own place.

The third challenge of success is in figuring out exactly how best to scale up small demonstration projects to a regional or national level. EC's president describes the various ways the organization has tried to take ideas to scale:

> One way we do it is building to the point of proof of possibility and write it up so that others can use it. We did this for the license bank. Ten

fishers joined, we did all the work including the shareholder agreement. We needed $500,000 to build the first one. When we knew it worked we wrote about it and the model has been used in a lot of places. A second way is to build an idea and then sell it as a business. We did this with Climate Smart. We prototyped it, did the math internally on how it could function. We then sold it on the open market and that paid our development costs. The third way is we own and take it to scale. For example, with electronic monitoring, we build the proprietary software to go on the fish boats. This is worth contracts from the federal government, so we kept it. It is bringing revenue into the organization. (personal communication)

Currently, the options around how to scale up ThisFish are engaging a lot of EC staff and board attention. The project is clearly a success and although other traceability projects exist, ThisFish has some unique features and the potential to reach a wider audience. Should EC scale ThisFish by itself (raise the capital themselves and keep it as part of EC); should they bring in an external partner with the capital to grow the project (but lose much of the financial benefit) or should they hive it off for some other organization to take to scale (without much financial benefit for EC but achieving maximum reach)? An EC board member suggested the decision really comes down to the goal: Is it getting the organization's programs to scale and building a bigger and stronger organization? Or is it transformation of systems that are harmful to people and place, which would require EC not just to reach scale with its programs but to influence others? The final sections of this case study show how EC has clearly chosen the latter path.

CREATING NEW NARRATIVES ABOUT THE ECONOMY

Storytelling has been an important part of EC's mission and work from the very beginning. One strand of the storytelling has been communities articulating and telling their own stories, the other strand has been EC's telling of its own story, both in words and through demonstration projects. Both strands lead to a new narrative about the economy. The mapping, community visioning and community development work help bring forth communities' own stories about themselves and what they want their future to be. EC's 1999 annual report describes mapping as a "common language for many coastal communities to communicate local values to others" (Ecotrust Canada 1999: 15), with EC's role to help local groups become proficient in this language and "to use it to tell stories of how the conservation economy is being put into practice" (ibid.: 16).

Current staff view ThisFish and other nascent EC traceability initiatives as not just meeting regulatory requirements but as a storytelling platform: "There is an added layer to lift the veil where it is interesting and important to the eaters of that food. It's about storytelling and connecting people to the fishermen" (personal communication). Some stories are told in actions rather than words. An EC staff member who works at the community level talked about the power of good stories in conveying concepts:

> What I do is show people examples. I know a woman who started a sawmill. She was an incredibly smart and persistent person. So I would bring lots of people to see her at the sawmill. And, everyone thought the point was this great sawmill she had created. That was part of it, but the other part of it was that people saw how much hard work and persistence was required to start something like that. Another part was that she was a woman succeeding in something unconventional for women to succeed in within a male-dominated community. These visits helped men appreciate women differently and they helped other women see her as a role model. (personal communication)

Finding the right words to communicate the vision, goals and activities in ways that mean something to a range of audiences is not easy. Inevitably, stories change with the tellers and the audiences and shift over time as contexts evolve. The earlier language of the "conservation economy" has shifted to language about the "triple bottom line" and "3E" as a way of making the concepts more accessible. The stories are being told differently but are still what the former EC President described as a "narrative of what it is like to be a fair society" (I. Gill personal communication).

EXTERNAL AND INTERNAL FACTORS AFFECTING THE PROCESS OF SOCIAL INNOVATION

Most successful organizations credit the quality of their staff, governance and management structures, planning and evaluating for the success of their operations. But for most, external factors also work to enable (or present barriers to) success. One external enabling factor for EC has been that the aftermath of the "war of the woods" created new spaces for its work as First Nations engaged in treaty negotiations, logging companies saw their old tactics could not win out and environmentalists began to think differently about conservation. The war in the woods was damaging in many ways but with time it left people looking for another way forward. EC's message that conservation alone was not enough, that industrial-scale resource extraction could not be sustained, that jobs and the environment and social fairness needed to be worked on together came at the right moment.

The availability of donor funding for new ways of working enabled a long period of innovation. Investment in coastal B.C. by big environmental funders started with the anti-logging protests and continued to around 2006. It provided EC with opportunities to experiment with new ways of working. Since the financial crisis of 2008, philanthropic funding has declined and necessitated a tighter organizational focus. But it may also be that the closer public scrutiny of mainstream financial institutions such as banks is now creating space for alternative economic models to be tested.

Despite all the external enabling factors, EC might not have been able to develop its model of responsive innovation without three important internal factors. The first factor is how the organization promotes innovation as an ongoing process. The second is the impact and influence beyond the relatively small-scale projects. The third is the relationship with communities, taking a lead from and providing leadership to the diverse communities of coastal B.C. and now beyond.

Maintaining the flow of innovation is a function of external and internal opportunities. When asked how innovation happens within EC, its current president identifies the organization's position between the community and the policy tables. EC is field-based, in that almost all staff members have practitioner experience and relationships in communities, and well enough regarded by larger institutions that it sits at policy tables and relates to regional and local government as well. Some social innovations emerge when problems identified by people in communities can be transformed into opportunities through the policy-level discussions:

> I think we have the advantage of being "far enough up the food chain" and large enough, that we are both in the conversations on the ground so we know [them] and people come to us and say we've got this problem can you help us. But, we're also far enough up the food chain that we're sitting at policy tables and regional discussions and local government discussions, and able to reflect where the possibilities lie and where there actually is an opening that we might jump into. And, that is different from organizations that are just on the ground, or just up. (B. Reid-Kuecks personal communication)

EC continues to encourage its staff to innovate. The current organizational structure holds a space where new ideas can develop. The Living Lab is an initiative that demonstrates where relationships with communities and partner organizations can be developed and nurtured and where new areas of work start and are tested. An idea becomes a business unit when the EC board has confidence that it shows potential for commercialization. One of the co-managers of the Living Lab explains:

> When we first envisaged the Living Lab we saw it as a cauldron that is cooking up different ideas. The bubbles are the ideas. We have to decide what goes into the cauldron in the first place. Once in the cauldron these ideas start to bubble up. Some bubbles are bigger than others and some

bubble up faster than others (these get formed into business units) and some never develop into anything. Others pop out of the fluid, like Climate Smart that has been spun off. (personal communication)

IMPACT AND INFLUENCE

Impact and influence are very difficult to document or measure and beyond the scope of this case study. EC itself has not yet conducted full impact studies, although it has documented the increased economic viability of the small-boat enterprises that are member-owners of the licence bank; the numbers of people trained and hired in the past two years as part of the marine monitoring program; the impact of EC management to triple bottom line objectives of Iisaak Forest Resources and the impact of the CLF.

One indicator of EC's influence is the dozens of partnerships that have been built with universities, non-profits, research institutions and for-profit enterprises. Another is the calibre of people recruited to the EC board and EC's increasing reach beyond B.C. as other places ask it to come and share its knowledge and expertise: "We are not asking to go to these places, they are calling us because we have demonstrated that it [the conservation economy] is not a crazy notion, and I think it is going to get easier and easier" (EC staff personal communication). One example of the spreading ideas is the request EC has received from the Northeast Superior Regional Chiefs Forum to help them operationalize the vision of a conservation economy for over 700,000 hectares of forest in the Chapleau Crown Game Reserve in Ontario. A representative of the Forum explains that the time was right to mobilize the conservation economy:

> We are getting really close to having to look at innovative models like this right across the board because: a) the environmental conditions are being pushed to the brink and b) the First Nations are rising up and saying we want our fair share. So we are becoming increasingly motivated to reconcile and come up with new ways of working together and that is where the conservation economy agenda flourishes. It is not just because it finds a better balance between the economy and the environment. It is also because it finds a better way to balance the needs and interests of the various groups who operate at a regional level and share interest in the land. (personal communication)

EC's ambition has always been to bring about system change that makes the conservation economy a reality. An EC board member told us that "real transformation can only occur when change happens across the layers of 'nested systems.'"

Organizations that innovate must be very clear about who they are and what their goals are. If the goal is system change then it requires EC to be both an implementing and an influencing organization. Demonstrating that projects can work in a particular place is not enough: EC must change the terms of the debate about the environment and the economy, highlight the barriers in policy and practices that stand in the way of change, build capacity for alternative thinking and implementing and inspire others to act.

But there is inevitably a tension between being responsive to people and place and the broader goals of market transformation and system change. Since the strategic repositioning of EC in 2009, the organization is looking to extend its impact beyond the communities and groups with which they have developed long-term relationships. As EC's president points out, "We want to see transformative change, we want to be able to scale things; we want to be thinking ahead about how to share these lessons, provide those opportunities for people in other regions" (personal communication). For EC, small localized projects are not enough. The year 2009 was what the president describes as:

> [an] inflection point when the organization went from being a deep community development organization focused on community development for the sake of community development to where the organization was doing community development to make a point ... At the end of the day it is about creating proof of concept that can be scaled, in this place and many others. (personal communication)

A professor from Simon Fraser University who has seen EC staff in action, learning "where the community starting points are and what they can do to build on these," thinks EC's work has been "way ahead of its time." He described how biologists talk about a "keystone species" as one that has a disproportionate effect on its environment relative to its abundance and suggested that EC might someday be seen as a "keystone organization": by taking risks and testing new ideas EC has the potential to influence others and by influencing others it may change the way the system operates (personal communication).

CONCLUSIONS

Ecotrust Canada describes itself as a "catalyst and broker." It is not a voluntary association, a membership organization or a co-operative but it has convened a number of groups that would meet those definitions and has had joint ventures with First Nations, worker associations and others. It does not itself organize citizen action to claim rights but focuses its programmatic activities on partnerships with communities working at the confluence of economy, environment and social equity.

EC certainly can claim to have helped build the capacity of groups of citizens to act collectively in new ways. It is a non-profit that embraces profit. It has its own vision but engages with communities, enterprises and First Nations to define their own visions for the future and create new ways of getting there. EC's staff are skilled professionals who approach their work with respect for community knowledge. This is obvious in the ways EC staff describe the people and communities with whom they work: the main motivation for staff is the chance to be working shoulder to shoulder with communities to shape a new kind of economy.

EC's innovative projects have been important in testing and validating an alternative approach to business that supports both environmental stewardship and social equity. Its impact is slowly extending beyond its home territory of British Columbia to other parts of Canada. The bottom line is as important to the conservation economy as to the conventional one, although that bottom line is triple rather than solely about financial rewards.

Perhaps even more important than the projects themselves are the stories these projects generate. By working with communities to create their own stories about themselves and their futures, EC makes the case for a different approach to the use of natural resources, for collaborative associations of producers and for 3E enterprise development. Through these innovations, communities see themselves, their assets and their agency in a new way. Ecotrust Canada is weaving stories that show a different kind of future is possible.

Notes

1. All references to personal communication are for interviews conducted in February and March, 2013.
2. For example, Individual Fishing Quotas (IFQs) can be bought and sold: in 2004 only 2 percent of IFQs were owned by people living on Vancouver Island, 3 percent by residents of the North island and 9 percent by the North Coast residents. This compares with the 44 percent owned by residents of metropolitan Vancouver and Victoria (Ecotrust Canada and Ecotrust USA 2004).
3. One of Ecotrust's first big initiatives was in British Columbia, helping the Haisla Nation negotiate the Kitelope Heritage Conservancy Protected Area in the world's largest unlogged coastal temperate rainforest with the West Fraser Timber Company and the Government of B.C.
4. The Forest Stewardship Council is an international not-for-profit that promotes best social and environmental practices for forest owners and managers through standard setting, certification and labelling of forest products.
5. Detailed information about the Aboriginal Mapping Network can be found on its website (nativemaps.org).
6. See also Ecotrust Canada (2013: 28): "The write-off rate in the CLF appears in the same range as for Aboriginal Financial Institutions of a similar size."
7. A program of an international non-profit named Marine Stewardship Council, intended

to recognize and reward sustainable fishing practices and influence the choices consumers make when purchasing seafood.

8. A designation of a fishing area in the Queen Charlotte Region of British Columbia by the federal Department of Fisheries and Oceans.

9. Any type of legal form that can hold fish quota — that is, a cooperative, non-profit, contractual arrangement or corporate entity. See Sutcliffe, Edwards and Edwards (2008) for more detail.

References

B.C. Multiculturalism and Immigration Branch. 2008. "The Diversity of Visible Minorities and Ethnic Origins in B.C." <http://www.welcomebc.ca/welcome_bc/media/Media-Gallery/docs/communities/visible_minorities_ethnic_origins.pdf>.

Ecotrust Canada. 1997. *Seeing the Ocean Through the Trees: A Conservation-Based Development Strategy for Clayoquot Sound.* Vancouver, BC: Author.

____. 1999. "1999 Annual Report." Vancouver, BC: Ecotrust Canada. <http://ecotrust.ca/sites/all/files/EC-AR1999.pdf>.

____. 2001. *North of Caution: A Journey Through the Conservation Economy on the Northwest Coast of British Columbia.* Vancouver, BC: Author.

____. 2009. "2009 Annual Report." Vancouver, BC: Author. <http://ecotrust.ca/sites/all/files/AR2009.pdf>.

____. 2011. *Reflections: Lessons Learned from Our Coastal Loan Fund.* Vancouver, BC: Author.

____. 2013. "Ecotrust Canada's Coastal Loan Fund: A Bold Institutional Experiment, 1998–2009." Vancouver, BC: Author. <http://ecotrust.ca/sites/all/files/Ecotrust_Canada_Coastal_Loan_Fund.3.20.13.web.pdf>.

____. n.d.[a]. "Terratruth." Vancouver, BC: Author. <http://ecotrust.ca/communities/terratruth>.

____. n.d.[b]. "The Living Atlas." Vancouver, BC: Author. <http://ecotrust.ca/communities/the-living-atlas>.

Ecotrust Canada and Ecotrust USA. 2004. "Catch-22: Conservation, Communities and the Privatization of B.C. Fisheries: An Economic, Social and Ecological Impact Study." Vancouver, BC and Portland, OR: Authors. <http://www.inforain.org/reports/Catch_22_Full_Report_November2004.pdf>.

Goad, J. 2007. "Land Use Practices in Clayoquot Sound: An Assessment of Success of the 1993 Protest." Unpublished research paper.

Magera, A., and S. Beaton. 2009. "Seafood Traceability in Canada: Traceability Systems, Certification, Eco-Labeling and Standards for Achieving Sustainable Seafood." Halifax, NS: Ecology Action Centre. <http://www.davidsuzuki.org/publications/downloads/2010/Seafood_Traceability_in_Canada.pdf>.

McIntosh, W. 2005. "Tsleil-Waututh First Nation and Ecotrust Canada: A Cooperation Model." In *Building Sustainable Relationships: A Compendium of Leadership Practices in Aboriginal Engagement and Sustainability.* Toronto, ON: Canadian Business for Social Responsibility. <http://www.cbsr.ca/sites/default/files/CBSRAboriginalEngBook.pdf>.

Reid-Kuecks, B. 2013. June 24. Presentation at the Forum on Citizen-led Sustainable

Change. Antigonish, NS.

Statistics Canada. 2006. "Aboriginal Peoples in Canada in 2006: Inuit, Métis and First Nations, 2006 census." <http://www12.statcan.ca/census-recensement/2006/as-sa/97-558/pdf/97-558-XIE2006001.pdf>.

Stefanick, L. 2001. "Baby Stumpy and the War in the Woods: Competing Frames of British Columbia Forests." *BC Studies* 130 (Summer): 41-68. <http://ojs.library.ubc.ca/index.php/bcstudies/article/viewFile/1581/1622>.

Sutcliffe, T., D. Edwards and D. Edwards. 2008. "Fisheries Licence Banks: A Start-Up Guide to Planning, Governance, Finance and Operations." Vancouver, BC: Ecotrust Canada. <http://ecotrust.ca/sites/all/files/LicenceBankToolkit.pdf>.

Thisfish. n.d. "Our Philosophy." <http://thisfish.info/about/philosophy>.

Tobias, T. 2000. "Chief Kerry's Moose: A Guidebook to Land Use and Occupancy Mapping, Research Design and Data Collection." Vancouver, BC: Union of B.C. Indian Chiefs and Ecotrust Canada. <http://www.ubcic.bc.ca/files/PDF/Tobias_whole.pdf>.

RESIDENT OWNERSHIP AND NEIGHBOURHOOD TRANSFORMATION

The Village at Market Creek

Tom Dewar

This is a story about neighbourhood change and resident ownership in the diverse neighbourhoods of southeastern San Diego. Like all strong community change stories, it builds on rather than ignores local history and context, while creating many new relationships, networks and shared practices. It also illustrates the value of an adaptive or trial-and-error approach rather than always sticking to the plan or following the rules. Like other stories in this collection, it is complex and hard to summarize — and still unfolding. In addition to providing a compelling example of taking residents and their aspirations seriously, it ripples with implications for both practice and policy in several fields, including local economic development, community organizing, city planning and development finance.

For our purposes here, the story begins in 1988 with the founding of the Jacobs Family Foundation (JFF). By 1997, the family members who ran the foundation had become dissatisfied with the results of their grant-making and started looking for new and better ways to carry out their mission. As one of Joe Jacobs's daughters, Meg, observed, "We were putting dribs and drabs of money and time here and there — but as the grassroots organizations got stronger, there were no apparent signs that the conditions in their communities were improving" (as cited in Korten 2009: 69). Looking back, former foundation president Jennifer Vanica explains that "We realized we needed to be more comprehensive in our approach, and to do that we had to be more microscopic in our geography" (as cited in Korten 2009: 69). In cooperation with local residents and organizations, JFF identified a dilapidated and dangerous industrial site as a priority for attention, as well as a symbol of the area's abandonment and lack of power. At the time work began, resident expectations were reportedly quite low, having been ignored so many times before.

The foundation bought the twenty-acre (eight hectare) site on which this eyesore stood and shortly thereafter moved their offices into the area. They also committed to listen to and plan with area residents. They hired an experienced community organizer, Roque Barros, and he, along with other staff and community residents, went out into the community to ask people directly what they wanted on that site, taking care to visit with residents from as many ethnic and racial groups as possible. Among the good ideas that surfaced, a local grocery store soon rose to the top of the list.

Work then began to focus on how to proceed in a way that kept residents in the middle of the multiple conversations underway, and most importantly, allowed them to have some "skin in the game," as Joe Jacobs, JFF's founder, liked to say. Out of this initial bold commitment came Market Creek Plaza (MCP), now a vibrant commercial and cultural centre with $34.8 million in retail sales operating on ten acres (four hectares) of the once abandoned factory site. MCP's first and largest tenant — a "Food 4 Less" grocery store — opened in 2001, and along with a range of other merchants, has since grown steadily in sales while hiring many area residents and using mainly local contractors. Over time, the initial vision and plan have gradually expanded, and been adapted, through a persistently community-driven planning and decision-making process. The vision and plan now embrace an updated Village at Market Creek on eighty acres (thirty-two hectares).[1]

An ownership and investment strategy was designed and implemented through which residents now have a 40 percent stake in the overall enterprise, with the goal of transferring all foundation assets and ownership of MCP over to community residents in the next twenty years or so. The ownership strategy was designed to ensure that all residents in the community were eligible to become investors and received solid investor education, developed by a Resident Ownership Team, to inform their decision about whether or not to invest. These and many other elements are described in more detail in the sections that follow.

The Market Creek story demonstrates that a strong and sustained process of citizen engagement can establish an agenda and action plan for achieving both profitable and equitable local development. At its heart is resident ownership, not only in economic terms but also in terms of many residents taking responsibility for themselves as well as their household, block and identity group. In this way residents come to own the community development process, and more importantly, they also own the results.

Much of the work to achieve these results is undertaken by community teams of various kinds and purposes. These teams range in size from 5 to 135 persons each.

Importantly, these groups are not permanent but come into and out of existence based on the work that needs to be done. In the overall mix of Market Creek, these various teams are constantly adjusting to the rhythms and realities of everyday life and are still busy doing a range of important tasks.

Only some dimensions of this complex story are highlighted here for the purpose of this case study. The first section presents the context within which the Village at Market Creek has emerged and moves forward. It highlights some aspects of the neighbourhood's demographics. Ideas and trends in the broader fields for which the experience here is relevant are also discussed.

The next section describes some key dimensions of the work, including the hands-on style of grant making adopted by JFF; the strong and persistent community engagement process it adopted; the development of an ownership structure which provided area residents with the opportunity to literally own a share of the project as small investors and an overall financial package that creatively gave Market Creek Plaza its legs and got it built and operating.

Finally, some key social and economic impacts of the Market Creek Plaza project are described including jobs, business development and sales and widening patterns of resident participation.

Each section includes brief discussions of some lessons being learned. These rely on the many interviews and meetings I had during and after several site visits over the period from 2010 to 2013. Finally, there are some concluding thoughts, including some implications of this still evolving story.

CONTEXT

San Diego is the eighth-most populous city in the United States and second-most populous city in California. It is located on the coast of the Pacific Ocean in Southern California, immediately adjacent to the Mexican border. The birthplace of California, San Diego is known for its mild year-round climate, natural deep-water harbour, extensive beaches, long association with the U.S. Navy and recent emergence as a healthcare and biotechnology centre. The population was estimated at about 1.3 million in 2012, an increase of about 7 percent from 2000.

In comparison with many U.S. cities of similar size, its land use patterns are lower density — almost suburban; and it has great disparities between wealthier and poor areas in terms of the condition of the housing stock. The low density brings weak links between any one area and the rest of the city (and its growing region), along with fewer amenities such as stores, parks, street lighting, traffic controls and public landscapes that reinforce safety, beauty and environmental quality (M. Bussell personal communication[2]).

In 2005, *Forbes Magazine* ranked San Diego as the fifth-wealthiest U.S. city

(Clemence 2005), based on the U.S. Census Bureau's American Community Survey, which measures median household income. At the same time about 10.6 percent of San Diego families and 14.6 percent of its population were below the poverty line, including 20.0 percent of those under age eighteen and 7.6 percent of those aged sixty-five or over. In 2006, San Diego was rated the fifth-best place to live in the "big cities" category by *Money Magazine*, based on weather, tax rates, median wages, population and real estate prices (CNN Money 2006). Last year, the San Diego County regional planning agency reported the city had a median household income of $45,733, and was relatively "safe" — in keeping with the 2010 *Forbes* report, which ranked San Diego as the ninth-safest city in the top-ten list of safest cities in the U.S., based on violent crime rates and traffic fatality rates (Levy 2010).

We can see that San Diego is relatively wealthy, safe and stable. This does not mean that disparities and persistent poverty are absent. The community area where the Market Creek story is unfolding demonstrates this. Originally named for the shape of its business improvement district, the Diamond Neighborhoods comprise ten different neighbourhood sub-areas, where residents total about 6.5 percent of the city's overall population and are much more diverse and much poorer than the overall profile of San Diego.

Asked to summarize the social dynamics of the area around Market Creek at the time JFF began its work there, one staff member of the Jacobs Center for Neighborhood Innovation (JCNI) described the two historically different sides of the Diamond area this way:

> One side had a long-standing base of working- and middle-class African Americans who bought their homes a long time ago, and mostly stayed. As some got older, they either sold or passed those homes on to family. On the other side there were newer residents from a growing variety of groups — they came in later, and in many cases also bought homes; but when the housing bubble burst, many were stuck or lost their homes. There have been many foreclosures in the Diamond [neighbourhoods] for those who bought later. (L. Islas personal communication)

Another resident added: "Overall, the different parts of the area didn't interact that much, and represent very different patterns of race and income, and age" (personal communication).

The broader context within which the Village at Market Creek emerged included some influential ideas about how community building, local economic development and even philanthropy should be done. Among the most important were: using a comprehensive approach to place-based community change, being an embedded funder and relying on an asset-building strategy. Beginning in the 1990s, comprehensive community initiatives (CCIs) arose as an ambitious strategy to address the challenges facing poor communities. In response to the apparent ineffectiveness of program-by-program approaches, CCIs were intended to do several things at once, with each strategy and activity ideally working in a complementary and strategic way. They aimed to implement a cluster of well-planned and appropriately-paced interventions in which the whole would be greater than the sum of its parts. Typically, they analyzed neighbourhood problems and assets, created a common plan, engaged community actors and identified a lead entity to coordinate all the partners. Each CCI sought to achieve multiple, interdependent results in areas such as local economic development, affordable housing, better employment and income, improved health and neighbourhood change. Getting such results clearly required effective collaboration between public, private and non-profit sectors (see Kubisch, Auspos, Brown and Dewar 2010; Torjman and Leviten-Reid 2003; Capraro 2012/2013).

Foundations were also drawn to comprehensive approaches because of the leadership or initiation roles they could play and the possibility to leverage their own limited resources to attract, inform and direct additional governmental and private sector support. This boundary-crossing style fit well with the chorus of development analysts and practitioners who pointed to the necessity of breaking down silos. These silos were widely viewed as a key part of the problem but difficult to change. To break through them, new collaborations and partnerships would be required to bring people, organizations and resources together in new ways.

Finally, and perhaps most fundamentally, the ideas of engaging residents and, to some extent at least, sharing power with them, were becoming more accepted. However, while the ideas were there and gaining support, actual practice on-the-ground had not caught up with them. Jennifer Vanica, president of JFF at the time Market Creek Plaza was designed and took its first steps, recalls:

> We were all very influenced by these ideas that were circulating at the time. And in fact, we wanted to not just do them but do them better.... The commitment to a particular place imposes a kind of focus, and interestingly, it allows for more comprehensive approaches ... because you see the different aspects of your strategic vision playing out in close proximity, and can better watch, listen and learn as you go along (personal communication).

KEY DIMENSIONS OF THE WORK AND LESSONS ALONG THE WAY

Let's now explore the most important dimensions of all this work. In doing so I want to consider not only what makes it citizen-led and innovative, but also to discuss what made it possible. Are there some key practices, and if so, what helped them get started, take root, and grow?

A family foundation with a focus and sense of urgency

As already described, JFF is a foundation that uses a hands-on grantmaking strategy with a geographic focus in the Diamond Neighborhoods of southeastern San Diego. In 1988, Joseph and Violet Jacobs founded JFF with funds set aside when the family business, the Jacobs Engineering Group, went public. In its first ten years JFF focused mainly on grantmaking and providing technical assistance to community-based non-profits located overseas. Starting in 1998, JFF began to align its financial assets more closely with its philanthropic mission by investing in ventures such as Urban America, a pioneering real estate firm that specialized in acquisition and development of commercial centres for inner-city markets. Inspired by their work, and "dissatisfied with the effects of its grantmaking strategies abroad," JFF leadership decided the foundation needed to change its mission and strategy and to focus instead on place-based community development through direct investment (V. Jacobs personal communication). In this way, they believed they would have more control over the impact of their investments.

Originally headquartered in Pasadena, California, where the engineering firm was located, JFF relocated to San Diego where the Jacobs daughters then lived. One of JFF's initial projects in the Diamond Neighborhoods involved the Elementary Institute of Science (EIS), an organization that offers after-school technology and science learning programs for children and is located at the intersection of Euclid and Market Streets — the heart of the Diamond. JFF worked with EIS to expand its efforts and played a key role in helping it move out of a "two-bedroom ramshackle house in a run-down neighbourhood" into a new $6 million state-of-the-art building. It also created a $2 million endowment aided by a large anchor grant from JFF (D. Anderson personal communication). This shift from relying on a grant-to-grant strategy to having an endowment, stable partners, ample space and a growing reputation as a regional resource was highly valued by EIS leadership and was described by them as being "transformative." The process and degree of change reportedly also inspired JFF leadership.

Soon after, JFF board and staff were meeting in a community centre when the subject of the abandoned factory site "right across the street" came up. After some preliminary research, JFF leadership decided to buy the site and publicly committed to work closely with the community and find something useful to do there. This set the stage for what was to come and allowed for a transition from what JFF had been doing to what it set out to do next in the Village at Market Creek. Its style became very similar to what has come to be known as an "embedded funder" (Brown et al. 2007: 1–2).

After 1999, nearly all of JFF's resources and efforts were focused on the Diamond Neighborhoods, mostly on the Market Creek Plaza project. They hired an organizer, started circulating through and getting to know the community and began looking for ways to "catalyze community change from within" (J. Vanica personal communication). JFF also enlisted a team of community residents to survey their neighbours about the community's priorities. Over eight hundred interviews were conducted, in four languages, and the information gathered framed discussions about next steps. These discussions became the basis for the community vision for Market Creek Plaza. Diamond Neighborhoods residents wanted more amenities in the area, "just like any other community." They also wanted jobs and better income. A top-ten list developed by listening to residents included priorities such as a grocery store, pharmacy and some restaurants.

Roque Barros, the lead organizer, recalls these initial discussions with area residents as both difficult and very informative. In some cases, racial tensions needed to be addressed. The process of community engagement had begun:

> We had streets where on one side there were Latinos, and on the other were the Samoans. We had to do something different and so recruited individuals from each group to join the outreach team, threw block parties, and started working directly to build new relationships and open up conversations. (R. Barros personal communication)

About that time, JFF's mission was amended to include "resident ownership of neighborhood change." To carry out the growing variety of work, JFF created a group of complementary organizations — often called the "Jacobs Network." It includes both non-profit and for-profit entities: JFF, JCNI, Diamond Management Inc. and Market Creek Partners — all of which are corporate structures; and Market Creek Community Ventures (to hold social enterprises), the Jacobs Community Development Group (a network of all Jacobs-related groups) and The Village at Market Creek (the project area name that came to include all the LLCs). All the entities in the network collaborate on Market Creek Plaza. Through it, for example, DMI and Market Creek Partners can acquire properties, build and subcontract construction, provide property management, run security and maintenance services as well as tenant leasing, business development services and broker property sales.

At present, JFF's largest grants are to JCNI, which was established as an operating foundation. This means it carries out work itself rather than making grants to others, like most traditional foundations would do. It's worth noting that most participants and informed observers rarely distinguish between JFF and JCNI even though JCNI does much of the hands-on work and JFF funds it. JFF and JCNI share a board and senior staff. As the project evolved over time, if something needed doing and there was no clear partner available to work with, JFF and JCNI simply created an organization to get it done. This makes the Jacobs Centre, with its many affiliated organizations, a very busy place, and working for Jacobs a "very full-time job," in the words of one community team leader. Someone working for Jacobs "cannot just be involved … on a casual or partial basis because … something always seems to be going on" (B. Bravo personal communication).

The sunset provision

Unlike most foundations, JFF is a limited-life foundation. From the outset, Joe Jacobs wanted it to go out of business in "one generation." At some point, the bylaws were formally amended to reflect this. Current plans are for the foundation to sunset around 2030 (Ostrower 2012). Over time several reasons for the sunset have emerged. "There is more risk taking, and greater focus. And let's face it, more urgency" (J. Vanica personal communication). While perpetual foundations cautiously manage their portfolio toward long-term investments, JFF can more aggressively manage its assets to leverage them more fully during the period of its operations as well as invest to build capacity that will outlast JFF's lifespan and protect resident interests. Pursuit of more leverage also means accepting increased risk in investments, such as an atypically high proportion of the Foundation's endowment held in stocks and bonds — about 50 percent. In addition, JFF also holds a high proportion of its assets in direct ownership of Diamond Neighborhoods properties (partner funder personal communication).

From the outset, the core strategy has been that as JFF spends down its own assets it will gradually build up self-generating systems of wealth creation. Thus, when JFF sunsets, its remaining assets will be turned over to the community and properties such as the Market Creek Plaza will transfer to self-management by neighbourhood organizations and institutions. From the outset, the Jacobs Network has been working through the leadership of its various members, including the foundation, neighbourhood resident teams and advisors to craft a succession process and continue building essential institutional capacity to support the work after JFF transitions out (Jacobs Centre for Neighbourhood Innovation 2010, 2011; R. Barros personal communication).

Thus, an important lesson being learned is that once JFF and its network committed to the Diamond, and to this set of strategies, it stayed the course. It has consistently and clearly communicated its commitment to the Diamond community and beyond. The sunset provision has been a decisive factor, bringing with it both focus and some urgency.

Deep and sustained engagement with the community

Even before JFF purchased its first property, it sought input from residents on the types of projects that would benefit the neighbourhood (Robinson 2005). At the centre of this community engagement process are community teams that come (and go) as the necessity to carry out important tasks dictates. Each team identifies and uses a range of individual, group and cultural assets. They also find and enlist allies to support their efforts. If necessary, they develop innovative new structures, such as cultural festivals and investor education workshops, to keep the work moving ahead. Specific work teams were formed around outreach, art and design, construction, business development and leasing, ownership development and childcare. "They are looking for specific contributions of time, experience, talent and connections" (L. Leilua personal communication). In this way, residents come to own parts of the work and understand their individual roles and importance in it. One young and active team leader noted:

> What feels most right about these teams is that we are ones doing the work. It is not about being recruited to help others, or agree to an existing agenda. No, that's not it. *We* make the agenda, and in carrying it out, we have to think about what we can and will do for ourselves, as individuals and as a group. (J. Venegas personal communication)

Thus, ownership here not only represents economic power or "buying a piece of the block," as the initial public offering campaign (discussed in the following pages) promoted; it also represents ways of doing things together that require a wide base of residents — each of whom is willing to join with others in actually doing the work. Roque Barros talks about "circles of ten" as the approach he liked to use here:

> It scales with everyday life. Most of us know about that many people and are in regular contact with them on a daily or weekly basis. If we ask people to work in those circles, it is simply easier, more comfortable, and yes, more effective at what needs doing in community building. ... Roles for team members include getting the word out about issues, events, and opportunities; identifying shared concerns and then developing alternative solutions; learning to listen to each other and, sometimes, helping surface tensions that would otherwise stay below the surface. (personal communication)

He also relied on a ninety-day cycle of "doing everything" so that people would not feel their work was endless or only vaguely related to results. Rather, it was driven by a succession of ninety-day planning cycles where each period has a solid action plan and a clear process for getting it done. Once its work is completed, a new ninety-day cycle could (and almost always would) begin. In this way residents stayed focused and busy — and accountable — but not fixated on long-term or abstract goals. Rather, they were focused on shorter-term, doable tasks and shared results.

In addition to these teams, the Village at Market Creek has large quarterly meetings. These are also an important element of the community engagement, providing an opportunity to present and discuss issues, report on progress and build shared vision. They are reportedly welcoming and well run, providing food, childcare, language translation and an opportunity to mix with a wide variety of other residents and community groups.

Thus we see that people and groups come together in this work around both large (such as quarterly meetings) and small tables (such as community teams and circles of ten). Both are important, but the smaller groups of people seem more able to help establish shared norms, work through disagreements and hold one another accountable (Block 2008). Through face-to-face conversation and increasing trust, many people will take their first steps toward becoming public voices and actors willing and able to express themselves outside their private, personal worlds and learning to listen and learn from others in a range of forums (Morgan 1984; Sennett 2012). One team leader observed:

> We knew we were just beginners. That was the point, right? And yet, we also knew it would not help if there was too much mumbo jumbo. We set the norms, and wanted people to be direct, clear, and patient. There was simply no other way to do it, and we had to be willing to ask for that ... and the great thing is, that is what we finally got. (personal communication)

Over the course of the first seven to eight years, nearly three thousand individuals participated in the Community Design and Planning Team and well over a thousand participated in fifty-two different working teams (Jacobs Centre for Neighbourhood Innovation 2009). As noted, the team process is fluid, with teams coming and going, based on work that needs doing. A value at work is not to waste residents' time and energy but put it to good use for as long as it takes to get the job done, but no longer. Neighbours organizing other neighbours brought residents into land-use planning, leasing, marketing, research, advocacy and ownership design. They helped shape the overall project through large visioning meetings and smaller strategy sessions. They hosted and went to living-room meetings in private homes, interviewed potential commercial tenants and contractors, helped develop strategies for getting applicants to apply for newly available jobs earmarked for residents and designed and carried out community surveys.

To support this range and level of resident participation, JCNI and community teams offered child care, food and meals, transportation, neighbour escorts and informal reminders as well as a great deal of necessary time and patience. This support was key. One mother of four children observed:

> JCNI has really encouraged me to participate. They built an indoor play area with a big glass window so that we can see our kids. Also, we talked about which hours would work best. I can't make afternoons because I start picking up my kids at 2:30. Also they provide food so I can bring my kids and they can eat. (personal communication)

These early demonstrations of putting residents at the centre of the community-building process and related decision-making helped set a standard of resident inclusion. Since then, participation has continued to grow and, just as importantly, newcomers to the process and new arrivals to the neighbourhood have often joined in. As Peter Pennekamp and Anne Focke (2013: 25) have aptly noted, in community democracy "change comes at the 'speed of trust,' and the development of trust is not linear."

JCNI and community leadership worked hard to value residents' time and knowledge and reduce barriers to involvement. As part of this commitment, JCNI paid stipends to some neighbourhood residents. Some community team members, such as those involved in outreach, who worked between ten and fifteen hours a week, were paid $6.50 and, later, $8.00 per hour to compensate them for their valuable local knowledge and problem-solving skills dedicated to the project (Jacobs Centre for Neighbourhood Innovation 2010, 2011). This practice of paying stipends to residents is controversial. Clearly, it does value residents and their experience. On the other hand, some believe it can create dependency or even cheapen resident involvement by lifting some people and their contributions above others, while others maintain that it is entirely appropriate to compensate people for their efforts, especially when it goes above and beyond the norm, as with team leaders and conveners (community coordinators meeting February 2013). Be that as it may, JCNI has recently discontinued resident stipends.

Importance of a high-profile core project — and visible results

Participants and observers agree that Market Creek Plaza has been the showcase project for both the Jacobs Network and community. As the first significant piece of retail activity in the Diamond in recent memory, MCP faced many hurdles. Now operating for almost ten years, it has provided practical and symbolic gains on both economic and social aspects of its "double bottom line." Completed in 2005 and anchored by the new, full-service Food 4 Less grocery store so many wanted, MCP has been successful in a number of ways. In retail sales, MCP has met or passed its target annual goal of $31 million every year since 2008 and most recently reported sales of over $34 million for 2011, which is down from a high of over $40 million in 2009 (see Figure 8-1). This ability to consistently meet or exceed the sales target keeps the project viable and growing.[3]

In employment terms, MCP now provides 92 full-time and 121 part-time jobs, of which 144 (68 percent) are held by Diamond area residents. The nearby Jacobs Center employers (including JCNI, Diamond Management Inc. and Market Creek Events and Venues) together have provided 63 full-time and 22 part-time jobs, of which 35 (41 percent) were held by area residents (as of February 2012). The fact that 91 percent of the initial Food 4 Less store staff came from the neighbourhood sent an important message about tangible benefits of "all that community engagement," and that most of the store staff continue to be local is clearly important.

The vision for business development at the outset of MCP roughly followed a rule of thirds with a goal of one-third local entrepreneurs, one-third franchises with potential for local ownership working in products and services sought by residents and one-third national/regional tenants. MCP has seen eighteen businesses open since 2001 with ten still open. Of those still open, three are locally owned and operated (two restaurants and a business services company), three are local franchises (two restaurants and a mobile phone store), three are national companies (Food 4 Less, coffee shop and a bank), and one is an outlet for a regional energy utility. Restaurants thus account for four enterprises that remain open and four that have closed. Of the total of eight businesses that closed, six were locally owned and operated and two were local franchises. This all means MCP has made progress but has fallen short on its ultimate goals for local ownership and franchises. It also reminds

Figure 8.1 Aggregate Economic Activity of Market Creek Plaza, 2004–2011

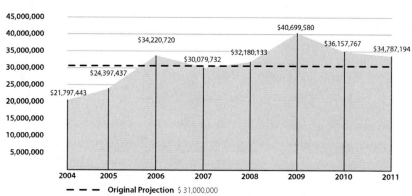

Note: This chart presents retail sales figures self-reported by the individual tenants. A few tenants in MCP no longer provide them so the total is underestimated. Two additional tenants — a Wells Fargo bank branch (which has reported steady growth in local deposits) and a utility bill payment centre — are not reflected in the figures presented.
Source: JCNI

us how difficult it is for small businesses to survive, much less thrive, especially in periods of economic downturn.

Contracting and employment goals for the initial construction of the plaza, as well as for its ongoing maintenance and related services, included the ambitious goal of 65 percent of jobs going to residents. In support of this goal, a formal structure (named the Construction Collaborative) was set up to work directly in association with contractors to help recruit, train and retain area residents as employees. Contractors who were not willing to work with the collaborative were disqualified from bidding on work. Further, an employment development team was formed and worked closely with Food 4 Less district management, union leaders and local employment programs. Their cooperative action helped achieve the 91 percent resident employment rate for initial jobs. Other businesses at MCP also relied on these practices and outreach to achieve local hires, including Diamond Management, which provides security, maintenance and property management to the Village at Market Creek.

Social enterprises were another goal, with Where the World Meets (which provided local entrepreneurs and artists with a way to showcase their products) and Writerz Blok (which began as a graffiti-arts program and has now expanded into mural projects and a line of urban wear) in the mix, although not yet at the level originally set as the goal. Another social business, Market Creek Events and Venues (MCEV), is a banquet and conference centre that opened in 2008 and has shown steady growth. In addition to employment for residents, it also provides training in the food and hospitality industries, along with strong working ties to key employers in the region. As a "social enterprise," MCEV started out with considerable support from grants, but has gradually increased its earned income and reduced its dependence on external funding. In 2010, for example, MCEV had $1.4 million in revenue, which was up 8 percent from the previous year and accounted for 66 percent of its total budget. Its goal is for earned income to cover 80 percent of its total budget, with remaining 20 percent to come from training grants. Other social enterprises in the village, such as Diamond Management and Writerz Blok, are also projected to make similar transitions and are each making progress.

The physical design and beauty of MCP are important results as well. MCP has become a major arts and culture destination for the city and entire San Diego region, offering a five-hundred-seat outdoor amphitheatre (with a stage that rises and falls according to water levels of the creek running through the Village), a festival park, a series of tapestries representing the various cultures in the community and numerous murals — including one with a tree of life composed of individually-coloured tiles each done by a child living in the neighbourhood and another called "community faces" featuring twenty-seven residents who have made significant contributions to the community. The art and traditions of the Native people who originally resided along Chollas Creek, in the heart of the Village at Market Creek, are also represented. The Jacobs Center building now has its own gallery space and a seemingly endless array of exhibits and art on display in its corridors, meetings room and offices. It also hosts many festivals, celebrations and other events.

The Community Development—Initial Public Offering

In early 2006, after six years of persistent effort and much negotiation, the State of California approved the sale of securities for Market Creek Partners, LLC, the company that owns MCP. With that approval, the Community Development — Initial Public Offering (CD-IPO) as it became known, could legally offer ownership shares in MCP to Diamond area residents. There were many issues that had to be addressed along the way.

First, who could invest? In preparation for the IPO, the Ownership Design Team decided it would be: a) residents of the Diamond Neighborhoods; b) people who owned businesses or worked in the Diamond; and c) people who volunteered time working with an area non-profit.

Second, the Design Team also had to demonstrate this offering would be fair to proposed investors, in the sense that it would provide enough good information to prospective investors that it wouldn't take unfair advantage of them. Since investors here have fewer assets than is typical, this was a challenge. Eventually, the team negotiated what became known as the 10-10-10 plan. That is, anyone could invest up to 10 percent of their income, no matter what it was; no more than 10 percent of their net worth (excluding big items such as homes, cars and retirement savings) and no more than $10,000 per person.

Third, they had to determine how much of the total investment would be made available to resident owners. The team decided that 20 percent of the total equity in the overall project would be ownership-qualified or available to residents. This meant that up to $500,000 was reserved for investments by the Diamond Community Investors (DCI), a partnership group of 425 community investors from the Diamond area neighbourhoods. In addition to the 20 percent set aside for resident investors, another 20 percent was to be held by the Neighborhood Unity Foundation (NUF), which operates as a resident-led and resident-benefitting grantmaker. As its capacity grows, it contributes to the sunset strategy, which relies on community capacity taking an ever greater role as JFF gradually exits. In addition to this total of 40 percent for residents, the remaining 60 percent was set aside for the Jacobs Center for Neighborhood Innovation (see Table 8-1), which allowed JFF to protect its interests and those of its charitable partners until they were refinanced out.

Table 8-1. Sources of Funding and Levels of Investment in Market Creek Plaza (MCP)

	Amount	Ownership
Diamond Community Investors (425 investors) (DCI)	$500,000	20%
Jacobs Centre for Neighbourhood Innovation (JCNI)	$1,400,000	56%
Diamond Management, Inc. (DMI)	$100,000	4%
Neighbourhood Unity Foundation (NUF)	$500,000	20%
Total financing eligible for ownership stake	$2,500,000	100%
PRI financing from other foundations	$3,250,000	Not eligible
Jacobs Family Foundation (JFF)	$2,000,000	Not eligible
Additional JCNI	$750,000	Not eligible
New Markets Tax Credit Program	$15,000,000	Not eligible
Total project funding	$23,500,000	

Data sources: Jacobs Center for Neighborhood Innovation (2009); J. Vanica personal communication.

In designing how benefits would be allocated from profits in MCP, the team decided to follow a rule of thirds: one-third for individual benefit, one-third for community benefit and one-third for reinvestment for long-term sustainability and ongoing development. NUF provides a mechanism both for community ownership (through holding an ownership stake in Market Creek) and for ongoing community benefit. Since its start, NUF has distributed all received benefits back to the community through grants.

Each investor from DCI could purchase shares in the development for $10, with a minimum purchase of twenty shares. Investors could opt into a payment plan for the investment and non-profits and churches could also invest in the project. Investments were capped at $10,000 and the average actual investment was $1,176. The year following the close of the IPO, DCI participants became eligible for a preferred return on investment of up to 10 percent (Green 2006). The investments from DCI were placed into the commercial centre's infrastructure, but not directly into the businesses operating there, which reduced some of the investment risk as long as property values held constant.

A distinctive aspect of ownership here is the principle of one investor/one vote. This was established for the purpose of stakeholder representation. That is, no one among the 425 members of DCI "could have a greater voice than any other" (G. Harris personal communication).

Once the IPO was announced, resident members of the Ownership Design Team played a key role in recruiting their neighbours to participate as potential investors. A former staff member central to the ownership process used here noted:

> Since members of the Ownership Team helped design it [IPO], they were better able to explain what the risks and benefits could be. Midway through the offering period, church networks in the neighbourhood also began to get involved, along with other resident groups who were unaffiliated with Jacobs. Interest slowly overcame caution, and people came forward. On the last day of the offering period, there was a line around the block. (G. Harris personal communication)

Jacobs met both its participation and investment goals, with 425 investors and $500,000 in investment. Materials given to potential investors clearly outlined the risks: the Jacobs-related company was new, profits were not guaranteed, the investment was long-term and it was possible that shares could not be sold unless the potential buyer also met investor qualifications. On the other hand, if the shopping centre makes a profit, the investment contract dictates that annual dividends would be paid first to DCI through a claim to the first $50,000 in profits, which represented a 10 percent preferred return. JCNI and NUF had the second claim with another 10 percent preferred return, followed by JFF and DMI for a 7 percent preferred return. Any profits beyond $205,000 would be dispersed equally among all shareholders.

In 2005, prior to the close of the IPO, MCP earned a profit of $128,000. In 2006, the IPO closed and MCP earned a profit of $99,855. In 2007, the net income of MCP was $111,236 (Jacobs Center for Neighborhood Innovation 2009), which allowed for a full dividend of 10 percent for resident investors. Eighty-two of them decided to reinvest in future community development projects (G. Harris personal communication). Since then, shares in MCP provided dividends to neighbourhood investors for a second time in 2008 (when 147 investors chose to reinvest their earnings from dividends), and again in 2009, 2010 and 2011.

It is still too early to know if the IPO will build an individual investor's net worth in the long run. However, there are some short- and long-term financial benefits worth noting. In the short term, the investment provides annual cash dividends. While the monetary amount is rather small — for a $1,000 investment, the dividend is $100 — it yields a higher rate of return (10 percent) than offered by most other savings vehicles now available, has only a moderately higher risk than a savings account and much less risk than the stock market. In the longer term, the large investment of time and energy in the education and personal development of prospective investors will pay off in ways that go beyond this specific ownership opportunity. One of the limitations of the IPO as an asset-building vehicle for low- and moderate-income individuals is the upper limit of $10,000 on the investment, which means it cannot compare to the equity that homeownership could provide.

However, the greatest promise of these shares is not as a substitute for homeownership but as an asset-diversification wealth-creation strategy. It also ensures that local people have a vested interest in the success of the venture.

It is important to note the decision by 35 percent of resident investors to reinvest. This seems to show a preference for asset building through savings over short-term consumption. The decision by many to reinvest caused the creation of a new tool called the Community Investment Fund. It was set up to receive these dividends. The reinvested money is held until the investors decide together the best use for it within the larger project, the Village at Market Creek. They are looking ahead and beyond MCP to other prospects. This commitment to long-term neighbourhood improvement through local investment and shared decision-making is perhaps the biggest news here. Reinvestment directly into the community is not mandatory and does not determine project growth, but the extent of it thus far is heartening. Expansion of this kind of voluntary investment is directly tied to expansion of wealth in the community.

Another dimension of the work to get this IPO approved bears mention. When JFF first began pursuing MCP, project risk was a major deterrent for the traditional financial institutions approached (B. Bravo, G. Harris personal communications February 2013). In fact, Jacobs approached ten banks and not one was willing to invest in MCP. When the Jacobs team began to pursue retail tenants (which would have strengthened the project to help it qualify for more traditional financing), no potential tenants would return their calls even though the Jacobs team (including key advisors) had over thirty years of development experience. Jacobs decided to move forward to purchase the property anyway, taking on the majority of risks and costs at the initial stage of the project (G. Harris personal communication).

Facing this response, a more traditional developer would likely try to move a project forward with little of its own money down and a long escrow. But here JFF leveraged its own assets (V. Jacobs personal communication). Once JFF purchased the property outright, more tenants were willing to sign on and JFF was able to redistribute its resources as other program related investment (PRI) partners came to the table. Once the Food 4 Less was up and running, income from the store could cover debt service. This willingness to take risks and go it alone, if necessary, is a major contribution from Jacobs. Unfortunately, it is not typically available, especially at the outset of these projects when it would make the most difference.

As momentum grew, it became possible to put together an overall financial package. In addition to the Jacobs/DMI program related investments (PRIs) amounting to 18 percent of the total, other foundations' PRIs contributed 14 percent and community capital (combination of DCI and NUF) provided 4 percent. But the biggest financial contribution — 64% — came from the federal government's New Markets Tax Credit (NMTC) Program.

By providing 64 percent of the total financing for MCP, the NMTC Program played a critical role in developing this project and its market-driven approach to resident ownership. One project advisor with JFF called NMTC a "saviour" of the MCP project and its financial strategy, adding that "these credits helped to keep the cost of money low, and keeping the cost of money low keeps more money in the community, the projects more profitable, and ultimately [makes] resident ownership possible" (personal communication). Indeed, Market Creek Plaza has been widely cited as a success of the NMTC program (Bystry 2005). In addition to the direct investments listed above, Wells Fargo Bank also became an investor here and opened a branch in Market Creek Plaza.

Thus, we see here another lesson being learned through the Village at Market Creek. Ownership is an attractive and popular goal. To make it real, however, takes hard work, high quality legal and technical assistance and persistence. The goal must be translated into specific and realistic steps that can be clearly understood by prospective owners. To make ownership widely available, some ongoing education and peer learning is essential. All this is done to ensure good choices rather than to promote ownership for all. Here, it is clear that ownership is about much more than having an economic share in Market Creek Partners, as important as that is. It is really about taking responsibility for what happens.

Art and culture as ways to build community

Few areas of teamwork in the Village achieved the kinds of impact that organizing around art and cultural heritage have, so they warrant special mention. Barros recalls:

> We discovered early on that cultural heritage and talent were a great way to approach people, and to invite them into our circles of connection. For many, going to another housing or a jobs meeting is not a great attraction. If they have been around a while, those kinds of meetings sound a bit tired. Plus, they were not very knowledgeable or expert on those subjects, so when they came, they basically had to sit and listen to others. (personal communication February 2013)

Another JFF staff member, Lisette Islas, added that many residents who might otherwise be shy or cautious about getting too involved may be more willing if approached in the right way:

> If you invite them out around their heritage, or artistic traditions, they have something to offer. Many are able and willing to contribute. Plus, there is tremendous variety of people skills and cultural traditions in this community. Too often all this richness has been kept below the surface,

or made available only on rare occasions. We were asking for it, and rapidly developing different ways to celebrate and feature it around the Diamond, and even across the city.... They like it, and we all benefit from it. (personal communication)

So, for example, organizers and community team leaders made special efforts to address the different cultural groups (at last count there were sixteen distinctly different groups) in the Diamond Neighborhoods by inviting each ethnicity to host a cultural event at the Jacobs offices, which has included sharing its distinctive food, clothing and traditions. Indeed, any visitor to the Jacobs Centre and adjacent MCP can see the extent to which art, murals, festivals, gatherings and artistic skills have been incorporated directly into the life of the community, as well as into the design of its buildings and public spaces.

A recent national learning exchange on resident-centred community building was held at the Jacobs Centre in 2012 and included JCNI staff and area residents. The findings of that exchange reinforce the community-building approaches being used here. For example, it is clear that residents want to contribute directly to doing the work and not just plan it; they enjoy working in teams provided those teams are productive and well-run. To get a variety of residents strongly engaged, you have to meet them where they are, engage them around things they know about and like to do and take the necessary time to listen, learn and gradually build relationships of trust (Kubisch, Auspos, Taylor and Dewar 2013).

Local government support

Throughout the life of the Village at Market Creek, support from the City of San Diego and its various agencies was sought. In February 2004, for example, the San Diego City Council approved a pilot village program for five neighbourhood areas across the city as an incentive-driven revitalization effort, and Market Creek was chosen. In order to qualify, pilot villages were required to meet certain "smart growth" principles such as having a transit stop within half a mile, a mixed-use development plan and population density minimums. In theory, the five designated pilot villages were all eligible for incentives including: (1) infrastructure upgrades or replacements; (2) deferral on fees; (3) funding for extras such as handicapped access, rebates on property taxes and revolving loan funds and (4) assistance with initiatives such as putting utility cables underground and affordable housing. All agreed these would be welcome in the Diamond. However, several Jacobs staff members, along with community leaders, told me that although Jacobs and Market Creek were "always promised" this help from the city, nothing much happened.

No one can deny the importance of local government resources and structure. They play a primary role in defining the local development process, and will continue to do so. The scale of resources the city controls makes it essential to keep trying to engage local government staff and elected officials. Among other issues, the city is often the go-between linking the community and key resources at the state and federal levels. The quality of relationships and opportunities for support of neighbourhood plans and projects cycles up and down, based not just on laws, habits and organizational momentum but also on the people in charge and their mindsets, as well as the incentives (such as tax and housing laws) that affect them. Clearly there is more to gain by working with local government rather than in isolation.

Looking ahead

In 2012, The Village at Market Creek received LEED Silver certification from the U.S. Green Building Council[4] for neighbourhood development. The ninety-acre (thirty-six hectare) area, which includes the entire Village, was cited for its walkability and transit connections, energy savings concepts and environmentally-sustainable practices. According to Charles Davis, Director of Project Development at JCNI, JFF spent about $90,000 to achieve LEED designation and produce planning documents to attract investors, guide developers and apply for grants related to this designation. JFF owns fifty-four acres (twenty-two hectares) of the master-planned area and hopes to eventually build a thousand housing units and 515,000 square feet in retail, office and industrial development. More than nine acres (four hectares) of undeveloped space around Chollas Creek are designated for preservation in their natural condition.

Through all of this, we see how the village continues to evolve and adapt. Sometimes, outside actors such as the city, catch up or change as well. Some partners, once only watching, get more interested as progress is made and new opportunities emerge. Importantly, the next phase of the Village at Market Creek will also allow a return to some of the residents' top priorities, such as affordable housing, that were part of earlier plans but had to be put on hold because of the economic downturn. Possible next projects will also be able to take advantage of continuing growth and momentum in sales, employment, business development and expanding ridership to and through the public transit stop at the centre of the Plaza.

CONCLUSIONS

The Village at Market Creek illustrates the value of strong community engagement and shared decision-making, as well as innovation and informed risk-taking. The primary catalyst has been and continues to be the Jacobs Family Foundation. The work has not only been resident-led, it has been designed, co-produced and accountable to area citizens. Much has been accomplished and much remains to be done. Over time a network of community teams and associations, as well as strategic partners and investors, have joined forces to transform abandoned industrial land into a now thriving (and still expanding) commercial and cultural centre.

Looking forward, it is clear that the Village at Market Creek and the Jacobs network have now moved into a new phase. Several leading staff members and advisors to the foundation describe the current moment as either the "end of the beginning" or the "beginning of the middle," in light of JFF's sunset provision. Challenges ahead will likely centre around issues of sustainability and how relevant organizational capacity and strategic investments can be found or created, both from the inside and outside the community to support the work ahead. As community priorities are revisited and strategies to achieve them rethought, it will be necessary to carefully look at who is at the Market Creek table, how and why they stay there, and what will be in it for them as the work unfolds. Further, the Jacobs network, like all community change efforts, will be under pressure to find more ways for leadership to be passed on to others, especially to new and younger residents (Mguni and Caistor-Arendar 2012).

This next stage also brings new leadership with the arrival of new JFF president and chief executive officer, Reginald Jones. In his introductory message to the Diamond community, he said:

> Over fifteen years ago, the Jacobs family and engaged residents had a vision for our community. It was an innovative plan for the Diamond Neighborhoods, driven by partnership and a community-led vision that would result in positive economic and social change. It has been an extraordinary journey, and it is not over. As with all journeys, unforeseen obstacles arise, and course corrections are needed in response to changing environments. This is where we are now, armed with a renewed commitment toward reaching our destination, as well as a refreshed excitement for this next leg of our journey. ("President's Introductory Message," *JCNI Newsletter*, Dec 2012)

The end of the beginning is a good time to reflect on some implications of the Village at Market Creek story for where and how the new economy is now emerging. Like other cases in this collection, this is not merely a story about local economic development. Nor is it a story of strong community building alone. Rather, these two stories are combined in ways that become aligned with resources and aspirations, which over time can change in ways that cause strains on governance and management. All of this requires a steadfast commitment to certain values and practices, such as keeping citizens at the centre and ensuring they have ongoing authority over what happens.

The work that runs through the Village at Market Creek builds on but also goes beyond local assets. It organizes residents to achieve collective power and coherent plans and then pursues these in pragmatic ways that are more concerned with results than with protocols. Like Market Creek Plaza, the next economy should provide work where there is work that most needs doing. This requires a community infrastructure that includes a range of organizations and leadership, each complementing the others. In addition, this infrastructure must be adaptable and able to align diverse interests and address persistent conflicts within the community while playing an active intermediary role between residents, their community-based organizations and working partners, on the one hand, and various outside interests on the other. The Village at Market Creek demonstrates persuasively that doing all this can bring concrete results: a widening base of support, a growing sphere of influence and ultimately, more wealth for both households and the community.

Interestingly, the people of Diamond Neighborhoods insist they have not developed a model, nor do they aspire to be one. Rather, they believe they are engaged in a process and set of strategies that keep evolving. It all requires innovation, a commitment to learn together and a willingness to take risks. As a result, the work here has been gradual, and not without setbacks and course corrections. Its time horizon and commitments extend beyond the attention span of most governmental or philanthropic initiatives. JFF has been patient and has worked with and for the community. It has been steadfast even when things got difficult.

Partners outside the neighbourhood have also been enlisted and play important roles as investors, advocates and allies. Many describe the profound ways in which they have been influenced and challenged by their direct involvement with the Village at Market Creek. "It has changed the landscape in San Diego," said one. When key work was identified for which no willing or able partner could be found quickly, the Jacobs network has often been willing to go it alone. This tendency, along with the abundance of process (such as larger and longer meetings, multiple consultations and residents being brought into key decisions) has put some outside partners off and slowed things down. Reflecting on resident-centred process and its repercussions, Jennifer Vanica notes:

> It's consistent with the saying that to go fast, you go alone; but to go far, you must go together. I never saw our progress in this work hung up by too much resident engagement and good community process. Sure, it got to some people, but the benefits were clearly there. (personal communication)

From the outset, JFF leadership has made sure the overall approach and plans are genuinely comprehensive, place-based and focused (Capraro 2013). To implement and adapt them, the Jacobs network has used a learn-as-you-go style that is highly dependent on building a learning culture. It also requires multiple forums that are open, safe and well run. To manage all this complexity and deal with the seemingly endless stream of emerging challenges has required a decentralized or horizontal style of leadership, one that fits the situation rather than some organizational model (Cabaj 2012).

The approach taken here not only recognizes cultural and racial diversity; it engages and features that diversity in its development. In many areas, such as arts and culture, this has featured a rich diversity of cultural traditions and made them into a key resource. Involving residents as ongoing partners requires a commitment to developing multiple engagement approaches and continuous outreach. Bringing residents inside the complexities and tough decisions of the work helps forge authentic ownership of both implementation and results. Partnering with residents in meaningful ways expands their perception of their own capacities and encourages them to undertake further organizing, policy advocacy and community-change work.

Building community ownership in areas such as Diamond Neighborhoods also requires anticipating and dealing effectively with race issues. They are embedded deeply into our society and institutions and, in the words of one community leader, they "cannot be worked around — they must be worked through!" (L. Leilua personal communication). Indeed, the approach here demonstrates the viability of ownership strategies that create new and more inclusive structures. Having a greater stake, or "skin in the game," as Joe Jacobs used to say, helps keep citizens directly involved and further, can increase income equality (of the kind generated here) and help promote further local development. All of this reinforces the idea that greater equity can be the basis for the next economy (Truehaft, Blackwell and Pastor 2011).

Notes

1. A map of the Village at Market Creek can be found at <thevillageatmarketcreek.com/>.
2. All references to personal communication are for interviews conducted in February, 2013.
3. The data presented in this paragraph were provided by Steve Aldana, JCNI Documentation Analyst.
4. U.S. Green Building Council is a national non-profit organization that has developed Leadership in Energy and Environmental Design (LEED) certification — a set of rating systems for the design, construction, operation and maintenance of green buildings, homes and neighbourhoods.

References

Block, P. 2008. *Community: The Structure of Belonging*. San Francisco, CA: Berrett-Koehler.

Brown, P., R.J. Chaskin, R. Hamilton, L. Fiester, M. Karlström, H. Richman, A. Sojourner and J. Weber. 2007. *Embedded Funders and Community Change*. Chicago, IL: Chapin Hall at the University of Chicago.

Bystry, D. 2005. "Case Study from Application to Construction: Clearinghouse CDFI Puts New Markets Tax Credits to Work." *Community Development Investments Review* 1, 1: 37–42.

Cabaj, M. 2012. *Situational Leadership and Management*. Toronto, ON: Tamarack Institute.

Capraro, J. 2013. "Can Successful Community Development Be Anything But Comprehensive?" *Shelterforce* Winter 12/13). <http://www.shelterforce.org/article/3344/can_successful_community_development_be_anything_but_comprehensive/>.

Clemence, S. 2005. "Richest Cities in the U.S." *Forbes,* October 28. <http://www.forbes.com/2005/10/27/richest-cities-US-cx_sc_1028home_ls.html>.

CNNMoney. 2006. "Best Places to Live." <http://money.cnn.com/popups/2006/moneymag/bplive_2006/frameset.2.1.exclude.html>.

Green, F. 2006. "Nonprofit Market Creek Plaza Offers Diamond District Residents up to a 20% Investment Stake." *U-T San Diego*. April 9. <http://legacy.utsandiego.com/news/business/20060409-9999-mz1b9neighbo.html>.

Jacobs Centre for Neighbourhood Innovation. 2009. "The Village at Market Creek: Social and Economic Impact Report, Calendar Year 2008." San Diego, CA: Author. <http://issuu.com/jacobscentre/docs/seir2008>.

____. 2010. "The Village at Market Creek: Social and Economic Impact Report, Calendar Year 2009." San Diego, CA: Author. <http://issuu.com/jacobscentre/docs/seir2009>.

____. 2011. "The Village at Market Creek: Social and Economic Impact Report, Calendar Year 2010." San Diego, CA: Author. <http://issuu.com/jacobscentre/docs/seir2010>.

Korten, A.E. 2009. *Change Philanthropy: Candid Stories of Foundations Maximizing Results Through Social Justice*. San Francisco, CA: Jossey-Bass.

Kubisch, A.C., P. Auspos, P. Brown and T. Dewar. 2010. "Voices from the Field III: Lessons and Challenges from Two Decades of Community Change Efforts." Washington, DC: The Aspen Institute. <http://www.aspeninstitute.org/sites/default/files/content/docs/pubs/VoicesIII_FINAL_0.pdf>.

Kubisch, A.C., P. Auspos, S. Taylor and T. Dewar. 2013. "Resident-Centered Community Building: What Makes It Different?" *National Civic Review* 102, 3: 61–71.

Levy, F. 2010. "America's Safest Cities." *Forbes,* September 11. <http://www.forbes.com/2010/10/11/safest-cities-america-crime-accidents-lifestyle-real-estate-danger.html>.

Mguni, N., and L. Caistor-Arendar. 2012. "Rowing Against the Tide: Making the Case for Community Resilience." London, UK: The Young Foundation. <http://youngfoundation.org/wp-content/uploads/2012/12/Rowing-Against-the-Tide-December-2012.pdf>.

Morgan, A.E. 1984. *The Small Community: Foundation of Democratic Life*. Yellow Springs, OH: Community Services.

Ostrower, F. 2011. *Sunsetting: A Framework for Foundation Life as Well as Death*. Washington,

DC: The Aspen Institute. <http://www.aspeninstitute.org/sites/default/files/content/docs/pubs/Sunsetting2.pdf>.

Pennekamp, P., and A. Focke. 2013. "Philanthropy and the Regeneration of Community Democracy." Dayton, OH: The Kettering Foundation. <http://kettering.org/wp-content/uploads/PhilanthropyAndTheRegeneration.pdf>.

Robinson, L. 2005. "Market Creek Plaza: Toward Resident Ownership of Neighbourhood Change." A PolicyLink case study. Oakland, CA: PolicyLink. <http://www.policylink.info/pdfs/MarketCreekPlaza.pdf>.

Sennett, R. 2012. *Together: The Rituals, Pleasures and Politics Of Cooperation*. New Haven, CT: Yale University Press.

Torjman, S., and E. Leviten-Reid. 2003. *Comprehensive Community Initiatives*. Ottawa, ON: The Caledon Institute of Social Policy. <http://caledoninst.org/Publications/PDF/55382041X.pdf>.

Treuhaft, S., A.G. Blackwell and M. Pastor. 2011. "Equity: The Superior Growth Model." *Race, Poverty and the Environment* 18, 2: 4548. <http://reimaginerpe.org/files/18-2.treuhaft-blackwell-pastor.pdf>.

PUSHING FOR GREEN SOLUTIONS TO URBAN NEGLECT

The Work of People United
for Sustainable Housing (PUSH)

Behrang Foroughi and Rachel Garbary

The city of Buffalo experienced a rapid economic and population decline starting in the 1970s as a result of de-industrialization and international outsourcing. Like other cities in the United States, the municipal government instituted a number of policies to attract large-scale investment and to create jobs. Decision-making about economic growth at that time, and for many years to come, was largely centralized in the hands of politicians and business elites. What is unique about Buffalo, however, is the way that a young organization made up of local activists — People United for Sustainable Housing (PUSH) — has managed to build a culture of active civic engagement among residents in one of the most marginalized areas of the city in less than a decade. This new culture includes citizen participation in decision-making at the municipal and neighbourhood levels and, perhaps more impressively, in the everyday interactions with hundreds of families and friends who are trying to (re)build a new kind of economy for those who choose to stay and live in Buffalo's West Side — an economy that is green, locally-owned, inclusive, affordable, equitable and grounded in relationships of mutual trust.

A GLIMPSE OF LIFE ON BUFFALO'S WEST SIDE

In the Green Development Zone, neighbourhood youth are installing solar panels and insulation in the latest housing renovation project. Just down the block, a PUSH energy advocate and a parent interested in making her family home more energy efficient and lowering her heating bills are discussing the benefits of a weatherization program. On their way to the next meeting, energy advocates cross paths with a community rally promoting environmental justice and opposing the extraction of natural gas through hydraulic fracturing in New York State.

Across the street is a cluster of people weeding potatoes and picking tomatoes at one of the local community gardens. A bike drives away with a cart full of vegetables for a barbeque at the Massachusetts Avenue Park a block away. Friends and neighbours gather for the second anniversary of the park, and spend the afternoon playing soccer, sharing a meal, and celebrating the successes of the past year. On the way home, community members stop for a dessert of fried plantains to support a PUSH member's dream come true, her own restaurant, "Mama's Kitchen," in the core of Buffalo West.

There are community members of all ages in the Grant Street Neighbourhood Center. While local youth use computers to complete their homework, in the next room a group of PUSH staff and residents are holding their weekly meeting and planning the next campaign. As the meeting wraps up, a workshop for youth and violence prevention is about to begin, a joint initiative led by PUSH and supported by the University of Buffalo. This is one of many community collaborations that are central to PUSH's strength and success.

PUSH Buffalo is a not-for-profit member-based organization in Buffalo's West Side. It was established to strengthen community relationships and to nurture local leadership capable of contributing ideas and taking action for the future of the neighbourhoods experiencing the highest levels of poverty in Buffalo. This case study provides a window into the life of PUSH. First, it outlines the social, economic and political conditions of the city in the late twentieth and early twenty-first centuries. It then discusses the evolution of PUSH as an organization and the significance of its achievements.

PRE-PUSH BUFFALO AT A GLANCE

Located on the eastern shores of Lake Erie and at the head of the Niagara River, Buffalo has historically been a centre of eastern trade routes in the U.S., as well as a major railroad hub and one of the largest grain-milling centres in the country. Throughout the first half of the twentieth century, Buffalo's significance as a manufacturing centre grew, especially during the Second World War. However, with a broader regional economic trend towards de-industrialization and international outsourcing, Buffalo's economy began to deteriorate in the 1970s. The city has remained, to the present day, unable to recover its status as an economic hub.

During the 1970s, Buffalo's prime economic industries were eroded by foreign competition and weakened by disinvestments (Goldman 2007). This period coincided with a nationwide trend of migration into suburbs; the population of Buffalo dropped by 23 percent between 1970 and 1980 (ibid.). This population decline severely affected the tax base, leading to a decrease in the provision of social services. The economic decline was further exacerbated when the city was teetering on the edge of bankruptcy in 2003. At the turn of the twenty-first century, thousands of job losses, vacant lots and abandoned homes were indicative of the enormity of Buffalo's economic and social strain.

In the years preceding the founding of PUSH, Buffalo struggled with poor fiscal management and development strategies at the time focused on large-scale economic endeavours that constituted the main driver of the city's economic "growth machine." These "growth machine" strategies, influenced by Peterson (1981) and promoted by business elites, were expected to attract large-scale financial investment, expand the workforce and increase population density. As an example, the Buffalo Niagara Enterprise (BNE) was an organization formed in 1999 by a number of the area's largest companies to generate a stronger tax base for the city through job creation and by advertising Buffalo as a desirable region to live and do business. BNE was among the best-funded privately-led booster organizations in the country at the time, operating on an annual budget of $7 million. However, BNE failed to achieve the expected improvements in Buffalo for a number of reasons. Goldman (2007) argues that BNE's development strategy was not supportive of residents in low-income areas and provided few opportunities for these residents to participate in local economic development decisions and activities.

Similarly, Logan and Molotch (1987) describe how the dominance of the pro-growth alliance of politicians and business elites hindered genuine citizen participation in policymaking, undermining public opposition to their development proposals by eliminating all potential challengers (Logan and Molotch 1987). They argued that city politicians depended on close relations with elite business leaders to maintain political power and to push forward their shared economic growth agenda. Similar to what occurred in other U.S. cities at the time (Detroit, for example) fuelling this growth machine led to the disempowerment and silencing of local, neighbourhood-level stakeholders (Hall and Hall 1994).

By the turn of the century, community leaders concluded that growth-machine development strategies were largely ineffective. Weak governance and financial mismanagement left Buffalo citizens bearing the brunt of de-industrialisation as manufacturing moved to countries with lower labour and production costs. With over ten thousand vacant land lots and abandoned homes throughout the city, the state took over the management of Buffalo's finances and created the Buffalo Fiscal Stability Authority in 2003 to develop a four-year development plan for the city and to establish stringent fiscal policies (Goldman 2007).

While the entire city faced socioeconomic decline, some districts and groups were affected more than others. One of the worst hit areas was Buffalo's West Side, one of the most ethnically and racially diverse areas in the city. At the time of writing, this part of Buffalo was populated mostly by Hispanics and African Americans; other sizable ethnic groups included Native Americans, Italian Americans, Burmese, Vietnamese, Sudanese, Somalis and Cambodians. Without decent job opportunities for unskilled workers, these migrants found themselves unable to rise above low-income or precarious employment. According to 2010 census data, roughly 41 percent of Buffalo's West Side residents, and over 60 percent of children in this area, were living below the poverty line (City-Data n.d.). This area also had a significantly higher population density than the rest of the city, a high percentage of single-mother households (26 percent), a large population of youth with little formal education and some of the highest energy bills in the city, due to the inadequate weatherization of the old housing stock. This was the context in which PUSH emerged as a community-based organization with a mandate to improve the quality of life in Buffalo's West Side.

THE STORY OF PUSH

Aaron Bartley and Eric Walker founded PUSH Buffalo in 2005. Both men had been involved in social justice activism for many years. Aaron returned to Buffalo after leading the Harvard Living Wage Campaign, which secured $10 million of annual wage and benefit gains for two thousand low-income service workers at Harvard University. Eric came to Buffalo from Beacon, New York with years of experience as a community organizer. He soon became engaged in local initiatives to address regional poverty. In 2005, Aaron and Eric met at a community gathering and decided to create a community-based organization as a response to the overwhelming desire of West Side residents to have a grassroots group to tackle issues of common concern, revealed through a door-to-door campaign. With support from Echoing Green, a New York-based non-profit that provides seed funding and technical assistance to social entrepreneurs, PUSH was established with two staff members in 2005.

Pathways to change: Environment, economy, and equity

As shown schematically in Figure 9-1, PUSH's work moves from community engagement and consultation to collaborative action along three interdependent pathways to social change. Its members have created various local organizations and partnerships to follow these three pathways, focusing on planning and advocacy on issues concerning the environment, the economy and equity.

Figure 9-1 Key Components of PUSH's Work

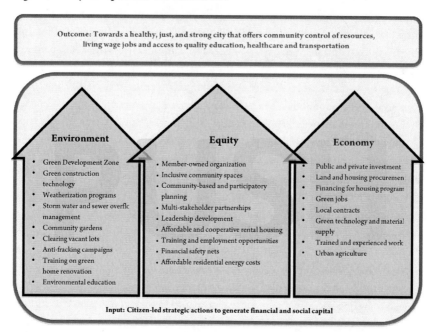

Outcome: Towards a healthy, just, and strong city that offers community control of resources, living wage jobs and access to quality education, healthcare and transportation

Environment
- Green Development Zone
- Green construction technology
- Weatherization programs
- Storm water and sewer overflow management
- Community gardens
- Clearing vacant lots
- Anti-fracking campaigns
- Training on green home renovation
- Environmental education

Equity
- Member-owned organization
- Inclusive community spaces
- Community-based and participatory planning
- Multi-stakeholder partnerships
- Leadership development
- Affordable and cooperative rental housing
- Training and employment opportunities
- Financial safety nets
- Affordable residential energy costs

Economy
- Public and private investment
- Land and housing procurement
- Financing for housing program
- Green jobs
- Local contracts
- Green technology and material supply
- Trained and experienced work
- Urban agriculture

Input: Citizen-led strategic actions to generate financial and social capital

Building PUSH Leadership

Over the past decade, PUSH has grown its member base to more than four hundred people. Most of its thirty full-time staff were initially volunteers who were encouraged to become more formal leaders over time — a deliberate strategy of PUSH. "Community leadership development resembles a five-rung ladder," explains one staff member: Participation in community events is level one; active attendance of PUSH meetings is level two and involvement in organizing community events is level three. Being at level three includes taking part in meetings for emerging leaders to reflect collectively on current PUSH activities and to discuss the neighbourhood's priorities. "Hard-core" leaders make up level four; they are the people who are "always there to help out and are super reliable" (personal communication).[1] These leaders are involved in PUSH's activities at least once every week. The uppermost fifth level comprises board members, who are elected by the membership. Most of the staff began at level one and eventually moved up to levels four or five before joining PUSH as paid employees.

One of the current staff members recalled her first interaction with PUSH. It took place when she was standing in a queue with hundreds of people on a cold November morning in hopes of receiving financial help from the government to pay her heating bill. "You have to go outside and have to wait many hours in the cold. It is demeaning. People can't afford to get time off work and go and stand in line for hours for this," she explained (personal communication). On that day, she approached a group of PUSH organizers who were providing hot chocolate, coffee, blankets and heaters to people standing in the cold and volunteered her assistance; she has been working with PUSH ever since.

PUSH's organizing director, Jennifer Mecozzi, is another such employee. She was a stay-at-home mother of four who initially got involved with PUSH through its door-to-door campaign. Jennifer has grown to become the focal point of PUSH's community organizing work, despite having no formal background in this field. Her story resembles that of Lonnie Barlow, an underemployed youth who gradually expanded his involvement with PUSH from writing a blog on its activities, to running campaigns to his current position as PUSH's communications specialist. By creating a variety of spaces for people to gather, voice their concerns and strategize, new leaders have emerged to take on the growing number of PUSH's activities.

The following sections discuss PUSH's activities in three interconnected thematic areas: advocacy and planning; environmental health; and energy justice. They outline the objectives, approaches, and actions taken in each of these areas, and bring the work of PUSH to life through the voices of its activists.

PUSH ADVOCACY AND PLANNING

Direct action campaigns
In 2005, residents in Buffalo's West Side were most concerned with abandoned housing, vacant lots, the lack of affordable rental housing and unemployment. In response, PUSH called on neighbourhood residents and other allies to participate in six direct action and legislative campaigns. During these campaigns, community leaders discovered that the New York State Housing Agency controlled roughly 1,500 vacant houses and land lots in Buffalo. Instead of rehabilitating these houses for the benefit of residents, the State Housing Agency sold the liens to corporate executives at a private investment firm.

PUSH members shared this information at community meetings. They painted large stencilled portraits of New York governor George Pataki on boarded-up houses owned by the State Housing Agency in their neighbourhoods. They organized protests outside the governor's Buffalo office. These actions enticed more residents to get involved. Eventually, state officials conceded to this pressure and the new governor, Eliot Spitzer, and representatives of PUSH entered into negotiations. PUSH's involvement as a stakeholder in these negotiations demonstrated the growth of its political influence and legitimacy among the residents of Buffalo's West Side.

Block-by-block campaign

These property negotiations also led to block-by-block campaigns as a result of which the state relinquished control of over more than 1,500 homes and opened a statewide funding stream for the rehabilitation of abandoned houses. PUSH subsequently formed a partnership with a non-profit developer, HomeFront Buffalo, and in 2007, PUSH's first six housing units were built. The tenants of these housing units became the first members of PUSH's housing cooperative and now serve as leaders in other PUSH activities.

Community planning congress

PUSH's first housing victory signalled to residents that a well-planned campaign could bring about change, which led to a rapid increase in membership. By 2007, the growing base of trained community organizers brought together over one hundred residents to their first community-planning congress, designed to develop a vision for a redevelopment plan along Massachusetts Avenue, located in the heart of Buffalo's West Side. Participating in large-scale planning for the city was a significant departure for residents from the growth-machine development strategies of the past and is a testament to how far PUSH had come in strengthening local leadership and fostering more inclusive development. The community-planning congress continues to meet annually with local residents to review the highlights of the year and to make joint plans for the future, ensuring greater local ownership and more relevant campaigns and programs.

Grant Street Neighborhood Center (GSNC)

Established in 2006, the GSNC is located on reclaimed space that once served as the Northwest District Branch Library, closed in 2005 due to budget constraints. The centre was established as a non-profit incubator for two community development organizations — the Massachusetts Avenue Project (MAP) and PUSH. The MAP, in partnership with PUSH, hosts the Growing Green Program, an urban agriculture initiative for youth. Growing Green's farm consists of over an acre of vacant lots reclaimed by PUSH, where youth grow produce to sell at local venues. The GSNC now serves as a drop-in community centre serving over sixty people from the neighbourhood every day.

The centre also serves as the central hub for PUSH, providing a convenient locale for community associations to meet and collaborate. The centre has been both an effect and a driver of social change: the community energy captured through PUSH has enabled the creation of the centre and it has created a physical space for PUSH members to keep up the momentum.

PUSH for the environment

Land and lot clearing

Abandoned land lots and empty houses were an eyesore for residents and a hotspot for criminal activity. These lots also took up valuable space that could be directed towards new housing developments. For PUSH, these interconnected issues presented an opportunity for a creative solution to multiple problems. PUSH leaders mobilized community members to campaign for the clearing of state-owned empty land lots. This campaign resulted in the relinquishment of nearly one hundred lots, which improved the appearance of the neighbourhood, provided space for the construction of new, affordable energy-efficient homes and created opportunities for local job creation.

Green Development Zone

After the success of the block-by-block campaign, PUSH members envisioned the creation of a Green Development Zone (GDZ) in the core of Buffalo's West Side. In 2009, with the goal of developing affordable green housing and developing vacant land in the GDZ, PUSH formed the Buffalo Neighbourhood Stabilization Corporation (BNSC) as a non-profit, development corporation, purchasing land and preparing it for development in consultation with the community, thereby preventing gentrification and displacement of low-income residents (Bartley 2011; PUSH website).

Participants of the Community Planning Congress laid out the boundaries, priorities, and a basic plan. Programs in the GDZ were designed to address the high cost of heating, including weatherizing older housing stock, developing new green affordable housing units, and using alternative sources of energy. Contractors provided on-the-job weatherization and construction training for local youth seeking employment, resulting in a network of "green contractors" as well as the first green construction cooperative in the area. At the time of writing this case study, 18 new units were constructed with more than fifty more on the way.

One housing unit in particular is drawing attention to the GDZ from energy advocates throughout the city. The "NetZero House" is designed to create as much energy as it consumes on an annual basis using the latest green technologies such as geothermal heating and a solar hot water system. Originally built around 1880, community volunteers and participants in the local green jobs training program collaborated on the renovation.

Massachusetts Avenue Park

In 2009, the Community Planning Congress brought more than one hundred residents together to develop the "Healthy Neighbourhood Park Concept Plan." This plan led to the Massachusetts Avenue Park Campaign, in which PUSH organized a team of community leaders to approach the municipal government for support. By 2011, the campaign received investment from Buffalo's Mayor, Byron Brown, members of the City Council, and Buffalo's Parks Commissioner for a sum total of $350,000. The following year, Buffalo's West Side became home to a new youth athletic field and pavilion, the largest publicly-owned green recreation space in Buffalo's densest neighbourhood, serving thousands of young people and their families.

PUSH for energy justice: National Fuel Accountability Coalition (NFAC)

Energy pricing became a social justice issue in Buffalo's West Side because of the connection between poorly insulated housing and high energy bills. In 2011, PUSH and a like-minded organization called VOICE-Buffalo[2] formed the National Fuel Accountability Campaign (NFAC) to take on utility companies for overcharging low-income households. According to New York State law, utility companies could apply a surcharge to motivate customers to weatherize their homes. Government subsidies were available for the weatherization, making it an attractive option for those who could afford it. The utility company serving Buffalo's West Side used this incentive program to charge all customers, including low-income homeowners, who were unable to afford weatherization despite the subsidization schemes.

Members of PUSH and the NFAC held protests at the utility company headquarters, and a hearing sponsored by the New York State Public Service Commission was flooded with speakers criticizing the injustice of the conservation incentive program for low-income homeowners. As a result, the Public Service Commission ordered the utility company to move roughly $19 million out of corporate advertising and into weatherization programs for low-income families. Approximately $4 million of that money was to be disbursed in Buffalo's West Side.

Push Green

NFAC paved the way for PUSH Green, a community-based energy efficiency program started in 2012. Funded by PUSH Buffalo and New York State Energy Research and Development Authority, PUSH Green focuses solely on green housing renovations and development. PUSH Green builds upon the Green Jobs–Green New York Act of 2009, a statewide initiative aimed to help New York reach its energy efficiency goals, bolster green job opportunities, and provide access to free comprehensive home energy assessments, installation services, and low-cost financing for home upgrades. PUSH Green serves as a liaison with the state, recruiting residents, small businesses, non-profits, and multifamily property owners into the state's energy efficiency program. In the other direction, PUSH Green provides information and guidance that helps local residents capitalize on cash-back incentives, and the on-bill recovery mechanism, allowing homeowners and tenants to finance energy upgrades with low-interest payments built into their existing utility bills.

PUSH Green also provides opportunities to make weatherization and home energy retrofits more affordable for customers through its Friends and Neighbours Program. This program encourages homeowners living within specific neighborhoods to apply for retrofits as a group, rather than individually. This way they can save costs on their energy efficiency upgrades collectively.

PROSPECTS AND CHALLENGES

PUSH faces obstacles typical of many voluntary and not-for-profit organizations, such as funding, recruitment, and community engagement; however, staff do not seem to get bogged down by these issues. Instead, as one staff member explained, "The challenges [of residents] we are addressing through our various actions *are* the major challenges we are facing." As one staff member explained, "PUSH is not about expanding for expanding's sake.... We take our direction from residents, not from the revenue the organization needs to keep going." Focusing on the residents helps PUSH remain relevant, active, and able to stay true to its founding principles and values.

Balancing grassroots activism with institutionalization

One of these values is maintaining a balance between "staying true to grassroots activism alongside the institutionalization of PUSH itself." Jennifer Mecozzi explains that in addition to the political mobilization and the direct action taken, PUSH strives to ensure that they take constant "time-outs" from the work for celebration to strengthen community cohesion. This, she highlights, is the key operational strategy PUSH relies on:

> As a grassroots leader brought up through the organization, I can say first hand how people are the voice, the forefront and the power that we have in PUSH. Everything we do is a clear result of input and pressure from the community to make some changes to improve their quality of life. It is not the norm for the people to be heard, for the people to even have the opportunity to speak to those in power or decision-makers. We try to make that the process. We stand behind them to encourage, offer the connections, work with community to develop strategy. (personal communication)

It has not always been easy to balance this grassroots activism with more "professional" developments as PUSH has evolved over time. One solution has been to branch out into a number of institutions. Although connected through core values and history, PUSH Buffalo, BNSC, PUSH Green, the Grant Street Neighbourhood Center are independent entities, complementing one another's work. For example, the BNSC owns the land lots within the GDZ; PUSH Green's Workforce Development organizers coordinate the development initiatives related to this land; and PUSH Buffalo coordinates the Community Planning Congress and leads direct action campaigns. By operating separately, these equally important elements of PUSH's operations are able to capitalize on their relative "value add" from their respective spaces and capacities, and keep politically charged issues where they are most appropriately handled.

Maintaining face-to-face contact with members

While social media can be a useful tool to raise awareness, maintaining direct face-to-face contact with residents has always been central to the way PUSH operates. This contact has become more difficult as the number of members increases. One of the strategies to overcome this challenge is the "snowflake" model of community engagement. Through door-to-door canvassing, community members who are more actively involved with PUSH's work pass information along to their own neighbours. This strategy helps improve dialogue between community members as people get to know their neighbours better and as awareness of PUSH events and campaigns increases.

Adopting Marshall Ganz's "Leadership story telling" is another strategy, involving successive unfolding of three stories, culminating in collective action: "We start with the skill of relationship-building, the story of *self*. Then we develop the skill of motivation or the story of *us*. Third, the skill of strategizing, the story of *how*. And fourth, the skill of *action*" (Ganz 2009). The idea is to bring people of the same place into the reality of making a new story together.

Unaffordability

On a more practical level, although PUSH has innovatively linked local job creation, affordable rental housing, and weatherization, the number of jobs created through its activities has so far been limited. Weatherization and renovation programs continue to be too expensive. While roughly 80 residential units in the GDZ and a total of 260 in Erie County have been retrofitted in only two years, the "push" continues for social programs to make weatherization and home retrofitting more affordable for low-income homeowners across New York State.

Looking to the future

PUSH leaders have deliberately not expanded its community organizing activities beyond Buffalo's West Side in order to remain a relatively small, place-based organization. However, PUSH's success and reach has become known in wider circles, and the organization is now actively involved in a number of partnerships and initiatives that span western New York State. PUSH members are now regularly invited to a variety of organizations and councils, including the Regional Economic Development Council, where PUSH now has a say in decision-making over how resources are spent and how policies are made for future developments in the region. This is a very different reality from the way that resource allocation decisions were made in the past.

CONCLUSION

Broadening the traditional notion of the economy to include values such as equity, the environment, inclusion and local ownership, PUSH Buffalo's programs have transformed one of the most marginalized neighbourhoods in the city — Buffalo's West Side — in less than a decade. The achievements are significant. Six direct-action campaigns have resulted in the reclamation of vacant lots and houses. Nearly 80 affordable housing units, including a locally-constructed "NetZero House" equipped with the latest green technology, have been erected in a new Green Development Zone. This zone has become a model for Buffalo and is increasingly attracting the attention of investors. Laws around energy pricing have been overturned, benefitting low-income families with more affordable programs to weatherize homes and reduce heating bills. Local youth have access to on-the-job training in green renovation and house construction as well as in urban gardening. And families now have access to state-of-the-art recreation facilities.

The PUSH magic, however, is not measured by the volume of its infrastructure developments; rather, it is found in its approach and member base. What started as the idea of two young activists now includes more than eight hundred members. These members are the organization, the reason for its existence, its driving force, the lifeblood and the heartbeat. Door-to-door campaigning and ongoing face-to-face relationships on tough issues, as well as celebration during lighter moments, have reinforced a collective identity that is now manifested in a cadre of hundreds of new activists and leaders, nurtured by PUSH and able to take action on demand. Unlike conventional external interventions, the work of PUSH has no end goal; rather, it is continuous outreach and leadership building through community organizing, astute campaigns and partnerships. For PUSH members, this is the real success.

Notes

1. All references to personal communication are for interviews conducted in February 2013.
2. A non-profit, interracial, urban-suburban coalition of twenty-eight faith-based congregations and community, business and labour leaders of Buffalo and Erie County.

References

Bartley, A. 2011. "Building a "Community Growth Machine": The Green Development Zone as a Model for a New Neighborhood Economy." *Social Policy* 41, 2: 9–20.

City-Data. n.d. "West Side Neighborhood in Buffalo." <http://www.city-data.com/neighborhood/West-Side-Buffalo-NY.html>.

Ganz, M. 2009. "Why Stories Matter." *Sojourners Magazine.* <http://sojo.net/magazine/2009/03/why-stories-matter>.

Goldman, M. 2007. *City on the Edge: Buffalo, New York, 1900–Present.* Amherst, NY: Prometheus Books.

Hall, M.F., and L. McIntyre Hall. 1994. "A Growth Machine for Those Who Count." *Critical Sociology* 20, 1: 79–101.

Ledwith, M., and J. Springett. 2010. *Participatory Practice: Community-Based Action for Transformative Change.* Bristol, UK: The Policy Press.

Logan, J.R., and H.L. Molotch. 1987. *Urban Fortunes: The Political Economy of Place.* Berkeley, CA: University of California Press.

Peterson, P.E. 1981. *City Limits.* Chicago, IL: University of Chicago Press.

PERMEATING THE MAINSTREAM
Rural Action for a Sustainable Future for Central Appalachia

Alison Mathie

On February 10, 2013, the *Athens Messenger* ran a lead story announcing that the non-profit organization Rural Action would be moving to new premises, a renovation of the mine office of Johnson Brothers Coal Company, closed in 1948. There is a satisfying symbolism in occupying this physical space. Rural Action's own history in South East Ohio is deeply rooted in the social and environmental consequences of coal mining and deeply committed to sustainable alternatives to the boom and bust cycles of industrial demand for the fossil fuels embedded in Appalachia: first coal, then oil and now shale gas.

With its main office on the edge of Central Appalachia in Athens, Rural Action's geographic area of focus is "one of the most ecologically and socially distressed regions of the country" (Rural Action 2012). Despite alleviation of the extreme poverty levels noted in the 1960s, cyclical losses of jobs gained have been a feature of the region's economic history (Gaventa 1987). In the last recession beginning in 2008, history repeated itself again: by 2011, the Appalachian region had lost all jobs gained since 2000, with unemployment levels running as high as 11 percent in Central Appalachia and outmigration "among the worst in the nation" (Appalachian Regional Commission 2011: 1).

This is the context in which Rural Action, among several like-minded partners in the region, is writing a different economic story for the region's future, one that builds and preserves, rather than extracts and depletes, the stock of the region's wealth:

This new story is practical, truth-tested in local knowledge and experience and drawing on the passions and innovations of people around the globe who are, in Paul Hawken's words, the blessed unrest — the millions who are organizing themselves, teaching, learning, trying every day to bring about ... a sustainable future — a world in harmony with natural systems, more just and fair to those in greatest need, aware of the fragility of life, and encompassing future generations. (Rural Action 2013: 2)

Spanning several decades, this case tells the story of Rural Action's roots in citizen action, its evolution as a member-based non-profit that promotes local community organizing for rural revitalization to its more recent alignment with strategies for wealth creation that can be scaled up to local and regional levels (WealthWorks n.d.). Promoting local food production systems, sustainable forestry, watershed restoration, environmental education, recycling and waste management and local energy projects, Rural Action has moved from the creative fringe to a position of influence, a central node in a network of local initiatives building a sustainable economy.

RURAL ACTION'S ROOTS IN CITIZEN ACTION

Citizen action to address poverty is at the root of Rural Action's history. The Civil Rights movement in the 1960s and resistance to the Vietnam War fuelled the politicization and activism of a new generation, including the founders of Rural Action. Rallying around demands for social and economic justice, grassroots organizations sprang up in Appalachia raising alarms about poverty and environmental degradation from the coal industry, identifying the legal pressure points and building alliances to strengthen their cause. Significantly, given Appalachia's growing reputation as a region of unrest at the time, Athens was where President Johnson gave his speech on the War on Poverty in 1964, outlining federal government initiatives to support social and legal services as well as grassroots community organizing. One of these programs was a domestic volunteer program, Volunteers in Service to America (VISTA), that had just been launched under the *Economic Opportunity Act* of 1964, allowing young university graduates to cut their teeth on community development anti-poverty programs. Many of these young men and women would go on to play an important role in Rural Action's future.

Twenty years later, when government funding for social and legal services was cut back under the Reagan administration in the 1980s, five individuals, including the future first director of Rural Action, felt compelled to take action. Board members Jon Sowash and Carol Kuhre recall a "poor people's rally" held in Athens in the early 1980s that mobilized over one thousand people by contacting "every food stamp office and anti-poverty program in the region." At the rally, everyone was asked to drop $1 in a basket, providing the start-up funds for what came to be known as the Appalachian Ohio Public Interest Campaign (AOPIC), an affiliate of the Ohio Public Interest Campaign (OPIC), which began to "fight tooth and nail against the huge roll backs of federal funding of benefits for poor people" (J. Sowash personal communication[1]). Tapping into activist experience elsewhere in urban and rural centres,[2] AOPIC arranged for community members and volunteers alike to learn techniques for adult education and community mobilization. What followed was a period of intense activity in local communities, drawing attention to precarious employment in the coal industry, to the environmental damage wreaked by longwall and strip mining and by polluting incinerators and landfills, and to the breaches of civil and social rights over years of neglect of this region.

AOPIC's approach was to support spontaneous citizen organizing that was already taking place. Citizens Organizing Against Longwall mining (COAL), for example, was challenging the use of a new mining technique that caused subsidence and interfered with aquifers on which farms depended for their water supply. AOPIC supported COAL's bid to change the laws that waived the responsibility of mining companies to provide compensation for this damage, flexing its muscle in state-level negotiations which eventually led to the ruling to enforce the right to compensation — a decision that eventually was adopted nationally. In the following years, AOPIC continued to force the state government to take regulations seriously. Its success in negotiating with different camps in the public and private sectors, and finally influencing national public policy, laid the foundation of credibility on which Rural Action would later build.

In 1989, frustrated with OPIC and its urban focus, the leadership of AOPIC decided to break away, renaming the organization the AOPI Center (rather than Campaign). However, an already overstretched staff could not bear the additional burden of fundraising without connection to the OPIC network. Also, by 1990 the affiliated citizen groups that AOPIC had supported in their fledging years were now competing for the same pool of funds or suffering burnout themselves. The question of AOPIC's future had to be addressed.

After lengthy consultations in which the closure of AOPIC was seriously considered, a four-month planning process was set in motion to give those people deeply entrenched in single-issue campaigns a chance to articulate their own ideas about what a sustainable economy would look like. From there groups began to network, forming committees to work out the details of a new and coherent vision for a sustainable economic future. These committees addressed diverse issues: sustainable agriculture, arts and heritage, economic development, education, energy, forests, health, housing, human needs, recycling and pesticide reform (Rice and Kuhre 2004).

While these small gatherings shaped and drove AOPIC's work, larger public forums were organized to bring a wider representation of local citizens, government officials and academics to the table. Rarely, however, did these events attract low-income participants. To address this, AOPIC deliberately reached out and held a series of meetings to generate ideas with residents in poorer rural areas about what healthy communities could look like. In 1991, after an extensive three-year process of local consultation, a *Strategy for Rural Renewal* was produced and Rural Action was formed. At this critical juncture, AOPIC had transformed itself from a resistance organization to an organization committed to sustainable development in the region, seeking to articulate, in Thomas Berry's words, "a new story to live by." Carol Kuhre and Michelle Decker launched the new effort on a shoestring budget and many volunteer hours.

RURAL ACTION AS DEVELOPMENT ORGANIZATION: RURAL REVITALIZATION AND COMMUNITY BUILDING

Associated with this shift was a new way of looking at community development and rural revitalization. Influential at this time were the ideas of John McKnight and Jody Kretzmann at Northwestern University in Chicago and the practice of asset-based community development. These ideas would become the basis for Rural Action's work during this phase:

> Contrary to earlier approaches to rural development in Appalachia, such as the War on Poverty of the 1960s, which were focused on the political, social and economic *deficiencies* of the region, Rural Action's work in Southeast Ohio is *asset*-based. (Rice and Kuhre 2004: 190)

An asset-based approach to community development combines three key features that would frame Rural Action's work going forward. First, it prioritizes community building by drawing attention to the often undervalued skills, talents and assets of all community members and nurturing the leadership capacity to mobilize these for community-based initiatives. In this sense, the approach sees active citizenship and the engaged community as drivers of positive change in a strong democracy (Rice and Kuhre 2004 citing Barber 1984). Second, considering the full range of assets accessible to a community, an asset-based approach orients people towards livelihood strategies over which community members can achieve some measure of control rather than remaining vulnerable to the swings of a globalized economy or to an industrial structure in which ownership of the means of production is in the hands of the few. Third, an asset-based approach not only shines the light on undervalued assets but also requires their protection, renewal and rebuilding if livelihoods are to be sustained. Taken together, these features share strong similarities with WealthWorks' Wealth Creation in Rural Communities Initiative in which Rural Action has participated in more recent times.

Throughout the 1990s, these features translated into Rural Action's three signature initiatives under its Rural Renewal Strategy: The Sustainable Communities Initiative, The Sustainable Economies Initiative and the Sustainable Environment Initiative. The Sustainable Communities Initiative concentrated on building local leadership and building community through self-organizing around specific projects. Rural Action organized training in leadership, in asset-based community development skills such as asset mapping and strategic planning and in grant-writing skills. As a starting point for community development activities, creative expression through storytelling and visual arts was often used. In eight different communities, for example, the Community Murals Project stimulated a collective remembering of survival through past struggles and of past achievement and then invited an imagining of what might be:

> Community-based art has always flourished in situations where people struggle for expression.... The people of Appalachian Ohio have similar sentiments: outrage at the industrial pillage of their environment, sadness over the loss of jobs and high poverty rates, pride in their past, and hopes and dreams for the future of their children, schools, communities, and region. (Kuhre 2001)

The Sustainable Economies Initiative, departing from the experience of rural Appalachia as a place from which resources were extracted and depleted, encouraged "a new way of looking at the creation of wealth ... [with strategies] to keep more local dollars local, use resources sustainably, and increase local ownership" (cited by Rice and Kuhre 2004). Starting with ReUse Industries to transform waste into an economic asset, Rural Action then ventured into The Good Food Direct Project, an early promoter of the concept of community-supported agriculture, and The Sustainable Forest Economies Project focusing on non-timber forest products (NTFPs). Finally, the Sustainable Environments Initiative took on the gargantuan task of reclaiming land and streams damaged by subsidence and acidification caused by the coal industry. Since 1994, several watershed restoration schemes developed by Rural Action have achieved success, undaunted by the skepticism of local authorities (Rice and Kuhre 2004).

None of these activities and accomplishments could have occurred without overcoming the challenges of building relationships with dispersed rural low-income communities or the confidence to collaborate with sometimes unlikely partners to get the job done. Carol Kuhre, Rural Action's first director, had witnessed effective community organizing strategies first hand during her previous work in the Philippines and this became the inspiration for her leadership. Locally, several board members had attended trainings at the Highlander Center in Tennessee and been involved in the welfare and legal rights campaigns of the 1980s. Together, a fierce sense of social justice, exposure to popular education methods, experience of patient relationship building and the principles of asset-based community development would prove to be a powerful combination.

Adding strength to Rural Action's work in both the short and long term was a dedicated volunteer force provided under the federally funded Volunteer In Service To America (VISTA) program. Through this program more than 360 volunteers supported Rural Action's work in rural communities from 1994 to 2009. Since then, this tradition has continued with the Ohio Stream Restore Corps, an AmeriCorps program working on reclamation of polluted streams, water quality monitoring, environmental education, trail access and waste and recycling (Rural Action n.d.).[3] An important feature of the VISTA program was the recruitment of both technical assistance providers and field workers from the community. These community fieldworkers were an entry point and knowledge source that facilitated the community organizing work from the outset (unfortunately this was discontinued with AmeriCorps). Exposed to the challenges facing central Appalachia, many of these volunteers, either local or from other parts of the U.S., went on to support Rural Action's work in later life as unpaid volunteers, supporters or employees.

Significantly, Rural Action retained its membership-based character from its AOPIC days, a feature that is a source of its strength and legitimacy today. Through participation in committees and annual meetings, members get engaged in the issues that the organization is grappling with and go on to influence and mobilize others. Some of its members are now sufficiently well-established financially to be major donors and to provide links to the partners needed to open doors of influence. At the time of writing (2013), Rural Action had a membership of just under one thousand, and 6 percent of its operating budget of $1.6 million came from membership dues and donations. Describing it as the "church-congregation" model of citizen organizing, Carol Kuhre emphasizes the importance of face-to-face relationship building at the local community level ingrained in her early in her career, and the value of a member-based organizational model for Rural Action as the basis for broad-based volunteer support.

The Monday Creek Restoration project that took place in the 1990s illustrates this confluence of voluntarism and community organizing well. Bernard (2010) describes the challenge. The watershed at the centre of the Hocking Valley's once prosperous coal field was scarred by the deep mines and surface operations that finally closed in the 1970s: "Household refuse, mine wastes and tailings, gob piles, rotting structures above and underground and acidic water impoundments bespeak disruptions of a century of mining" (Bernard 2010: 47). Due to the inundation of old mines and resulting acidification, waters ran orange and turquoise with pH levels below 4.5, "a threshold below which no fish species and few macro-invertebrates can withstand" (ibid.: 48). A local teacher described "growing up in a small community and playing on coal slag piles and in orange creeks and not realizing those were not natural landforms until she was entering high school" (M. Decker personal communication). In the mid-1990s, the streams in the watershed were dead and declared "unrecoverable" by the U.S. Environmental Protection Agency (Bernard, 2010: 44).

However, the scientific case for restoration advanced by hydrogeologists Mary Stoertz and VISTA volunteer Mary Ann Borch, combined with Rural Action's capacity to raise funds, engage the interest of local communities, mobilize volunteers and collaborate with key strategic partners, would prove this statement wrong. By 1997, three years into the project, fourteen partners were involved: "other nonprofits, a university and technical college, and several State and Federal agencies, including the U.S. Forest Service which in Wayne National Forest manages 38% of the watershed" (Bernard 2010: 50). Also by this time, the watershed had been mapped so that progress could be tracked, volunteers had cleared surface debris, trees had been planted, school children had begun to talk of "fishable and swimmable streams" and proposals had been written to fund the continuation of this work. By 2008, ten years and $6 million later, the Monday Creek Restoration Project had become a model for other attempts to clean up the pollution left in the wake of coal mining in the Eastern Coal Lands. Since then, life has begun to return to the streams, astonishing long-time residents. Newly built trails now draw tourists to a destination that had once been avoided.

To this sweeping summary, Scott Miller, currently a member of Rural Action's board and the director of the Voinovich School of Leadership and Public Affairs at Ohio University, adds some of the texture of the real struggles, strategies and serendipity that occurred. A VISTA volunteer himself on the Monday Creek Restoration Project, he describes his role as "emissary" to local communities, attending local city council meetings to persuade local citizens and their elected representatives of the value of this work: "Often they were not interested, or didn't believe it would work, or thought the money could be better spent" (personal communication). He describes how the project coordinator, Mike Steinmaus spent many years working and living in a local community, becoming part of it, contributing as a volunteer firefighter, establishing trust.

At that time — in the late 1990s — fortuitously, the Clinton administration was offering federal support for engaging local stakeholders in a discussion about watershed restoration and this added heft to the effort. Local citizens, local communities, state and federal agencies, universities, nonprofit organizations, philanthropic organizations and others were all drawn in. In this way, state and federal agencies became the enablers of the slow but steady generative work of community organizing necessary for the restoration work to take place, with Rural Action acting as the catalyst of this participation and collaborative effort. As Scott Miller says, "It's a mix of science, participatory democracy, passion and commitment" (personal communication).

Replicating the success of the Mountain Creek Restoration Project, Rural Action now has volunteers from an AmeriCorps program dedicated to stream restoration and building local environmental stewardship. Local participation has occurred gradually as layers of skepticism are lifted by evidence of tangible environmental recovery. As one longtime resident wrote, "In the 1960s the creek was dead, now in 2012 there are bluegill and smallmouth bass in the river. If you need me to do anything, call me" (personal communication).

FROM DEMONSTRATING ALTERNATIVES TO INFLUENCING THE MAINSTREAM

> Before, we were on the fringe of the mainstream. Now the mainstream comes to us (Scott Miller personal communication).

Being "on the fringe of the mainstream" has several connotations. It can suggest "being on the outside looking in," but more commonly it implies questioning the mainstream, working around the edges where one can operate without interference and quietly influence by example. Being on this creative fringe is by its very nature experimental and innovative, sometimes radically so, or perceived to be so out there as to be beyond serious consideration. When the roots of Rural Action and other like-minded organizations were taking hold in the 1970s, ideas about sustainability and alternative economies bordered on that radical edge,[4] often inspired by counter-cultural activism and idealism of people from outside Appalachia who came to settle in and around Athens. Regionally, this activism merged with widespread Appalachian resistance for which the Highlander Center in Tennessee served as a gathering place (Fisher 1993; Ansley 2012; Fisher and Smith 2012). As Michelle Decker points out, "These outsiders found some special soil in which to grow" (personal communication).

Over time, this alternative activity has edged its way into the centre, growing and maturing into successful social and economic enterprises and permeating the mainstream. The intractability of poverty, the instability of social inequality, the legacy of environmental damage and a growing concern about the effects of climate change have started to raise doubts about the wisdom of solutions tied to the prevailing industrial model. The optimism of post-Second-World-War growth, refuelled in boom periods, has given way to concerns about the limits to growth. In this context, Rural Action has tested new strategies that localize economies and develop regional resilience, even as another prospect for boom-and-bust economic growth presents itself in the form of shale gas extraction.

Building such social and economic resilience is at the heart of Rural Action's partnership with the Wealth Creation in Rural Communities initiative of WealthWorks, running formally since 2010. Building on Rural Action's asset-based community development approach, the initiative is based on the premise that sustainable development requires wealth creation and synergy among multiple forms of capital. These range from tangible forms of capital such as financial capital, built capital (infrastructure) and natural capital (water, soil, biodiversity) to less tangible forms such as the networks and relationships of trust that constitute "social capital," the "individual capital" of skills and talents, creative "intellectual capital" and the influence inherent in "political capital." In line with this thinking, the stock of wealth created is as important as the flow of jobs created or dollars of income generated in the process (Ratner and Markley 2014).

The initiative's practical approach to creating local wealth is through the development of product value chains. For Rural Action, this has been tested in its Wealth from Forests initiative, promoting a supply of Forest Stewardship Council (FSC) certified wood products to meet demand in urban markets and the production and processing of non-timber forest products (NTFPs) such as ginseng. Waste diversion and recycling through the Appalachia Ohio Zero Waste Initiative (AOZWI) is a second initiative. And at its most developed is its sustainable agriculture initiative, linking local food producers to local wholesale and retail markets and large institutional consumers.

The basic idea of the approach is to add value as close to the source as possible and retain it locally by marketing value-added products effectively outside the region as well as stimulating the multiplier effect of local consumption. An important component of the approach is identifying where low-income people can take up new employment opportunities in production, small business and services.

Transactions in value chains transform relationships in the marketplace with producers, traders, aggregators, processors and consumers relying on mutual solidarity for the system to work. In turn, these primary transactional relationships are complemented by widespread "networks for wealth creation ... webs of organizations that are developing institutions and collective strategies that build local assets and create wealth that stays local" (Castelloe, Watson and Allen 2011: V). Rural Action, for example, is a member of the Central Appalachian Forestry Alliance (CAFA), a multi-state collaboration established in 2009 "to increase certified sustainable forest management, strengthen value chains from forest floor to showroom floor, explore new powerful value streams, and build the capacity of key organizations and enterprises in the region" (Central Appalachian Forestry Alliance n.d.). It is also a member of the Central Appalachian Network (CAN), an eighteen-year-old collaboration of six anchor organizations in the region focused on sustainable development. These members share ideas of what works, whether technical methods of super-insulating local hoop houses to extend the growing season or innovations in financing, aggregation, processing and distribution of agricultural products. Through research, evaluation, convenings and technical assistance associated with these innovations, CAN has produced a regional strategy to accelerate the growth of the food systems sector and potentially other sectors as well (Castelloe, Watson and Allen 2011; M. Decker personal communication).

These formal networks are built on a base of linkages between "economically isolated assets, producers and consumers to build effective market demand at scale" (Ratner and Markley 2014). Using the value chain approach, these wealth creation programs have therefore complemented Rural Action's strong local-level initiatives to build on local assets but have streamlined this work into a coherent vision for the regional economy. CAN and CAFA claim that despite the economic and environmental distress in much of the Central Appalachian region, "the land still offers Central Appalachians a path towards a diversified, more robust economy owned by the people who live there" (Central Appalachian Network and Central Appalachian Forestry Alliance n.d).

Yet the situation in 2013 is highly unpredictable. The expectation of the shale gas boom has driven land prices up. Some people can sell or lease land and pay off a lifetime of debt; some see an opportunity to reinvest in agriculture or forestry; some see taxation of the industry or corporate responsibility "dividends" redirected to Community Foundations and non-profits; some hold out for increased business and employment opportunities in construction and energy sectors. On the other hand, collateral environmental damage remains a threat and a disincentive to invest: concerns are being raised about forest losses for pipeline construction, the contamination of water supplies through hydraulic fracturing or "fracking" at deep well injection sites, noxious wastewater impoundments and increased truck traffic.

Addressing these concerns, Rural Action initiated the Look Before You Lease program to advise landowners on the possible environmental consequences of leasing land for shale gas operations and to explain the alternatives to doing so. Combining the expertise of four different organizations and several local landowners, the educational approach has helped Rural Action maintain its reputation for thorough research and broad consultation.

While President Obama has promised "a supply of natural gas that can last America a hundred years" (State of Union address January 24, 2012 as cited in Hond 2012: 21), detractors suggest that this prediction may be seriously overblown (Semeniuk 2013), and oil price shocks may weaken the promise of a shale gas boom. In any case, experience of other boom and bust cycles suggest that Rural Action should continue to encourage long-term investment for a robust land-based local economy and for renewable energy solutions that can operate at scale. The message Rural Action promotes is that a value chain approach to wealth creation offers a viable economic strategy for the long term while also offering resilience to endure upswings and downturns of the dominant economy. The following brief account of its Wealth from Forests, Appalachia Ohio Zero Waste Initiative (AOZWI) and its Sustainable Agriculture programs illustrates this message.

Wealth from forests

In order to add value to timber products that were historically exported from this region as raw commodities, Rural Action began to develop a value chain for locally manufactured wood products certified by FSC through its Green and Regionally Oriented Wood (GROW) products value chain program. In the first two years, wood products from this program yielded $300,000 in sales and the program was ready to be launched as WoodRight Forest Products LLC in early 2013, a social enterprise owned and operated by Appalachian Sustainable Development in Virginia and Rural Action in Ohio. As illustrated in Figure 10-1 below, Woodright LLC links the players in this chain, acting as a broker for green products. It boosts domestic demand in high-end building markets by providing information, product sourcing and other services to builders and architects willing to pay the premium for green building products. On the supply side, WoodRight provides FSC certification assistance for the "chain of custody" mechanism that tracks certified wood products from harvest to point of sale.

The business model is a collaborative regional network that can advance the kind of market development necessary for this green-building sector to thrive at scale. A community development financing institution has invested (with loans guaranteed by a local foundation); this creative financing solution has been able to "anchor an entire value chain and unleash activity all through it" (WealthWorks 2014).

Actively supported by the Central Appalachian Forestry Alliance (CAFA), whose mission is to preserve biodiversity and promote a stronger forestry sector, the development of WoodRight and the wood product value chain is complemented

Figure 10-1: WoodRight and the Wood Products Value Chain

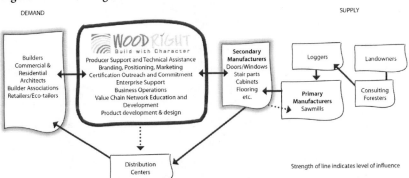

by other sustainable forestry initiatives. For example, the future supply of timber products requires forest management for the long-term sustainability of a quality forest. Only 4 percent of family forest owners in Ohio have registered management plans to date. Rural Action's strategy has been to demonstrate the short-term potential for economic gain from managed forest and encourage landowners to become active managers of their forests in the long term, especially in those areas that have suffered neglect. As a testament to Rural Action's influence on forest management, its Call before You Cut campaign has been institutionalized by the Division of Forestry in Ohio and five other states. Other Rural Action initiatives in the region include a mechanism for landowners to enrol their woodlands in a carbon offsetting scheme in which landowners are paid for the increased carbon uptake of their forests resulting from better management practices.

Since the late 1990s, NTFPs have also been promoted as a source of supplementary income. Scott Bagley, a consultant on low-impact forestry and a current member of Rural Action, explains:

> We see economic development around NTFPs as an entry point to promote holistic forest management which combines NTFPs with some timber removal. The income the landowners earn is just extra; it is not a get-rich-quick fix or a full-time income strategy. (personal communication)

NTFPs have been of interest to both multi-generational residents of the region as well as newcomers who have settled in the region during the last thirty years. Also, there is now a noticeable back-to-the-land movement by people who are two generations removed from those who migrated to find work elsewhere. These returnees are seeing more opportunity in forest land, especially given the rise in ginseng and other NTFP prices since the late 1990s.[5]

Along with the potential of wood products in sustainably managed forests, an income stream from NTFPs such as ginseng offer reasons to invest in and protect forests, especially as the temptation to lease or sell land in anticipation of high land prices for shale gas development becomes a threat.[6]

Appalachia Ohio Zero Waste Initiative (AOZWI)

Rural Action's newest program, launched in 2010, promotes a zero waste economy, combining its community development expertise with Ohio University's Voinovich School of Leadership and Public Affairs' expertise in local government and public policy.

Rural Action's work with waste grew out of public concern about landfill space in the 1990s, when new legislation was being written at the state level for the management of solid-waste districts. Rural Action members provided written testimony at numerous public meetings to make the case for recycling and recovery services to reduce the reliance on landfills and incineration. It made sense; as Carol Kuhre pointed out, people in communities where Rural Action worked saw "waste" in a very different light:

> For them [rural Appalachian people], these were not junk piles, they were resource piles. Many of them were tinkers. There was a value built into the culture in transforming "junk" into something useful. They were children of the depression. (personal communication)

In this spirit, Rural Action began to work with community members to start ReUse Industries, a repair and reuse program, and hosted a state-funded program called Economic Development from the Waste Stream, a multi-year effort to find and promote regional examples of businesses using waste materials. Subsequently, this experience led a local foundation to invite Rural Action to partner with Ohio University and to assess the potential for building a local economic effort around innovative recycling ideas for a zero-waste economy:

> This project is not just about recycling. ... With experts estimating that recycling can create up to ten times as many jobs as landfills and incineration, trash should be viewed as a representation of potential jobs, financial opportunities and resources, not as something disposable. (S. Miller personal communication)

For the AOZWI partner organizations, a zero waste economy has three core elements: public education; improved infrastructure and viable business ventures. Tying these together, AOZWI has hosted community meetings to discuss waste recycling and recovery ideas, secured investment to upgrade infrastructure and encouraged innovation in new technologies that can translate into new business ventures. For example, engineering students from Ohio University recently designed a portable conveyer belt to sort recyclables at big public events, such as music festivals (M. Decker personal communication). Other innovations in the pipeline include viable systems for the collection, aggregation and resale of recyclables; the promotion of cottage art and craft industries using recyclables; the secondary processing of plastic into pellets; housing deconstruction and materials recovery and compost aggregation and bagging operations. There is potential for this sector to create jobs for both low-skilled and high-skilled labour, especially in an environment where the demand for environmental services to the shale gas sector is likely to expand and where stricter recycling regulations could generate the raw material for a thriving waste-recovery sector.

Sustainable agriculture

Rural Action's sustainable agriculture program is at the heart of its commitment to a resilient land-based economy. It is a core player in a network attempting to stimulate the local economy by shifting local consumption to locally grown and processed food.

Current estimates indicate that only 3 percent of food consumed is being sourced locally and that only when the market share derived from local food increases to 10 percent will it be viable for full-time farmers to reinvest and for the local food system to be self-sustaining (T. Redfern, L. Schiller personal communications). Rural Action and its partners say that reaching the 10 percent threshold could take anywhere between ten and twenty years but they are confident that it is possible.

So far, on the supply side, services have been established to train local growers in this sector and introduce them to technologies to extend the growing season. There are incubators for local food-processing businesses in two locations; opportunities for direct sales through new farmers markets or through new produce auctions and other mechanisms for aggregation, distribution and marketing, advertised through Rural Action's *Ohio Foodshed*, a website linking consumers to local food producers. On the demand side, consumer education through initiatives such as the 30 Mile Meal program, promoted by a collaboration of Athens-based local food groups as well as the Athens County Visitors Bureau, have contributed to stronger public awareness of the value of local food and to higher demand from local restaurants and other local institutions, such as Ohio University and Hocking College's Culinary Institute. Educational programs in the schools and school food programs are a strong indicator that the shifts in food preferences continue into the next generation. In this way, collaborative strategies shaping public opinion, creating demand, supporting a sustainable supply and influencing government and food-sector policy are combining to build a value chain for a local food system in southeast Ohio.

The example of the produce auction at Chesterhill illustrates these collabora- tive relationships well. In 2003, Rural Action was funded by the Appalachian Regional Commission to explore ways of increasing local-food sales to institu- tions. That same year Jean and Marvin Konkle retired to Chesterhill, moving from Bainbridge, Ohio where a produce auction was thriving. They met Rural Action business-development staff and decided to become members. At the time, Tom Redfern, coordinator of Rural Action's sustainable agricultural program, was work- ing on how to aggregate produce to supply potential institutional buyers. After introducing the Konkles to Ohio University extension, he soon became the glue that supported and connected them to agricultural and community networks as they started enlisting support for the idea of a produce auction in Chesterhill with local producers. By 2005, an auction property had been purchased and the first auction held. By 2007, Ohio University dining services began to purchase local produce and by 2009 the local foods website linking producers to consumers was launched (Voinovich School of Leadership and Public Affairs 2010; T. Redfern personal communication).

Produce auctions are not new to Ohio but since 2004 they have doubled in number (from six to twelve) and become significant economic drivers in their respective regions. What is interesting about Chesterhill is that 60–70 percent of the produce comes from members of the Amish community. Their reluctance to travel to urban markets means they rely on the market coming to them. This in turn creates a rural food destination for a wide variety of participants. At auction, the biggest consumers are entrepreneurs who use the auction to build up their own supplies for retail sale at both informal and formal farmers' market settings. As Tom Redfern points out, "It's an easy entry entrepreneurship opportunity, especially in food desert areas. They can buy and resell" (personal communication). For large institutional buyers, the range, quality and volume of produce make it worth their while to purchase directly at auction. In the last three years, the uptake of these opportunities at Chesterhill has resulted in a 40 percent growth in sales.

To increase supply, training and educational opportunities have been offered to local producers led by Rural Action and The Appalachian Centre for Economic Networks (ACENet). Innovative technologies such as plastic hoop houses to extend the growing season have been demonstrated, as well as food safety and marketing programs, all taught with a view to building peer-to-peer learning opportunities and encouraging membership in associations that can provide mutual support and influence policy at state or federal levels. Rural Action and ACEnet see cumulative benefits of these activities:

> All these are pieces of wealth. We have earned a lot of social capital at the state level, we have contributed to physical capital in the form of the produce auction, and the peer-to-peer learning has enhanced our intellectual capital. (T. Redfern personal communication)

ACEnet's program director, Leslie Schiller, concurs: "It's not just wealth creation, but health creation" (personal communication).

The question now is how to achieve that 10 percent slice of local food consumption. According to Tom Redfern, the pattern in Ohio has been the expansion in the number of small "hobby" farms and large farms. To sustain the growth of a local food system, medium-sized farms (grossing $200,000-$1,000,000) are needed for a vibrant local economy to take off and generate taxes, savings and demand for services. As one resident pointed out, "Fifty years ago this was dairy country. People could send kids to college with a two-hundred-acre [eighty-one-hectare] farm or fifty cows." With horticulture, more production can be done with less acreage. However, while the self-insured Amish are a special case, for other producers a major obstacle to the expansion of production is health insurance. Many farmers are supported by a spouse with health-insurance coverage from their off-farm employment. Universal coverage as urged under the *Patient Protection and Affordable Care Act* (enacted in 2012) has yet to stand the test of time. Without such protections, the danger is that local food systems will operate as a parallel universe rather than permeate the mainstream and food produced (by farmers for sale or by gardeners for domestic consumption) will be one of several strategies for income patching, rather than a viable livelihood by itself (L. Schiller personal communication).

A NETWORK OF COLLABORATIVE ACTION

According to Tom Redfern, the percentage of food consumed that is sourced locally (currently 3 percent) is as much an indication of the extent to which producers and providers in the value chain support each other as it is about a shift in consumer demand for local food. The goal of 10 percent is achievable if partners in the value chain help each other grow to stimulate both supply and demand. The more inclusive and mutually supportive the system, the denser the network and the more exponentially it can grow. It illustrates well how, as a collaborative venture among market partners, the value chain puts network theory into practice.

Collaborating in networks has been in Rural Action's DNA. In the early 1990s, a pioneering collaboration of multiple institutional partners and volunteers was the Monday Creek Watershed restoration project. In this and other collaborations that followed in the forestry and waste recycling and recovery sectors, web-weaving has been deliberate. The basis of these relationships is mutuality — "organizations not only reference each other but showcase each other" (M. Decker personal communication). By way of illustration, Rural Action's work in sustainable agriculture is tightly woven with the work of ACEnet, an incubator for small-scale food processing enterprises in two locations, Athens and Nelsonville, and a core player in the development of this and other local food systems around the country. Illustrating a long history of partnership, ACEnet's program director, Leslie Schiller, was involved in AOPIC in the 1980s and since the early 1990s she has been on the Rural Action board. Both organizations became the anchors of CAN when it was formed in 1992. The founder of ACEnet was herself a champion of network weaving. There is now a dense network of partnerships in the inner circle of the local-foods value chain itself and in its outer circle of facilitators and supporters.

The CAN network, with Rural Action and ACEnet as key partners, has seen the cultural divide between sustainable agriculture and the industrial agricultural models of the 1990s (tobacco production, for example) bridged to the point where

ACEnet and Rural Action now run training courses for extension staff across the state. These courses focus on best practices in the local-food value chain to support Rural Action's Know Your Farmer, Know your Food and 30 Mile Meal programs. Grocery stores increasingly recognize the value of these organizations as intermediaries to educate and prepare producers to enter their wholesale food systems and facilitate primary market partnerships with institutions such as Hocking College, Ohio University and local restaurants. With the support of the Ford Foundation in the last four years, CAN has been able to strengthen its role as a vehicle for partners in the network to align their roles, avoid duplication and leverage funding. Within southeast Ohio, ACEnet and Rural Action are the "connective tissue," (M. Decker personal communication) animating a culture of cooperation — "social capital" in wealth creation terms.

By connecting the right people to one another and making its programs accessible across the region, Rural Action establishes a foundation for community building that is at the core of its work. Tom Johnson, the Perry County mayor, for example, has set an economic revitalization program in motion in one of the most depressed counties of the region. Under his leadership, tapping into ideas through a number of Rural Action portals and sharing these with local citizens, the county has developed a heritage tourism project, innovative water and sewage disposal systems, clean and green energy initiatives, a negotiated deal with shale gas companies for an association of landowners and enterprise development for businesses in ceramics, tourism, agriculture and services. He credits Rural Action with the ideas for recognizing and building assets, making community engagement a reality. As mayor, he has been at the forefront of efforts to retain wealth at local levels from extractive industries, lobbying for an increased portion of the state-levied severance tax on shale gas companies to be redistributed to communities experiencing the most impact and developing innovative financing models for investment in community-led initiatives. Establishing a community foundation is one such example. The idea of wealth retention appeals to Perry County residents who often say, "If we had a nickel for every lump of coal taken out of the county, we'd be the richest county in the state" (T. Johnson personal communication).

KEEPING MOMENTUM GOING

Political will has grown in recent years to align funding streams across agencies to meet community needs and continue support for sustainable agriculture initiatives through USDA. The challenge, however, is to register public demand for issues of environmental sustainability, food security and poverty to be addressed so that the work continues irrespective of political stripe. Different levels of government have to work hand in hand to reassure the agricultural sector of ongoing support to small and micro-business development, farm-to-school funding and the development of farmers' markets. Financial investment at all stages of the value chain is needed but particularly for small entrepreneurs who are ineligible for most private equity investments and therefore require innovative forms of equity financing rather than more credit. As another form of investment, publicly-supported health insurance can lower the financial risk of full-time self-employment as well as alleviate the financial strain on low-income households.

Securing the core funding required so that Rural Action can keep the momentum going and continue to innovate is essential. The network building required to do the actual work of Rural Action is rarely supported, let alone the networking and building of social capital required to maintain a diverse funding base in an increasingly squeezed funding environment. The frustration is compounded by that sense of loss when young talent is attracted to the work but has to move to other employment when job security becomes an issue.

If Rural Action is to maintain its credibility as an adviser to landowners and food producers on climate change issues, it needs to attract resources or partners who can tackle the hard task of tracking the changes in forests, soils and pollination systems that impact the viability of a land-based economy in the future.

MOVING ONWARDS, OUTWARDS AND UPWARDS

While the language of assets, capitals and wealth building for sustainable development is not new (Flora and Flora 2012; Chambers and Conway 2001; Mathie and Cunningham 2008), Rural Action's use of the wealth creation framework has consolidated a way of describing long-time efforts to promote sustainable economy and has focused attention on types of wealth not typically considered in conventional economic-development models. And so, in Rural Action's world, there are conversations about place-based assets, about unlocking *individual capital* and generating the *intellectual capital* for family-friendly farming to pass down from one generation to the next, or for new models of worker-owned farming to take off. *Social capital* in the networks and value chains has resulted from a focus on relationship building among market partners. Natural assets for a land-based economy are discussed in terms of the ability to continuously restore and generate productivity and reduce dependence on the global food system. New equipment for producers, buyers and distributors in the value chain is the *built capital* and the degree to which the market partners have been able to influence policy represents *political capital*. Success is judged by whether all forms of wealth have grown, not one at the expense of another.

Given the repeated patterns of precarious employment and wealth extraction in depressed areas of Appalachia (see Gaventa, Smith and Willingham 1990), this language speaks of transforming the economy in potentially radical ways. Rural Action's innovation has been to demonstrate new forms of economic production that pass the test of broad-based wealth creation and foreshadow the idea of distributed systems of production in a "Third Industrial Revolution" fuelled by renewable energy (Rifkin 2011; Markillie 2012). Yet the dominant economic landscape sits squarely in old industrial growth prescriptions:

> Shale gas development is our region's newest extractive practice, echoing in many ways the extraction of the past but also operating at an unprecedented scale ... There are many unknowns about the long-term effects ... and it requires new information, broad coalitions, new organizing, and new policies. So far, communities have little voice in the process and its rapid rollout has given people, governments, and institutions little time to prepare. (Rural Action 2013: 4)

Given this new reality, offering a sustainable pathway for development in the region means that Rural Action has to keep chipping away at systemic change, inserting this language of sustainability in mainstream discourse and shifting public attitudes to raise expectations of sustainability and equity in local economic development. It continues to work at the level of consumer demand by increasing purchasing preferences for fresh local produce and increasing the value placed on having clean streams in the backyard, sustainable forest resources and pollution-free air. It is encouraging institutional partners to take leadership roles as buyers of local products and generators of locally-based business opportunities.

It means thinking long term. Rural Action has earned recognition for environmental education with school children to encourage responsibility for ecological stewardship into the next generation. Similarly, tastes and preferences for local foods are being shaped in a "food to schools" program supported by Hocking College, whose culinary arts students use schools as a lab for food-preparation work. In keeping with rural traditions, a strategy of developing multiple sources of livelihood is now built in to the training of a new generation of owner-producers, not just wage earners. Often, however, the funding periods to test, innovate and take innovative ideas to scale are completely insufficient and the pressures to deliver desired results in tight timeframes have endangered the very capacities on which long-term success depends (Ross Strategic 2013).

Yet Rural Action's strategy for constructing a different story for central Appalachia has followed a time-honoured process in keeping with the advice of Meadows (1999: 18):

> In a nutshell, you keep pointing at the anomalies and failures of the old paradigm; you keep speaking louder and with assurance from the new

paradigm in places of public visibility and power. You don't waste time with reactionaries; rather you work with active change agents and with the vast middle ground of people who are open-minded.

Rural Action has followed this strategy of "Speaking louder and with assurance … in places of public visibility and power," and has been forthright in its commitment to social and economic change. "Working with active change agents and with the vast middle ground of people who are open minded," it has been the hub of networks of innovation, constructing local food and sustainable forestry value chains or a zero waste economy, and has taken environmental education to a new level. Collaboration with organizations that have shared the risk of innovation has been the hallmark of its successful influence in the institutional environment. As Kania and Kramer (2011: 36) argue, "Large-scale social change requires broad cross-sector coordination … [not] the isolated intervention of individual organizations." Rural Action has demonstrated this, not only in the value chains in which it plays a key brokering role but also in the networks in which it links to public and private sector allies for all its work.

Going forward, systemic change in policy and regulatory regimes will be a hard nut to crack, especially given the different state jurisdictions in the region. Access to investment funds by local producers and entrepreneurs will rely not only on favourable federal and state policies but also on a shift from grant making to social investment as "the language of resistance gives way to the language of business" (M. Decker personal communication). Innovative financing strategies for providing equity investment to small-scale operations, such as crowdsourcing, are beginning to emerge, facilitated by rules associated with the *Jumpstart Our Business Startups (JOBS) Act* that passed into legislation in 2012 (Cortese 2013). More profoundly, health insurance should make a significant difference in mitigating the risks of entrepreneurs and their employees. The *Patient Protection and Affordable Care Act* (Obamacare) to ensure that no one will be excluded from getting insurance is a new story unfolding (Hamblin 2013).

LEADERSHIP AND MEMBERSHIP

Regardless of the changes of the political and economic environment over the last forty years, Rural Action's leadership and membership has been an "arc of continuity" (M. Decker personal communication). Many of the active citizen leaders of the 1980s went on to take leadership roles in the non-profit sector or were early innovators and adopters of sustainable-development practices. They have continued to support each other's work through ever-deepening networks. In turn, these leaders have mentored a new generation of leaders, sometimes supported by federally-supported volunteer programs. For example, the current director of Rural

Action worked with the founding director in the early 1990s, then built experience and expertise elsewhere before returning to take the helm. At the same time, the volunteer programs (VISTA, followed by AmeriCorps) have attracted a cadre of talent, developing leadership skills at a young age, with many volunteers going on to take leadership roles in Rural Action or in partner organizations. Another brand of volunteer leadership has been nurtured through the membership of Rural Action. With close to 1,000 members, Rural Action reaches 650 households directly and has a ripple effect in those members' communities, through their efforts raising public awareness, fundraising, volunteering or creating local projects.

Maintaining broad-based support, however, requires leadership that can steer a consistent course amidst diverse and sometimes shifting opinion. There is no question that there are tough choices to be made. Rural Action's staff, for example, understands the public support for job opportunities and economic gain promised by the shale gas boom, but has voiced concern that increases in inequality will occur in communities as a result and that the increase in private wealth will not necessarily translate into an increase in public wealth. Advocacy for strongly enforced regulation and taxation will require persistence. Given the potential environmental impacts of shale, some members of Rural Action would prefer a policy against shale gas to be articulated, while others see the urgency of shaping new development by ensuring that the supply, construction and waste/recycling sectors and employment in environmental monitoring are locally designed and owned. Says Perry County's mayor, Tom Johnson: "If we don't get in front of this, they'll take everything we've got." (personal communication)

At what point are the goals of an environmentally-sustainable economy at odds with the urgency of new revenue streams from shale gas? Rural Action's membership is grappling with such questions and hopeful that the history of organizing in these rural communities will feed public debate about the costs and benefits of hydraulic fracturing ("fracking") and how to sustain a viable economy that ensures environmental protection whether shale gas extraction continues or not. At a recent annual meeting of Rural Action members the conundrum was finally discussed openly. In the words of the director:

> It was like lancing a boil … Then fracking came out … a story by one of our speakers about being a child when the coal came and twenty-six wells went dry on his farm, and the lessons he learned (policy matters, place matters). What it did was to put the topic on the table and have us agree that we have to get together. This [shale gas] is coming. Our response can shape corporate behaviour. Just resisting won't move the needle. (M. Decker personal communication)

To move the needle, Rural Action is positioning itself to influence rather than back away, insert itself in the mainstream rather than hang back on the edge.

CONCLUSION

Rural Action began as a citizen-led movement, challenging the power of industry to expropriate resources and leave poverty and environmental damage in its wake. Now members of Rural Action are juggling the possibilities of economic benefits from shale gas with the imperative of demonstrating that a radically different type of economy is viable and necessary. Walking this fine line is seen as the best course of action to influence as broad a base as possible given the challenge of reconciling often conflicting interests and the complexity of the problems at hand. Building momentum for change comes with public deliberation at the community level, where the risks of innovation for a new economic model may be felt most keenly, as well as at policy and boardroom levels where the imperative for change may otherwise be ignored. As Rural Action's director, Michelle Decker, writes in the introduction to the new *Strategic Plan for 2013–2018*:

> We believe in development that starts with the people most affected. We believe many solutions exist to our problems, but many communities are not prepared to take advantage of them and the business models and investment strategies we need for the future have not yet been built. But we have an amazing opportunity to do things differently and to create access to new opportunities. (Rural Action 2013)

Rural Action is both in the vanguard of a new economy and in the trenches of dealing with immediate issues faced by local communities as shale gas development proceeds. It is a unique and valuable combination and its history of moving beyond resistance gives it a powerful and legitimate voice.

Notes

1. All references to personal communication are for interviews conducted in January and June 2013.
2. Urban activism in major cities provided some inspiration to AOPIC though the rural context presented unique challenges. Particularly influential during this period was the Highlander Center in Tennessee, which was providing training and support to civil rights and anti-poverty activists where rural poverty and environmental degradation was felt most keenly.
3. VISTA was brought under the AmeriCorps program in 1993, under the Clinton Administration, and was renamed AmeriCorps VISTA.
4. The term "sustainability" was already being used then in different quarters to describe an economy in equilibrium with basic ecological support systems (Stivers 1976).

5. Wild-simulated ginseng, promoted by Rural Action, now fetches between $500–$1,000/lb (compared to $80–$100/lb for woods-cultivated ginseng, according to Rural Action), and is mostly exported to Asian markets.
6. According to Rural Action staff, land prices in some counties have risen from $500/acre to $2,000–3,000/acre in 25 years, and in areas where land is being sold to shale gas companies, the price can be as high as $10,000/acre.

References

Ansley, F. 2012. "Talking Union in Two Languages: Labour Rights and Immigrant Workers in East Tennessee." In S.L. Fisher and B.E. Smith (eds.), *Transforming Places: Lessons from Appalachia*. Urbana, IL: University of Illinois Press.

Appalachian Regional Commission. 2011. "Economic Overview of Appalachia 2011." <http://arc.gov/images/appregion/Sept2011/EconomicOverviewSept2011.pdf>.

_____. 2012. "County Economic Status in Appalachia, FY 2013." <http://www.arc.gov/research/MapsofAppalachia.asp?MAP_ID=64>.

Barber, B. 1984. *Strong Democracy: Participatory Politics for a New Age.* Oakland, CA: University of California Press.

Bernard, T. 2010. *Hope and Hard Times: Communities, Collaboration and Sustainability.* Gabriola Island, BC: New Society Publishers.

Castelloe, P., T. Watson and K. Allen. 2011. *Rural Networks for Wealth Creation: Impacts and Lessons Learned from U.S. Communities.* Asheville, NC: Rural Support Partners. <http://www.ruralsupportpartners.com/docs/RuralNetworksforWealthCreation.pdf>.

Central Appalachian Forestry Alliance. n.d. *Brochure.*

Central Appalachian Network and Central Appalachian Forestry Alliance. n.d. *Opportunities for Land-Based Economic Development in Central Appalachia.*

Chambers, R., and G.R. Conway. 1991. "Sustainable Rural Livelihoods: Practical Concepts for The 21st Century." *IDS Discussion Paper No. 296.* Brighton, UK: Institute of Development Studies. <http://opendocs.ids.ac.uk/opendocs/bitstream/handle/123456789/775/Dp296.pdf>.

Cortese, A. 2013. "The Crowdfunding Crowd Is Anxious." *New York Times,* January 5. <http://www.nytimes.com/2013/01/06/business/crowdfunding-for-small-business-is-still-an-unclear-path.html?pagewanted=all>.

Fisher, S.L. (ed.). 1993. *Fighting Back in Appalachia: Traditions of Resistance and Change.* Philadelphia, PA: Temple University Press.

Fisher, S.L., and B.E. Smith. 2012. "Placing Appalachia." In S.L. Fisher and B.E. Smith (eds.), *Transforming Places: Lessons from Appalachia*. Urbana, IL: University of Illinois Press.

Flora, C.B., and J.L. Flora. 2012. *Rural Communities: Legacy and Change,* fourth edition. Boulder, CO: Westview Press.

Gaventa, J. 1987. "The Poverty of Abundance Revisited." *Appalachian Journal* 15, 1: 24–33.

Gaventa, J., B.E. Smith and A.W. Willingham (eds.). 1990. *Communities in Economic Crisis: Appalachia and the South.* Philadelphia, PA: Temple University Press.

Hamblin, J. 2013. "What Is Obamacare?" *The Atlantic,* April 2. <http://www.theatlantic.com/health/archive/2013/04/what-is-obamacare/274509/>.

Hond, P. 2012. "The Gas Menagerie." *Columbia Magazine* (Summer): 14–23. <http://

magazine.columbia.edu/sites/dev.magazine.columbia.edu/files/pdf/The%20Gas%20 Menagerie.pdf>.

Kania, J., and M. Kramer. 2011. "Collective Impact." *Stanford Social Innovation Review* (Winter): 36–41. <http://www.ssireview.org/pdf/2011_WI_Feature_Kania.pdf>.

Kuhre, C. 2001. "Introduction." In A. Lipka and S. McDaniel, *Community Murals: Handbook and Case Studies*. Trimble, OH: Rural Action.

Markillie, P. 2012. "A Third Industrial Revolution." *The Economist*, April 21. <http://www. economist.com/node/21552901>.

Mathie, A., and G. Cunningham (eds.). 2008. *From Clients to Citizens. Communities Changing the Course of Their Own Development*. Rugby, UK: Practical Action.

Meadows, D. 1999. "Leverage Points: Places to Intervene in a System." Hartland, VT: The Sustainability Institute. <http://www.donellameadows.org/wp-content/userfiles/ Leverage_Points.pdf>.

Ratner, S., and D. Markley. 2014. "Linking Rural Assets to Market Demand: Wealth Creation Value Chains in Rural America." *Local Economy*. doi: 10.1177/0269094214535713.

Rice, C.S., and C. Kuhre. 200). "Rural Action: Participatory Planning for Healthy Communities in Appalachian Ohio." In W.R. Lovan, M.R. Murray and R. Shaffer (eds.), *Participatory Governance: Planning Conflict Mediation and Public Decision-Making in Civil Society*. Burlington, VT: Ashgate Publishing.

Rifkin, J. 2011. *The Third Industrial Revolution: How Lateral Power Is Transforming Energy, the Economy, and the World*. New York: Palgrave MacMillan.

Ross Strategic. 2013. *Interim Evaluation of the "Wealth Creation in Rural Communities" Initiative*. Washington, DC: Author.

Rural Action. 2012. "Internal Report."

____. 2013. "Rural Renewal 2013–2017: Rural Action's Strategic Plan."

____. n.d. "Our History." <http://ruralaction.org/about-us/our-history/>.

Semeniuk, I. 2013. "Geologist's Provocative Study Challenges Popular Assumptions About 'Fracking.'" *Globe and Mail*, February 19. <http://www.theglobeandmail.com/technology/ science/geologists-provocative-study-challenges-popular-assumptions-about-fracking/ article8869710/>.

Stivers, R. 1976. *The Sustainable Society: Ethics and Economic Growth*. Philadelphia, PA: Westminster Press.

Voinovich School of Leadership and Public Affairs. 2010. "Chesterhill Produce Auction: A Rural Appalachia Case Story." Athens, OH: Ohio University. <http://www.ohio.edu/ voinovichschool/upload/CAN-CASE-STORY-CHESTERHILL_TO-PRINT.pdf>.

WealthWorks. 2014. "Enterprise Financing for WealthWorks Value Chains: Overview and Guide." WealthWorks Initiative. < http://www.WealthWorks.org>.

____. n.d. "Economic Development the WealthWorks Way." <http://www.creatingruralwealth. org/the-initiative/the-initiative/>.

RECLAIMING LAND, REAFFIRMING CULTURE
The Deep South Community Agricultural Network

Phil Davison

> You see all of this land — we own it. It's ours! We, the people of the South, African Americans, who once worked in these fields as slaves, thinking we had nothing — no freedom, no place to call our own and feeling like we had no power. We struggled and fought and shed tears ... but we also sang for joy as we began to overcome. We never gave up. I know this land has a painful past but it also holds a wonderful future. There is wealth in this soil and I want our people to claim it and use it! (Alabama farmer[1])

This is a story rooted in the vibrant social, political, economic and racial realities of the Deep South and in the struggles, passions and innovations of African Americans to reclaim their land and reaffirm their culture as key assets for wealth creation and empowerment. It is an emerging narrative of hope and opportunity from a region of the United States where citizen-led change is steeped in the Civil Rights Movement and in the dreams and inspiring actions of people who stepped forward in towns such as Selma, Birmingham, Jackson and Montgomery to overcome injustice and challenge seemingly insurmountable obstacles.

The case examines how the Deep South Community Agricultural Network draws upon this rich history of civic engagement and action to develop agricultural assets for the purpose of sustaining the natural resources and improving the livelihoods of rural African-American families in Alabama and Mississippi. The Network comprises twelve community-based and institutional organizations that have a long history of working in the rural communities of the region.

In Alabama, these organizations include the Alabama Sustainable Agriculture Network, National Wildlife Federation, The Cottage House, Perry County Center for Economic Development and The United Christian Community Association. In Mississippi, the organizations include Children's Defense Fund, Mississippi Action for Community Education, Quitman County Development Association, Southern Rural Black Women's Initiative, Winston County Cooperative, Tougaloo College and Mileston Cooperative.

Since 2011, members of the network have worked with McIntosh Sustainable Environment and Economic Development (SEED) in partnership with the Ford Foundation's Wealth Creation and Rural Livelihoods Initiative. Initial research funded by the Ford Foundation identified and assessed the existing and possible agricultural assets, defined a set of investment and capacity needs for growing these assets and uncovered the opportunities and challenges related to the growth and development of agricultural assets in rural communities. Motivated by the results of this research, the network developed agricultural assets in rural areas of Mississippi and Alabama. This case outlines the activities of the Deep South Network and explicates the lessons learned from the work of its members.

Although the network is only a few years old and the agricultural assets are not fully developed, the effects of the work in communities and the impacts of the wealth creation discourse on the lives of people in Mississippi and Alabama are compelling. As one farmer points out, "There's something happening here, something built on the sacrifices of African Americans ... our struggles, our successes, our pain, and our history. It's something that folks across this country need to know about and learn from."

At the conclusion of this case, a centuries-old story told by one of the farmers in the network is shared. This story poignantly illustrates the tenacity and historical underpinnings of the African-American struggle in the Deep South to build and sustain wealth despite overwhelming odds.

SETTING

> We know how to challenge things that need to be challenged, speak up when it's required, and take ideas from the table to the community — make things happen. Taking action is part of our history living in the South. It's in our DNA. (Mississippi farmer)

There is a growing hunger in both Canada and the U.S. for broad public conversations on how to create new kinds of economies that are rooted in communities (Mathie and Cunningham 2008; Bernard 2010; Castelloe, Watson and Allen 2011). People across the political spectrum are wondering what kinds of activities citizen groups should be undertaking for their communities with and without support from governments. Further, development practitioners are asking what kinds of activities citizen groups should be initiating and what types of investments and partnerships with governments and the private sector they should explore (Boshara and Sherraden 2004; Dabson, Jensen, Okagaki, Blair and Carroll 2012).

In Mississippi and Alabama, where rural communities have historically felt economic and social challenges more acutely than in the rest of the United States, there is a growing interest in supporting citizen-led actions and community-based social movements that build upon the region's Civil Rights Movement history to address current economic realities. It is here in these two states where many of the civil rights struggles began, bringing historical, cultural and political changes that transformed America over the past fifty years. However, despite these changes and the uplifting fundamental shifts in the socio-cultural and political system, Mississippi and Alabama still experience entrenched poverty, low education rates and systemic racism. An undervaluing of education, limited local control of resources, continued out-migration of youth and a social narrative that highlights what people do not have and cannot do rather than what they possess and can do have led to weakened community capacities and the disenfranchisement of many rural communities.

And yet, a more hopeful discourse is also emerging. People are realizing that if they use the assets found in local communities, the potential contributions of rural communities to the overall wealth of citizens in Mississippi and Alabama can be significant. Consider, for instance, that many people throughout these two states and in much of North America are more concerned than ever before about their food and how it is produced. They want to know if their food is safe to eat, where it came from and how it was grown and harvested. In order to meet demand for healthier and more sustainable food choices, farmers must be knowledgeable about the entire food system. They must be informed about key issues so that they can guide customers on what to buy and eat. Independent restaurants and multi-unit operators are also joining this wave of change and seeking more locally grown products (Clancy and Ruhf 2010). Given this context, there is great opportunity for farmers in the Deep South. However, several challenges remain.

In Mississippi and Alabama, most small farms are owned by African Americans but many are no longer used for farming (Alabama and Mississippi Value Chain Project 2012). In addition, much of the farming knowledge resides with older African Americans who have few options to pass on their knowledge (or their land) to a younger generation since most youth do not see farming as a viable career or even hobby. Yet, within this context of languishing rural land and untapped agricultural knowledge, opportunity emerges in the form of the increasing demand from predominantly urban areas. The challenge for rural African-American communities in meeting this demand is to revive small farms, encourage a new generation to become involved in farming, incorporate new agricultural practices into existing knowledge and adopt a new approach to rural development that focuses on wealth creation rather than only income generation. Meeting these demands requires rural leaders and farmers to explore new ways of thinking about economic development to ensure that wealth sticks.

The individuals and organizations that comprise the Deep South Community Agricultural Network have a long history of working with rural communities and farmers to protect and encourage the use of African American owned land. These individuals and organizations appreciate the tenacity required to use land as an asset in building wealth among African Americans in the Deep South. The Wealth Creation in Rural Communities Initiative taps into this powerful history and uses many of the creative ideas of member organizations to support new ways of thinking and acting that address the current economic realities of rural communities in Mississippi and Alabama.

GETTING STARTED

> You start thinking that there must be something else, another way of doing things — a big idea. So you talk to people and before long, you find out there is another way but it takes a while to see it, even longer to describe it, then time to develop it, longer still to learn more about it and get some support and expertise, and then even though you're not completely ready, you have to step out and take action. You can't sit around waiting for someone else to do something. You have the idea, you have the land, you have the skills, you've talked it over — you act. (Alabama farmer)

Many of the organizations and individuals in the Deep South Network have a long history of working in community development. However, like others doing similar work elsewhere in the U.S. and Canada, they felt that rural communities needed to do economic development differently given their challenging circumstances. Further, they noted the need to create sustainable wealth that remained rooted in local communities rather than income that disappeared into national ventures. They also realized that some of the current citizen-led efforts could benefit from a broader and more integrated coalition that, while rooted locally, could cross community and state boundaries.

The rich context of advocacy work and community development in Mississippi and Alabama, coupled with a renewed desire to work collectively and differently, enabled the organizations now comprising the Deep South Community Agricultural Network to respond quickly to the concept of wealth creation and value chains as put forward by the Ford Foundation. As one member of a partner organization explained:

> The Ford concept of wealth creation and using local assets wasn't something out of left field or foreign to these organizations. These folks have a rich and powerful history of doing similar work and they understand how to mobilize community support and use local resources. They know how to get things done and how to lead. What they need is funding to bring people together and the technical expertise to help them grow their agricultural assets in a sustainable manner.

In the spring of 2008, the Ford Foundation brought together rural development practitioners, researchers and policy makers with expertise in value chains, entrepreneurship, culture and triple bottom line[2] financing to explore what an integrated approach to development might look like and how it could be designed to produce multiple forms of wealth. A working group formed and over the next year its members conducted research and shared results. Notably, they extended their research beyond print documents and digital files and took time to take a "learning journey in Central Appalachia" where they met with people in the forest and wood products sector (Yellow Wood Associates 2012) to see first-hand the benefits of bringing diverse groups together to discover common interests and develop new ideas.

Within a few months, using the research they had conducted and the experiences of their own vocations, the group members developed a conceptual framework for an integrated wealth-creation approach that could be used in rural communities. This framework became a key component of the Wealth Creation in Rural Communities Initiative (WCRC).

To help test the framework and its concepts, the Ford Foundation and its partners provided four multi-year grants to organizations in Central Appalachia with which the foundation had worked previously (ibid.). Since collaboration was viewed as central to the potential success of the conceptual framework, funding agreements for each of the grantees stipulated that their work would be completed through partnerships. The wealth creation concept as developed by Ford viewed each grantee as the hub of a collaborative network working to create a new kind of value chain and thereby build multiple forms of wealth.

As these projects unfolded, work continued on the development of the wealth creation concept based upon feedback and learning from grantees. The working group established a resource and policy development team to process this feedback and to research and develop the policy context needed for sustainable wealth creation. This team also helped build the capacity of the intermediaries (individuals who were working in the field with the grantees) by sharing what was being learned with them and providing them with support and training. The resource and policy development team continued to serve as a focal point both to strengthen the approach itself and ultimately to help influence and bring to scale the wealth creation rural development framework in other areas of the country.

In the Deep South, the overall conceptual framework for wealth creation as developed by the WCRC is similar to that developed in Central Appalachia but the process for developing the network and local assets is somewhat different as the focus is on smaller exploratory grants to emerging organizations that may not have worked with Ford previously. These exploratory grants give each group a chance to identify potential assets and key partners in order to test the viability of wealth creation ideas. This decision required Ford to provide additional support for organizational and leadership development of the grantees, particularly as they took initiatives to scale. This additional assistance has been critical to introducing the approach in the South. In a report prepared by Yellow Wood Associates and the Wealth Creation Management team on the Deep South Initiative, the authors note: "We anticipate this investment in personal growth resulting in increased professionalism will stand these individuals, their organizations, and the region as a whole in good stead for years to come" (Yellow Wood Associates and the Wealth Creation Management Team 2012: 8).

UNDERSTANDING WEALTH CREATION AND VALUE CHAINS

Wealth sticks with you, your family, and your community. It's like the soil on this farm — always there, deep and rich. If you feed it, stuff grows and everyone benefits. But income, well it just slips away, you can't hold it no matter how much you make. It's like the dust on that road — blowin' away in the wind. You run after it, trying to stuff it in your pockets, knowing you'll never catch it or get enough, but you think you can [laughs]. If you approach your work this way, you can spend your entire life making an income and retire with no wealth at all. (Alabama farmer)

The Wealth Creation in Rural Communities Initiative, funded by the Ford Foundation, identifies seven forms of community wealth or capital: intellectual, social, individual, natural, built, financial and political (Yellow Wood Associates and the Wealth Creation Management Team 2012). Several of these forms of wealth are tangible (financial, built and natural) while others carry less tangible attributes (social, political, intellectual and individual capital). However, all can be measured in terms of outcomes, rather than only activities, and it is expected that a community can build each form of wealth without harming the others (e.g., increasing built wealth without sacrificing natural wealth).

By broadening the traditional definitions of wealth to include forms of wealth that benefit individuals and communities (e.g., well-being, political collaboration, shared communication), the wealth creation framework aims to be more inclusive than traditional community-development models, which tend to focus on economic and financial outputs while ignoring social, political, intellectual and individual capital. In the wealth creation framework, people can see themselves contributing to and building wealth in ways that they may not have considered and, in so doing, they are more likely to feel confident in their ability to create sustainable livelihoods. One of the farmers in the Deep South noted:

> I realize that the experiences that I have from working on the farm as a kid and watching my Dad work the land are actually valuable. They [the experiences] are what this project calls individual forms of wealth. It's wealth that I carry but never put any stock in its value. It was just part of my life growing up and I figured that was all it was, but now I see that I have a lot of skills and abilities and they are worth something.

The principal mechanism for developing and mobilizing the seven forms of wealth is the value chain, which is a supply chain comprising all the activities involved in bringing a product or service from conception to production to consumption in a sustainable manner (Feser and Isserman 2009; Yellow Wood Associates and the Wealth Creation Management Team 2012). Most importantly, the value chain expands the meaning of value beyond money and products to include the broader personal and community values and traditions of all those who participate. The purpose of the value chain is to use these community assets to retain and add value locally rather than have the assets extracted, removed from the community, and their value added distantly.

Value chains use a systems or wealth-creation approach to business and when combined with the broad wealth framework are designed to create multiple forms of wealth for all partners. They are based upon shared economic, social and environmental values and provide the infrastructure for producers, processors, marketers and buyers to work together and derive mutual benefits from meeting a market demand. The focus is on building long-term investment for partners rather than only generating short-term income.

GOALS, SUCCESSES, AND OUTCOMES

The Deep South Community Agricultural Network aims to establish at least two value chains for members so that local products can be sold into wholesale and retail markets (Littles and Peterson 2013; Shipman and Miller 2013). The revenues earned are re-invested to support the continued development and growth of value chains and to encourage the involvement of youth and other community members. The network members have had a number of successes including:

- Organizing groups of farmers in the sub-regions of Southeast Alabama, the Mississippi Delta and a two-state sub-region of West Alabama and East Mississippi;
- Developing a farmers' cooperative in Mississippi;
- Gaining food handling and processing certification from state and federal departments;
- Marketing and selling more than $250,000 worth of produce (e.g., collard greens, turnips, sweet potatoes, cabbage and pink-eye peas) to local schools, grocery stores and upscale restaurants in 2013;
- Training growers on universal farming protocols (e.g., planting procedures, use of fertilizer, irrigation methods) and providing them with technical assistance to maximize product yield;
- Acquiring liability insurance for farms;
- Purchasing equipment and infrastructure for shared use (refrigeration, irrigation, transportation);
- Creating entry points to wholesale markets for small farmers;
- Providing mentorship opportunities for youth to enter agricultural work;
- Creating job opportunities on farms that need support with harvesting, travelling, planting.

Although the Deep South Community Agricultural Network is only a few years old and data on specific value chains is limited, the partners in the Network have seen emerging results in each of the seven areas of wealth. The examples described in this section originate from the qualitative data shared by the network members during the interviews held in March of 2013 and also from their presentations. Significantly, the impressions of the Network members suggest that an intentional recognition of cultural power is a prerequisite for the effective use of other capitals. This prerequisite relationship is discussed under an eighth form of wealth not explicitly defined within the original Wealth Creation framework but included in this paper — cultural capital.

Intellectual capital

This form of wealth comprises the knowledge, innovation and creativity in a community. Investment in intellectual capital often comes through research and development and support for activities that encourage innovation, learning and knowledge building.

In the Deep South Community Agricultural Network, many of the farmers spoke of new ways of seeing their land as a result of working with research and technical staff from local universities and colleges. The planting and fertilization protocols established by the university and college partners have enabled farmers to increase crop yields and improve quality while reducing the use of pesticides and other chemicals. Another form of intellectual capital noted by the farmers is the food handling and processing certification they have gained from state and federal departments. A Mileston Cooperative member explained:

> The farmers in the co-op now have certification and collective insurance. The certification gives us the ability to sell our produce to larger stores and the insurance allows us all to keep our costs down because we all share in the liability.

The skills gained from building and maintaining the small greenhouses (also called hoop houses) also led to a number of intellectual capital outcomes. Farmers learned how to keep their soil free from pests by employing a simple, sustainable, organic process called solarizing. Instead of spraying the soil in the greenhouse with pesticides, solarizing involves covering the ground inside the greenhouse with sheets of plastic during the hottest month of the year — July. The soil essentially gets baked in the hot sun and any pests within are killed. Depending upon crop cycles, this process occurs either before or between plantings. One Alabama farmer observes:

> I saved a lot from using the sun to kill all the pests and weeds instead of spraying everything. At first, I didn't think this solarizing process would work ... and so I sprayed [pesticides] in one of the hoop houses and tried the solar sheets in the other one. Well guess what — it works, the sun kills the weeds and bugs just as well as the pesticides ... and I get just as good a crop as when I spray ... So now, I use the sun to kill my bugs!

In Mississippi, Mileston Cooperative involved community youth in the assembly and repair of several greenhouses. The results of this engagement were youth who developed skills, who used those skills to earn income and who planned to apply the practical skills to additional post-secondary study. One young man explained his newly acquired intellectual capital as follows:

I didn't know that I had skills to do this sort of work, putting these hoop houses together and working with all these folks. I feel better about myself, like I have more potential ... I can help other people. I want to do well in school and life, be a person that my family can be proud of. I might even start a small business repairing these greenhouses.

Measurements of intellectual capital often focus on the behavioural changes and outcomes that result from new knowledge and understanding of new possibilities. Thus, for example, in Mississippi and Alabama, the way in which young people spoke about their skills, the new ways in which people viewed the land, the exposure that farmers had to more sustainable agricultural practices and the lessons shared by older generations of African American farmers led to changes in behaviours and actions (e.g., more self-confidence, new protocols for planting, use of small greenhouses to solarize the land, irrigation practices that conserve water) that strengthened the wealth creation value chain.

Social capital

Social capital encompasses the intangible aspects of trust, relationships and networks that support civil society and lead to the sharing of ideas and experiences among people who previously may not have been connected. As one of the Deep South Network members in Mississippi noted, "Our history here in the South shows us how coming together makes us [African Americans] stronger and more knowledgeable. We could write a book on the power of social capital!"

The efforts of the network members demonstrate a desire to use and build upon the rich social capital and deep culture of Mississippi and Alabama in order to establish trust among farmers and partners and create networks in communities that can grow the value chains. Examples of social capital being used include recognizing and incorporating prior agricultural knowledge and farming practices, showcasing community achievements and participating in community events, growing and marketing traditional foods and ensuring that existing organizations that work with African Americans are involved in and lead the initiatives of the network. At a meeting in Alabama, one of the farmers highlighted how social capital was realized through the initial efforts of the Network:

When this project started and we first came together, I noticed that folks took time to listen to each other. There was none of this attitude: "You need to do things this way" or "Look, you farmers don't know what you're doing." Instead, people took time to listen and we all had an opportunity to learn from each other. ... I felt like my experiences and my opinions were valued. Yes, I did learn some new ways of farming ... and there were things that I changed on my farm but I gladly did those things because I felt like I was involved and included in all the discussions. I never felt like an outsider ... I felt like I was a leader meeting and working with people who wanted to support me.

Individual capital

Individual capital as defined in the Ford wealth creation framework is the stock of skills and physical and mental health of people in a region or community (Hoffer and Levy 2010). Measuring individual wealth focuses on the behavioural changes and outcomes that occur when new skills have been mastered or human health has improved.

In the Deep South, training and support from the intermediaries and Ford partners to build the skills of farmers and their organizations to meet demand in the wealth-creation value-chain framework resulted in increased engagement in value-chain transactions. At a meeting in Birmingham, several farmers noted how the technical training and educational support from other partners in the network changed their perspectives on the viability of farming and also their farming practices:

> The planting and fertilizing protocols have changed the way that I [understand] farming. I see how I can get a better crop and more of it, from using what Dr. [name of institutional professor] has put in place. I wouldn't have planted things this way before he came along but now I see the results and how sticking to the protocols puts more money in my pocket.
>
> At first, some folks didn't use the protocols — they just did what they wanted. Well, their crops didn't grow well. The leaves on their collard greens turned brown and they couldn't sell their crops. That's when they realized that perhaps they should change the way they put stuff in the ground.

Members of the network also spoke of how they hoped that the early success of the value chain would encourage other African-American communities in Mississippi and Alabama to become involved. In addition, several members felt that by getting their families and communities back on the land eating habits of youth and families might change, which could help alleviate health concerns across the region. One emerging value-chain venture involves getting fresh produce into local school cafeterias. A network member observed:

> Like many people in this country, our community members and especially our kids eat too much pre-processed and packaged foods. If we can change

the way our kids eat and how they view farming, we can help folks become healthier. Getting locally grown food into the schools is the first step.

Perhaps most importantly, the network members spoke of the increased self-confidence and increased desire to "do something to change things" that they observed in themselves and in others involved in the Deep South Community Agricultural Network. One farmer explained:

> I didn't realize how much I actually knew about farming and getting things done [laughs]. And now I want to do something to change things in my community. ... I see other people who've been working on this project saying the same thing. ... They feel better about themselves ... like they have something to offer and can participate in things going on in their community. They feel like someone is listening and they are citizens again.

It seems that the wealth creation approach with its explicit recognition of local knowledge, skills and culture helps build self-confidence, which leads to increased individual capital and a renewed desire to become more involved in local community affairs. This aspect of the wealth creation approach will be discussed in more detail later in the paper.

Natural capital

Natural capital consists of the environmental assets of a region — renewable and non-renewable. While these assets (e.g., land, water, minerals and atmosphere) cannot be created, they can be maintained and restored.

As noted earlier, much of the farmland owned by African Americans in the Deep South is not being used for farming or has been taken over by large farming corporations. The work of the Deep South Network and its member organizations such as the Southern Black Women's Initiative and Mileston Cooperative is bringing underutilized farmland back into production using a wealth creation and value-chain approach. One network member observed:

> Some of these farms are small and we realize that people need support to get started. Most can't afford to drill a well, install irrigation equipment, or build a hoop house so we work with Ford and other organizations to get funding so that people can get back on the land. It takes time to show people that their land is an asset — one that can help them earn an income and build wealth in the process. It also takes time to show people new ways of farming that are more sustainable than just pouring fertilizer and weed killer on the soil. That's why we partnered with the colleges and

universities to bring in agricultural experts who can show the farmers new protocols that will preserve the land and increase yields.

In Mississippi and Alabama, getting people to use standardized farming protocols and built structures such as greenhouses, new wells and irrigation systems ensured that land belonging to African Americans was not left to become overgrown, unused and undervalued. Further, by investing in land (a sustainable resource), the Network ensured that this asset will continue to produce wealth for future generations.

Built capital

Built capital includes the infrastructure created, used and shared that does not degrade other forms of capital, especially natural capital. The creation and improvement of built capital is both an end product of the Deep South value chains (e.g., a farmers' market) and also a means to an end (e.g., an irrigation system). The value chains in the Deep South are beginning to provide sufficient revenue to justify and support investments in built capital which are necessary for improving production quality and increasing sales.

Even in these early stages of the integrated wealth creation work in the Deep South, there are a number of noticeable built capital items that have resulted from the Network's activities, including greenhouses, wells, irrigation systems, shared farming equipment, a farmers' market, transportation vehicles, refrigeration units and storage facilities. At a farmers' meeting in Mississippi, members of Mileston cooperative commented on their increased built capital:

> We share our equipment and we are all working to get irrigation systems set up to help us have better crop yields. We're now renovating an old service station — changing it into a farmers' market which will give our members a place to sell their products. We're also setting up shared refrigeration areas so that we can store our greens and peas … keep them fresh so that they maintain good quality and fetch a better price. None of us could afford to do this on our own but by working together we have the ability to invest in our farms.

While these built capital items are not available in every community participating in the Network, several do exist in most of the communities involved and plans are underway to increase built capital in order to help farmers meet increased demand for their produce and to expand their activities across both states.

Financial capital

As wealth-creation value chains become fully functional and developed, they should show a profit for the people and organizations involved. Financial capital consists of monetary assets generated over and above the costs of production that are invested in other forms of capital and/or financial instruments that are unencumbered. Financial capital can be built in a variety of ways including budget surpluses, fees, tax revenues and bonds. These funds provide both rainy-day insurance and investment opportunities to help citizens and communities weather risks and uncertainties and invest in projects that increase other forms of capital.

The Deep South Network is just beginning to build financial capital through establishing a farmers' market and farmers' cooperative in Mississippi (in partnership with Mileston Cooperative), acquiring liability insurance for the farmers in the Network and earning income. At the end of 2013, the Network members collectively sold over $250,000 of collard greens, peas and turnips to high-end restaurants. While this may seem like a small amount of money, it is significant when one considers that the network only entered this market recently and also accumulated other capital as noted previously.

Political capital

Political capital is understood as the ability to influence the distribution of wealth resources, including setting the agenda for how these resources are supported (e.g., policy, financing). While the Deep South Network is still in the early stages of building political capital, its partner organizations have a long history of political activism. During interviews with members of several of the partner organizations, they indicated that they understood the importance of intentionally building political capital among and between allies in local, state and federal government to leverage and influence decision-makers. For instance, while standing in a field with other farmers and network members watching an irrigation system being installed, one farmer expressed how political action was needed to get local municipal officials to stop delaying permits for drilling wells and installing irrigation systems on African-American farms. As he leaned over the tractor, he explained his perspective on what was going on:

> These officials here in [name of town] they know what such a delay in getting a permit for a well means to a small farmer. It means you don't get your crop in the ground because you don't have enough water to guarantee proper irrigation. So they [the local officials] will wait or they'll sit on the paperwork because they really don't want us competing with these other mostly white farmers. ... That's not right and is it because we're an

African American? I'm not sure but we're trying to let people know at the political level that this situation has to change.

It appears that bureaucratic and regulatory inconsistency at the local level is proving to be a key barrier to scale the wealth-creation value chains. Thus, the capacity to influence resource allocation decisions that are favourable to wealth-creation value chains is required. The network members have discussed and taken various actions to deal with this issue, including organizing members and using an intermediary (usually one of the network members with advocacy experience) to identify the key resource allocation decision-makers who, when influenced, can bring about change at the local level that would help speed up the permit and payment process. While the organizations and individuals in the network often have the necessary capacity and experience to deal with local issues, the network as an entity increasingly recognizes that it also needs to take action on behalf of the membership. The advocacy roles for the Deep South Network are still emerging; however, given the deep experiences of the members in carrying out such roles, it is foreseeable that the network will play a significant role as an advocacy organization in the future.

Cultural capital

The rich history of African Americans in Alabama and Mississippi and their complex connections to the land have created a distinct culture that is defined not only by race but also by a state of mind and a sense of place. Members of the Deep South Network would often note that they possess a powerful understanding of culture that comes from decades of tenacious efforts by men and women who struggled to build capital and communities and support families while being denied basic civil rights. While it is beyond the scope of this paper to explore the Deep South culture in detail, it is worth noting how culture comprises an eighth form of wealth in Mississippi and Alabama and, in some ways, links all the other wealth components. A member of the network explained her understanding of cultural capital in this way:

> Our families, our history, our spirituality, our faith, our land, our struggles, our activism, our knowledge, our celebrations, our songs — these all shape our identity as African Americans here in the South. We are more than the colour of our skin, and our culture is deeper than narrow definitions of race.

Another farmer who helped build the cooperative structure for the farmers in Mississippi noted:

Our African-American culture builds unity and gives us a strong voice and defines our community's identity. All of our work here at the co-op starts with our culture and everything is built upon it — our buildings, our networks, our events, our plans.

One of the university intermediaries described the importance of tapping into cultural capital:

When you work here in the South, you have to know how it [culture] is used and how it can be built upon to strengthen your work and our future. If you tap into it, all of your work is stronger and people lean into what you're doing rather than sitting around watching you. ... I think one of the strengths of the wealth creation approach is that it builds upon culture. In fact, I'd argue that it's our culture that glues all of this work together.

Cultural capital enables communities to work together to recognize and enhance the resources and assets they possess. In the Deep South, it seems that as people tapped into cultural capital, they began to recognize their natural wealth (land) as an asset rather than a liability and were strengthened in their efforts to build agricultural value chains that increased other forms of wealth — social, political, individual, etc. In effect, cultural capital appears to tie together, enhance and enrich the other seven forms of wealth.

LEARNING FROM EXPERIENCES

We're changing the way people, both young and old, think and talk about the land and farming. But it takes time. You see, many African Americans here in the South, they don't see the land as an asset, as something that has value. They see land as something that slaves worked on and they don't want anything to do with farming. We have to change that view — there's too much that's been sacrificed. (Network partner)

The following section discusses some of the learning that is emerging from the Deep South Community Agricultural Network. Each of these lessons helps to build wealth, support leadership development and encourage participation.

Focusing on what people can do

Throughout the interviews and during the farm visits, it was clear that all partners understood the importance of focusing on what people could do and could change rather than on what they could not do or change. As one of the university partners explained, "A program targeted at communities which have experienced hardship in the past must be designed to motivate their members by making their experiences attractive rather than punitive."

The Deep South Network uses a positive, forward-looking discourse to validate experiences and empower participants and their communities. Promotional literature and documents talk about the value of local knowledge and highlight the assets of local communities and the skills of rural people. One farmer explained this more positive focus in this way:

> When they [the people from outside the community — McIntosh SEED, Tugaloo College] came here, they took time to listen to us and they respected what we already knew. There was never an attitude of, "We know best." Sure they challenged us to do some things differently, especially with the planting protocols, but even that was done in a helpful manner ... not in a way that showed disrespect. It was like we were all on a learning journey.

The experiences of the organizations in the Deep South Network demonstrate that when the skills that already exist in the community are recognized and enhanced, citizens develop a greater appreciation of their informal or experiential learning and exhibit an increased desire to become involved in their community. One of the college intermediaries who had worked with farmers in Mississippi for many years offered the following observation concerning the importance of recognizing and validating the skills that people already possess:

> What I've learned is that more people will participate in these initiatives ... and [will] take a greater leadership role if their previous experiences are recognized. Unfortunately, we live in and I work in an environment that is deeply socialized to privilege the attitude of learning equals schooling. ... It is a paradigm that virtually excludes any serious consideration of the individual and all of their informal learning. This is a development approach that we need to toss out!

The Deep South Network appears to utilize a more inclusive community-development practice, one that helps reveal, recognize and use what people already know and can do. In a turbulent economy where even highly qualified individuals face sudden, unexpected and demoralizing change, the importance of understanding, recognizing and using all of one's skills and knowledge has never been greater.

Changing the policy–practice discourse

Many community-development policy discourses and the resulting practices target economy-driven programs — employment support, back-to-work activities and education-to-work programs. In essence, the focus is on income generation rather than on wealth creation. The Deep South Community Agricultural Network illustrates that the current community-development policy discourse within local and state governments often privileges the exchange value of community development (income) rather than its use value (wealth creation). A longtime farmer and member of the Southern Rural Black Women's Initiative outlined her views on the negative results of privileging income over wealth in this way:

> We try to help women farmers see the value in growing produce in a sustainable way so that they can stay on their farm and make a living. Unfortunately, a lot of folks just want to make quick money but you can't farm that way. You might get a small amount of money in the short term but you'll never have enough to invest in the farm and eventually, you'll just let the land go because you don't see it as an asset.... For many years that's been the way folks around here have farmed ... and it's a common way to do development work — short-term income projects that put immediate cash into pockets but do nothing to build wealth over the long term.
>
> In my opinion, this way of doing development work has nothing to do with building capacity or developing leaders.... It also doesn't help us build a sustainable-agriculture business for African Americans because the focus is only on short-term income measures. We can't keep working and talking this way.

While community development policies and practices should give some attention to the income needs of citizens, the wealth-creation discourse and resulting practices help broaden this focus to include longer-term investment measures. In the Deep South project, this means investing in irrigation systems, planting protocols, greenhouses and building local capacity by offering training (e.g., in budgeting, bookkeeping and marketing). Such long-term efforts strengthen the capacity of people to act. A university partner observed:

> What I really like about what we are doing here in Alabama is that we are helping build a sustainable farming enterprise. We are using what people know about farming and ... combining that [knowledge] with expertise in new planting protocols and technical skills.... We are investing in infrastructure ... that will help the farmers over the long term, especially as they go to scale. And we're focusing on local foods and markets that have a future.

Recognizing the value of individual capital

Of key interest in the theoretical literature on development is whether the benefits of individual and community social capital can be altered through deliberate interventions and if these interventions result in a change in the perception of oneself as a citizen (White, White and Regan 2006). Wealth creation initiatives such as the Deep South Network are deliberate interventions (albeit with the consent and involvement of the individuals concerned) that respect the networks, norms of reciprocity and trust and the traditions that exist in a community. But such programs also play a role in challenging these norms and encouraging local action. Thus, while the network partners may understand their work as doing learning development, the programs they develop are most successful when they are done by members of the community.

When a wealth-creation approach such as the Deep South Network is led by community members, it helps foster a greater sense of possibility and skill recognition among residents (individual capital) while also helping to expose the social and political capital necessary to challenge and change local circumstances (agency). It appears, for example, that members of the Deep South Network change their attitudes and obtain enhanced feelings of personal self-worth — their individual capital — when they recognize and validate existing assets, which then shapes their behaviour and encourages their civic interactions — their agency.

A person's individual capital — or more plainly, a person's feeling of confidence and self-worth — determines how he or she negotiates life passages and challenges in daily life, work and learning and can also determine how he or she acts.

Supporters of wealth creation and asset-based approaches assert that people with improved self-confidence are more likely to take calculated risks, have a future-oriented focus and have a desire to be more active in the community. Often, the result of such improved confidence is a desire to learn (Sherraden et al. 2005), which increases a person's skill capacity and encourages their motivation to act.

One of the main lessons learned from the Deep South Community Agricultural Network has been that the people who have the opportunity to create wealth speak of feeling like stakeholders, like active citizens in the society in which they live. A farmer from Cottage House explained how she noticed a change in the way farmers talked about their skills and abilities since being involved with the Network:

> I think our farmers now feel more confident in themselves and their abilities and they feel more motivated to work together.... It's not that they didn't have the capacity to step up and build a better farm before this project ... they just didn't feel like it was worth it ... and they didn't feel like anyone would support them. They also didn't think that anyone would listen to them and learn from what they already knew. There are a

lot of experienced people living in these rural communities ... and they have so much to offer if given the chance.

This feeling of being an active citizen with experiences and knowledge to contribute — individual capital — is a primary factor in motivating people to participate and act — agency — in citizen-led initiatives such as the Deep South Community Agricultural Network.

Recognizing cultural capital and developing local leadership

The Deep South experience illustrates how culture powerfully contributes to wealth creation and leadership development because the identity and historical experiences of African Americans have significant influence on the culture of Mississippi and Alabama and on American culture as a whole. Cultural capital includes the practices, social networks, history and traditions that reflect the values and identity of a group of people:

> Cultural capital includes the dynamics of who we know and feel comfortable with, what heritages are valued, collaboration across races, ethnicities, and generations, etc. Investments in cultural capital create or sustain the values, traditions, beliefs, and/or language that become the currency to leverage other types of capital. (Yellow Wood Associates and the Wealth Creation Management Team 2012: 14)

As discussed earlier, cultural capital enriches social capital and is perhaps deeper as it goes beyond relationships and networks and delves into ethnicity, race and beliefs. In the Deep South, building social capital to grow the value chains requires the Network members to be intentional in their efforts to grow cultural capital. Recognizing and using cultural capital ensures the strength and diversity of relationships needed to further the success of the value chain and wealth creation efforts. Further, and perhaps more importantly, cultural capital roots all activities in the historical context and encourages the development and participation of local leaders. One of the college partners noted:

> Without cultural capital, the Deep South value chains would not take root and the local leaders would not participate. ... I think one of the direct results of this approach [wealth creation] is that it helps people in the community realize their leadership potential. It gives them a strong voice ... [because] the language and practices of generating wealth resonate with the long-standing civil rights activities of our past.

Engaging and connecting intermediaries

Intermediaries (also referred to as value-chain managers) work alongside farmers at the local/community level in both Alabama and Mississippi to build relationships among and between all of the network partners. They have solid experience in community development and, in the case of the Deep South Network, have experience with farming and/or organizational development and management. They help support the value chain by bringing in partners to build existing capacity or strengthen a particular activity. One of the intermediaries described her work as a "link builder:"

> I help articulate the vision of the value chain but it's not my vision, it's the vision of the farmers. When I see that we have a link that needs strengthening or that is missing, I seek out partners to work with us. ... So for instance, when we needed technical expertise on growing protocols, I went to the university ... [and] sought out agricultural experts who could work with us.

The intermediaries/value-chain managers are also well versed in community issues and, given the cultural context of the Deep South, are African American. They know the community organizations and most often are leading several local citizen-led agencies and engaging in local civic engagement activities. They understand how to work collaboratively and take time to listen carefully in order to fully appreciate the experiences of the network members. On a breezy spring day as one of the intermediaries drove along a rural highway, he related a story of working with local farmers over the past year:

> When I started, they didn't really trust me — at least not completely. It took a year of working on the ground, going to meetings, eating together, visiting them in the fields, meeting their family members, talking late into the evening while sitting on a front porch ... all of the things that you do here in the South to build trust and relationships.
>
> At some point, I think they realized that I really cared about them and about their farms ... I also know what it's like to live and work in a rural community and they saw that experience in me. Before long, I was invited to so many events, I couldn't keep up! I was asked to speak, to pray, to share stories [laughs]. That year ... getting to know the farmers and their families helped me see the humanity of this work and I suppose helped me build relationship wealth.

The intermediaries gain support from each other and gain direction from project managers who have broader responsibilities for the overall Deep South

Initiative and who provide strategic input for and coordination of the network across Mississippi and Alabama. During group and individual interviews, the intermediaries noted that without the support of the project managers (from McIntosh SEED), they would find it difficult to "raise their work and the value chain efforts beyond the local level" and would be challenged to learn from other value-chain managers in Mississippi and Alabama:

> If McIntosh SEED wasn't involved with this project and providing the overall coordination and direction ... and bringing us together from across Mississippi and Alabama to learn from one another, we would not be as successful in our work and the value chains would be limited and fragmented.... Sure, we'd have some local efforts but they would be small and no one would be learning from each other.... Frankly, there wouldn't be a Deep South Network without the work of McIntosh SEED ... [because] to make all of these individual, local projects work with and learn from each other, you need an organization to provide coordination at the regional level.

Using a distributed management process

All of the partners engaged in the Deep South Initiative are focused on developing practices and collective strategies that build local assets and create wealth that stays local. However, "staying local" while working with multiple partners over the vast geographical area of Mississippi and Alabama requires a distributed management process. The advantages of distributed management (e.g., having local decision-making within a regional structure) consist in allowing participants to benefit from a broad range of ideas, to share responsibilities, to make efficient use of resources, to avoid duplication of efforts and to enable intermediaries to respond to demands from grantees and other interested parties in a timely and localized manner.

In Mississippi and Alabama, the network is beginning to develop a collaborative framework based upon a distributed management process. In addition to the advantages already noted, this distributed management structure has enabled partners to think strategically about their work, share resources, have greater influence throughout both states and, most importantly, work collaboratively rather than competitively.

This support for collaboration is especially important in the South, where a history of limited wealth-creation resources and systemic racism has led to a culture of competition between organizations and individuals, even those working for common goals. While the process of building trust and relationships takes time, the work that project participants are doing within the initiative is leading to significant progress in overcoming this challenging history (Yellow Wood Associates and the Wealth Creation Management Team 2012).

Balancing local-national-global perspectives

A challenging issue expressed by several of the farmers is how communities should balance local needs within the context of state, national and international policies and economies. That is, governments, institutions, NGOs and businesses in Mississippi and Alabama can develop local and state strategies to encourage wealth creation but these strategies cannot ignore the impact of global shifts in policy and trade. Even with the best wealth creation strategies, some communities face significant turmoil from job losses as companies move their operations elsewhere. One of the intermediaries from Tougaloo College explained:

> The wealth creation approach has to adopt a learning model that encourages growth from within — at the personal level, but it must also give consideration to how national and global issues affect people's lives.... People need to think about the bigger picture but they also need to make sure that they don't lose their farm.

In essence, the Deep South wealth creation approach enables people to think at a systems level — locally, regionally and nationally. It is a sustainable approach that prepares people to be competitive within a local-global marketplace.

Building relationships and trust
between rural and urban communities

The experience in the Deep South and in most of the states and communities involved with Wealth Creation in Rural Communities (WCRC) is that there is growing demand in urban areas for many things that rural areas can provide. The challenge is connecting producers with service providers and buyers across the region. In Alabama, one of the farmers described his efforts to connect rural producers with urban consumers:

> I have the land and I grow the crops and I've built the hoop houses ... but connecting with folks in the city, the people who are going to buy what I grow, well ... that's not something I know much about. I also don't have a lot of time [to connect with markets] because it takes most of my day just to keep things going ... you know, planting, watering, and checking to make sure everything is growing. So what I do is work with other folks — members of my family and other people in the community, some Black and some white, who have connections and experience [with marketing]. They know the restaurants who want to buy my greens and so I let them make the deals while I grow the crops.

In Mississippi, members of Mileston Cooperative use the cooperative structure to bridge the rural-urban divide and help market and distribute their produce. One of the members described how the cooperative helps rural farmers:

> Our farmers, they know the land and they know the community and they have lots of skill in growing the crops but many need some help in getting their crops to market.... So we're building a farmer's market here in town that will give them a spot to sell their crops along with other members [of the co-op]. They could sell their produce on their own and many do that ... but as they start growing more produce and try to reach out beyond the local community, they need support. That's where the cooperative structure helps [because] we can reach a broader group of consumers.

The members of the Deep South Network are working to connect producers and buyers in order to show how each part of the region, rural and urban, can benefit from investments in wealth creation value chains, and how products and services produced in rural areas can address the demands of urban areas. One of the intermediaries explained the urban-rural relationship in this way:

> We need each other to survive.... We have to start dancing together rather than ignoring each other. It's not a question of whether a rural lifestyle is better or [that] an urban setting provides more opportunity. Those divisions are no longer true — maybe they never were but we all bought into this false notion. I think the [wealth creation] framework gives us all a structure to express shared values — values that not only cross racial lines but urban-rural ones. It's time we worked together, not run in opposite directions.

The value-chain experiences and outcomes of the WCRC Initiative should help identify new opportunities to establish rural-urban connections that are mutually supportive rather than exploitive.

SUSTAINABILITY

> I realize that we're just getting started [and] we don't have a lot of big numbers to give you or examples of how we've built all sorts of wealth and made big sums of money ... but we're putting down deep roots in land ... [and] in communities that have sat idle for far too long ... in land that we possess and communities in which we live but we see as having no value.... But now, because of this [network] we are nourishing our soil, our souls and our communities. We are building a future for our

families, creating wealth from what we already own — our land and our people! (Mississippi farmer)

From the Deep South experience, it is clear that the wealth-creation framework is a powerful development approach. The value-chain and wealth-creation language helps frame the work and provides direction for those who participate in the network. This language also provides a way to measure the impacts of various activities designed to build wealth and ensure the sustainability of the value chains. Further, the approach has recognized existing skills and experiences and has tapped into the cultural capital of African Americans in Mississippi and Alabama. A Mileston Cooperative member observed:

> What we are doing here is working. When I talk to [the farmers in] the co-op they tell me that this approach is a good one ... [because] it builds on what they already know and helps them to develop new skills and [find] new markets for their produce.... I notice that they are more involved in the co-op and [they] come out to meetings more often.... I think they are more involved because [the concept of] wealth really speaks to them and they now understand how wealth is something that can be passed on to their families in a way that income cannot. So they want to be involved.

The predominant perception among the network members is that increased wealth and successful value chains are being realized. Farmers, community members, intermediaries and interested organizations unanimously agree that the effort they have invested in the network is worth it, that the benefits of the work — the wealth — outweigh the costs. The distributed management structure and the wealth-creation framework are widely viewed as successful, enabling cross-cultural communication as well as collective and individual growth.

As with any emerging innovation, there are several challenges to be addressed. The intermediaries noted that a uniform record-keeping system is needed for producers in order to manage workflow and respond to inquiries for data. Several farmers spoke of the need for more investment for small farmers to meet increased demands for produce and to expand into larger and more competitive markets. Network organizations felt that a marketing and recruitment strategy was needed to encourage youth to view farming as a viable and legitimate career. The university and college partners indicated that the farmers need to be encouraged to follow the growing protocols. Many of the farmers talked about the need to challenge local and state policies that benefit large-scale commercial farmers but limit the viability of smaller farms owned by African Americans. Further, one key challenge raised by all of the network members is how to sustainably scale the initiative so that farmers are able to meet the increased demands for their goods and services.

A farmer in Mississippi felt that several recent initiatives would help in this regard:

> I think that the [establishment of a] farmers' cooperative and the farm-
> ers' market are going to help small farmers to work together to meet the
> demands [for locally grown produce] but as we start moving across the
> state, we're going to need to have more of these sorts of things [markets
> and co-ops].

Despite these challenges, the members of the Deep South Network seem confident that as the network matures and grows, it will have people with the necessary skills and partners with the required capacity to manage expansion and sustainability challenges. One Mississippi farmer observed:

> Will we have some hiccups? Of course, you can't do this work and you
> certainly can't learn anything if you don't make some mistakes.... But we
> have enough experience now to know what's likely to cause us problems
> and we have enough people involved who can help out. We can't stop at
> this point and say, "Well that's all we need to do. Let the community and
> the farmers work on their own." No, we have to move forward and let oth-
> ers know what's going on and we need support to maintain and expand
> this work throughout the Deep South. There's no turning back now.

CONCLUSION

> Folks see that these efforts are paying off — not in cash, although that's
> nice to have. No it's more than that ... it's hope ... and that [hope] helps
> you stand up and take action ... which is the first step in building wealth.
> (Alabama farmer)

The Deep South Community Agricultural Network celebrates and continues the Civil Rights Movement by reclaiming and reaffirming the stock of natural and human assets within the region to empower African Americans to create a new future built upon the creation of wealth. Specifically, the organizations see oppor-tunities to build sustainable livelihoods in the region by using people's knowledge of the land and strengthening agricultural value chains. When people create good livelihoods for themselves and their families, they build and grow their own assets. They generate and hold financial assets; they acquire new skills, education and knowledge and they collectively build upon and sustain the natural and cultural assets of their region.

Rural communities in Mississippi and Alabama already have an abundance of fertile land and a large number of landowners who carry generational knowledge of the soil, climate and other environmental assets of the region. The Deep South Community Agricultural Network builds on these assets to link farmers into a value chain where they work together to meet the food demands from high-end restaurants, large-scale institutional buyers and local schools while investing in a shared infrastructure and receiving the training required to succeed in a competitive marketplace.

The network has been successful in establishing trust, building identity capital and motivating agency among its members by becoming a vehicle for regional cooperation and innovation. African-American farmers see how the collective power of the organization deepens the impact and expands the scale of their individual efforts. By building upon the experiential knowledge of local people and by helping them to recognize the potential of the assets they possess, the network has changed the previous and disempowering narrative of "have not" to that of "have much." This project presents a profound opportunity for Mississippi and Alabama to develop value-chain resources that empower citizen organizations, build wealth for individuals and support leaders of local communities and governments who are seeking to find new ways to invest responsively in citizen-led activities.

This case study also reveals that a wealth-creation approach does not rely on blind optimism or magical thinking. It does not offer quick fixes to social ills or over-promise results. It is not based on ideals of sweeping social transformation but it does seek fairness and equity. Further, while the supporting theoretical constructs and discourse provide a descriptive language for analysis and action, the approach is not based on theory alone. This is an approach based on direct, systematic observations on how a growing number of highly effective communities think and act with regard to what their citizens have and can be — assets — rather than on what they do not possess and cannot do — deficits. Deficit-based thinking is rooted in mistrust and fear. Wealth-based thinking arises from aspiration and agency.

The roots of Deep South capital

The following narrative illustrates metaphorically how capital is rooted and wealth is built over several generations in the Deep South. It is told by an Alabama farmer and longtime community development practitioner as she stands in her flower garden on a warm spring day.

> *Interviewer:* So tell me the story of these lilies.
> *Farmer:* The story of the Hutchenson Plantation lily?
> *Interviewer:* Yes.
> *Farmer:* Well it was my great-great-great-grandmother. She came from Pretoria, Africa. She was a slave and was working on this particular plantation in South Carolina … the Hutchenson plantation. The slave master

had her working in the garden because she did so well with the flowers. That's what she'd spend her time doing while keeping the children because everyone else was out working in the fields.

But the day came when the soldiers arrived and rounded up everybody and took them to different places. She had no possessions, nothing at all ... except a piece of the root [of the lily] about eight inches long and a piece of an iris in her apron pocket. She also had some cuttings from what we call the wedding rose. She had just finished trimming them and she knew how to propagate roses.

She took that [the rose cuttings, lily and iris root] with her everywhere she went; and over the years, every time someone would get married, she'd give them a piece of the rose, the iris and also what we now call the Hutchenson Plantation lily. It was her way of keeping us connected ... of reminding us of our past ... of the power of small things in creating beauty and giving hope in times of struggle.

This one [points to a lily stem] comes up as a very pink rose [colour], and every time somebody got married in our family she would always dig up one root and give it to them because that one root would multiply. And so, when I got married, I was given one root from my grandmother who had gotten one from her grandmother just as she had gotten one from her grandmother — three grandmothers.

Everywhere I've moved, I would have to dig up pieces of them [rose and lily] and take them with me [laughs]. That was the family tradition. So now, I have all these flowers here which came from her and from one root. I only took one root and you see how they've multiplied [gestures to a garden full of lilies and irises].

The lily is very beautiful and powerful. It grows almost four-and-a-half feet tall and the stem and flower that comes out has a beautiful pink colour. It looks like a bell. ... And at night around six o'clock, if you want to smell something really good when it's in bloom, hmmmm, it's a calming smell.

I like to walk here in the evening and know I'm connected to this place ... and to an African-American history that is rooted in this rich soil, and to my grandmother's endurance. It's like that old hymn that talks about wealth beyond all measure [laughs]. That's what our work is about, remembering who we are and what is possible, and that's why I do what I do. That's why I stand up for my community.

This story provides a powerful metaphor of the tenacity and historical underpinnings of African Americans in the Deep South to build and sustain wealth despite overwhelming odds. It is a story that shows how wealth can be built from the smallest of things — tiny roots that spread out, grow and produce strong stems and beautiful flowers that give hope, shape identity and encourage agency. It is a fertile narrative that reveals how cultural capital roots and grows wealth.

Notes

1. In March of 2013, individual and group interviews were conducted with twenty-two members of the Deep South Community Agricultural Network in various locations — homes, farms, offices, greenhouses, meeting rooms, cars, restaurants — throughout Alabama and Mississippi. These first-hand impressions are shared in this case and supplemented with information from funder reports, press releases, information bulletins, policy briefs and other documents that examine the work of the network and discuss its conceptual underpinnings.

2. Triple bottom line refers to the financial, social and environmental effects of an organization's policies and actions that determine its viability as a sustainable organization. It is often used as a metric to measure business involvement in sustainability.

References

Alabama and Mississippi Value Chain Project. 2012. *Assessment, Planning and Measurement, September 2012.* Deep South Community Agricultural Network.

Bernard, T. 2010. *Hope and Hard Times: Communities, Collaboration and Sustainability.* Gabriola Island, BC: New Society Publishers.

Boshara, R., and M. Sherraden. 2004. *Status of Asset Building Worldwide.* Washington, DC: New America Foundation.

Castelloe, P., T. Watson and K. Allen. 2011. "Rural Networks for Wealth Creation: Impacts and Lessons Learned from U.S. Communities." Asheville, NC: Rural Support Partners. <http://www.ruralsupportpartners.com/docs/RuralNetworksforWealthCreation.pdf>.

Clancy, K., and K. Ruhf. 2010. "Is Local Enough? Some Arguments for Regional Food Systems." *Choices: The Magazine of Farm, Food, and Resource Issues* 25, 1. <http://www.choicesmagazine.org/magazine/article.php?article=114>.

Dabson, B., J. Jensen, A. Okagaki, A. Blair and M. Carroll. 2012. "Case Studies of Wealth Creation and Rural-Urban Linkages." Columbia, MO: Rural Futures Lab. <http://community-wealth.org/_pdfs/articles-publications/cross-sectoral/paper-dabson-et-al12.pdf>.

Feser, E., and A. Isserman. 2009. "The Rural Role in National Value Chains." *Regional Studies* 43, 1: 89–109.

Hoffer, D., and M. Levy. 2010. "Measuring Community Wealth: Report for the Wealth Creation in Rural Communities project of the Ford Foundation." <http://community-wealth.org/_pdfs/news/recent-articles/04-11/report-hoffer-levy.pdf>.

Littles, J., and C. Peterson. 2013. "The Deep South Wealth Creation Network: Partner Building Agricultural Value Chains in Alabama and Mississippi." Powerpoint presentation.

Mathie, A., and G. Cunningham (eds.). 2008. *From Clients to Citizens. Communities Changing the Course of Their Own Development.* Rugby, UK: Practical Action.

Sherraden, M., A. Moore-McBride, E. Johnson, S. Hanson, F. Ssewamala and T. Shanks. 2005. *Saving in Low-Income Households: Evidence from Interviews with Participants in the American Dream Demonstration.* St. Louis, MO: Center for Social Development, Washington University in St. Louis.

Shipman, B., and W. Miller. 2013. "The Deep South Wealth Creation Network." Powerpoint presentation.

White, D., S. White and S. Regan. 2006. *The Citizen's Stake: Exploring the Future of Universal Asset Policies.* Seminar report. London, UK: Institute for Public Policy Research.

Yellow Wood Associates. 2012. "Wealth Creation in Rural Communities —Building Sustainable Livelihoods: Cross Regional Convening." <http://yellowwood.org/wealth-creation-in-rural-communities-wealthworks-411.html>.

Yellow Wood Associates and the Wealth Creation Management Team. 2012. "Formulating a Sustainable Economic Development Process for Rural America: Fourth Interim Report." <http://www.yellowwood.org/assets/resource_library/resource_docs/formulating%20a%20sustainable%20economic%20development%20process%204th%20interim%20report.pdf>.

REACHING BACK TO MOVE FORWARD TOWARDS A FUTURE OF HOPE

The Story of Sandhills Family Heritage Association

Yogesh Ghore

> We were land-based agrarian people from Africa. We were uprooted from Africa, and we spent 200 years developing our culture as black Americans. And then we left the South. We uprooted ourselves and attempted to transplant this culture to the pavements of the industrialized North. And it was a transplant that did not take. I think if we had stayed in the South, we would have been a stronger people. And because the connection between the South of the 20s, 30s and 40s has been broken, it's very difficult to understand who we are. (August Wilson cited in Shannon 1997: 659)

The Sandhills Family Heritage Association (SFHA) is reviving the unique African-American culture in the Sandhills region of North Carolina. One of the first African-American organizations in the United States to combine land protection with community economic development, SFHA demonstrates how cultural connections to the land can be converted into a broad array of economic, social and environmental benefits. The key principle of the Association's work is embodied in its emblem, the mythical Sankofa bird that moves forward while looking backward with the egg of the future in its beak. The word Sankofa comes from the Akan people of West Africa and translates into English as "go back to fetch it." SFHA is helping community members reach back and gather the best of what the past has to teach in order to move forward.

The seeds of SFHA were sown when its founder Ammie McRae Jenkins returned to her birthplace in the Sandhills after living for decades in the city of Durham some 120 km away, where she had worked for eighteen years as a computer programmer and instructor at Durham Technical Community College and later as a health and beauty spa owner. What started as a personal quest to learn about her family's history soon became a broader endeavour to document the rich cultural heritage of the African-American community in the Sandhills. Ammie's conversations with the elders revealed one thread that ran through every family story shared: the deep connection of local African-American families to the land. Land had always been central to their social, economic and political life as well as to their cultural identity. However, with the introduction of Jim Crow laws[1] and the racial and economic discrimination that ensued, Black landownership began to decline. The decline of Black landownership and the discrimination against African-American farmers continued even in the civil rights era (Daniel 2013). The stories of Sandhills families recorded by Ammie provided ample evidence of the detrimental effects the loss of land had upon their livelihoods and the unique African-American culture in this region. It was natural, therefore, that land and the cultural traditions tied to landownership acted as a magnet drawing together a group of African Americans concerned about preserving and passing on their heritage, which eventually developed into SFHA.

Today, SFHA delivers programs in heritage preservation, outreach education, protection of land and economic development with a view to fostering self-reliance and a sense of self-worth among the African-American community in the Sandhills. Inspired by the local traditions of giving, SFHA leaders reaffirm these traditions through the ways they engage with the community and other public and private organizations, which they describe as "culture-based philanthropy." SFHA's work offers important lessons and insights, especially with regard to Black land loss, the inclusion — or, rather, non-inclusion — of African-American communities in the mainstream economy and the capacity of active citizens to influence systemic social change, even when these grassroots Davids have to face the Goliath of mainstream development. Perhaps the key contribution of SFHA to social innovation is that it offers a vision of development in which economic well-being is attained through preserving and drawing on local cultural heritage, rather than at the cost of disregarding or even destroying it. However, in order to clearly appreciate this and other innovations that SFHA's work presents, it is important to understand the historical context that shaped it.

CONTEXT

The Sandhills comprise eleven counties in south-central North Carolina: Cumberland, Harnett, Lee, Moore, Richmond, Scotland, Hoke, Robeson, Chatham, Montgomery and Wake. This area holds national significance for a number of reasons. Besides being recognized as one of the last strongholds of longleaf pine forests that rank among the most diverse ecosystems in North America, it is also home to one of the world's largest military complexes, some of the finest golf courses in the United States and a unique African-American culture. The Sandhills region has witnessed the dramatic journey of African Americans from slavery to self-reliance. This journey amply demonstrates the inventiveness and tenacity of African Americans, their entrepreneurship and strong cultural ties to the land and the many contributions they have made to the region.

African-American heritage in the Southern United States dates back to the early seventeenth century, when the first Africans were forcibly brought to this region to work on tobacco, rice and cotton plantations. In the pre-Civil War United States, enslaved African labour played a critical role in economic development, especially in the South. The high rates of slavery were generally associated with tobacco plantations in Virginia and rice plantations in Southern Carolina; the dry, nutrient-poor soils of North Carolina's Sandhills could not support these crops. Instead the demand for enslaved Africans in this region came mainly from the naval stores industry — the production of tar, pitch and turpentine for the construction and maintenance of wooden ships (Aragon 2000). In the mid-1800s, North Carolina produced over 95 percent of the naval stores in the country (North Carolina History n.d.). Slave labour there was used primarily to produce turpentine, a volatile fluid obtained by the steam distillation of pine resin, which had a multitude of uses in and beyond the naval industry. "It was a dirty job," notes Ammie Jenkins, "many people got sick from the fumes" (personal communication).[2] Besides the naval stores industry, enslaved Africans also worked on farms, constructed buildings, sailed ships and did domestic chores (UNC n.d.). Among other things, they built the longest plank road in North Carolina between 1849 and 1854, stretching 129 miles (208 km) from Fayetteville to the village of Bethania near Salem.

The social dynamic of slave life on farms in North Carolina was somewhat different than it was in other Southern states, where large-scale plantations typically featured hundreds of slaves and a clear hierarchy of specialized field and domestic workers. By contrast, most slaves on small farms in North Carolina were required to work in the fields and at various other jobs at different times of the year.[3] Another consequence of living in smaller groups was that slaves in North Carolina generally had more interaction with slaves on other farms. They often looked to other farms to find a spouse and visited different farms during their limited free time. The relatively intense social interactions and versatility characteristic of the local slave population were conducive to the development of a close-knit African-American community with a strong entrepreneurial spirit in the region after the abolition of slavery.

The emergence of land-based Black culture

After the institution of slavery was formally abolished in the United States in 1865, African Americans fought hard for their economic independence and acquisition of land was central to that struggle (Grant, Wood and Wright 2012). Many freed slaves became tenant farmers or sharecroppers on the land of their former owners. This eventually enabled some of them to become landowners as the cash-poor whites sold off their land in parts (Aragon 2000). The land did not come cheap or easy, though. African Americans had to work very hard for many years as sharecroppers or in industry in order to be able to acquire farms of their own. Yet land was so important to them that in the period immediately following emancipation, most African Americans wanted to become landowners even more than they wanted voting rights or education (Mitchell 2000). Landownership was much more than owning a piece of property; it provided a source of livelihood as well as a means to economic and political independence. Ammie Jenkins explains the importance of landownership for African Americans in the Sandhills in this way: "Land was a dream of independence, it was power to our ancestors.... It was one thing around which they achieved self-sufficiency and built communities" (personal communication).

Owing to the persistent desire of African Americans to acquire land and their hard work to fulfil that desire, Black landownership in the United States rose steadily until the early twentieth century. By 1920, nearly one million African Americans owned roughly fifteen million acres (six million hectares) of farmland across the country, and 25 percent of Black farmers owned the land they worked (Grant, Wood and Wright 2012; Mitchell 2000). Almost all of the Black landowners lived in the South. In the Sandhills region, many of the former slaves owned 50 to 100 acres (20 to 40 hectares), and a few owned much larger amounts of land, including Ammie's great-grandfather who owned 658 acres (266 hectares).

After acquiring land, African Americans converted it into farms where the entire family would dwell and work together. This way of living shaped a culture of self-reliance and entrepreneurship. The Sandhills region in particular boasts a strong history of Black entrepreneurship; local African-American businesses included the production of natural remedies, carpentry, barbershops and eateries, to name a few. Ammie pieced together the following account of what her family's economy looked like in the early 1900s:

The one hundred-acre [forty-hectare] farm of ... grandfather Neill McRae, Sr. [was] agriculturally diversified and self-sufficient. Structures ... included a house, hay barn, mule stables, smokehouse, wood shed, ice house, chicken coop, cane syrup mill, and privy. Besides grains such as corn and wheat, the family raised livestock and a variety of fruits and nuts such as pears, grapes, peaches, apples, plums, blackberries, dewberries, persimmons, pecans, and black walnuts. These items were grown for family consumption, and also sold directly off the farm to local customers, as was honey gathered from the orchard bees. Deer, rabbits, squirrels, and raccoons were hunted for recreation as well as for meat to supplement the homegrown beef, pork, and poultry (as cited in Aragon 2000: 42).

Black-owned farms were generally able to supply the needs of the resident families without external assistance. When additional cash was needed, family members would work in the tar and turpentine industry or plant more cash crops such as corn, cotton or tobacco. Ammie refers to those years as a golden period in the history of African Americans in the Sandhills, a time when "we were a self-sufficient community" buoyed by a spirit of entrepreneurship and sharing. A century later, these traditions of entrepreneurship, self-reliance, and sharing would become the guiding lights for SFHA.

Ironically, the end of slavery, while making it possible for African Americans to achieve self-determination and economic independence through landownership, did little to ease social segregation and racial tensions (Aragon 2000). These tensions, along with other factors that will be discussed in the following section, eventually led to epidemic losses of Black-owned farmland across the United States.

Decline of African-American landownership

The decline of Black-owned land in the rural parts of the Southern United States over the twntieth century is a well-documented trend. After the 1920s, there was a general decline in the number of farmers across the country but its rate was markedly uneven with regard to race (Richardson 2013). Wood and Gilbert (2000) and Mitchell (2000) have established that the number of Black farmers in the U.S. plummeted by 98 percent between 1920 and 1997, whereas the number of white farmers declined by 66 percent over the same period. The overall amount of Black-owned farmland also declined sharply: according to the 1997 U.S. Census of Agriculture, African-American farm owners or operators across the country, including part-owners, owned a little over two million acres (eight-hundred thousand hectares), a dramatic decline from the fifteen million acres (six million hectares) they had accumulated between emancipation and 1920. As noted by Mitchell (2010: 22), "In 1920, black farm owners accounted for one out of every seven farms in the United States; today [in 2000] these farms account for less than one percent of all U.S. farms."

The period following emancipation and enactment of Jim Crow laws in the 1890s was marked by vigilante "justice," lynchings, race riots and attacks on successful African-American businesses and farms (Conrad, Whitehead, Mason and Stewart 2005). Traumatized by the rampant violence and lack of legal protection in the South, African Americans fled en masse to the North, leaving behind their land, livelihoods and ancestral culture. Their exodus continued for much of the twentieth century, involving over eight million people (Gregory 2005). Many of them never prepared wills determining who would inherit their property; after their death, ownership of their land was automatically passed on to their heirs. Mitchell (2000) estimates that at least half of African Americans who had owned land in the South died without a will; therefore, a significant proportion of Black-owned land in this region, especially in its rural parts, had heir property status. Heirs own such property as tenants in common. All heirs hold an undivided interest in the entire property, which cannot be physically distinguished but can be transferred or sold to someone outside the family or ownership group. Such an unstable type of ownership spurred the decline of Black-owned land, since any heir had the right to partition his or her interest and cash out.

Land developers would often use this loophole, convincing just one inheritor to sell their portion of an heir property, whereupon the sale of the entire property

Figure 12-1 Number of Black-operated farms in the U.S., 1900–1997

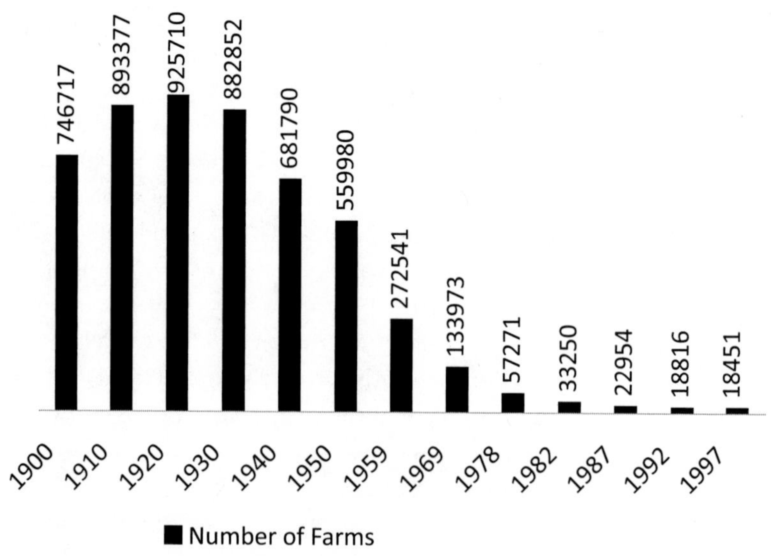

Source of original data: Wood and Gilbert 2000.

could be forced since it had not been legally apportioned to the other heirs. The growth in the number of heirs over generations, leading to increasingly fragmented property ownership, further contributed to Black land loss. These factors are still in place today (PBS n.d.). Indeed, Mitchell (2000: 9) argues that "a sale for partition and division is the most widely used legal method facilitating the loss of heir property" in African-American communities.

Those African-American farmers who remained in the South would often experience various forms of discrimination from local offices of the United States Department of Agriculture (USDA), such as untimely delivery of operating loans or non-provision of information about the availability of technical and financial support programs (Grant, Wood and Wright 2012), which could prevent them from being able to plant their crops at the optimal time or purchase new equipment and necessary supplies. The expansion of corporate agriculture further exacerbated the decline of family farms across race lines; however, African-American farmers were affected especially severely because they were also hit by discriminatory practices of USDA and other agencies (C. Brown personal communication). Daniel (2013) highlights an irony whereby the expansion of Black-owned land was most pronounced during the period when race-based violence and discrimination in the United States reached its worst level since the Civil War, while the decline of African-American landownership peaked during the heyday of the Civil Rights Movement when new government programs incorporating the latest scientific and technological achievements promised to usher in an era of universal prosperity.

Fort Bragg

In addition to the factors discussed above, the Sandhills witnessed one specific phenomenon that caused the loss of Black-owned land in this area: the creation of what has now become by far the largest army installation in the country.[4]

During the First World War, the U.S. Army was "seeking an area having suitable terrain, adequate water, rail facilities and a climate suitable for year-round training" (U.S. Army n.d.). The Sandhills region met these criteria and a military reservation now known as Fort Bragg was established there. Today, Fort Bragg is one of the largest and busiest military complexes in the world, with an area of 251 square miles (650 km^2) and a population of approximately 140,000, including nearly 80,000 military and civilian personnel and over 60,000 military family members (militarybases.com 2012).

The mapping of the original African-American land holdings in the area carried out by SFHA revealed that much of today's Fort Bragg acreage was once owned by Black farmers. Many of them never wanted to leave their hard-earned and well-tended land but were forced to do so under eminent domain provisions.[5] To facilitate the takeover, the authorities persuaded local landowners that they would prove themselves as loyal American citizens by letting the military use their land. A board member of SFHA recalls:

> Military people came in big numbers, with horses and guns, and when you see them for the first time, it puts a fear in you. Many people got afraid but they had no rescue because the military itself was there "to protect them from the enemy"! Many felt powerless in that situation and ended up giving the land for as little as nothing, practically a giveaway. (personal communication)

However effective these tactics may have been, Ammie remembers that the military had to escort the last Black farmer out of the Fort Bragg area because he did not want to give up his land voluntarily.

Since its creation, Fort Bragg has continuously expanded its area and operations. Many Sandhills farmers who started out with fifty to one hundred acres [twenty to forty hectares], are now down to five to six acres [less than three hectares] or even less, and some have lost all of the land they once owned (focus group discussion with SFHA members). When Ammie started interviewing elders in communities surrounding Fort Bragg in 2001, she found that many local residents feared its further growth. Their fears soon came true: in 2005, the U.S. Base Realignment and Closure Commission recommended a significant expansion of Fort Bragg to carry out the relocation of forces from recently closed bases across the country. As a consequence, its core area was enlarged and a buffer zone was established, which restricted non-military development around the base. With the expansion of the core military area, additional land was also required for housing, infrastructure, services and other activities associated with the maintenance of the base. If Fort Bragg continues to grow, it threatens local landowners with further land loss and land use restrictions.

Culture at risk

Despite facing the hardships of slavery, racial discrimination, segregation and enormous financial burdens, African Americans created a strong culture closely tied to the land they once worked on and later owned. The decline of landownership profoundly impacted the African-American community. First, African Americans agonized deeply over losing the one thing they had thought they could leave as an inheritance for their descendants. Second, losing their land meant losing the income they derived from using that land for agricultural and other purposes. Further, losing their land put them at risk of losing their cultural traditions inextricably linked to the land. The land was much more than just a natural resource for African Americans; it was the lifeblood of their culture. As a board member of SFHA observed, "The land — it's about [your] whole life … hunting for food;

growing food; income. It's a secure place you can call home. All of these things you lose when you lose the land" (personal communication).

It was into such circumstances that SFHA was born.

THE UNFOLDING OF SFHA

SFHA was formally incorporated in 2001 but its roots can be traced much further back to a momentous experience Ammie Jenkins had in 1978, when she returned to the Sandhills to visit her birth place for the first time after she had to leave it twenty-three years earlier. She came back to fulfil one of her ailing mother's final wishes:

> Mama wanted to see the old home place before she died. But she got so sick that she couldn't go, so she asked me and my sister if we could go. ... She just wanted something to remind her of her old home place. ... And she said, "If you go, look around, and if there's an old canning jar or even a jar lid, bring me that." And we wanted to do that for her because we knew she wouldn't be around much longer. (A. Jenkins personal communication)

Ammie herself never wanted to return to the Sandhills, worrying that it would bring back unhappy memories. After her father died of lupus in 1954, at age thirty-five, her mother and six younger siblings were harassed by racist hate groups and fled from the family farm, which was eventually appropriated by Fort Bragg (PBS NewsHour 2007). But eventually Ammie and her sister went there and once they started up the little dirt road leading to their old home site: "We just forgot about all the bad stuff and ... started bringing back all the good memories" (A. Jenkins personal communication).

The experience of revisiting her old home place helped her rediscover her ties to the land and also rekindled in her a desire to research her family history. Ammie started interviewing older family members and soon found herself collecting the stories of other families across the Sandhills. The people she talked to would often refer her to other old-time residents and eventually her undertaking snowballed into more than eighty tape-recorded interviews with people aged seventy or older.

In most of these interviews, people talked at length about the land they used to own. Ammie learned that many African-American families in the Sandhills had once possessed diverse and self-sufficient farms exceeding one hundred acres (forty hectares), similar to the one she grew up on. "That's a lot of land," she observes, "I know these people's descendants and they don't know anything about the land; so where is that land now?" (personal communication). Many of the people she talked to appeared to have the same concern: "The land is disappearing" was their common lament. Ammie knew all too well from her personal experience how drastic the consequences of land loss can be. Once their family farm was lost, she remembers, "we went from being self-sufficient to 'Where do we go from here? We have nothing,' to the point of accepting handouts and that type of thing" (as cited in PBS 2007).

Now that Ammie saw that the entire culture she belonged to was in jeopardy, she knew she had to find a way to preserve it.

* * *

While conducting interviews, Ammie noticed that residents of the Sandhills had a number of common concerns, and eventually she started organizing group meetings to discuss these concerns. As these meetings progressed, participants also started talking about what their community had achieved in the past. One of the accomplishments they remembered with special pride was the old civic centre built by African-American men and women with financial and other contributions from the community. It quickly became a local hub of African-American social life, being used by the entire community for any activity that could not be held at the Church. It also became a political hub in the days of the Civil Rights Movement, when local Black leaders used it as a place to get together and strategize. Other collective achievements brought up at these meetings included the construction of churches and the creation of businesses and community gardens.

The discussion circles catalyzed by Ammie's interviews, which usually met after church services, either in somebody's home or simply in the street, became a regular feature of the community's life. It then occurred to Ammie that they could make a real difference by forming "some type of a group where we could speak as one having a common concern, which was the loss of our land, the income and everything else that goes with that loss of land" (A. Jenkins personal communication). She ran her idea by several friends, including then mayor of Spring Lake, Marvin Lucas, with whom she had gone to high school, and Betty McMillan, president of the Ladies Auxiliary to the North Carolina Veterans of Foreign Wars. Everyone was enthusiastic about the prospect. "All I did was just encourage the idea," remembers Lucas, "and she took the bull by the horns" (as cited in Solano 2011). The Sandhills Family Heritage Association was launched in 2001 with the goal of "building self-sufficiency and self-worth through preserving our cultural heritage and our natural resources" (A. Jenkins as cited in Cohen 2007). Ammie gave up her spa business in Durham and moved back to the Sandhills to devote herself to achieving this goal.

During the early period of her community organizing work in the Sandhills, Ammie came in contact with Mikki Sager of the Conservation Fund, a national non-profit with a dual mission of environmental protection and economic development. As director of the Fund's Resourceful Communities Program, Mikki immediately saw the congruence of Ammie's aspirations with the program's mission of fostering a network of grassroots organizations implementing the triple bottom line of sustainable economic development, social justice and environmental stewardship in North Carolina communities. She also found in Ammie "that unique combination of somebody who is both a visionary and a doer" (as cited in Solano 2011). Ever since the inception of SFHA, the Resourceful Communities Program has been its key partner, providing financial support as well as capacity building assistance, both of which have been crucial for its continued existence and growth.

SFHA is a membership-based, non-profit organization with a volunteer board of eight members representing all the five Sandhills counties in which it works. Its current membership exceeds 175 people. SFHA membership is not restricted to African Americans and includes current and former residents of the Sandhills. The association has only two staff members, Ammie (executive director) and her part-time assistant. Most of its work is being accomplished by volunteers who include members and non-members alike.

KEY FACETS OF SFHA'S WORK

What had begun as a personal quest evolved into community organizing and what had begun as a heritage-documentation project evolved into a commitment to keep that heritage alive and draw on its strengths to build a better future; that's how SFHA came to be. Its mission is articulated as building communities of HOPE through Heritage preservation, Outreach education, Protection of land and natural resources and Economic self-sufficiency (Sandhills Family Heritage Association n.d.).

Heritage preservation

In keeping with the Sankofa principle of looking back in order to move forward, much of SFHA's work is focused on documenting the rich history and culture of African Americans in the region. By now the association has conducted and recorded over 130 interviews with Sandhills elders. These interviews have formed the basis of two books compiled by Ammie Jenkins. One of these, *Preserving our Family Heritage*, presents the stories of local African-American families dating back to slavery. These stories range from the simple everyday struggles of farming in white America to various agricultural, forestry and technical innovations created by African Americans in the Sandhills (Jenkins n.d.). The second book, *Healing from the Land*, illustrates the deep connection between African-American elders and their natural environment as reflected in their use of various resources from the forests, waters and fields "to sustain life and heal themselves" (Jenkins 2003).

SFHA makes systematic efforts to correct the one-sidedness of the mainstream historical memory, which has tended to overlook the contributions of African

Americans in the Sandhills region (McCann 2008). In addition to documenting African-American heritage, the association has partnered with the North Carolina Department of Public Instruction to prepare new online history lesson plans for state schools. These lessons draw upon SFHA's oral-history interviews to demonstrate the rich tapestry of Black cultural expressions in North Carolina and the important historical contributions of African Americans in local communities. They also illustrate the cultural impacts of civil-rights activism in the Sandhills.

SFHA has also been active in showcasing the achievements of African Americans through heritage tourism. It has developed an African-American Heritage Trail featuring sites that provide glimpses into the life of African Americans in the Sandhills from the period of slavery to the Civil Rights Movement, including the oldest educational facilities founded for Black students, old churches built by Black congregations and museums exhibiting African-American artifacts. In collaboration with several partners including Fayetteville Convention and Visitors Bureau, Town of Spring Lake and local churches, SFHA organizes heritage tours for families and youth groups, guided by its volunteers.

The development of heritage tourism is closely related to SFHA's work in revitalizing historic places such as the above-mentioned civic centre. At the time when SFHA was formally launched, the old centre stood empty and in disrepair (Sandhills Family Heritage Association 2004). The Association acquired the building and petitioned the Town of Spring Lake to designate it as a historic landmark owing to its past role as a hub of the local African-American community. The designation was awarded in 2007 and the facility, named Sandhills Heritage Center, has now become a feature of SFHA's heritage tours, boasting a replica of the historic plank road and a brush arbour,[6] constructed by the association's volunteers. The centre also hosts a thriving weekly farmers' market, initiated by SFHA as well. The association's plan going forward is to develop the centre into a fully-fledged hub of community life that would host a library, a business incubator and SFHA offices, as well as providing space for various cultural events, celebrations and meetings.

Yet another signature element of SFHA's heritage preservation work is the Sandhills Sankofa Festival. Held annually since 2002, it offers a one-of-a-kind opportunity to promote the music, dance, storytelling, food, crafts and other local African-American traditions on a continuing basis.

Outreach education

For SFHA leaders, keeping the land stewardship and entrepreneurial traditions of African Americans in the Sandhills alive is just as important as documenting them. This goal is being achieved through an intensive education outreach program aimed to foster a greater public awareness of these traditions and to ensure that they are passed on to future generations.

"One of the biggest impacts we have had is through our outreach education," observes Ammie, "because this is something we have done from the very beginning of the organization in 2001 on a monthly basis" (personal communication). SFHA offers at least twelve workshops a year for Sandhills residents, covering a wide range of subjects: estate planning, heir property ownership, financial management, forest stewardship, gardening and heritage appreciation. Hundreds of people have attended and benefitted from these workshops. In addition to the local workshops, SFHA also hosts regional trainings in community organizing, asset mapping, communication skills, fundraising, conflict resolution and other aspects of community development for grassroots leaders in partnership with the Conservation Fund's Resourceful Communities Program. The attending leaders then bring their newly-acquired knowledge and skills into their communities.

Recognizing that the success of its mission largely depends on the involvement of the younger generation, SFHA has developed apprenticeship and service learning programs targeting youth. One example is its gardening project which paired community elders and young people in order to document and pass on knowledge about growing traditional African-American food crops. Another example of SFHA's outreach work targeting young people is the project, Building Bridges to Healthy Communities (carried out in partnership with the University of North Carolina at Chapel Hill in 2008), in which Sandhills youth were taught to conduct interviews with the local citizens about public health and environmental issues in their communities. During the course of that project, the youth were also taught the basics of building partnerships aimed to address these issues. SFHA's most recent youth-oriented outreach initiative is a model apprenticeship project, Youth Engaging in Agriculture, launched in 2012 in collaboration with the North Carolina A&T State University. This three-year project connects limited-resource local youth with mentor-farmers to provide in-depth practical experience in the production and marketing of locally-grown crops, which the apprentices can use to start their own farming businesses. In the third year of the project, the participating youth interested in continuing farming as a career will be provided with guidance for locating rental farmland and securing loans from USDA or other institutions.

Protection of land and natural resources

SFHA was born out of Ammie's conversations with Sandhills elders, which revealed the fundamental role that owning and tending land have played in shaping the unique African-American culture in the region. It is not surprising, therefore, that the association has been committed to helping sustain African-American landownership and traditions of land stewardship since its inception.

Land goes for a premium in the Sandhills as the continuous growth of Fort Bragg and the expansion of other economic activities create an ever-increasing demand.

To satisfy it, developers and real estate companies are keenly looking to acquire new land. Ammie speaks sadly about the predatory tactics that some of them employ. sFHA is addressing this threat by educating African-American landowners about their legal rights and options and by connecting them to support services when they are considering selling their properties. It also helps them obtain clear title to their properties, document their family trees, complete affidavits of heirship and organize family reunions to discuss the status of jointly-owned land.

Access to land management services is important to maintaining landownership. However, many Black landowners in the Sandhills feel uncomfortable initiating contact with the relevant offices due to prior discriminatory practices of representatives of these or other government agencies against African Americans. sFHA works with the landowners and agency personnel to help them build effective working relationships. The case of the North Carolina Forest Service provides a good example of sFHA's mediating work. This agency's mandate includes developing forest-management plans for the interested landowners for a nominal fee or even free of charge. These plans provide valuable information on the habitat requirements and life cycle of various tree species, as well as insect-related and other tree diseases, and include recommendations for attaining the landowner's management objectives (Harris 2006). However, sFHA members found that no African-American landowner in the Sandhills had ever requested this service. The agency staff, in their turn, had never made any concrete steps to reach out to Black landowners. To address this issue, sFHA hosted a workshop for the local landowners interested in having management plans developed for their woodlots and then helped individual landowners connect with appropriate Forest Service staff. These efforts have yielded the creation of the first forest-management plan for an African-American landowner in the Sandhills.

sFHA also organizes Sandhills residents to advocate their position regarding land issues with various stakeholders. Its work with Fort Bragg is an example that deserves to be discussed here. As mentioned earlier, in 2005 the U.S. Base Realignment and Closure Commission recommended the closure of several military bases across the country and an increase in Fort Bragg area to accommodate their personnel. sFHA board members were invited to participate in the consultations on the projected expansion. Fort Bragg authorities proposed a five-mile (eight km) buffer zone around the base, which threatened Sandhills landowners with another massive loss of land and further land-use restrictions. During the initial consultations, sFHA representatives insisted that the information about the proposed expansion should be shared with local landowners. sFHA also undertook its own research to determine which properties would be affected and conducted discussions with the owners of these properties to assess the possible impact of Fort Bragg expansion on various aspects of their lives. Along with that, sFHA leaders insisted that consultations on Fort Bragg expansion should be conducted in the African-American community in open meetings allowing the public to participate. They saw to it that Sandhills residents showed up at the meetings armed with detailed information on their land-based economic activities and encouraged them to express their concerns openly about the negative effects of Fort Bragg expansion on their life. Ammie remembers:

> We were at the table to discuss how it is going to change the lives of our people.... Why are they upsetting the lives of people who had already been displaced once [by the creation of Fort Bragg]? It seems like a replay of history. (personal communication)

While SFHA and the community were not able to prevent the establishment of a buffer zone and associated land-use restrictions, they did succeed in that the buffer zone was reduced from the proposed 5-mile (8-km) radius to a 1-mile (1.6 km) radius outside the core base area. Without challenging the law of eminent domain as such, SFHA has also helped those residents who had to give up their land to Fort Bragg receive compensation equivalent to its market value by providing them with appropriate information and training or by connecting them with experienced lawyers.

Entrepreneurship and economic development

Today's economic landscape of the Sandhills is dominated by military facilities, big-box stores and sprawling golf courses. These development models are hardly conducive to preserving the culture of land-based self-reliance that became a hallmark of the African-American community in the Sandhills after the abolition of slavery. Nor have they helped this community achieve wealth even in the very narrow economic sense of the term. On the contrary: the interviews conducted by SFHA reveal that one of the major reasons why Black landownership in the area has dropped so precipitously in the recent decades is because many Sandhills families were simply not earning enough income to pay land taxes.

SFHA's work in the area of economic development is focused on "creating land-based jobs and income opportunities so people can help pay their taxes and hold onto their land and so they can continue to do the type of work they enjoy doing and at the same time preserve the cultural heritage that is tied to the land and have something to pass on to the next generation" (A. Jenkins as cited in Cohen 2007). For example, the association works actively with the North Carolina Forest Service to help the local landowners develop sustainable timber harvesting practices. Before SFHA entered the scene, many African-American landowners in the Sandhills were not aware of the services provided by this agency. However, through patient and persistent work with both the Forest Service officials and the landowners, SFHA has helped them develop constructive working relationships. The Forest Service helps the landowners determine when their woodlots are mature enough for harvesting and assess the volume and value of their timber before sale. It also provides information and advice on cost-share, tax and other financial-incentive programs available to non-industrial private forest owners in North Carolina to promote sustainable forestry. These services are particularly important in the Sandhills where some timber companies are reported to prey on small-scale woodlot owners in order to gain an unfair market advantage.

Thanks to SFHA, local landowners such as Ed and Sheila Spence are now better equipped to make informed decisions regarding the harvesting and sale of their timber and other resource management issues on their land. The Spences attended SFHA's educational workshops and were inspired by its vision of land-based entrepreneurship. They became the first landowners in the Sandhills to work with the North Carolina Forest Service on developing a management plan for their woodlot, the process that has helped them determine sustainable harvest levels and appropriate silvicultural practices.

The establishment of the Sandhills Farmers' Market represents another notable achievement in SFHA's work to promote land-based entrepreneurship. The Association started working on the idea of creating a local farmers' market in 2006, aiming to enhance income opportunities for Sandhills landowners and to improve community access to fresh, healthy food. To begin with, it had to persuade the Spring Lake Board of Aldermen to amend the town's zoning ordinance, adding a farmers' market as a permitted use. Once the amended ordinance was approved, SFHA commissioned a design firm to develop a market site plan. Next, SFHA representatives had to present their project to the town's Board of Aldermen and Board of Adjustment. Once the proposed market had received an approval to operate from the boards, SFHA quickly fulfilled numerous requirements concerning market layout and hygiene and obtained a business licence. The first ever African-American operated farmers' market in Cumberland County was born. Despite the many bureaucratic hurdles that the market creation involved, it was a labour of love for SFHA, a tangible step towards reviving the local tradition of land-based entrepreneurship.

In both its push for the farmers' market and its efforts to protect Black-owned land around Fort Bragg discussed earlier, SFHA has proven itself an effective organizer, capable not only of bringing community members together for a cause of common concern but also of keeping the momentum going until a satisfactory outcome has been achieved.

ASSERTING PRIDE IN AFRICAN-AMERICAN CULTURE

Historically, African Americans in the Sandhills were subjected to discrimination and disparagement. To a certain extent, racial discrimination in the region continues today, albeit in less blatant forms. A board member of SFHA observes: "Black people [are often put] in a negative context ... 'they are lazy people; they do not want to work; they do this or that'" (personal communication).

SFHA is determined to change this:

> We've got to get rid of that image and not buy what they are selling. We need to continue to work to uphold our own dignity and speak out what we believe. We need to stick together as a group. (SFHA board member personal communication)

The Association's efforts to foster a sense of dignity and cultural identity among African-American citizens in the Sandhills follow a two-pronged approach which combines community rebuilding with community organizing and advocacy.

Community rebuilding

SFHA seeks to bring a sense of pride and self-determination back to centre stage in the life of African Americans in the Sandhills. The association's leaders have realized that collecting and sharing family stories is key to fostering a strong sense of shared identity and belonging. They have learned first hand that recognizing the hardships our ancestors had to deal with, the accomplishments they made, the values they lived by deepens our sense of personal history and place. In this way, all of us come to know who we are and how we got to where we are today.

SFHA leaders believe that the perfect model for rebuilding a strong African-American community in the Sandhills is found in its own ancestry. At the same time, they emphasize that they are not in the business of merely reenacting the past ways. "I'm not talking about living in the past," maintains Ammie, "but I'm talking about recognizing those things that we had that are of value and building on those assets" (as cited in PBS 2007).

SFHA leaders thus do not view their oral-history documentation initiative as an end in itself. Rather, they see it as a form of asset mapping, a stage setter for a deliberate community-rebuilding process focused on helping African Americans in the Sandhills regain economic self-reliance through creating income opportunities linked to land stewardship and heritage preservation work.

Community organizing and advocacy

In view of the progressive loss of Black-owned land in the Sandhills, Ammie sometimes speaks of SFHA as an organization "in an emergency phase" (as cited in PBS 2007). As such, the association must engage in advocacy to ensure that the concerns and desires of the community it represents are taken into consideration by those in power. This requires effective community organizing.

In the two examples of SFHA's advocacy work mentioned earlier in this paper (reducing the buffer zone around Fort Bragg and pushing for the establishment of a farmers' market in Spring Lake), the association relied on the same principles: identify the burning issues of community-wide concern; encourage as many community members as possible to show up at meetings with authorities; ensure that people come to these meetings armed with information pertinent to the issues at hand; encourage them to voice their concerns and desires regarding these issues and make it clear to the authorities how these specific concerns and desires relate to the big picture of the overall community well-being. In both instances, this strategy has enabled SFHA to achieve its key campaign objectives: the buffer zone around Fort Bragg was reduced to a small fraction of its originally proposed size; the farmers' market came to life. Significantly, the association's community organizing and advocacy efforts have also yielded an enhanced sense of self-worth in the African-American community.

CULTURE-BASED PHILANTHROPY

One of the key drivers of SFHA's work is the principle of giving back to the community. In following this principle, the association helps keep up the practice of giving that has been the backbone of African-American community in the Sandhills since slavery. Ammie's childhood memories, corroborated by her interviews with local elders, led her to conclude that:

> [This practice was] the connection ... that tied all the people together. When we grew up, even though we didn't have a lot, I don't know of anyone who went hungry.... Some of the older people in the community wonder when they see the news that people in New York and other big cities are hungry: they don't understand how that could happen with all the people around them.... Because on the farm if you see your neighbours hungry, you feed them. There is no such thing as people starving or wanting food, because what I don't have, you have. It was inherent in our culture that you help your neighbour; it was a given. (A. Jenkins personal communication)

In its community rebuilding work, SFHA seeks to revive the traditional forms of giving that had a formative influence on African-American culture in the Sandhills. One example is the custom allowing those in need to collect excess crops, known as "gleaning." In her book *Healing from the Land*, Ammie describes it in this way:

As in many rural Southern communities, [our] home gardeners ... have kept up the practice of gleaning — the traditional Biblical practice of gathering crops that would otherwise be left in the fields to rot or be plowed under after harvest. In the Sandhills, many who continue gleaning do so as an embodiment of their Christian beliefs. (Jenkins 2003: 44)

To ensure that this tradition is passed on to the next generation, SFHA's Gardening and Gleaning project teamed up local youth with the farmers and gardeners interested in donating their surplus crops. Ammie explains how the project succeeded in engaging youth who were not necessarily interested in farming:

We let *them* choose who they would like to partner with, and every one of them chose their grandmother.... Also, when we went to the young people, we didn't just say, "You're going to be doing gardening and gleaning."... We figured we could get them if we included technology; so we had them do interviews, take photos and create a booklet telling about their experience and what they had learned. (personal communication)

The leaders of SFHA also rely on local giving practices to harness a variety of philanthropic resources. Most of the association's work gets accomplished by volunteers and through partnerships — which also represent a form of mutual giving, albeit not commonly regarded as such (Price, Shank and Jenkins 2008). Examples include its collaborative projects with local universities (outlined earlier) as well as relationships with local churches and various public agencies, which donate spaces for community meetings and other activities organized by SFHA and disseminate information on various community affairs at its request. Besides serving their specific purposes, all these partnerships also help strengthen what SFHA leaders call "culture-based philanthropy," based on the values of sharing and cooperation which the Association seeks to uphold.

FOSTERING SYSTEMIC SOCIAL CHANGE

When SFHA was formed in 2001, it was intended to help preserve the cultural heritage of African Americans in the Sandhills rather than to bring about social transformation. While implementing its original mission, however, the association's work gradually took on the features that clearly qualify it as a catalyst of systemic social change. Based on the preceding discussion, one can highlight at least three such features:

- A holistic vision of development, embracing preservation of cultural heritage, social justice, economic sustainability and environmental stewardship;

- Deliberate engagement of community members, including elders, women and young people at all stages of work, from the identification of issues and planning of activities to implementation and evaluation of results and
- Focus on programs that advance community self-reliance and self-determination.

The Association's programs foster systemic change through various channels: shifting the attitudes towards landownership in the African-American community, especially among its young members; helping local landowners understand and assert their rights with respect to land; forging effective working relationships between African Americans engaged in farming or forestry and extension services; providing training and technical support for community-based entrepreneurship and facilitating implementation of local land-use and economic-development policies that help support a culture of self-reliance and self-determination in the African-American community.

This change-fostering work is taking place at a critical moment in the region's history. The latest U.S. census, held in 2010, provides ample evidence that the South is experiencing a profound change in its demographic makeup, which owes much to the massive return of African Americans to their ancestral areas. A discussion of census data by *New York Times* reporters reveals the magnitude of this trend: "The share of black population growth that has occurred in the South over the past decade," they observe, "[has been] the highest since 1910" (Tavernise and Gebeloff 2011).

According to experts, such as demographer William Frey of the Brookings Institute and historian Clement Price of Rutgers University, a key factor behind the current shift of African Americans to the South is the decline of heavy industry which served as one of the major employers for black people in the urban areas of the Northeast, Midwest and West. With this decline, observes Price, "the black urban experience has essentially lost its appeal with blacks in America" (as cited in Tavernise and Gebeloff 2011). Yet, as Frey points out, there is both "a push and a pull involved with the movement": "a big part, aside from the economy, is the kind of historic roots that blacks have had there [in the South]" (as cited in Tanneeru 2009).

The reverse migration of Blacks is pronounced in the Sandhills and many of the African Americans who have returned to this region were prompted by a desire to reconnect with their communities of origin and ancestral traditions. The story of Ed and Sheila Spence, who came back "to the peace and reward of being close to the land" (Spence Family Farms n.d.) in their native Sandhills after long military and teaching careers in California, is a case in point. "My grandparents were sharecroppers," explains Ed. "We literally lived off the farm … but they never owned any of the land. And so this was special for us to be able to do the same thing that we did when I was a child, but now we own the land" (as cited in PBS *NewsHour* 2007).

SFHA was instrumental in helping Ed and Sheila make their dream a reality. It linked them with its resource network and extension services which provided research that helped them develop a management plan for their woodlot. Through its own training programs, the association also helped the Spences become reacquainted with gardening practices that sustained their ancestors and its educational workshops provided them with a good understanding of current policy and legal issues affecting land owners in the region.

In less than a decade, Ed and Sheila developed a small forestry operation designed to offer a sustainable supply of timber and a thriving farm producing a wide variety of fruits and vegetables. They also raise grain-fed cows, goats and hens. Thanks to SFHA's efforts to promote community-level entrepreneurship, they now sell their produce not only at their farm stand but also at the Sandhills Farmers' Market in Spring Lake. "We are always sold out," observes Ed with pride (personal communication). He and Sheila are convinced that one can make a good living as a farmer in the Sandhills these days. Significantly, the Spences now assist SFHA in its efforts to promote farming as a worthy and viable occupation among the younger generation of Sandhills residents. For instance, in 2012–13 they provided hands-on mentoring to eleven local youth participating in the association's farm apprenticeship project.

This example illustrates SFHA's role as a one-stop centre providing education, training, income opportunities and support networks to help Sandhills residents create rewarding lives in tune with the tradition of economic self-sufficiency tied to land stewardship that lies at the heart of local African-American culture. In so doing, the association also fosters a sense of community identity and pride based on preserving this cultural heritage and actively passing it on to future generations. By pursuing this multifaceted yet unified strategy, a small organization with just two staff members is achieving something that the big-box development model currently dominating the Sandhills doesn't seem capable of: it is re-awakening the entrepreneurial spirit in the African-American community and thereby empowering its members to achieve greater control over their lives.

LESSONS

Based on our discussion of the key aspects of SFHA's work and its major results, we can identify a number of factors that have enabled it to become an effective agent of social change:

An exceptional servant-leader at the helm

Throughout its history, SFHA has been blessed with a unique combination of "a visionary and a doer" its leader brings. The association's key partners and supporters recognize Ammie's leadership skills as the cornerstone of its success. "She's one of those people who can see the big picture," says Mikki Sager of the Conservation Fund, "but she also can get right down into the nitty gritty and roll her sleeves up and push fish dinners across the table at the Sankofa Festival" (as cited in Solano 2011).[7] State Representative Marvin Lucas concurs: "If you want a catalyst in any community involvement activities and someone who really wants to establish a historical profile, then you should get Ammie Jenkins" (ibid.). There is little doubt that one of the association's core strengths, effective community organizing, owes much to Ammie's humility and her commitment to serving the community that nurtured her sense of identity. "We are standing on the shoulders of the people who went before us," she says. "My life's work … is about giving back to the community that helped me" (ibid.).

Being one with the community

SFHA started out as an oral history project dedicated to capturing the traditions that have largely shaped the local African-American culture. While its work has greatly expanded over time and is now focused on carrying on, rather than merely documenting, these traditions, it still hinges on the same core element: attending to community members, being with them. This means not just hearing and recording what people in the community have to say but getting a sense of how they view life, what concerns they have, what they want to accomplish. The engagement of community members at all stages of the association's work, from the identification of burning issues to the evaluation of results, is therefore not a political gesture intended to draw support for its programs; it is the force that shapes and drives its agenda. As Mikki Sager has observed, "What SFHA is doing is very simple and common sense. It is about knowing your history and heritage, and it is about what people think is right, it's not about what someone else thinks is right" (personal communication).

Building bridges between generations

SFHA leaders have realized from the outset that their community rebuilding efforts will be futile if they don't reach different age groups, especially the youth — for how else can the traditions that are the community's lifeblood be carried forward into the future? Accordingly, many of the association's programs deliberately bring people of different generations together as a means of passing on traditions and sharing knowledge and skills. The following observations by Sheila Spence indicate that these programs also help young people get a sense of their roots and thereby foster community cohesion:

We had a youth program. My granddaughter and I participated in that program, and it was very enlightening to her. Without her being out in the field, in the heat of the day, picking peas, she would have never been able to realize what it was like for our ancestors to be working on share-croppers' farms or be enslaved, to have to do that. (as cited in PBS 2007)

It is important to note that SFHA leaders do not conceive of the sharing of knowledge and skills as a one-way street where traffic is only supposed to flow from the older generation to the younger. On the contrary: the association's programs provide ample opportunities for local youth to put their own skills and talents to good use. For example, SFHA often relies on young people proficient with computers to assist older community members with land title research or help them obtain information about government incentive programs for sustainable farming and forestry operations (C. Brown personal communication).

A clear vision and roadmap to get there

SFHA's work rests on the solid foundation of a simple yet profound vision that "sees the goals of economic development and heritage preservation as inextricably linked" (McCann 2008: 41). For SFHA leaders, the medium through which these goals are linked is land and maintaining African-American land-stewardship traditions is a compass for developing a sustainable local economy:

> I would say that Sandhills Family Heritage Association is all about pre-serving our land and natural resources. And the reason I think that is so key is because everything else is connected to the land and our natural resources: our culture, our livelihoods, our food, our medicine — all of those things that help to make us self-sufficient. (A. Jenkins as cited in The Conservation Fund 2013)

The various activities SFHA is spearheading — whether it be historical re-enactments, workshops addressing land ownership issues, farm apprenticeships or the annual Sankofa Festival — are not silo projects; they are woven together into a single canvas, a coherent roadmap to regaining the community's economic self-reliance and an increased sense of self-worth that it brings.

Forging relationships that work

SFHA neither attempts nor intends to be a jack-of-all-trades. Most of its work is carried out in partnership with a wide range of actors, including other non-profits, local churches, universities, government agencies and individual farmers, to name a few. Here is just one example of the synergistic relationships SFHA leaders are so good at forging:

Look at the [farm] apprenticeship program alone: that is a partnership between farmers, students, the North Carolina A&T University, and our organization. Through this partnership SFHA creates a win-win for all the partners involved: the farmers get young apprentice trainees to work for them; the young students earn stipends and the real-life agricultural experience; and the university completes its field component. (A. Jenkins personal communication)

A prominent feature of SFHA is that its leaders' devotion to collaboration extends to its advocacy work as well. For example, when SFHA had to deal with the buffer zone issue, its leaders opted for working with, rather than against, Fort Bragg to find a solution that both the community and military authorities could feel positive about. This commitment to non-confrontational advocacy owes much to the high esteem Ammie has for Martin Luther King's philosophy of non-violent direct action. In a recent talk she gave at Dr. King's birthday celebration at Fort Bragg, she remembered her first encounter with his ideas: "I did go to one of the strategy meetings [organized by Dr. King's followers]. And I found out if you could not protest and be non-violent, they did not want you to participate" (as cited in Reinier 2014). This happened in the early 1960s, during Ammie's years at High Point College. As its first-ever African-American student, she remembers, "I was the target of a lot of spit balls" (ibid.) and "heard the 'n-word' so much I almost thought it was my middle name" (as cited in Solano 2011). But Martin Luther King's message that "we must learn to live together as brothers or perish together as fools" has nonetheless stuck with her and now rings through SFHA's commitment to building relationships across racial, cultural and ideological differences. The fact that its membership is open to non-African Americans attests to that.

FINAL MESSAGE

"I don't know if the young generation of today would survive the way my generation did," says Ammie, "and one reason is the fact that they don't know their history" (personal communication). These words can be read as an allusion to her personal story. For much of her life, Ammie kept away from revisiting her family's past, worrying it would only bring back painful memories. But eventually she resolved to face that fear and experienced a "miracle" that would deeply change her life and many lives around her. A visit to her old home place set her on a path to uncovering the cultural traditions that had shaped her ancestral community. Walking that path gave her a sense of empowerment and inspired her to create the Sandhills Family Heritage Association at the young age of sixty.

The association's work of preserving the heritage of African-American community in the Sandhills is focused on sustaining the traditions that shaped its culture rather than simply documenting them. And because these traditions are tied to good land stewardship — the ability to "live off the land without messing it up" (M. Sager personal communication) — sustaining them is a prerequisite to survival. This is, then, what the association's work is ultimately concerned with: reclaiming, reviving and perpetuating the cultural traditions conducive to our survival, in the deep sense that involves self-determination, self-reliance and self-esteem.

SFHA offers a vision of economic development that is inextricably linked to the recovery of local cultural traditions. In stark contrast to the development models dominating the Sandhills today — military facilities, big-box stores and golf courses — it promotes an economy that draws upon a broad range of local assets and seeks to create multiple forms of wealth. Its work indicates that maintaining a broad-based "portfolio of wealth" may be critical to attaining sustainable prosperity.

Notes

1. State and local laws that enforced racial segregation in the Southern United States between 1877 and the mid-1960s.
2. All references to "personal communication" are for interviews conducted in January 2013.
3. During the pre-Civil War period, 53 percent of the state's slave owners owned five or fewer slaves and only 2.6 percent of the slaves in North Carolina lived on farms with over fifty slaves (UNC n.d.).
4. Community-asset mapping conducted by SFHA in 2003 identified the proximity of Fort Bragg as one of the key reasons behind the loss of Black-owned land in the region (Conservation Fund 2007).
5. Eminent domain refers to the power of government agencies to take private property for public use, providing "reasonable compensation" in return.
6. Brush arbour is an open-sided shelter constructed of vertical poles with a roof of brush. Such structures were used as worship places by local African-American congregations in the 1700s and early 1800s.
7. Found at <http://www.fayobserver.com/2011.02.27>, currently unavailable.

References

Aragon, L.V. 2000. *Sandhills Families: Early Reminiscences of the Fort Bragg Area*. Fort Bragg, NC: Public Works Business Center.

Cohen, T. 2007. "Non-Profit Promotes African Heritage." *Philanthropy Journal* (online). <http://www.philanthropyjournal.org/archive/130591>.

Conrad, C.A., J. Whitehead, P. Mason and J. Stewart. (eds.). 2005. *African Americans in the U.S. Economy*. Lanham, MD: Rowman and Littlefield.

Conservation Fund. 2007. Case Study: Sandhills Family Heritage Association Community Asset Mapping. <http://people.tamu.edu/~jpackard/cases/NA06SFHA_Sager.pdf>.

Daniel, P. 2013. *Dispossession: Discrimination against African American Farmers in the Age Of Civil Rights*. Chapel Hill, NC: University of North Carolina Press.

Grant, G.R., S.D. Wood and W.J. Wright. 2012. "Black Farmers United: The Struggle Against Power and Principalities." *The Journal of Pan African Studies* 5. 1: 3–22.

Gregory, J.N. 2005. *The Southern Diaspora: How the Great Migrations of Black and White Southerners Transformed America.* Chapel Hill, NC: University of North Carolina Press.

Harris, V.L. 2006. "Falling in Love Again." *Minority Landowner Magazine.*

Jenkins, A. 2003. *Healing from the Land.* Spring Lake, NC: Sandhills Family Heritage Association.

Jenkins, A. n.d. *Preserving Our Family Heritage.* Spring Lake, NC: Sandhills Family Heritage Association.

McCann, M. 2008. "2008 Community Traditions Award: Sandhills Family Heritage Association." *North Carolina Folklore Journal* 55, 2: 37–42.

Militarybases.com. 2012. "Fort Bragg." <http://militarybases.com/north-carolina/fort-bragg>.

Mitchell, T.W. 2000. "From Reconstruction to Deconstruction: Undermining Black Landownership, Political Independence and Community Through Partition Sales of Tenancies in Common (Land Tenure Center Research Paper No. 132)." Madison, WI: University of Wisconsin–Madison.

North Carolina History Project Encyclopedia. n.d. "Naval Stores." <http://www.northcarolinahistory.org/encyclopedia/103/entry>.

PBS. n.d. "Black Farming and Land Loss: A History." <http://www.pbs.org/itvs/homecoming/history.html>.

PBS NewsHour. 2007. "Organization Helps Preserve African-American Family Land." <http://www.pbs.org/newshour/bb/social_issues/july-dec07/prize_09-17.html>.

Price, C.R., C. Shank and A. Jenkins. 2008. "Sandhills Family Heritage Association (Case Profile, the Transforming Philanthropy in Communities of Color Project of the National Community Development Institute)." University of Chapel Hill, NC: University of North Carolina at Chapel Hill.

Reinier, W. 2014. "Dr. Martin Luther King Jr. Birthday Celebration at Fort Bragg." The Official Homepage of the United States Army (*News*, January 22). <http://www.army.mil/article/118591/Dr__Martin_Luther_King_Jr__Birthday_Celebration_at_Fort_Bragg/>.

Richardson, D. 2013. "Saying One Thing and Doing Another: Agriculture and the Duality of Institutionalized Racism in the Modern United States (Review of P. Daniel, *Discrimination against African American Farmers in the Age of Civil Rights*)." *H-Net Reviews.* <http://www.h-net.org/reviews/showrev.php?id=38616>.

Sandhills Family Heritage Association. 2004. "Annual Report."

____. n.d. "Programs." <http://www.sfha-nc.org>.

Shannon, S.G. 1997. "A Transplant That Did Not Take: August Wilson's Views on the Great Migration." *African American Review* 31, 4: 659–66.

Solano, A. 2011. "Cape Fear Profile: Ammie Jenkins Is Rooted in Tradition." *The Fayetteville Observer*, February 27.

Spence Family Farms. n.d. "About Us." <http://spencefamilyfarms.com/about.php>.

Tanneeru, M. 2009. "Family Roots Lure Many African-Americans Back to South." CNN *Living.* <http://www.cnn.com/2009/LIVING/wayoflife/07/10/bia.return.south/index.html?iref=nextin>.

Tavernise, S., and R. Gebeloff. 2011. "Many U.S. Blacks Returning to South, Reversing Trend." *New York Times*, March 24. <http://www.nytimes.com/ 2011/03/25/ us/25south.html?pagewanted=all&_r=0>.

The Conservation Fund. 2013. "Resourceful Communities." Video documentary. <http:// www.youtube.com/watch?v=svnEvgU1j5E>.

UNC University Library. n.d. "Slavery in North Carolina." <http://www.lib.unc.edu/stories/ slavery/index.html>.

U.S. Army Fort Bragg. n.d. "Fort Bragg History." <http://www.bragg.army.mil/Pages/ History.aspx>.

Wood, S.D., and J. Gilbert. 2000. "Returning African-American Farmers to the Land: Recent Trends and a Policy Rationale." *The Review of Black Political Economy* 27, 4: 43–64.